D1759134

* 8 1

SOUTH DEVON COLLEGE LIBRARY

WITHDRAWN

SOUTH DEVON COLL. LIB.	
81960	372.21
ACC.	CLASS

PROMOTING EVIDENCE-BASED PRACTICE IN EARLY CHILDHOOD EDUCATION: RESEARCH AND ITS IMPLICATIONS

ADVANCES IN APPLIED EARLY CHILDHOOD EDUCATION

Series Editor: Tricia David

ADVANCES IN APPLIED EARLY CHILDHOOD EDUCATION
VOLUME 1

PROMOTING EVIDENCE-BASED PRACTICE IN EARLY CHILDHOOD EDUCATION: RESEARCH AND ITS IMPLICATIONS

EDITED BY

TRICIA DAVID

*Centre for Educational Research,
Canterbury Christ Church College, UK*

2001

JAI
An Imprint of Elsevier Science

Amsterdam – London – New York – Oxford – Paris – Shannon – Tokyo

ELSEVIER SCIENCE Ltd
The Boulevard, Langford Lane
Kidlington, Oxford OX5 1GB, UK

© 2001 Elsevier Science Ltd. All rights reserved.

This work is protected under copyright by Elsevier Science, and the following terms and conditions apply to its use:

Photocopying
Single photocopies of single chapters may be made for personal use as allowed by national copyright laws. Permission of the Publisher and payment of a fee is required for all other photocopying, including multiple or systematic copying, copying for advertising or promotional purposes, resale, and all forms of document delivery. Special rates are available for educational institutions that wish to make photocopies for non-profit educational classroom use.

Permissions may be sought directly from Elsevier Science Global Rights Department, PO Box 800, Oxford OX5 1DX, UK; phone: (+44) 1865 843830, fax: (+44) 1865 853333, e-mail: permissions@elsevier.co.uk. You may also contact Global Rights directly through Elsevier's home page (http://www.elsevier.nl), by selecting 'Obtaining Permissions'.

In the USA, users may clear permissions and make payments through the Copyright Clearance Center, Inc., 222 Rosewood Drive, Danvers, MA 01923, USA; phone: (+1) (978) 7508400, fax: (+1) (978) 7504744, and in the UK through the Copyright Licensing Agency Rapid Clearance Service (CLARCS), 90 Tottenham Court Road, London W1P 0LP, UK; phone: (+44) 207 631 5555; fax: (+44) 207 631 5500. Other countries may have a local reprographic rights agency for payments.

Derivative Works
Tables of contents may be reproduced for internal circulation, but permission of Elsevier Science is required for external resale or distribution of such material.
Permission of the Publisher is required for all other derivative works, including compilations and translations.

Electronic Storage or Usage
Permission of the Publisher is required to store or use electronically any material contained in this work, including any chapter or part of a chapter.

Except as outlined above, no part of this work may be reproduced, stored in a retrieval system or transmitted in any form or by any means, electronic, mechanical, photocopying, recording or otherwise, without prior written permission of the Publisher.
Address permissions requests to: Elsevier Science Global Rights Department, at the mail, fax and e-mail addresses noted above.

Notice
No responsibility is assumed by the Publisher for any injury and/or damage to persons or property as a matter of products liability, negligence or otherwise, or from any use or operation of any methods, products, instructions or ideas contained in the material herein. Because of rapid advances in the medical sciences, in particular, independent verification of diagnoses and drug dosages should be made.

First edition 2001

Library of Congress Cataloging in Publication Data
A catalog record from the Library of Congress has been applied for.

British Library Cataloguing in Publication Data
A catalogue record from the British Library has been applied for.

ISBN: 0-7623-0753-6

∞ The paper used in this publication meets the requirements of ANSI/NISO Z39.48-1992 (Permanence of Paper).
Printed in The Netherlands.

CONTENTS

FOREWORD

Throughout the world, early childhood (internationally defined as the years from birth to eight) is high on the agendas of governments. Equally, in many countries, there is a call for policy and practice to be more closely linked to research and many advocates of particular viewpoints will enlist the support of selected research evidence to lobby for their special interest.

Issues of philosophies and values and the ways in which these influence not only the policies which gain ascendancy but also how (and if) research is funded and the methods adopted, are important aspects of the field which must be confronted and shared. The more participants in this exciting and important field debate with other stakeholders such as parents, politicians and, where possible the children themselves, the greater our shared understanding of children, their lives and learning, will be. Thus I must acknowledge that this book could never hope to cover all the research evidence and debates about policy and practice in which we need to engage, it is merely one contribution.

Having said that, I must also state that I feel very privileged that my contributors, all eminent specialists in their own fields and countries, as well as internationally, have so thoughtfully helped in the production of this reader. My first thanks are to them.

I am grateful too to the publishers for their unending patience; to the secretaries of the Centre for Educational Research at Canterbury Christ Church University College during the period of the book's production – Louise Duff, Roma Woodward, Gill Harrison and Annie McLaren; to co-members of the British Educational Research Association Early Years Special Interest Group, most of them my friends and colleagues over many years – for their vibrancy, integrity, commitment and challenges.

Finally, I must add my usual acknowledgement to my husband Roy and all my family, especially my five grandchildren – Coralie, Eliot, Kieran, Oliver and Sam – from whom I am learning something new all the time.

Tricia David
Canterbury
April 2001

INTRODUCTION: THE YOUNG CHILD IN CONTEXT: PRACTICE, POLICY AND RESEARCH

Tricia David

Most societies take babies and children, even childhood itself, for granted, rarely questioning their long-held beliefs and assumptions – except when the young cause trouble. In only a few countries or regions do members of society pause and debate how their current global, national or local context impacts on the lives of children, or what exactly they think childhood is for, what children should be and what they should learn. Two examples of societies where such thinking is happening are, firstly, the Reggio Emilia region of Northern Italy, where children are encouraged to be 'rich and competent', using 'the hundred languages of children' to express their own ideas and to grow up as capable, independent thinkers (Edwards et al., 1998). Secondly China has instituted 'parent schools', to guide families, because the one child policy and commercialisation have so changed the way of life and nurseries are expected to counter the effects of grand-parental and parental adoration. The massive changes in Chinese society mean that parents are unsure about their responsibilities, feeling inexperienced they need reassurance (Powell, 2001).

At the same time, much of the knowledge that wise, elderly relatives in many minority world countries have gleaned from their experiences and observations, often trivialised in years gone by, is being confirmed by recent research and this body of knowledge about young children's socialisation and learning is being ameliorated through the gathering of research information from a number of fields, such psychology, sociology, history, neurophysiology. Overall, practitioners and researchers in the field can build on the work of the last hundred years of research and theory including that of Freud, Winnicott, Bowlby, Piaget, Vygotsky, Isaacs, Skinner, Bruner, Bronfenbrenner, Donaldson and many others, developing their own theoretical perspectives based on further research, observation and discussion.

In this publication I have invited a number of eminent colleagues, all leaders in their fields and countries, to contribute an overview of an area of research which has important messages for policy-makers and/or practitioners concerned with the earliest years of childhood. Clearly this is a selection in a number of ways – book length is limited – but also as editor I must acknowledge my own limitations as white, western/ northern and having my own beliefs about democracy and social justice, values which I believe should underpin services for children and their families. Further, a few of the invited authors found it impossible to clear the time to write a proposed chapter, so that I was at the mercy of forces other than my own planning and the final book does not contain all I had intended. As a result, the 'picture' presented is partial and to some extent fragmented. I hope that readers will find both challenges and enjoyment in the work my colleagues present. For my part I have been excited and fascinated by the many parallels in the different chapters and I have found that each contribution helps me think more deeply about the situation here in the south of England, an area with many pockets of serious disadvantage and child poverty, despite its apparent affluence. Equally, their work has helped me ponder the implications for young children in our global future. Thus I trust the text will prove useful firstly as a reflective tool, especially for practitioners, policy-maker and researchers.

Secondly, I hope those who have not themselves carried out research will feel intrigued enough to want to consider taking this step, since nothing can help one become a more competent reader of research reports than actually doing research oneself, so gaining a better understanding of the challenges and demands, as well as recognising the pitfalls. Developing this critical ability towards research in the early years field is vital if we are to debate findings and their relevance to contemporary childhood and society. Further, the sign of a lively and engaged workforce is its depth of interest in its own field. Wishing to know more by seeking to develop practice through one's own investigations and building on those of others, fulfils this measure of an engaged and well-educated workforce. As several of the contributors point out, research from other countries and cultures, regions and settings may provide illumination and food for thought, but often results should be applied extremely tentatively to a different context. For this group of readers, I hope the book will be both a spur and a reference text.

The book is divided into sections and the areas covered are as follows:

- *The child, the family and the community*
- *The wider context: policy-making and its impact*
- *Curriculum matters*
- *Researching early childhood education and care.*

In *The child, the family and the community*, Anne Meade reviews the available evidence about brain research, with reservations about some of the current hype on this topic and stressing the plasticity of the human brain, prepared as it is for lifelong learning. She also discusses some pointers for practice in the early years field. Naturally, this article, exhorting recognition that children's brains are at their most plastic and thirsty for appropriate experiences during the earliest years, is also of great importance for policy-makers and parents. For example, for too long U.K. governments have acted as if children under three do not need learning opportunities, as if they have no brains at this stage and need only 'care'. Yet it is during this period that the patterns of learning are laid and that the inborn urge to explore and experiment can be extinguished and replaced by learned dependency or apathy as a result of thwarted explorations.

Also in that section, Lars-Erik Berg informs readers about recent research in Sweden concerning the relationships between fathers and children and their views of divorce and separation by birth parents. Here we see the impact of societal attitudes, for Berg's findings are much more positive than those of earlier research, carried out mainly in the U.S.A and the U.K., where perhaps white Anglo-Saxon attitudes created a climate of disapproval which resulted in pain for the children involved, as well as for the parting parents. During my own time as a headteacher, I became aware that staff would occasionally attribute certain negative behaviours in children to parental divorce, rather than to the way in which the divorce was being handled or to attitudes among family members and the community. Trying to persuade parents to be more positive for the sake of their children and staff to recognise that children could be helped rather than excused for inappropriate behaviour which was sometimes going unchecked, became an important aspect of my leadership role as the numbers of family break-ups mounted. Lars-Erik Berg's chapter will give hope to many parents but it will also cause practitioners to think about their approaches to parental separation.

The final chapter in this section by Leonardo Yanez and Arelys Moreno concerns the part communities can play in developing provision for young children. It highlights the mistakes that can be made by over-zealous planners who do not include local people in a democratic process. Here in the U.K., we could learn much from this report, especially in relation to the Sure Start initiatives. Their findings remind one of the work of Paulo Freire and demand an exploration of the philosophies and values that underpin any initiative. This reminds us that research is not value-free, that philosophical and ethical reflection is a vital part of the research process throughout.

The second set of papers, called collectively: *The wider context: policy-making and its impact*, include chapters by Peter Moss, Celia Valiente, Olusola Obisanya and Pam Calder. Here the authors explore the ways in which policy-makers' decisions have an impact on the services provided for young children and their families, raising issues ranging from staff qualifications and training, to reliance on the private sector in a majority world country; the movement of political parties towards the centre and the effect on childcare policies; and the ethical arguments for governments to take early childhood services very seriously.

In the section entitled *Curriculum matters*, Stig Broström discusses the question of who should create early childhood curricula and how curriculum design might be approached. In many countries, in the past, babyhood and infancy were often seen as the domain of the mother, other female relatives or wet- and nursery-nurses, who were not thought to be clever (Steedman, 1988), the ability to provide appropriate care for such young children being thought natural. What they might be expected to learn during this phase would have depended on the type of society into which a child was born and even today, there are very different expectations of what and how children will learn, dependent upon whether the society is largely *individualist* or *collectivist* (Rosenthal, 2000). Recognising that children come into the world avidly keen to learn and that therefore a curriculum exists even when it is not consciously planned or written down is the first step towards realising that professional practitioners should at least have some clarity about what they understand their society to be asking of them. In a similar way to the acknowledgement that a curriculum of some sort will exist in any setting, it is important to realise that assessments of children's achievements will be on-going. Thus, assessments by professional early childhood educators need to be made more consciously and through appropriate techniques. As Anne Smith (1999) argues in her discussion of the New Zealand early years curriculum framework, the Te Whariki,

> It was particularly important to develop informal assessment practices which were an integral part of the normal early childhood activities and interaction. Checklists and worksheets just would not be appropriate with a holistic curriculum focusing on encouraging children's dispositions to learn. Carr (1999) argues that formative assessment is a type of action research, and that it is therefore valid for teachers to choose ethnographic and interpretive methods such as the narrative-based "learning stories" approach which she has developed (Smith, 1999: 15).

Since literacy (print literacy) and numeracy are so high on many governments' agendas it seemed important to explore the available research evidence for both and chapters by Bridie Raban and Carol Aubrey provide a wealth of information and debate. The fact that these 'curriculum areas' have been covered and not others such as physical development; creative development; personal, social, moral, spiritual or cultural development; or knowledge and understanding of the world (to use but one possible type of curricular framework) does not indicate my prioritisation of these areas, more, it is intended to indicate the way in which the research supports the idea that children's learning is holistic, rooted in everyday events in which they themselves are interested and that both literacy and numeracy in the earliest years need to be approached through playful, meaningful experiences. It is only through examining research evidence that the dangers inherent in a narrow curriculum which overemphasises literacy and numeracy and encourages or enforces an inappropriate, overly teacher-led approach with this age-group that the alternatives can be promoted (Anning, 1998; David et al., 2000).

Glenda MacNaughton focuses on gender and, using research evidence, she argues that we need to recognise that equal opportunities lack an appreciation of the complexity of the power-knowledge issues which continue to dog this aspect of society in general and early childhood services in particular. The importance of examining specific research concerning other aspects of social justice and inclusion, such as those relating to race, special needs, poverty, language and religion was not overlooked and a number of these were included in the original plan for the book. That young children are very quickly aware of the ways in which society classifies them or members of their peer group and their families is now widely recognised, as is the acknowledgement that powerful socio-cultural forces in children's eco-system (see Bronfenbrenner, 1979) help shape the people they are and their understandings of the world. Paul Connolly's (1998) study of young British African-Caribbean boys demonstrates the complexity of their active involvement in shaping their own identities.

The section concludes with Sally Lubeck and Patricia Jessup's review of evidence about the dangers inherent in the possible globalisation of the curriculum. They use research data from the United States and the United Kingdom to illustrate their discussions. At a time when the OECD (Organisation for Economic Cooperation and Development) is about to publish its comparative report on surveys of 12 nations' ECEC (OECD forthcoming), it is important to bear in mind that such work can very helpfully produce guiding principles but not a blue-print for services, because of the issues of context and history.

The final set of articles actually debate issues concerning research itself. Ann Lewis charts the arguments concerning research involving children and she uses many practical research examples to illustrate her review. Carol Aubrey and Helen Penn, in their separate chapters, are both concerned about the ways in which research findings are used comparatively, rather than cross-culturally, and both call for early years researchers, policy-makers and practitioners to be wary of over-generalisation from one context to another – and the overlooking of different strengths and values in societies whose priorities may not concur with those of the apparently 'more successful' contexts. Urie Bronfenbrenner (1952) once pointed out that if researchers became too entangled in and anxious about ethical issues they would be immobilised and end up abandoning their projects. Thus he advocated rigorous attention to ethical issues but not the abandonment of research. In a similar way, we should not be daunted by the difficulties pointed out in the critiques of research approaches but examine what can be learnt, in terms of both substance and methodology, from every report we read.

In exploring all the areas of research included in this book, it is important to bear in mind constantly both the individual child and the context – the time and place – in which they are growing and learning. The childhoods children experience will be subject to not only their innate inheritance in terms of physical and psychological characteristics and well-being, but also to what is available to them as food and activity for their bodies and for their minds. Children themselves will be active participants in shaping those childhoods but the histories, economic and social conditions of the societies to which they belong will be powerful forces influencing not only the children but their parents, other family and community members, early childhood professionals and policy-makers. Our assumptions about young children and early childhood will colour *how* we 'see' and *what* we actually 'see'. Debating with colleagues from a wider international group, including parents, policy-makers, practitioners and researchers, is one way to expose those aspects we 'see' differently, as well as exposing those aspects some of us fail to 'see' at all. Such a forum also acts as a spur to the question of *why* we 'see' in particular ways, in particular countries at particular times. This book is intended to provide a contribution to that forum.

REFERENCES

Anning, A. (1998). Appropriateness or effectiveness in the early childhood curriculum in the U.K.: some research evidence. *International Journal of Early Years Education*, 6(3), 299–314.
Bronfenbrenner, U. (1979). *The Ecology of Human Development*. Cambridge, Mass: Harvard University Press.
Bronfenbrenner, U. (1952). Principles of professional ethics: Cornell studies in social growth. *American Psychologist*, 7(2), 452–455.

Carr, M. (1999). *The four Ds: assessing teachers as researchers in a research project on assessment in early childhood*. Paper presented at the Third Warwick International Early Years Conference, University of Warwick, 12–16 April 1999.

Connolly, P. (1998). *Racism, Gender Identities and Young Children*. London: Routledge.

David, T., Raban, B., Ure, C., Goouch, K., Jago, M., Barrière, I., & Lambirth, A. (2000). *Making Sense of Early Literacy: a practitioner's perspective*. Stoke-on-Trent: Trentham Books.

Edwards, C., Gandidni, L., & Foreman, G. (1998). *The Hundred Languages of Children*. New York: Ablex.

OECD (forthcoming). *Comparative Report of ECEC in Twelve Countries*. Paris: OECD.

Powell, S. (2001). Early childhood in China: a case study of contemporary Shanghai. Unpublished doctoral thesis, University of Kent at Canterbury.

Rosenthal, M. (2000). *Quality in early childhood provision*. Keynote address presented at the University of Malta International Seminar, New Dolmen Hotel Malta, November 28–December 1, 2000.

Smith, A. (1999). *The role of an early childhood curriculum: promoting diversity versus uniformity*. Keynote address presented at the Dublin Conference Enhancing Quality in the Early Years, Dublin 19–20 December 1999.

Steedman, C. (1988). The mother made conscious: the historical development of primary school pedagogy. In: M. Woodhead & A. McGrath (Eds), *Family, School and Society* (pp. 82–95). Hodder & Stoughton/Open University Press.

SECTION I:

THE CHILD, THE FAMILY AND THE COMMUNITY

1. ONE HUNDRED BILLION NEURONS: HOW DO THEY BECOME ORGANISED?

Anne Meade

INTRODUCTION

The brain is one human organ that is not fully formed at birth. Nevertheless, an amazing amount of the brain has developed by the time a child is born. One hundred billion brain cells called neurons have formed – the same number as in adults' brains. These are in their right locations, but most are not connected, nor are they mature. In other mammals, the cortex is far more mature at birth, because animals do not have nearly so much learning ahead of them. In humans, different regions and different layers of the brain develop on different time frames over an extended period.

This chapter describes how the brain develops and how it functions. An explanation of brain-imaging technologies follows. Brain imaging (also known as neuro-imaging) has been able to reveal more about what is formed at birth, and when and where subsequent development occurs. These images have drawn attention to the importance of the early years. I will weave together some neuroscience findings with other child development findings in a later section. Finally, I will suggest some implications for early childhood education, bearing in mind that "you can't derive pedagogy from biology" (Brandt, 1999: 237).

Promoting Evidence-based Practice in Early Childhood Education:
Research and its Implications, Volume 1, pages 3–26.
Copyright © 2001 by Elsevier Science Ltd.
All rights of reproduction in any form reserved.
ISBN: 0-7623-0753-6

BRAIN DEVELOPMENT

The brain is part of the central nervous system, as is the spinal cord. The other part of the nervous system is called the peripheral system (which includes the sensory nerves for input and motor nerves for acting out what the brain says). The central nervous system has a genetically programmed sequence of development. Put simply, it develops from 'tail' to head. The top of the head, the cerebral cortex region of the brain, develops last.

There are four main stages in brain development:

(1) cell division;
(2) cell migration;
(3) the formation and elimination of synapses (connections) between neurons; and
(4) myelination (wrapping) of neurons – in particular their axons.

Neural Cell Division

The growth in number of neurons occurs at a phenomenal rate in the womb. The process of cell division to achieve the end-result of 100 billion cells is not evenly spread over the period from gestation to birth. It produces the vast majority of brain cells during the first half of the foetal period.

Rita Carter (1998: 14) describes the diversity of neurons.

> There are long thin [neurons] that send single snaking tendrils to the far reaches of the body; star-shaped ones that reach out in all directions; and ones that bear a dense branching crown like absurdly overgrown antlers. Each neuron connects with up to ten thousand neighbours. The bits that join up are the branches, of which there are two kinds: axons, which conduct signals away from the cell nucleus, and dendrites, which receive incoming information.

Neural Cell Migration

Genes direct the cells to migrate to approximate locations in the brain.

> [*T*]he remaining and most intricate part of brain sculpting is accomplished by neural cell *migration* . . . . . New neurons . . . shimmy their way along to a predestined zone in the thickening brain . . . . . Neurons migrate immediately after being born. By the end of neurogenesis . . . all the main brain structures are in place . . . [but] not yet hooked up (Eliot, 1999: 26).

Sensory cells are said to be 'plastic' for a period after they arrive – they can change their function. When neurons become hooked up to each other and wrapped by myelin (see below) they lose much of their plasticity. Migration to a specific location and layer in the cerebral cortex has significance for defining later functions. As neurons shimmy up 'columns' from the inside out, they gather information from those they climb over.

Synaptic 'Blooming' and 'Pruning'

Information is transmitted between axons and dendrites on neurons by brief electrical pulses (See Edelman's 1992: 20 diagram: A Neural Cell and Synapses). There is a microscopic gap in junctions between the axon of one neuron and the dendrites of another. Information must cross these gaps via hook-ups called synapses. Synapses start forming two months from gestation *within* the womb and continue forming well into childhood, some into adulthood. Most synapses form between birth and 3 years of age. Indeed, young children's brains form lots more of them than adults'. This oversupply results in 50 to 100% more synapses than adults have. The oversupply allows for 'pruning' – a withering away – where lack of activity weakens connections.

Chemical neurotransmitters carry the information pulses across synapses. Synapses can be excite or inhibit electrical activity in the brain. When excited a chain effect is set up, which ends in some output to muscles, or thought.

The Committee on the Developments in the Science of Learning has an analogy of sculpture to describe the process of synapse consolidation.

> Some neuroscientists explain synapse formation by analogy to the art of sculpture. Classical artists working in marble created a sculpture by chiselling away unnecessary bits of stone until they achieved their final form. Animal studies suggest that the "pruning" that occurs during synapse overproduction and loss is similar to this act of carving a sculpture. The nervous system sets up a large number of connections; experience then plays on this network, selecting the appropriate ones and removing the inappropriate ones (Bransford, Brown & Cocking, 1999: 104).

This still begs a question. Does synapse *blooming* signify learning? Or is synapse *pruning* associated with learning? John Bruer (1999) challenged those who jumped to the conclusion that the prolific growth of synapses signifies an enormous amount of learning in the first three years. Others are cautious in the interpretations of 'blooming', and lean toward associating learning with the strengthening of synapses. The jury is still out on this debate. Many agree with William Greenough who suggests that each process is associated with a different type of sensory information storage (Greenough, Black & Wallace, 1993).

Greenough argues that blooming happens when mammals first meet sensory experiences that they are genetically primed for. He is referring to experiences like seeing in the daylight. There are critical periods associated with these experiences. For the most part, they do happen, so most of us have such synapses. If an animal is deprived of an *expected experience* in a critical period (for example, because of a severe visual impairment), dendritic growth, and connections between neurons related to that experience, is stunted.

Yet the 'jump start' from expected experiences is not the whole story. The rest of the organisation of neural cells is determined by individual experience. The formation, retention and/or strengthening of synapses are said to be *experience dependent* – dependent on what happens in the lives of individual children (and adults). Even this is not the whole story. Changes in chemical neurotransmitters and in capillaries that supply blood to the brain occur.

Scientists are confident that genes are largely responsible for establishing the sequence and template for brain wiring. Lise Eliot comments, '[Then] 'nurture' steps in and finishes the job .... Synapses that are highly active – that receive more electrical impulses and release greater amounts of neurotransmitter – more effectively stimulate their postsynaptic targets. This heightened electrical activity triggers molecular changes that stabilize the synapse' (1999: 30).

Circuits of stable synapses reflect *patterns* of greater physical and mental activity. Animal researchers have found that greater physical and mental activity – providing that it is in a complex environment and involves social stimulation as well – not only produces more synapses, but also more blood vessel formation and bigger cell bodies (Bransford et al., 1999). The pruning of synapses and the formation of circuits make mental processes more streamlined. However, when synapse pruning and myelination in different regions are past their peak, the potential for 'rewiring' reduces.

Myelination

Coinciding with synapse pruning is a wrapping (myelination) process. Myelination of axons by a fatty sheath serves two purposes: to insulate them to reduce muddled connections, and to speed information flows.

Circuits or Maps

Each system in our brains, for example the visual system, is made up of many circuits or 'maps', which entail a mass of connections between cells (Edelman, 1992). Circuits for sensory systems are quite localised; circuits for other functions may be more distributed. The structures of the brain and the location of some of these maps are described by Rita Carter.

> At the very back of the main mass of brain, tucked under its tail and partly fused to it, lies the cerebellum ... [that] was our mammalian ancestors' main brain .... Each half of

[successor], the cerebrum is split into four lobes .... Each lobe processes its own clutch of things: the occipital lobe is made up almost entirely of visual processing areas; the parietal lobe deals mainly with functions connected with movement, orientation, calculation and certain types of recognition; the temporal lobes deal with sound, speech comprehension (usually on the left only) and some aspects of memory; and the frontal lobes deals with the most integrated brain functions: thinking, conceptualising and planning. They also play a major role in the conscious appreciation of emotion (Fig. 1).

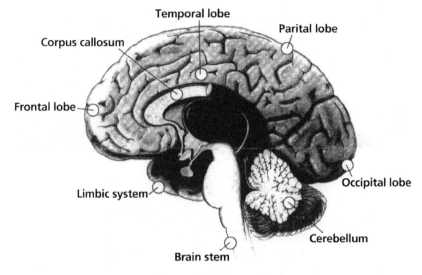

Fig. 1.

If you slice the brain in half down the centre line so that the two hemispheres fall apart, you see that beneath the cortex lies a complex conglomeration of modules: lumps, tubes and chambers .... and criss-crossing ropes of axons interconnect them all .... The bands that connect [the modules] are covered in a sheath of ... myelin, which acts as insulation, allowing electricity to flow swiftly and directly along them. The corpus callosum joins the two hemispheres and acts as a bridge between them, constantly shunting information back and forth so that most of the time they are effectively one (Ibid., 1998: 15–17).

The 'lumps, tubes and chambers' describe the limbic system. The 'criss-crossing ropes' are communication routes linking many areas of the brain.

[*The limbic system*] part of the brain is unconscious, but it has a profound effect on our experience because it is closely connected to the conscious cortex above it and constantly feeds information upwards. Emotions – our most basic cerebral reactions – are generated in the limbic system. But the limbic modules have ... other functions besides.

The brainstem is formed from the nerves that run up from the body via the spinal column and it carries information .... Various clumps of cells in the brainstem determine the brain's general level of alertness and regulate . . . processes of the body, such as breathing (Ibid., 1998: 17).

How then does the mind works? Rita Carter uses the metaphor of a 'fire-dance' where the neurons get "fired up, joined up and dancing" (1998: 19). She emphasizes that it needs to be on a large scale. Each brain does its own 'firing up' for and to itself.

In addition, Edelman (1994) says that cells not only fire together but change together chemically over a period of time. And each individual's experiences are unique. 'If one were to number the branches of one neuron and to number in a corresponding manner the neurons it touched, the numbers would not correspond exactly in any two individuals . . . – not even in identical twins' (Ibid.: 25). He emphasizes the complexity of the dynamics of the brain, and uses the 'jungle' as a metaphor for these dynamics – a jungle full of sound and light patterns and movement and growth patterns (Ibid.: 29).

NEUROSCIENCE

Neuroscience is about how the brain gives rise to mental processes. Animal studies, and research related to head injuries, neurological illnesses, and medical interventions on humans, used to be the main sources of neuroscientific knowledge. Now, technologies are available to see the human brain at work. These technologies are like x-rays that reveal our bones. Put simply, what shows up in brain images is electrical- or fuel-use activity. The images show both the locations of brain activity, and their timing.

There is a convergence of findings from neuroscience, cognitive science and development psychology. Together their findings give people a better understanding of the relationship between the brain and the mind. Educators are particularly interested in this, and are keen to find out if neuroscience can guide their teaching. Remember, however, *behavioural neuroscience* is still in its infancy. Not surprisingly, therefore, researchers in this field are mostly cautious about using brain research to explain learning, or to select educational practice. However, they supply some missing links and broaden knowledge about human development.

Pat Wolfe and Ron Brandt (1998: 10) comment that educators need to develop their understanding of the brain or run the risk of being caught out by 'pseudo scientific fads, inappropriate generalizations and dubious programs' (1998: 10). An example of such a fad is left brain, right brain training, or stimulus programmes for infants. About the latter, Siegel advises: 'Developmental studies . . . suggest that infants do not need to be overwhelmed with sensory stimulation to achieve 'normal' levels of development of their brains' (1999b: 8).

The relationship between neuroscientists and educationists can involve misunderstanding and even fairly heated disagreements. Some publications have set in train some struggles between existing and new disciplines.[1] The struggle, in part, seems to be about definitions of knowledge and learning – classical academic knowledge versus a wider knowledge base. Classical theories of knowledge hold that the world is made up of objects and relations between them. Research on emotional intelligence (e.g. Gardner, 1983; Goleman, 1997), and on states of the mind, have altered our views of the mind and the brain. For example, Daniel Siegel, a neurobiologist, now offers a theory that 'human connections shape the neural connections from which the mind emerges' (1999a: 2). His emphasis on neural changes is relatively new, but the link between human connection (viz. person-to-person interaction) and children's learning is not (see, for example, Dewey, 1938; Rogoff, 1990).

NEURO-IMAGING TECHNOLOGIES

There are two main classes of technologies that produce images that complement what is known about the brain from medical research or can be inferred from observations of human behaviour. They are (a) those that permit direct visualization of the *structures* of the brain (the spatial domain), and (b) those that provide pictures of *processes* in the brain (the temporal domain) (Nelson & Bloom, 1997: 970).

Neuro-Imaging Procedures

These procedures fall into three classes:

(1) **Metabolic procedures** (e.g. Positron Emission Tomography (PET), and functional Magnetic Resonance Imaging (fMRI)) where the measurement is of the *use of fuel* – oxygen or glucose – in various parts of the brain. The pattern of glucose use is strikingly similar to changes in cortical synapses;

(2) **Electrophysiologic procedures** (e.g. Electroencephalogram (EEG), and Event-Related Potentials (ERP)) where the brain's *electrical activity* is scanned via electrodes on the scalp to show where activity happens and on what time frame. EEG images show spontaneous natural rhythms, whereas ERP recordings show activity following the introduction of a stimulus;

(3) **Magnetic procedures** (e.g. Magnetic Source Imaging (MSI)) where neuronal activity and the consequential *bioelectrical signals* are detected via magnetic measurement.

Advantages	Disadvantages
Metabolic (use of fuel) **PET** can: • Show brain metabolism, e.g. synaptic development, • Identify brain structures used for different tasks, • Identify which parts of the brain are developed at different ages, • Compare behavioural and pharmaceutical treatments of disorders.	*Metabolic (use of fuel)* **PET** involves: • subjects being confined in a scanner, • ethical constraints because radio-active material is introduced, • high costs. In addition, relatively lower quality: • spatial resolution of images, • temporal resolution of images (thus, it reveals little about when thinking is happening).
fMRI can do all the above. In addition, fMRI is: • non-invasive, • a faster procedure, • able to identify any similarities in primate and human structures (e.g. visual cortex), • able to reveal any similarities in brain activity in adults and children (e.g. non-spatial working memory)	**FMRI:** • involves subjects being confined in a scanner and to keep very still, • reveals little about when thinking is happening, • emits a relatively high level of noise.
Electrophysiologic procedures **EEG** can: • show electrical activity associated with ongoing cognitive activity, including emotional activity, • link type of emotions to specific brain structures. It is non-invasive, and relatively inexpensive.	*Electrophysiologic procedures* **EEG** has: • relatively poor temporal resolution, • relatively poor spatial resolution.
ERP is: • a fast procedure, • suitable for infants & children, • able to measure timing very precisely, • able to show neurological impairments (e.g. auditory mechanism impairments that affect rapid speech processing).	**ERP** has: • improved but not good spatial resolution, • considerable risk of poor measurement data due to muscle or eye movement.
Magnetic procedures **MSI:** • can combine the measurement of the structure and function of the brain, • gives superb time measurement • gives superb measurement of brain structures, and • is non-invasive.	*Magnetic procedures* **MSI:** • requires a special test chamber, • is not very useful for images of deeper structures of the brain.

Fig. 2. An overview of neuro-imaging techniques (Adapted from Nelson & Bloom, 1997).

A summary of the advantages and disadvantages of each technology is set out in Fig. 2 on the previous page. This section also provides an overview of some of the terms used in technical reports.

BENEFITS OF NEUROSCIENCE

Many potential benefits of neuroscience have not yet been realised. Further advances in the technologies are needed before any imaging data can be gathered in children's day-to-day settings. As well, neuroscientists and educational researchers are yet to come together to develop and implement the complex research designs that are needed to answer some educational questions.

To date, some benefits of relevance to educators include:

- describing the neurological bases of, and demonstrating the efficacy of different treatments for, disorders,
- revealing the effects of environmental influences, like substances and chemicals, on brain development;
- advancing understanding of neurobiological bases of early learning and development, including understanding of difficulties;
- explaining how the brain retains and retrieves information; and
- demonstrating the relationship between emotions, and learning and development;
- validating some theories of child development.

I will not describe neurological disorders, nor their treatments. Rita Carter focuses on them in her book *Mapping the* Mind (1998). A brief example of showing the efficacy of different treatments for disorders was when two alternative treatments were used for two groups of patients who had an obsessive-compulsive disorder. A PET scan showed that both the behavioural and pharmaceutical treatments changed the brain in the exactly the same way (Nelson & Bloom, 1997). The educational/therapeutic programme *was* efficacious, and the scan explained what had happened in neurobiological terms.

Other benefits from neuroscience will be explored in more detail below.

WHAT HAS BEEN FOUND ABOUT ENVIRONMENTAL INFLUENCES ON PRENATAL BRAIN DEVELOPMENT?

Pasko Rakic (1988) has found that the cerebral cortex is vulnerable to influences from the environment from within days of conception. His explanation for the long-lasting effects is that early environmental factors may disrupt the cell migration process so that cells may 'end up in the wrong place at the wrong time and form inappropriate synapses' (Shore, 1997: 23, summarising Rakic, 1988).

Lise Eliot (1999) has synthesised medical research about environmental influences, and these are summarised below.

Nutrition. If nutrition is deficient – in particular in calories and protein – from mid-way through gestation to about 2 years of age, brain development can be too. It can result in a smaller brain. The earlier the poor nutrition begins and the longer it lasts, the greater and longer the effects. If children are malnourished in periods of myelination, it doesn't go well. The usual result is more muddled connections.

Malnourished children raised in stimulating environments don't suffer the same level of effects. It would seem that neural activity – those 'fire dances' – can ameliorate the effects of malnutrition.

Effects of substances and chemicals on brain development. Agents in moderate doses that harm a foetus (as well as large doses leading to gross abnormalities) tend to have a greater effect when taken early in the pregnancy, and if taken with other agents, for example, smoking. The effects include slower sensory, motor or language development.

Alcohol drunk in excess kills neurons, disrupts cell migration, and interferes with dendritic development and precise synaptic connections. Lower intakes can have an impact too. The most common outcomes are growth and mental retardation.

Cigarette smoking is associated with a decrease in oxygen in the brain, leading to low birth weight, premature births, and SIDS. Low birth weight and prematurity increase the chance of neurological impairment in thinking.

Illegal drugs, including marijuana, are linked to higher rates of defects and retardation, according to some research. Premature births are also more likely.

Caffeine, artificial sweeteners, and MSG effects have all been studied. No ill effects are evident.

Maternal emotion and stress. A pregnant woman who is unhappy, stressed, or anxious, in poor health and/or lacks social support transmits the effects to her baby and the nervous system of the baby activates in sympathy. The mother's stress alters the hormones in the brain that control the blood flow to the placenta, growth and movement of foetuses, and lactation after birth. All are important for the baby's brain development. Babies of anxious mothers tend to be fussier and possibly delayed, and themselves produce higher levels of similar hormones after birth.

NEUROBIOLOGICAL BASES OF CHILDREN'S LEARNING AND DEVELOPMENT

The Role of Genes

Daniel Siegel provides a succinct summary of the role of genes – and experience

> Genes contain the information for the general organisation of the brain's structure, but experience determines which genes become expressed, how and when. The expression of genes leads to the production of proteins that enable neuronal growth and the formation of new synapses . . . . Early in life, interpersonal relationships are a primary source of the experiences that shapes how genes express themselves in the brain (Siegel, 1999a: 14).

The Role of Experience

Brad Shore (1996) describes the human brain as an "ecological brain" that is dependent throughout its life on environmental input. Human brains start learning in the womb. Two examples of prenatal learning relate to touch and hearing experiences. First, a possible explanation for the high proportion of right-handed people is that the right arm has more room in the womb and, therefore, has had more experience of different touch sensations before birth. Second, there are now several studies that indicate that infants recognise sounds they have heard in the womb – styles of music, for example.

The Development of the Sensory Peripheral System[2]

In the postnatal period, there are critical periods when infants and young children need to have typical visual and auditory experiences in order for them to be fully brain sighted and fully brain hearing. Hearing and vision are the only aspects of brain development where there is strong evidence that it is virtually impossible for later experience to correct any abnormal brain functioning that is established in critical periods. If typical experiences don't occur in those periods, other cells may take their place and the brain is rewired. Because of this 'rewiring' capability, Mark Johnson (1998, p. 14) argues that the division of the cortex into regions, such as the hearing sub-region, is heavily dependent on experience.

The *hearing* area of the brain is one of the first to mature. Nevertheless, babies' brains process auditory information at least twice as slowly as adults. Like other aspects of development, handling complex input, such as language, comes later. And language input can be complex unless adults adjust it – which they do. Lise Eliot (1999) provides a neurobiological explanation as to the value of 'motherese'. It is simpler. Also, it's louder and more direct style helps babies distinguish it from background sounds, which is important as babies' hearing circuits are not able to process fine distinctions in sound (Eliot, 1999: 249).

Aspects of *language* development are guided by a genetic timetable that is linked to the development of hearing. Evidence is accumulating that this language timetable may include critical periods. For example, the ability to discriminate between letter sounds (phonemes) becomes restricted to those of the mother tongue at around 12 months of age (Johnson, 1998: 32). Also, researchers using ERP technology to compare brain activity for different language systems – sign language versus spoken language – have concluded that children display sensitive periods in development for different aspects of language input (Dawson & Fischer, 1994: xvi).

The visual cortex has many sub-regions each processing an aspect of *sight,* such as colour, shape, motion, and so on. At about 3 months, infants start to recognise things they have seen in the immediate past. The visual cortex has achieved maturity by then (Herschkowitz, Kagan & Zilles, 1997). The critical period for this sensory system occurs early on.

Perhaps because there has been so much experience of *touch* in the womb and during birth, new-born babies can feel a lot better than they can see, hear or taste. There are four different elements to our touch system: touch, temperature, pain and a sense of our own body. Each has its own neural circuitry developed by experience. Being touched has an influence on physical growth, the emotions and the mind. Touch is particularly important early in life. Studies of babies raised in orphanages where staff fed them well found they still ended up stunted if seldom cuddled. Myelination of touch neurons occurs from birth and continues for about six years.

The Development of the Motor System

The motor neural system takes far longer to mature. It is more complex. Myelination starts later (at about 6 months old), and is slow. To compound the situation, some of the axons needing myelin are particularly long – running from, say, the brain to the fingertips. Neural motor development progresses from head to toe, and from the centre (the brain) to the periphery (muscle control of, say, fingers). Maturity of the motor system is completed around puberty. Young children are generally clumsy because of neural immaturity. As circuits mature, movement becomes more purposeful and smoothly co-ordinated. Once myelination is underway, practice refines motor circuitry. This is true for adults, e.g. playing sport, and for babies, e.g. learning to walk independently.

Physical activity is important not only to improve brain circuitry. It also stimulates the supply of blood to the brain, which is essential because the 'brain runs on empty' (Greenough, personal communication, 2000).

One final point is that there is not the same amount of cortical space given over to making different body parts work in all individuals. 'The final composition of cortical space is fought out between different body parts based on the relative amount of sensory experience' (Eliot, 1999: 127). This indicates the importance of a wide range of input in the early years.

Language Learning

Neurological research about language development mostly focuses on whether particular parts of the cortex are critical for language development, and on regions used for different language skills. These are difficult areas to research. Mark Johnson suggests there is a degree of plasticity in young children's neural language systems (1998: 31). Studies comparing brain activity for sign and verbal language support this. Johnson also notes, 'different regions of the cortex may be involved in the acquisition of language from those which are important for language in adults' (Ibid.). Neural language research shows that the left-brain is dominant for language activity, although both hemispheres have a role to play.

'Mass action' aptly describes language activity in the brain (Carter, 1998: 12) Different parts of the brain respond to hearing, seeing and speaking words, for example. Also, different parts of the brain are active when working on word meaning, on word recognition, or on searching for a word. When these skills are more automatic there less activity in the prefrontal cortex. (Passingham, 1993: 250).

Elizabeth Bates and colleagues (1992) note that the attainment of adult-levels of brain metabolism by about 9 months of age correlates with the onset of infants beginning to comprehend specific words. In the second half of the second year there are bursts in vocabulary and grammar progress; these coincide with an increase in synaptic density. The time when language growth becomes more complex at around age 4 years coincides with pruning.

MEMORY – HOW THE BRAIN RETAINS AND RETRIEVES INFORMATION

The brain's ability to process information – to capture, store and retrieve records of information in circuits of connected brain cells – is what makes learning possible. A recent conclusion about the prefrontal cortex is that stored records of information in the brain – memories – also include social skills and moral knowledge, not just knowledge of events and objects (Dolan, 1999).

Memory is important for mentally generating and selecting actions in making plans. Passingham (1993) points out that only humans are equipped with the ability to select between ideas. This uniqueness to humans gives us a clue about the complexity involved and the length of time that will be needed to develop the capacity to deal with it.

Few adults or older children remember events that happened before they were aged three or four years, except those surrounded by a high emotion. This has puzzled developmental psychologists for decades. Brain research provides the answer – the complex circuits responsible for storing longer-term memories take several years to develop.

In the prefrontal cortex, myelination is not finished until early adolescence. An important part of the circuitry for long-term memory includes input and output pathways between the hippocampus and the cortex. Myelination of these is very slow – in some it doesn't start until the second year. Until the prefrontal cortex builds up maps of 'where' and 'when' things happen, which are made more robust by myelination, children can't consciously remember early events – their brain 'equipment' isn't ready.

Infants and toddlers do acquire information and store it in short-term memory, and later for increasing periods of time. Deliberate storage is evident from about seven to 10 months of age. This coincides with the completion of cell formation in the hippocampus. There is an increase in synapses per neuron, and significant chemical changes too. From about seven months old, capitalising on these neurobiological developments, an infant can start to use her working memory to recall where an object has been hidden and reach for it after a delay.

At this age, infants can use their working memories to categorise people as familiar and unfamiliar. They become more upset by 'discrepancies'. As infants develop better memories of familiar faces they react against strangers about whom they have no memory, and against the absence of their mother about whom they have a good memory (Herschkowitz, Kagan, & Zilles, 1997).

"Memory is composed of multiple separate systems" (Squire, 1995: 62), which associate with different abilities. Important categories of memory systems include:

- The short-term memory (also known as working memory) and long-term memory system,
- The conscious (explicit) memory and unconscious (implicit) memory system, and
- Memory for events and autobiographical narrative memory.

Each of these has a different brain organisation. Larry Squire states that explicit memory covers facts and events, while implicit memory includes skills, and habits (Ibid.: 67). Implicit memories include all the learned skills and behaviours, including emotional regulation that we are no longer aware of. In childhood, or sometime in the past, they became habitual because of a lot of practice.

> Early experience can affect subsequent behavior, but the mechanism by which experience persists does not include a record of the event itself. Behavior simply changes. Thus, following multiple and varied encounters, experience can result in altered dispositions, preferences, conditioned responses, habits or skills, but these changes do not afford any potential for an awareness that behavior is being influenced by past experience (Squire, 1995: 73).

Implicit memories are acquired and stored from an early age in the cerebellum. It is possible that this is where much learning derived from play is stored. Implicit memories include perceptual and bodily 'how-to' forms of memory that are stored as schema – generalisations or patterns from repeated experiences.

Explicit and implicit memory can function independently of each other, but usually support each other. Mark Johnson concludes, '. . . most memory tasks likely engage multiple memory systems' (1998: 29). Actually memory activity involves more than memory systems. *All* nerve cells are capable of change in response to experience – they modify their structure or synaptic connections in response to electrical activity.

Recognition and Novelty Preference

Novelty preference is the mechanism that leads babies, toddlers and young children to spend a lot of time seeking out new forms of stimulation; things that they don't recognise. Novel experiences feed the senses with new experiences, and thereby keep the electrical activity in young children's brains humming.

Recognition is the basis of novelty preference, as the baby needs to decide whether an experience is familiar or not. Recognition of the familiar is a straightforward process, and calls on implicit memory. Passingham (1993: 222) says that some tasks don't require people to generate a response, others do. Recognition fits into the first group. His scans show that the second group – generating a response – activates more of the brain. (Recall is also more complex, because the object or event is not in front of you; retrieval needs to be a conscious act.)

BRAIN DEVELOPMENT AND EMOTIONS

Emotion is a function of the brain as is intelligence. Infants' first communications are emotional ones. Simple emotions combined produce complex ones. Rita Carter describes complex emotions as "sophisticated cognitive constructs that are arrived at only after considerable processing by the conscious mind and an elaborate exchange of information between conscious cortical areas of the brain and the limbic system beneath" (1997: 81). Like other complex neural processes, complex emotion circuits are slow to develop.

Feelings are created in the brain stem and information about them passes up through the limbic system. There it is modulated by memories of experience and parental training. When it flows to the cortex, emotional information is translated into mood or motivation. EEGs show that the cortex and limbic system are active as feelings are kept in check – if they are – a process called 'emotional regulation'. The limbic system also imprints emotion on memories.

There are differences in the right and left frontal regions in processing emotional information. '[T]he left frontal region is activated during emotions associated with *approach* . . . [actions] (e.g. joy, interest, anger), whereas the right frontal region is activated during *withdrawal* emotions (e.g. distress, sadness and disgust)' (Dawson, 1994: 347). Any asymmetry in approach and withdrawal emotions, in effect, explains temperament. The balance can be altered by experience, which may be positive, e.g. supportive experience for shy, withdrawn children, or it may be negative, e.g. poor mental health of a mother or an insecure attachment relationship between the mother and child (Dawson, 1994: 371).

The infant comes into the world programmed to connect with others, to be soothed by them when distressed, and to develop schema of self and others. This program motivates interpersonal communication and joint attention. Ongoing communication between, and joint attention by, caregivers and infants sculpts the circuits in young brains that develop social schema.

During the early years of life, the basic circuits of the brain are developing which will be primarily responsible for a number of important mental processes involving emotion, memory, behavior and interpersonal relationships. These processes include: the generation and regulation of emotion; the capacity for 'response flexibility' or mindful, reflective behavior; the autobiographical sense of self and the construction of 'self narrative'; the capacity to understand and care about the mind of others; and the ability to engage in interpersonal communication . . . . [P]atterns of communication between caregiver and child have an important impact on the development of these processes (Siegel, 1999b: 6).

Positive attachment in the first year of life provides a buffer against stress effects, in that year and beyond (Gunnar, 1996). Caregivers who are warm and consistent assist infant brains to modulate emotion. Infants who have insecure attachments and inconsistent caregiver reactions get stressed. Individuals of any age who are stressed react by producing higher levels of cortisol that can trigger the destruction of neurons and synapses. In infants, these cause developmental delays. Moreover, they can set atypical neurological patterns for life, unless an intervention is mounted.

As explained earlier, infants and toddlers cannot consciously recall what happened to them. However, experiences with caregivers and early educators have a powerful and lasting impact. They are significant for developing a sense of self. Siegel says that relationships create 'subjective-self' and 'self-with-other' circuits between 9 and 18 months when the cortex is developing. 'Beyond this period, a 'narrative self' over time emerges in which autobiographical narratives play a major role in defining self' (Siegel, 1999b: 9).

Responsive relationships that result in secure attachments are important. A minority of parents are not capable of giving appropriate emotional nurturance because their own histories. They can't give their children a sense of 'feeling felt' (Siegel, 1999a: 89). Yet 'feeling felt', which Siegel also calls 'mental state resonance', is necessary for healthy secure attachments and for limbic systems. Children most at risk are those with disorganised attachment to parents who are frightening.

[These children] have been found to have the most difficulty later in life with emotional, social and cognitive impairments . . . including affect [emotional] regulation, social difficulties, attentional problems . . . and significant problems in the development of a coherent mind (Siegel, 1999a: 109).

A recent set of studies with Romanian orphans who have been adopted by parents in other countries indicates that the first year may be a critical period for good attachment relationships to establish key neural circuits[3] (Nelson & Bosquet, 2000: 38). An earlier longitudinal study, the Minnesota Parent-Child Project (Egeland, Carlson & Sroufe, 1993), also found that infants who experienced warm and responsive care turned out later to be more socially competent with peers.

Lise Eliot reports the good news about appropriate limbic system development. Children at age 4 years with better regulation of emotion, and better integration of mind and emotion, turn out best later. An indicator of these states is an ability to wait longer for a reward. Those who could wait longer during a test of impulse control an extra turned out to be higher achievers and better adapted socially – with their peers and adults – when they reached adolescence (Eliot, 1999: 291).

Eliot also summarises the bad news when the limbic system is impaired by neglectful/stressful experience in childhood. This includes: children's brains are markedly smaller (shown by MRI scans); there is abnormal electrical activity in the limbic brain regions; and the hippocampus is still stunted in adults (Ibid.: 324).

When development moves in the direction of more integrated states, while all systems are becoming more and more complex, there are happier outcomes.

VALIDATING EARLY CHILD DEVELOPMENT KNOWLEDGE

The brief summary of research above contains many examples of a convergence between neuroscience and child development knowledge. Neuroscience can also help explain some puzzling findings from observations of behaviour. Together they provide a broader knowledge base. The convergences include:

- Many developmental delays derive from environmental influences on the foetal brain: mother's nutrition, ingestion of drugs, and stress.
- Nutrition is important for infant and toddler brain development.
- Neural development goes from simple to complex, primal to higher-order. This matches learning trajectories from basic and concrete to complex and abstract.
- Neurons can (and need to) inhibit some responses and activity. Some behaviour needs to be regulated or constrained.
- There are critical periods in the first few years of life when children need to have appropriate sensory and perceptual input to develop their neural sensory regions. Sensitive periods for optimal development of other domains, such as language may also exist. Child development studies have identified many of these optimal periods.

- There is interplay between nurture and nature – the influences are bi-directional.
- Experiences in complex environments, i.e. environments that entice mammals to use all modalities including social interaction, enhance brain development. Both early childhood and child development research has identified the importance of enriched environments.
- Touch and hearing experiences are particularly important for very young babies.
- Significant neurobiological changes need to take place *before* infants and young children can do most things – physical and/or mental. The timing is set by genetic programs, then experience is essential for brain development. Much child development knowledge is about stages or sequences of development.
- The brain has specific regions to handle some neural functions such as processing sensory information; and some substitution of cells (plasticity) is evident when a modality is under-utilised. Human development and medical research has identified that some sensory abilities are strengthened as a partial substitute when others are impaired.
- Most neural functions require interplay between several regions.
- Plenty of practice is beneficial to motor co-ordination and skill once the brain is sufficiently mature for each particular physical activity to occur.
- Stable synapses (connections) reflect where the individual has invested great physical and mental activity.
- The brain is more active, particularly in the prefrontal regions, when the mind has to handle something new or recall something in the abstract. Learning studies have noted differential performance according to the demands of the task.
- The brain structures that are essential for memory processes include the same or adjacent structures that handle emotion. Their interaction results in memories being imprinted with emotion. The connection between thought and emotion is a major topic in psychology.
- Implicit memories are stored in different brain structures from conscious memories. Implicit memories are laid down by lots of practice that we are unaware of. Early years knowledge highlights the importance of varied repetition (as distinct from drilling).
- Novel experience keeps babies' and young children's brains buzzing with electrical pulses, and involves their prefrontal cortex. This links to child development research that children pay most attention to that which is less familiar. This is what engages their interest (a positive emotion).

- Emotional information passes up and down between lower brain structures that create emotion and higher brain structures where analysis and planning take place. Child studies have shown that encouraging children to 'use their words' can regulate emotional expression.
- Temperament relates to the balance of excitory and inhibitory neurons in individual brains. Nurture (experience) can modify temperament, although not transform it.
- The development of a baby's frontal cortex and chemical brain functioning are affected by the mother's mental health and by the security of attachment between the child and mother. Satisfactory limbic system development needs at least one adult to provide the child with plenty of experiences of 'feeling felt'. Attachment theory and early education literature on 'joint attention' converges with this.

Some themes emerge above. They include: the importance of a rich variety of experiences to support the multitude of aspects of neural development needing experience to develop, the links between emotion and thought, and the significance of the limbic system and prefrontal cortex for development in the early years.

IMPLICATIONS FOR EARLY EDUCATION: A PERSONAL REFLECTION[4]

While researching this paper, I have asked myself often: What is the role of play for brain development? Play is behaviour that is universal, and is a dominant behaviour for an extended period in babies and young children. It is also common amongst young primates. It has to be significant, and yet it is hardly mentioned in the neuroscience literature.

I think that brain research contains considerable implications for the role of play in early childhood education. I have several reasons for suggesting this. First, all types of development are practised in play which indicates it affords appropriate experience for most (all?) regions of the brain.

Second, play seems to have a relationship with the blooming of synapses. There is a time-period correlation between the early childhood years, when children's play is extensive and involves physical, social and mental effort, and the period of excessive synaptic growth in the brain. Is this type of play where children are using all modalities – the senses, physical activity, emotion, and mental representations – particularly conducive to synaptic growth?

Third, play of the kind where children's interest and motivation are optimal seems to have a relationship with the sculpting of the brain. Four processes could be occurring.

(1) Caregivers who are attuned to their infants transmit positive feelings that become associated with play, motivating more play.
(2) The play experiences where children display the greatest expressions of interest may be the ones that optimise synapse stabilisation because of positive motivation and because there is likely to be repetition.
(3) The selection processes as to play topics, approaches and partners will activate the prefrontal cortex and limbic system, and therefore conscious memory.
(4) Synapses associated with experiences not chosen begin to wither away.

Support comes for this hypothesis from research on early childhood programmes. When child-centred programmes are replaced with direct instruction, there is little time for play. Such programmes have been shown to be detrimental for children's learning and achievement (Schweinhart & Weikart, 1997; Sylva & Nabuco, 1996). My interpretation of their findings is that when play is limited, fewer modalities are active and emotions such as motivation adversely affect brain functioning. On the other hand, there is a positive relationship between interest and learning – usually found in child-centred programmes (Fivush & Hudson, 1990).

Fourth, play is generally a time where children display high levels of motivation. Emotion, thought and action are in harmony – the dynamic system that is the brain is in balance.

Fifth, play seems to be important for laying down implicit memories of skills, dispositions, and schemas. My entrée into brain research was studying children's schema learning in New Zealand (Meade, with Cubey, 1995), following on from research on schemas by Chris Athey in the U.K. (1990). Both studies found 'threads of thinking' in children's play in child-centred programmes (Nutbrown, 1994). Children showed periods of fascination with particular schemas (such as grids or circles) when they explored an array of experiences. They created experiences to repeat their exploration of the form, albeit in novel ways.

Sixth, implicit memory formation can relate to dispositions. Research related to the implementation of *Te Whaariki: Early Childhood Curriculum* in New Zealand (Ministry of Education, 1996) has revealed how much activity for the development of dispositions occurs in the early years (Carr, May & Podmore, 1998).

Seventh, play in a complex environment affords children lots of opportunity to satisfy their novelty preference.

Animal studies signal the value of complex environments for brain development (Greenough, Black & Wallace, 1993). It is highly likely to be true for humans. What is a complex environment for young children?

- One where children can use a mix of modalities – their mind, social and communication skills, and their bodies – during a high proportion of experiences;
- One where children can extract meaning from an array of activities;
- One that contains a wide array of equipment and resources that children can explore;
- One where their need for novelty at frequent intervals is addressed;
- One where children can engage in pretend-play where they move in and out of role/s.

Brain research, in my view, also has implications for the *approaches* adopted by educators. On the one hand educators need to be mindful that there is a vast array of aspects of the brain that need many and varied experiences, especially in the early years when foundation circuits are formed. Adults' visions as to experiences needed are likely to be more limited than children's are (our brains tend to increasingly limit our creative thinking over the years they are honed). Therefore the opportunities we provide may constrain young children's brain development if too many time and space rules are applied. It follows that educators need to allow children adequate scope for creating their own experiences, while being mindful of children's choice of experiences. Educators need to be proactive in offering new opportunities to any children who limit their choices.

One common source of educators' constraints is the belief that early years curricula pertain to academic learning focused on objects. However, neuroscience tells us that encompassing socio-emotional learning in the first few years is also highly important. All children need experiences that, *inter alia*, facilitate their theories about self and others. For children who have experienced lots of stress triggering a chronic alarm state, early education could do even more. Educators who intervene with warmth, responsiveness and training to be responsible may help to reset the balance of brain.

NOTES

1. Bruer (1999) seems to be an example of this sort of struggle.
2. In the space available, the neurological development of only some of the senses is discussed.

3. Nelson concludes that human contact in this period also needs to include cognitive challenge and linguistic input.

4. As there is little neuroscience that has directly researched the effects of early childhood education on brain development, I am drawing on my extensive knowledge of early childhood education to consider the implications of neuroscience for the field.

REFERENCES

Athey, C. (1990). *Extending Children's Thinking: A parent-teacher partnership*. London: Paul Chapman Publishers.

Bates, E., Thal, D., & Janowsky, J. S. (1992). Early language development and its neural correlates. In: I. Rapin & S. Segalowitz (Eds) *Handbook of Neuropsychology* (pp. 69–110). Amsterdam: Elsevier.

Brandt, R. (1999). Educators need to know about the human brain, *Phi Delta Kappan*, (November), 235–238.

Bransford, J. D., Brown, A. L., & Cocking, R. R. (Eds) (1999). *How People Learn: Brain, mind, experience and school*. Washington, D.C.: National Academy Press.

Bruer, J. (1999). *The Myth of the First Three Years*. New York: Free Press.

Carr, M., May, H., & Podmore, V. (1998). *Learning and Teaching Stories: New approaches to assessment and evaluation in relation to Te Whaariki*. Wellington: Institute for Early Childhood Studies.

Carter, R. (1998). *Mapping the Mind*. London: Weidenfeld & Nicholson.

Collins, P. E., & Depue, R. A. (1992). A neurobehavioral systems approach to developmental psychopathology: Implications for disorders of affect. In: D. Cicchetti & S. L. Toth (Eds), *Rochester Symposium on Developmental Psychopathology: Volume 4, Developmental Perspectives on Depression*. New York: University of Rochester.

Dawson, G., & Fischer, K. W. (Eds) (1994). *Human Behavior and the Developing Brain*. New York: The Guilford Press.

Dawson, G. (1994). Development of emotional expression and emotion regulation in infancy: Contributions of the frontal lobe. In: G. Dawson & K. W. Fischer (Eds), *Human Behavior and the Developing Brain*. New York: The Guilford Press.

Dewey, J. (1938). *Experience and education: The 60th Anniversary Edition*. West Lafayette, Indiana: Kappa Delta Pi.

Dolan, R. J. (1999). On the neurology of morals. *Nature Neuroscience*, 2(11), 927–929.

Edelman, G. M. (1992). *Bright Air, Brilliant Fire: On the matter of the mind*. New York: Basic Books.

Egeland, B., Calson, E., & Sroufe, L. A. (1993). Resilience as process. In: *Development and Psychopathology*. Cambridge: Cambridge University Press.

Eliot, L. (1999). *What's Going On In There? How the brain and mind develop in the first five years of life*. New York: Bantam Books.

Fivush R., & Hudson, J. A. (Eds) (1990). *Knowing and Remembering in Young Children*. Cambridge: Cambridge University Press.

Gardner, H. (1983). *Frames of Mind: The theory of multiple intelligences*. New York: Basic Books.

Goleman, D. (1997). *Emotional Intelligence*. New York: Bantam Books.

Greenough, W. T., Black, J. E., & Wallace, C. S. (1993). Experience and brain development. In:
    M. H. Johnson (Ed.), *Brain Development and Cognition: A reader*. Oxford: Blackwell
    Publishers Ltd.
Gunnar, M. (1996). *Quality of care and the buffering of stress physiology: Its potential in
    protecting the developing human brain*. Minnesota: University of Minnesota Institute of
    Child Development.
Herschkowitz, N., Kagan, J., & Zilles, K. (1997). Neurobiological bases of behavioural
    development in the first year. *Neuropediatrics, 28*, 296–306.
Johnson, M. H. (1998). The neural basis of cognitive development. In: D. Kuhn & R. S. Siegler
    (Eds), *Handbook of Child Psychology: Cognition, Perception and Language* (5th ed., Vol.
    2, pp. 1–49). New York: John Wiley & Sons, Inc.
Meade, A., with Cubey, P. (1995). *Thinking Children: Learning about schemas*. Wellington: New
    Zealand Council for Educational Research/Victoria University of Wellington.
Ministry of Education (1996). *Te Whaariki: Early childhood curriculum*. Wellington: Learning
    Media Ltd.
Nelson, C. A., & Bloom, F. E. (1997). Child development and neuroscience. *Child Development,
    68*(5), 970–987.
Nelson, C. A., & Bosquet, M. (2000). Neurobiology of fetal and infant development: Implications
    for infant mental health. In: C. H. Zeariah, Jr. (Ed.), *Handbook of Infant Mental Health*.
    New York: Guildford Press.
Nutbrown, C. (1994). *Threads of Thought: Young children learning and the role of early education*.
    London: Paul Chapman Publishers.
Passingham, R. E. (1993). *The Frontal Lobes and Voluntary Action*. Oxford Psychology Series,
    No.21. New York: Oxford University Press.
Rakic, P. (1988). Specification of cerebral cortical areas. *Science, 241* (July 8), 170–176.
Rogoff, B. (1990). *Apprenticeship in Learning: Cognitive development in social context*. Oxford:
    Oxford University Press.
Rose, S. (1997). *Lifelines: Biology beyond determinism*. Oxford: Oxford University Press.
Schweinhart, L. J., & Weikart, D. P. (1997). *Lasting Differences: The High/Scope preschool
    curriculum comparison study through age 23*. Ypsilanti, Michigan: High/Scope Press.
Shore, B. (1996). *Culture in Mind: Cognition, Culture, and the problem of meaning*. New York:
    Oxford University Press.
Shore, R. (1997). *Rethinking the Brain: New insights in early development*. New York: Families
    and Work Institute.
Siegel, D. (1999a). *The Developing Mind: Toward a neurobiology of interpersonal experience*.
    New York: The Guilford Press.
Siegel, D. (1999b). Toward a Biology of Compassion: Human relationships, the brain, and the
    development of 'mindsight' across the lifespan. An invited presentation for Pope John Paul
    II and the Pontifical Council for the Family, Vatican City, December.
Squire, L. R. (1995). Memory and brain systems. In: R. Broadwell (Ed.), *Neuroscience, Memory
    and Language, Decade of the Brain* (Vol. 1, pp. 59–75). Washington, D.C.: U.S.
    Government Printing Office.
Sylva, K., & Nabuco, M. E. (1996). Children's learning in day care: How shall we study it? A
    paper given at the ISSBD Conference on Behavioral Development, Quebec City, August.
Wolfe, P., & Brandt, R. (1998). What do we know from brain research? *Educational Leadership,
    56*(3), 8–13.

2. DIVORCE AND FATHERING IN LATE MODERN SWEDEN

Lars-Erik Berg

Winnicott's concept of 'good enough mothering' has become well known. Few talk about the corresponding term 'fathering'. However, the question of practical, everyday life fathering has been a hot topic over the last three decades (Lamb, 1997). There is a range of reasons for this. They seem to be related and linked to one point: the fear of what may become of children who miss their fathers.

This has become an officially recognised problem at the highest level: as ex-U.S. President Bill Clinton said: 'The single biggest social problem in our society may be the growing absence of fathers from their children's homes because it contributes to so many other social problems' (Fost quoted in Lupton & Barclay, 1997: 2). This problem is firmly linked to the social problem of divorce. In Sweden the general rule remains that when parents separate, the mother stays in the family home with the children, while the father moves, and that he – at best – takes his children to his new home regularly, at least two days every fortnight. However, this can be regarded as too little contact, resulting in different sorts of suffering.

One of the ways children suffer is – besides emotional deprivation connected with the father's absence – the children receive a mixed and diffuse picture of masculinity and fathers' roles, and that this results in a reduction in the likelihood of developing a positive gender identity, especially for the boys. It is thought that the result will be – at worst – identity problems, violence, stereotypical habits and disturbed conceptions of gender roles for both sexes. It is often assumed this may pave the way to a poor capacity for social and

Promoting Evidence-based Practice in Early Childhood Education:
Research and its Implications, Volume 1, pages 27–42.
2001 by Elsevier Science Ltd.
ISBN: 0-7623-0753-6

emotional interactions between the sexes. At the extreme, this bad view of development portrays young boys ganging together, raping girls, and committing violence, robbery and even murder on innocent people like children and the elderly (see for example Lupton & Barclay, 1997: 78). Such dramatic scenarios are found to be at the core of concern for the father's role.

Meanwhile, it has been demonstrated in many countries that the involvement of fathers in their children's lives, as demonstrated in paternal direct interaction with the child, together with accessibility and responsibility for the care of the child, has been growing for the few decades that social researchers have directed their interest to fathers (Pleck, 1997: 67). Thus there is a contradiction between the growing parental interest generally among fathers and the belief in increasing maladjustment among children. We relate this contradiction to the continuing increase in the divorce rate.

I do not seek to deny that there is a need for attention to this worrying prospect. But the situation demands closer exploration, 'staring at hell easily turns one blind'! For one thing, increases in rates of divorce do not equate with declining paternal interest in children. One could argue that there is an interest in their children shown by most if not all fathers, even 'bad' fathers who do not often see their children. Research both in the USA, England and Sweden indicates this. Fathers sometimes face serious obstacles when trying to see their children and to practise paternal responsibility. For reasons of space, I will not discuss this research here, but give two references of different sorts. A huge body of mainly quantitative material can be found in the anthology edited by Michael Lamb (1997). Another source, this time mainly qualitative and discussion material, is Adrienne Burgess (1997). Both works contribute to the debate about the blessings to be found and those which could evolve in relations between fathers and children.

I will now go on to provide a structured view of the qualities which define the facts and the dreams reported by some fathers and their children in an interview study in Sweden in the mid-1990s.

First a few words about my empirical material. The interviews, from which I present evidence, enabled me to discover some of the happier points relating to divorce than those indicated above. My empirical material constitutes interviews with 25 fathers and their children.[1] The work as a whole explores the relations and identity development of divorced fathers and their children, but here I cover material that examines opinions and activities of importance concerning the father in relation to his child.

In some cases in my empirical material the fathers and mothers, while separated, have joint custody, but most of them have 'exchanged' shared custody arrangements for regular interaction appointments. Most of the father-child pairs in our study showed a higher frequency of meeting than two days every fortnight. In fact this higher frequency was so common, that it made us suspect that the pattern of two days every fortnight might be more a myth than a reality in Sweden today. A pattern of Thursday evening to Monday morning was quite common, as was also the pattern of Friday to Sunday every second week *and* every Wednesday. In a few cases the pattern was 50–50, that is, the parents shared their children's company equally. In our sample, most of the fathers had moved from the family home and the mother had stayed there with the children. So the residency pattern was not a myth.

What appears below is mostly 'qualitative' material, concentrating on the 'happier' aspects, without denying that the research data also provided a basis for writing 'misery' stories. Only dominant trends will be discussed, and these are picked from the more positive findings, rather than from the sad ones. The reason for this choice will be successively revealed.

DIVORCE AS DISASTER OR POSSIBILITY; CHILDREN'S VIEWS

Much literature on divorce gives us the definite impression of divorce as a human disaster. The reasons are economic, social and emotional. An overview of this literature shows that especially the English and American research reports confirm this pattern. Writings on the topic in the USA and the U.K. are often reports of misery, and at best stories about people fighting misery in a successful way.[2] It is, however, possible to reverse the focus, to study divorce not as a disaster but as a sort of tentative solution to severe family problems. Thus divorce could be seen more as offering new possibilities and as a problem-solving process, rather than as a destruction of human resources. A corollary to this view is that the 'absent father' can be complemented by the 'engaged father'. This notion helped me to explore what I found to have been created in the interaction between father and child.

This idea of reversing the focus did not emanate from myself. I was bound by the assumptions and traditions in my own society to have a negative view of divorce, and both I and my co-worker began the interviewing process prejudiced in this way. (Regard it as a form of interviewer bias!) However, the children themselves forced us to open a more sensitive eye and to 'see' the potential for 'happy' interpretations of divorce. The children we interviewed have a very simple and rational way of seeing their parents' divorce, unaffected by moralistic arguments. Their message is: If parents are incapable of giving support and help and love to each other any longer, then they should divorce as a matter of course. The children themselves see nothing peculiar with that! And when directly asked about the legal right to divorce, they regard this as a self-evident human right. These young moral philosophers do not even contemplate the idea that legal restrictions could be morally or rationally possible.

But this very plain and pragmatic attitude does not imply that they regard divorce as a trifle. Some of them also told us about grief and anger, when we ask about their feelings during the divorce process. But the pattern they reported is that bad feelings are restricted to a short period. Here there is a weak gender-related pattern too. No boy reported having given way to intense feelings, neither in the present of the interview time, nor when they tried to remember the dramatic phases. The girls were more sensitive to feelings of both grief and anger. But overall only one girl reported acute tensions, telling us about the very dramatic divorce process between her parents. When reviewing it for our research some ten years later, she still wept a little during our interview.

We are aware that the picture our research obtained from these children may be limited. Some bad feelings have probably been unconsciously repressed, and some have been consiously 'reasoned away' in the reconstruction of their 'stories'. Nevertheless, there is something to be learnt for us all. These children led us to doubt the 'absolute truth' in those psychological doctrines which maintain that for the child's sound psychological development it is essential both parents are 'concretely present' every day. Reasoning of this sort is found in some of the literature mentioned above.

Our material does not confirm such findings. Neither does it confirm the picture of the divorced father as the absent father. We believe that some research confuses the main facts of divorce – absent fathers and bad emotional/ social conditions. We would like to present a tentative explanation for our conclusions. We find a fairly sharp difference between the 'typical' Swedish divorce and, especially, the American one as discussed above. The latter happens in a culture which stigmatises divorce to a much higher degree than seems to be the case in Sweden. There is one point in particular we wish to mention. Fürstenberg and Cherlin (1991) tell us that the normal pattern in divorce processes means that children are told about the problem very late in the proceedings, often only a short time before the father leaves the home, and that both parents tell the children as little as possible in order to 'save' them from the bad story.

In our research in Sweden the reverse seems to have been the rule: the children have generally been told at an early stage. The reasons have also been recounted to them: for example – 'Mummy does not love me any more, and so we have decided to divorce.' The next difference seems to be the fact that most of the children in our study were told that they would continue to see Daddy regularly. Finally many of the children said they had been told in a detailed and reasonable way that they, the children, had no causal part whatsoever in the divorce. A few of these children had grown to adulthood by the time of the interview, and they showed a warm emotional dedication to their parents for just this reason: they admire them for their capacity to be so thoughtful and caring in discussing the whole matter with them in spite of their own intense bad feelings during the process.

One very striking fact is that the children especially do not regard divorce and relatively brief time together as obstacles to good fatherhood. So what good outcomes can be found emanating from the father-child relationship when time is so short? I will give two types of answers to this question. The first concentrates on what capacities fathers and children believe grow out of the divorce condition as such, and the second tries to depict a 'good father', as seen from the standpoints of our participants.

MORE PROBLEMATISING VIRTUES AND WISDOM

To begin with one can recognise that being forced to reflect on the theme of divorce causes reflection and problem-solving. There are indications that fathers who have gone through a divorce become much more attentive to their children, and more thoughtful concerning relational problems in a group like the nuclear family. Reflection on family problems becomes more intensive, so that this is no longer the exclusive domain of social scientists, but of fathers and children themselves. Some researchers maintain that reflexivity concerning fatherhood becomes more mature among those fathers and children who have experienced the vicissitudes of divorce (Lund, 1987; Giddens, 1991, 1992; Bauman, 1991). The problems appear in an intense light and demand conscious examination.[3]

This is very evident from our research material. Some fathers went to extremes in recognising this, and some said that the divorce was – regarded from this point of view – almost a blessed event. Without it they would have gone through their lives spending time on work and sports for ever, without realising all energy residing in responsible parental relations. They use words like sensitivity, sensibility and prudence about this phenomenon.

Some special issues are mentioned. You get *closer* to yourself, more able to *single out yourself from the other* and consider what are your *own wishes and objectives* in relation to your children. You become more capable of *reflecting* and you realize that some painful life events, like divorce, cannot and *should not be escaped* but handled in a prudent way. The divorce has made these fathers more mature and has given them a better sense of judgement in human problems.

What is remarkable here is that the same could be said about the children, and this is true for the older teenagers as well as for some of the younger children. Many of them showed themselves highly capable of discussing, narrating and reflecting on the divorce theme. These children were able to reflect on the questions as they applied to themselves and even the younger ones were capable of realising there can be happiness in new family relations and new siblings. This theme was frequently raised by the older children. A couple of the younger teenagers (12 and 15 years) even gave details about their new siblings. Children also explained the good feelings associated with having *two real homes*.

MORE ENGAGEMENT IN THE CHILDREN

There is one theme that is at first sight somewhat paradoxical. It is related to what is said about the 'happy' consequences of divorce, but it relates more directly to the father-child relationship. We have some specially lucid illustrations of the attitude in question. One father said that when you are divorced and do not have so much time with the children, this is exactly the point in life where you can 'interact with them much more'. Another father said that divorce makes you a 'much better parent'.

These utterances are consciously provoking. There is a message: when you get into divorce, you find yourself in a situation where you have *individual responsibility* for the children's welfare. If you do not make a decent job of your 'parent work', there is no one else to blame other than yourself. This is somewhat of a revelation to many of these fathers. Parenthood is not an automatic affair.[4] It is not fullfilled by the child being born and money being earned to provide for the material needs of the family.[5] To be a parent and a father is an ongoing issue of indulging in relationships, the intense and varied emotional character of which is not fully realised by many men, if they do not have to exert individual responsibility. Many of the fathers told us that the interaction becomes much more total, and that this basically results in a good feeling, even if this intensive way of parenting can prove tiring.

A special aspect of this is often mentioned in the literature, and confirmed in our material. One of the main aspects of identity for girls and women is to be the one who knows best about family life. Thus some women have a tendency to dominate men on this subject (Chodorow, 1978). Men are often ill-equipped to combat this assumption of maternal power. Thus they feel a kind of relief and are more able to take the initiative when left alone with their children.

The traditional father role in industrial society was distant and passive with regard to the children. This traditional role is explicitly renounced by the fathers in our study. The counterpart to this finding is that not a single child in the study reported a feeling of constant 'father deprivation'. Some talk of their unhappiness when their father moved out to another home, but this was for a limited period, and they reported no permanent bad feeling about it. All these children felt that they had a father who is committed to them and to his fatherhood.[6] Children also told us with pleasure that in this situation you really have both your parents totally, if you separate your time between them. This is not to deny the intense feeling of wellbeing reported when both parents and the whole original family and other relatives and friends meet on special occasions like Christmas and birthday celebration. A few children ascribe a central position to the father on these occasions.

VARIATION IN LIFE FOR FATHERS AND CHILDREN

There is a readiness for both fathers and children to take up the more positive aspects of divorce. We need to underline the paradox that the divorced condition makes the relationship between father and child more intensive, close and warm, as well as more varied in terms of spare time projects like travelling and visiting relatives and friends. Fathers especially also report that the very experience of exhaustion in connection with the intensive interaction gives a special warm character to the relationship. Time now is filled up with varying activities, some of which are very project directed, like going on some carefully planned, special excursion, while others are more meditative, like reading long, goodnight stories.

This variation of experiences also resounds in other areas of their lives. Both parties, but especially fathers, recognise that one and the same thing or person have different co-existing characters, for example: the ex-wife is often realised as a person with both good and bad traits; the fathers' own fathers have come to be reflected on much more, and they are also found to be both good and bad. In some cases the project fathers had intensified their interaction with their own fathers, with the happy result that the children experience closer grandfather contact than might otherwise have been the case. The restricting conditions around family life are also contemplated much more, together with the intensive interaction with the children. It is as if the more emotionally loaded character of this interaction results in more intellectual activity concerning human social life.

All this is in line with Giddens' (1990) proposition of increasing *reflectivity* in late modern society, as it is with Zygmunt Bauman (1991) who recognises postmodern life as *ambivalent*, ambiguous and therefore as subject to constant decision-making about types of actions and ways of living. These tendencies are supported in our material, and it is astonishing that even young children exert both activities in a creative way. Put another way, Giddens and Bauman help us to understand the unconventional character of our material, both from fathers and from children. We had expected more ready-made and stereotypic attitudes and much more data on divorce as a disaster. However, we found mature individuals with deep reflective-sensitive capacities in both fathers and children.

Finally, we must report that there is a tendency for fathers from different socio-economic strata to have this reflective capacity. Social class differences concerning both intellectual reflection, language use and emotional sensitivity were found to be small. Macro social changes have impacted on intimate family life. The picture depicted by our research is in sharp contrast to that presented theoretically by Chodorow (1978) during the seventies in the USA.[7]

LESS QUARRELING – CHILDREN'S REACTIONS

One further point must be mentioned on the theme of divorce as *not* being a disaster for the children and it is one which should be understood in relation to social psychological identification theory. An unhappy relationship between the two adult partners in a family is the heaviest burden to bear, according to the children in our study. This is why divorce can easily be regarded as a sort of relief. Why?

Small children do not have a personal identity independently. They literally do not know who they are, and the parents in two different ways constitute the main device through which they come to learn who they are. Children 'build themselves' through their parents. They identify themselves through their parents' eyes. This process entails 'material' from the individual children themselves; the parent reacts to the actions of each child, and these reactions are received and moulded in the childish mind. But there is also the other process of the child taking up 'material' directly from the parent: 'My father looks like this, and makes these things. Then I'll do as he does, and I'll become like my father!'[8]

Now, if the parents are constantly quarrelling, this becomes material for a negative identity construction in the child. Such children constitute themselves with a constant quarrel within the soul. The quarrel is not an external condition, as it might be for the parents themselves, but an internal one, contributing to the self. The quarrel is still worse in the mind of the child than between the parents. These two can blame each other, but the child can not blame either of them. The quarrel becomes 'internalised' we say. This is why all these children tell us unanimously that stopping the quarrelling was the best thing they ever experienced and this is why the divorce is seen as a relief.

Notably, there is no tendency for the children to ascribe guilt in the process as most adults do. They do not even regard the divorce as something which implies guilt on any part. It is seen as a process in life which some people go through and some not, and there is nothing more to it than that, if they are free to continue seeing both parents in a reasonable way. The depressing and desperate character of divorce might be attributes ascribed by adults, but the children we have interviewed did not do so.

Divorce in itself is not necessarily bad for the children, but parental conventional reactions to it are, especially when these involve quarrelling and apportioning of guilt to each other. This research has cast more light on the theme of divorce, in particular demonstrating that these recent Swedish stories of divorce seem so much less unhappy and depressing than the material we find in some of the other research literature. Possibly divorce has finally become a much more 'normal' phenomenon in contemporary Sweden than it was in the USA of the seventies and eighties, and perhaps this is one of the reasons why these children are not father-deprived.

The only unhappy children we find in our material are in fact those older children who reported a 'bad' divorce between their parents several years ago. And we note especially that the quarrelling which stopped only when the combattants stopped meeting, is what has remained as an evil memory for those children. Because of the unresolved character of these children's experiences, a few of them show contradictory attitudes towards their parents, of the type where the father (and the mother too) is seen explicitly and implicitly as both a good and bad person.[9] Such feelings must be burdensome to reconcile.

WHAT IS DADDY LIKE? THE PORTRAIT OF A MODERN ENGAGED FATHER

Looking at the confusion concering both masculinity and the father role that both our material and the literature displays, it is no wonder that fathers have more diffuse notions of themselves than those held by their children. The child does not wonder who Daddy is, but Daddy himself does. This paradox is not a Swedish peculiarity, but it seems to be a steadily increasing global phenomenon, at least in so called advanced industrial societies. 'Fathers are not what they used to be. Fathers no longer model themselves on the image of the sovereign patriarch, the head of the family, who orders his wife and children around, *but they have not developed a new identity, either*' (Lupton & Barclay, 1999: 14, italics mine).

Fathers worldwide seem to have a hard time identifying themselves as fathers, and this gives them some problems. But their children do not mind. They are not burdened by sex or parent role stereotypes, and they have no pride invested in the problem, in the way their fathers have.

Let us first conclude that almost all the fathers in our study disclaimed any knowledge about masculinity. The few who answered preferred to maintain that there are no big differences between men and women. Next in frequency were the few who claimed that 'it is like hell to be a man today'. Just two revealed that they like traditional differences between the sex roles, but they want to exert this difference with modesty and at great distance. Only one man made a real argument supporting his position that there are definite differences between the sexes: he claimed that language separates men from women.

Of special interest is the fact that no one in our sample claimed that there are definite differences between the sexes concerning children. It was generally felt that fathers can and should do the same things and have the same attitudes to children as mothers do. Another interesting finding was the idea that individual differences were said to be greater and more interesting than sexual differences. Thus *individualism* seems to have taken over from *gendered* culture in the opinions expressed.

These two findings held for the children in the study too. But again: while fathers have a problem because of their ignorance about both men's and fathers' roles, children do not. The children often fail to detect any significant differences between their expectations of daddy and mummy, but as far as they are concerned, it is quite acceptable that this is so. They feel no need to be treated in different ways by the two parents. When children talk about how their fathers actually behave, there is a slight tendency for them to be more inclined to project-orientation, while mothers are slightly more 'passively' being-oriented. This is in accord with traditionally conceived roles, and the children can accept the situation, there is no problem in their conception of the whole gender complex in the family.

Let us end this report about attitudes to fathering in today's family culture with a list of the rankings given to particular aspects of fathers which are most appreciated – the traits in fathers which, according to our research, are most appreciated by fathers themselves, and how children respond to this. We have scrutinised the discussions with our respondents, and thus we can give a rank order of fatherly traits. (Numbers indicate the frequency with which a trait is explicitly mentioned by the fathers, but do not indicate the weight that is ascribed to the trait by each person. This is left to our judgment.)

Relatively few of our participants (11) considered being a *role model* for behaviour to be important. However, when we listen sensitively to the interview material, we found that the discussion seemed rather superficial, paying merely lip service to this idea. It was something that tended to be said at first, perhaps out of habit, while thinking of what 'really' to give as an answer.

Next in rank order came involvement and the capacity to be a *supporter* (10). Here there was also mention of the will to be *present*, to be together with the child in a concrete way. In several interviews this theme soon became a subject of rather intensive discussion. Our respondents liked to talk about it, and they carried on talking for a while, giving examples. A similarly emotional involvement in what was said was displayed intensely by nine (9) interviewees during focus on another theme, which I call *communicativeness*. The fathers in particular endorsed the view that emotional and straight communication was one of the most needed and most lacking resources in social life between parents and children today. Some of our fathers actually became upset when thinking of this, and one of them began to weep in our presence when talking about lone children and bad communication conditions in today's society.

Next in order is *stability* and steadiness (7). It is easy to think stereotypically of this as a difference between men and women. But in our research not one participant thought stability something that fathers should show more than mothers. It was seen as a virtue that should be common to both parents and it was related to parental duty to show the child in a clear way how the world is 'constructed'.

In fact this aspect of stability can be seen as a general summary of three traits which follow next (each seen as important by six participants), *everyday involvement*, *drawing borders* for decent behaviour, as an important component of education and *showing children the outer world and men's world*.

Emotionality and *sensitivity* and being a good *playmate*, were each claimed by five (5) participants to be important ingredients in fathers' roles and relationships in today's cultural climate. The last mentioned is well known in the psychological literature, but is seldom explicitly related to emotionality, which is often linked more closely with mothers' ways of relating to their children, which are often reported to be less playful than those of fathers. We think it is significant that play and emotionality are often mentioned together among these fathers. This group believed play to entail a necessary dimension of emotionality and that men should and can cultivate this capacity.

Next in frequency comes *'being oneself'* (4). At first glance this seems to be just a stereotype: of course people should be themselves, what else could they be, and so what? But scrutinization of the data revealed a special, partly hidden and unconscious, emphasis on the theme. The fathers mean that in traditional culture there is pressure on fathers not to be themselves, that a father should conform to some sort of general pattern, and as a result not show his true self.[10] Alternatively, the individuality of the special father is hidden behind 'traditional behavioural norms' for fathers. By expressing these views, our fathers demonstrated their support for what they think is a blessed emancipatory process for men and fathers in today's culture.

A few fathers told us that a good father should be a good *pal or buddy* (3). However, this was not supported by the majority. Some of the fathers who did not mentioned this as a nice property of a father did discuss the idea, but theorised that a father should not be a constant playmate or a pal, neither for boys nor for girls. They believed this would be abnegating parental responsibility. There is, for most of these fathers, a clear and actively theorised distinction: the father as playmate should be well-defined, and when play is over, the 'fostering responsibility' of the father re-enters the scene; he is no longer just a pal, but somebody who is in charge in many ways, and who should thus take on responsibility for the child in a way which has little to do with the sort of responsibility a friend might have.

Somewhat surprisingly, only two fathers (2) voluntarily mentioned the notion that a good father should show his daughter what good and constructive *masculinity* is like. This is a common psychological theme, frequently based on Freudian and Lacanian psychoanalysis. But the fathers in our sample did not have respond positively to these ideas. First, they did not appear to consider it a particularly interesting issue in thinking about the relations between parents and children, because the whole culture abounds with myriad gender-related pictures. They felt there is no need, really! Second: this is something that is not restricted to fathers in regard to daughters. Rather, it is a question for both sexes and both generations. Mothers should be good gender models for children of both sexes, as should fathers. And so it was concluded that there is no difference whatsoever between the sexes regarding this responsibility.

The last aspect we think it important to mention was a special reference to *responsibility*, and the father who raised this issue argued that it is a special duty of fathers to show reciprocity in human responsibility relations; a father should show his children what it is like to assume and to give responsibility to other people. However, the list of preceding aspects give an abundant picture of fatherly responsibility. In fact, the only point where parental and fatherly responsibility is not clearly implicated is the point of the *pal*, and at this point all but the three young fathers who mention it as a good thing, say that the father should refrain actively from being only a pal. Practically all other traits mentioned implicate parental responsibility on the part of the father in one form or another.

There is an old cultural stereotype that fathers are and should be more active, 'instrumental', tool-oriented and the like. That they play football rather than read fairy tales, they take children out in the world rather than talking with them about relational problems and so on. It is interesting to find that neither the fathers nor the children in our study paid much attention to traditional opinions of this sort. Still, going out to see relatives and friends at the week-end was a very common and appreciated shared activity. However, this is done without thinking of it as something different from what the mother would do.

We should point out that our list was mainly deduced from what the fathers had to say. They were much more forthcoming than the children, in the interviews, so the data are richer. However, we do have some direct and some indirect measures of the children's opinions. Among the indirect measures we find the fact that in most of our cases there is documentation showing a close relationship between the fathers and their children. In fact only three of the fathers indicated that they have little contact with their children, (and in these cases there were severe difficulties over cooperation with the mother). A second indirect measure is that the children all seemed to be satisfied with the father they have. None expressed severe dissatisfaction, and many of them, being asked about the 'ideal daddy' said that their own is in fact this ideal. Finally, many children, even the small ones, explicitly mentioned, without our prompting, that they wanted to see more of their fathers.

But there is also a direct measure for the children. We asked them to give a picture of the 'ideal father'. The following brief summary gives some of the key characteristics they listed:

- a father should *listen,*
- he should be *present,*
- and he should *do funny things* with his children.

The first two of these are among the highest ranked and most frequent characteristics also listed by the fathers in our research. Similarly, the last is also mentioned explicitly by many of the fathers.

In some cases father and child had only two or three days a fortnight together, so the issue of such narrow time constraints became a focus of our interviews. But it was striking that both parties expressed their higher validation of quality rather than quantity – much better to have a happy father a little time, than to have an unhappy father every day. In fact, the children were the ones who expressed this opinion most clearly. It was more common for the children to defend the possibility of divorce than for the fathers to do so. Even in cases of direct infidelity the children held that the father (or mother, there is no gender discrimination!) who falls in love with another person than the other parent, should have the right to live with the new partner. And some children explicitly drew a causal relationship between the new love and a happier father, who is more intensely present as a father whenever he has the opportunity.

There was one point where some of the children, mostly the young ones, expressed disappointment: they wanted to see their fathers more than they do. But this wish was reciprocal. The children did not blame their father, but had a realistic knowledge of the constraints that reign over everyday life for working fathers and mothers.

This research began with the objective of studying the actual and wished-for relations between fathers and children. We took the standpoint that there would be a quantitatively lacking relationship in the divorced family. Through this approach, we arrived at what seems to be the essence of this relationship. Exactly because of the shortage of time together both parties come to know better what they want, and what possibilities there actually are; the father/child relationships we studied matured into social competence, as well as deeper emotional intelligence.

NOTES

1. Fathers were interviewed twice with at least one year's interval. Children were interviewed at the time of the second interview with the fathers. Very few children under 6 years were interviewed, and they gave comparatively little information to us; we did not have the time or economic resources to penetrate and pursue this aspect. A few interviews with children at the border between preschool and early school age gave us much material, but by far the richest material from children came from teenagers and young adults who gave deep and intensive reflections on both past and present experiences of living with divorce and/or a step family. This, of course, gives us validity and reliability problems, as we are often dependent upon these adolescents' memories/ reconstructions. However, we think we could not have acquired any of this material without using this method of interviewing children who try to remember their earlier childhood experiences. The whole project was carried through by the author and his co-worker Thomas Johansson. Most of our material is reported in the book 'The Second Parent', 'Den andre föräldern', Carlsson bokförlag, Stockholm.

2. Just two examples from this tendency towards 'misery writing': an overview by Fürstenberg and Cherlin (1991) and a case study (already a classic) by Wallerstein and Kelly (1980).

3. The point also conforms to the well known theses of 'optimal frustrations' in Piaget, Vygotsky and other developmental psychologists.

4. Some research indicates that having children, for women, is a conscious and deliberate choice to a much higher degree than for men, who regard it more as a matter of course. This was recently confirmed in a Swedish-English comparative study by Kearney et al. (2000).

5. The father portrait of the 'bread-winner', of which much is spoken in the English literature (e.g. Lewis & O'Brien, 1987) is totally dismissed by these fathers. In fact some of them do not even understand why we mention it.

6. Of course there is the possibility of false answers in order not to make the father feel bad. We cannot deny this, but we notice that the fathers on many occasions were blamed for other reasons in a way which is sometimes almost vigorous and even rude. It does not seem that the children are afraid of saying something bad about their fathers. Their respect for the father does not take this passive form. Also, children's interviews were made in confidence, without the father present. The only exception was for some very young children.

7. The traditional picture is also confirmed in today's USA culture (see for example: Lupton & Barclay, 1997, especially chapter 3 – for a survey of both scientific and popular father images).

8. Most of these identification processes are, of course, unconscious and much more subtle than this crude picture admits. I have presented them more fully in Berg (1999).

9. We know that economic conditions play a heavy role in most divorce literature, for example lone mothers suffering bad economic conditions with their children in the USA. Economic circumstances play a very small role in our material, in spite of the fact that many of our respondents are working class fathers among whom some have experiences of unemployment.

10. It is easy to think, again, in terms of male distance, anonymity, instrumentality and the like, in terms that Chodorow (1978), Dinnerstein (1976) and many else have analyzed.

REFERENCES

Bauman, Z. (1991). *Modernity and Ambivalence*. Oxford: Polity Press.

Berg, L.-E., & Johansson, Th. (1999). *Den andre föräldern*. Stockholm: Carlssons bokförlag. English title: *The Second Parent*.

Burgess, A. (1997). *Reclaiming Fatherhood. the Making of the Modern Father*. London: Vermillion.

Chodorow, N. (1978; 2nd ed., 1995). *The Reproduction of Mothering*. Berkely: California University Press.

Dinnerstein, D. (1976; 2nd ed., 1980). *The Mermaid and the Minotaurus*. New York: Harper & Row Publications.

Fost, D. (1996). The lost art of Fatherhood. *American Demographics*, *18*(3).

Fürstenberg, F., & Cherlin, A. (1991). *Divided Families*. Cambridge, Mass: Harvard University Press.

Giddens, A. (1990). *The consequences of Modernity*. Cambridge: Polity Press/Blackwell.

Giddens, A. (1991). *Modernity and Self Identity*. Cambridge: Polity Press.

Giddens, A. (1992). *The Transformations of Intimacy*. Cambridge: Polity Press.

Kearney, J., Plantin, L., & Manson, S-A. (2000). *Fatherhood and masculinity*. University of Sunderland: Center for Social Research and Practice.

Lamb, M. (Ed.) (1997). *The Role of the Father in Child Development*. New York: Wiley & Sons.

Lewis, C., & O'Brien, M. (1987). *Reassessing fatherhood*. London: Sage.

Lund, M. (1987). The non-custodial father: common challenges in parenting after divorce. In: C. Lewis & M. O'Brien (Eds), *Reassessing Fatherhood. New Observations on Fathers and the Modern Family*. London: Sage.

Lupton, D., & Barclay, L. (1997). *Constructing Fatherhood*. London: Sage.

McLanahan, S., & Sandefur, G. (1994). *Growing up with a Single Parent*. Cambridge, Mass: Harvard University Press.

Pleck. (1997). Paternal involvement levels, sources and consequences. In: M. Lamb (Ed.), *The Role of the Father in Child Development*. New York: Wiley & Sons.

Wallerstein, J., & Kelly, J. (1980). *Surviving the Breakup*. London: Grant McIntyre.

Winnicott, D. W. (1964/1976). *The Child, the Family and the Outside World* Harmondsworth: Penguin.

3. YOUNG CHILDREN, COMMUNITIES AND LEARNING: VENEZUELA – A MODEL FOR THE PUBLIC MANAGEMENT OF CHILDHOOD PROGRAMMES BUILT UPON LOCAL STRENGTHS AND DIVERSITIES

J. Leonardo Yánez and Arelys Moreno de Yanez

This essay is a reflection on the general set of problems encountered when implementing care and early childhood programmes in Venezuela. We also analyse political and conceptual change in management at this educational level and some of its immediate consequences. We approach this reflection from the point of view of programme implementation. More detailed information can be found in the attached bibliography.

As in the rest of the countries in the region, Venezuela has developed various help programmes in childhood care and development; each one of them has its advantages, innovations and limitations. Despite the relative success of each experience, every government team has constantly had a tendency to invent new curricular models.

Promoting Evidence-based Practice in Early Childhood Education:
Research and its Implications, Volume 1, pages 43–75.
Copyright © 2001 by Elsevier Science Ltd.
All rights of reproduction in any form reserved.
ISBN: 0-7623-0753-6

In 1995, we proposed and implemented a change in strategy; instead of creating new curricular models, we made a change in the method of implementing educational and daycare public policy (Sánchez & Yánez, 1996). The effort was led by the Ministry of Education, with the support of the Ministry for the Family and various non-governmental organisations to whom we owe the modest success of this experience.

Our theory is that accepting multiple ways of tackling the issues of childhood care and development – with follow-up policies, registration and direct transference of funds, networking and technical support for organised civic society – allows for the provision of more effective care for this vulnerable sector of the population. These activities should operate as part of planning and coordination networks with other local initiatives already in existence, as well as with academic institutions, health services and other relevant sectors in each region.

The care models designed by technicians at a centralised level only work in the context they were designed for, but they are distorted when applied to the ethnic, geographical and economic diversity which is typical of many countries. Therefore, it is more desirable to build upon already existing capacities and arrangements and to create a favourable environment in terms of the quality of the care and an effective cost-profit relationship.

TEMPORARY SOLUTIONS TO PERMANENT PROBLEMS

In Latin America there is a high correlation between the poor population and the young population. This is one of the reasons why governments and multilateral organisations have provided incentives for care programmes directed at early childhood. The compensatory programmes, directed to the sector of the population most affected by macro-economic adjustments, do not correspond with the structural poverty of the region. Frequently, short-term measures are applied, in the hope that once the crisis is over, these programmes can be replaced by formal systems of institutionalised care.

The reality has been different. It has been proved that informal programmes directed towards daycareand childhood development are needed on a permanent basis. In addition, despite not having a clear legal and normative frame to function in, they have expanded and been consolidated. This situation frequently creates tensions, conflicts and contradictions among the different sectors in charge of their implementation and control. For instance, the preschool centres subsidised by the Municipality of Cacaras (Unampre) in extremely poor areas of the city, have not obtained recognition from the educational institutions, because of the negative response from another department of the same Municipality to the request for the relevant permits to operate.

WHY DO WE FIGHT AMONG OURSELVES FOR THE 'POOR'?

Frequently, the conflicts concerning legality and legitimacy which these programmes face lead to the existence of parallel programmes run by different branches of the same executive powers: Ministries of Education, Health, Family, Childhood Protection, Autonomic Institutions. These agencies fight over the same infant population and the result is high costs, owing to the lack of co-ordinated planning. When all their respective statistics are put together, the result is an overestimate of the real coverage of the education and care programmes, while in fact many families living in extreme poverty remain invisible to the eyes of the very same institutions.

During a visit we made to one particular community, we watched two daycare homes, one sited opposite the other. One was financed by the Ministry of Youth while the other was financed by the Foundation for the Child. Each one had its own team of supervisors and sponsors, so efforts and expenses were duplicated, not to mention the great rivalry and distrust created between both institutions. At the end of our visit we mentioned these facts to the members of both teams, and someone said: 'Certainly, I don't know why we fight over the poor, there are enough of them for all of us'.

This 'sectarism' and territorialism among social welfare institutions is a constant issue in Venezuela. The selection of managers for this field rarely takes account of candidates' knowledge, skills or merits; therefore, with each new administration, everything starts all over again. It is not unusual, then, for newcomers to feel great apprehension towards their predecessors and so end up reinventing the wheel; after all, they know very little about the programmes they are going to manage, or how to benefit from accumulated past experience. Furthermore, a professional civil servant is generally the survivor of a system poor in rewarding achievement, but rich in excessive guarantees of job security. The combination of both factors produces a passive and conformist attitude which in the end resists the need for innovation in the face of the challenges which public administration constantly faces in a country with a large population living in poverty. This is why these civil servants enjoy little credibility and trust among their peers and hence amongst management.

PROGRAMMES OF CHILDHOOD CARE AND DEVELOPMENT

During the past decades, care and preschool programmes based in the family and community have appeared in Latin America. After the first Lima Seminar on Experiences in Initial Non-School-Based Education in 1978 (Torres, 1999), the progress of these programmes has been assessed in various meetings and annual regional conferences, where each country presents its innovations and achievements.

The region has greatly advanced in implementing childhood programmes and many lessons and examples have been drawn from them. In particular, the contrast between what is happening in communities and what is planned at high governmental levels and multilateral organisations, which frequently seem to operate in different worlds (Alvarado, 1997).

Documentation about these programmes from the various countries of the region is now plentiful, although, generally, access to this documentation is limited, and its character too quantitative. For this reason, we have chosen here to make more public some of the most well-known and extensive programmes in Venezuela. Although the Venezuelan programmes for daycare have a long history and are pioneers in the region, we have considered it valuable to add a brief description of the Peruvian 'Wawa wasi', for being initiators in development programmes based in the community with official support from the Ministry of Education. This would have a favourable impact in the region, in the search for integration between early childhood education and care, although there is still work to be done to ensure its general acceptance.

WAWA WASI OR WAWA UTA, NON-SCHOOL-BASED EDUCATION PROGRAMMES IN EARLY EDUCATION IN PERU: AN INITIATIVE WITH ITS ORIGINS IN THE COMMUNITY

Towards the end of the 1960s, a new idea was developed in Peru that was to evolve and expand through Latin America and other world regions: childhood care and education based in the family and the community.

In 1967, due to a seven year drought in the Puno Department, in the Peruvian highlands, a significant increase in infant mortality was registered in the area. As a result, Caritas (a religious organisation) decided to put into action a plan centred around the training and teaching of literacy to artisan mothers.

In order to look after the small children while the mothers went to the lessons, care centres were organised in neighbours' houses. To this experience the name Wawa wasi (quechua) or Wawa uta (aymara) was given, meaning Children's Homes. A group of 21 teachers devoted themselves to systematising and following up the experience, training assistants and parents who would educate the children. In 1973, the Ministry of Education expanded the model and created the Non-School-Based Programme of Early Education (PRONOEI). This was taken to other regions of the country with variations, following the different local versions of the idea.

In the beginning of the programme, a member of the community, generally a man with knowledge of the Spanish language, took care of a small group of children, while his neighbours looked after his 'chacra' (small plot of land). With this action of solidarity it was assured that the minder could devote enough time to the children, without compromising his earnings.

In view of the success of the experience, some international organisations decided in 1978 to sponsor an international gathering where a practical plan to reproduce it in other countries of the region could be presented.

During its history, the programme has undergone continuous changes and transformations. For example, when the Ministry of Education introduced a modest payment to the minder, the neighbours stopped tending the chacra, thereby causing a tremendous drop in the number of men volunteering to work for PRONOEI. Even though its value is recognised, this programme faces resistance within the same educational sector. Despite teachers recognising that the minders in the programme are frequently better than the properly qualified primary school teacher, children still face problems in accessing primary education. Furthermore, there is a big gap between the resources assigned to this mode and those invested in more formalised, and much more expensive, modes of education (Moreno, 2000).

A government rule determined that the centres for childcare should be located a certain distance apart to expand their coverage. But in practice one can usually find various programmes competing for the same children. Nowadays, the Ministry for Women has begun putting into practice a variety of the Wawa wasi, whose main aim is the nutritional care of children aged 0–2 who are at social risk. This new development in the work of the government agencies adds to the already existing competition for resources and target populations.

Day Care Homes (HCD) in Venezuela: A Solution Based in Community Practice

One of the oldest programmes based in the community is the Venezuelan Day Care Homes project. The Child Foundation, an institution chaired by the first lady of the Republic, began the project in 1974 (González, 1998).

A group of experts was set up to analyse the situation of children living in poverty while their mothers worked, and to try to find a solution to their day care.

When it was discovered that the children of working mothers were frequently looked after by female neighbours, it was decided to strengthen this kind of community arrangement for daycare by adding specialised help in health, nutrition, education and legal aid for the family. Thus, in October of that year, the programme Day Care Homes was born. One of the female neighbours (*minder mother*) undertakes to look after five children aged from birth to five, whose mothers work outside their homes (*biological mothers*), for up to 12 hours a day. During this time the children are fed, washed and cared for. With the help of a technical group in each community, the healthy development of the child is monitored and advice is given in feeding and in activities to help the cognitive, psychomotor, social and emotional development of the children. Each minder receives a feeding subsidy and a bonus that, although below the national minimum wage, allows her to be at home with her own children. In addition, the working mother pays a small sum to supplement the wages of the minder.

In 1978, under the patronage of UNICEF and the technical support of the U.S. High/Scope project, the programme was assessed (Fundación del Niño, 1978). In terms of child development, the programme showed a high level of quality. In terms of impact on the children, the evidence led UNICEF to propose the extension of the model to other regions. During the following years, the experience was developed and expanded, on a small scale, to different regions of the country.

Until this moment, the emphasis of the programme was on the working mother. She, as well as the minder, subsidised the programme with her time and money. The spread was modest and the quality of the childcare high.

In 1989, when faced with the fast-increasing impoverishment caused by the adjustments of the country's macro-economic plan, it was necessary to resort to compensatory programmes in order to reduce the impact on children – the most vulnerable segment of the population. The Daycare Homes programme (HCD) was 'well established as a model' (González, 1998: 13) and was incorporated into the Plan for Confronting Poverty. However, it became over-extended, leading to sacrifices a 'quality' programme may resort to when stretched on such a scale. The programme was then taken over by the Ministry for the Family, a government agency, and was injected with substantial economic resources and restructured into bigger units, called Multi-daycare Homes (MCD), that would be managed jointly with various non-governmental organisations. It was then decided to transfer funds to those organisations capable of managing the programme, under strict ministerial supervision. This initiative sought to favour civic organisations concerned with the challenges that the care of children in poverty create. Thanks to state subsidies, assistance is now provided free of charge, and the fees which were previously charged to parents are covered.

The aim of the changes in the management of the daycareprogramme was to massively extend the coverage of the population in a relatively short time (Senifa, 1997). In fact, the results were successful and the coverage went from the care of 4000 children throughout the country to more than 350,000 in less than 4 years.

Normally in Venezuela, every change of government brings about profound changes at almost every level of state management. Frequently these changes ignore 'institutional memory' and every time they start a painful process of learning and reinventing what was already known. Thankfully, the Daycare Programme survived the test. The new government team of 1994 decided to develop more control mechanisms for both the administrative and curriculum aspects. The aim was to improve quality and achieve better administration. Unfortunately, however, the result was an increase in controls and processes for transferring funds, which led some of the organisations closer to the real project to abandon it, since they did not have the backing of strong financing. Furthermore, the non-governmental organisations had to choose between being subordinate to the Government – in terms of their own quality ideals – or breaking away from the programme and carrying on independently.

Despite these problems, the programme has shown resilience and although its growth stopped and the target population varied considerably from the poorest sectors to a relatively better off population (Ruesta, Yánez, Zarikian & Díaz, 1995), it continues to demonstrate its potential as the answer to providing for early childcare and learning, as well as its organisational strength.

From Family Model to School Model

In 1994, as a case study on child environment sponsored by the Bernard van Leer Foundation (Ruesta, Yánez, Zarikian & Díaz, 1995; Woodhead, 1996, 1998) both models of care, HCD and MCD, were studied using an ethnographic method. Important qualitative differences were identified between the two modes of the daycare programme. It was found that the home/family-centred   model (Daycare Homes-HCD) offered greater opportunities for child development and learning than the semi-school model (Multi-Daycare Homes – MCD). Because the HCD functions within a family, the children have the opportunity to interact with the older children as well as with its other members. The minder must organise her time well, so stimulating the older children's autonomy. She can devote more time to meeting the specific needs of each child and can often get extra help from other members of the family setting. A common scene is the minder mother feeding a child in her lap, distracting and then singing the child to sleep.

The MCD, on the other hand, operates in communal premises rented from a third party. The carers do not live there, they are simply there during working hours. In these settings it was found that feeding, washing and resting routines were timed and controlled, in a production line pattern, to the detriment of the children's individual needs. Children who had not finished eating when it was time to tidy up, did not eat. Although the best answers to questions about child development were given by the carers in the larger establishments, the evaluators considered that on the basis of their observations and criteria relating to individual children's learning needs, the best practice was observed in the family settings (HCD).

Child Education Programmes Based on the Strengthening of the Family

With the aim of increasing the coverage of preschool education in Venezuela, in the rural and marginal urban communities, non conventional strategies for preschool education have been created as alternatives to the classroom. The most successful of these programmes were the *Family Programme* (PF), inspired by initiatives brought from the United States (Head Start and Portage), and the *Centres for Child and Family*, inspired by the local experiences of communal promoters twinned with the Peruvian Wawa wasi.

Around 1979, the Ministry of Education launched a new programme that combined media strategies (radio and television) with a face to face strategy known as the Family Programme. The programme was based on a prescriptive approach where parents were 'taught' how to bring up their children, from birth to 6 years old. The programme aimed to reassert parental roles and family integration, as well as reassess traditional raising methods and provide instrumental and conceptual tools for family education (Colmenares, 1996).

The Family Project starts with the premise that the child is the starting point and the family its generating core. Intelligence is considered as the first right of every child and it can be learnt and taught through early intervention and suitable stimuli.

The programme contains multiple elements; it approaches the training with regard to children's health, nutrition and learning, relying on the mother, father and family's mediator. The Family Programme operates in two ways: face to face, through facilitators who guide pregnant and breast-feeding women who attend child and mother centres, clinics, and so on, and through radio and television.

From 1986, this programme was attached to the Preschool Education Office (Ministry of Education). Its mission was given a new direction towards increasing coverage and improving of the quality of preschool education. To this end, the facilitators, now teachers, were professionalised and regional coordinators were appointed for supervision.

The programme expanded rapidly. It was established in 19 urban maternity units and 17 rural establishments. It spread through television, radio, cinema and telephone thanks to the help of the private media, without any cost to the government. The model was transferred to other countries and the programme was assessed.

However, the programme also faced great difficulties, such as desertion by volunteers and resistance from health professionals and various factors led to its gradual deterioration. These included: a lack of emphasis on the eradication of legal, social, family and economic barriers to the child's upbringing and development; a defective registration system; difficulties in recruiting the required high standard of professional personnel; and the typical lack of continuity in public administration due to government changes.

Child and Family Centre: Preparing the Family for their Children's Introduction into the Formal System

The Child and Family Centres Programme (CNF) was launched in 1985 with the support of the Bernard van Leer Foundation and the participation of the Metropolitana University. Five years later, in 1990, the rural version appeared. From the Ministry of Education's point of view, it was hoped that the programme would help to increase the number of children in preschool education (Yánez, 1994).

Although the necessary infrastructure to increase the coverage of preschool education had been established, it was apparent that the poorest families did not send their children to preschool, because it did not answer their real needs. The hours provided by these educational preschools actually prevented the mothers from taking and collecting the children, due to transport costs and their working hours. The demands for materials and money by parent-teacher associations were higher than these families could afford and, additionally the mothers who were deemed most in need of this service did not understand about educational provision for such young children. Therefore, the central aim of the CNF was to strengthen very poor families, and the communities in the upbringing of their children. To this end, shared activities to improve the environment were initiated and a group of community promoters were trained in early intervention, as well as in being able to offer help to families with children under 7 years old in the areas of health, nutrition, psychological development, education and legal aid.

One of its most important achievements was that the benefits given by the social programmes (Food Grants, Milk Grants, School Bags) awarded through the education system could also reach those who most needed them, including children aged from birth to three, who had been omitted from other educational projects.

By 1994, the programme was in theory implemented in all the federal entities, with a total of 105 working units. However, when outside help ceased, technical supervision decreased considerably. Nowadays this programme barely reaches 13,000 children all over the country. The CNF became classroom programmes of very low quality, with some exceptions worth mentioning. For example, the Pacomin Programme, with the help of a non-governmental organisation, with networks in the oil industry and help from the Bernard van Leer Foundation, maintains a clear philosophy of social participation and integral community development. As for the rest, there only remain a few isolated examples in other regions of the country.

It is worth mentioning that the programme survives with an acceptable level of quality, as defined in the original tenets of the programme, in those communities where civic or basic organisations have retained a certain degree of independence from ministerial authorities and are able to combine the benefits available from various private and state institutions.

The Management of Preschool Education: A Responsibility Shared Between the Civic Society and the State

Quality Integral Pre Schools (PIC)
The Constitutional Law on Education provides that standard Pre- school Education starts with birth and ends when starting school, preferable at 6 years old. It also establishes total care for the child within the context of his/her

family and community; therefore, the care programmes based in the family and the community fit perfectly into the valid legal framework.

Although the current legal regulations restrict Preschool Education to one year of school attendance, preferably from 5 years old, one article leaves the possibility open for the Ministry of Education to modify this and in 1995 it was proposed to take a new political and conceptual direction in Preschool Education in Venezuela (Sánchez & Yánez, 1996).

The conceptual reorientation of Preschool Education was intended to increase the coverage throughout the country, without sacrificing quality. The efforts were directed not at creating new programmes but towards recognising the activities that the same civic society carries out in looking after children aged 0 to 6 and their families. The aim was to bestow on existing informal provision, focussed on the family and community, a legal and institutional framework less vulnerable to the constant changes brought about by the high instability of public administration.

The greatest part of the social project's funding assigned to preschool education was used in infrastructure and to a lesser, though important, degree in the training of classroom teachers. It is not easy for high level civil servants from the financial sector, from the government and the World Bank, to understand the meaning of programmes based in the family and the community. It was necessary therefore to create a model which was easier to understand, with the aim of being able to channel some resources, even if marginal, to the development of a new form of managing preschool education in equal partnership with non-governmental organisations.

Within this context, the idea of **Quality Integral Preschools** (PIC) was launched in the middle of 1995, as a strategy to tackle the integral coverage of care and early childhood education, with the proactive participation of families and communities, together with the institutions that serve them (Yánez, 1996; Sánchez, 1997; Hernández et al., 1998).

The strategy was set within: (a) the valid Constitutional Law on Education; (b) the commitment made by the nation to the International Convention on the Rights of the Child; (c) the nation's 9th Plan; and (d) the Ministry of Education Action Plan.

PIC (Quality Integral Preschools) is the label given to a preschool educational unit (in classroom, family or community), when it expands its educational community beyond the formal sphere and considers as its target population every child who lives in a particular sector of the community. This strategy promotes the formulation of community-based and family-based approaches within the educational activity of the preschool unit.

A **preschool education unit** is defined by the human team made up of teachers, assistants, promoters and representatives, under the coordination of a manager, with its own mandate for registration and a permit to administer the standard curriculum. The key defining element is the unit's manager, a post which facilitates the organisation and administration of the network. In this way, educational preschool activity is a process of social development based on acting within the physical, social and cultural environment of individual children and their families. This strategy is a first step towards breaking away from the prevailing form of education centred on infrastructure.

PIC does not offer a substitute for any current care programme in the classroom, family and community fields, but it tries to join up the various existing efforts, aiming to guarantee a high standard of educational activity, sociocultural relevance and the simplification of the system's management, whilst not opposing the need for diversification in operational models.

Respect for the contractual conditions of the teachers is combined with the greater importance given to non-governmental and basic organisations which co-ordinate educational activity and which serve as a link between the educational unit and the family and community childcare arrangements. In this way, it is possible to bring the educational activity to the children, wherever they are, with greater cultural relevance, since the parents participate actively in the system's organisation.

An element worth mentioning is that the PIC is formulated by drawing on the practice observed in different regions of the country. The study of ten local experiences, sponsored by UNICEF, allowed the sketching out of the general outlines of the idea, while each participating educational community was allowed the opportunity to develop its own action strategies (Ramírez, 1996).

The model is coherent with the decentralisation process that is taking place in the educational sector. The State promises to guarantee initial education for all, but not to provide it. Its new role is to create a cooperative and stimulating environment for the particular answers that the different communities give to their own problems of childcare and education. The formulation of these initiatives in the formal education system is built upon local capabilities. Each Preschool Education unit is responsible for the children in its community, and not only for the ones that have a place in the available classrooms. At the same time, the shared responsibility of State-Civic Society concerning initial educational activity is retained.

The secondary consequences of this decision present an encouraging prospect for the promotion of private and community initiatives around childcare and education. As an example, an initiative from the Open National University in cooperation with the Ministry for Youth's Employment and Training Office, trained around 300 women as 'educating mothers' in a farming region of the country (Lara). The certificate given to these women has helped them to enter more easily into governmental care programmes as well as to start their own 'micro-enterprises for childhood help', joining PIC's community networks. Among those involved in the 'informal preschools' network in Lara, adopted as one of the PIC's models, there were more than 3000 children from rural and urban marginal communities.

In Caracas, the non-formal preschools subsidised by the municipality of Caracas have more than 25000 children, and their participation in the PIC represents an enhancement of the involvement of impoverished communities. Examples of these networks, although they are still in their infancy, are found all over the national territory, since their expansion depends more on the initiative and pro-activity of local authorities and organisations than on the action of the central authorities of the educational administration.

The improvement of the system of 'formal' registration of children in the family and community modes makes evident the magnitude and variety of the participants who contribute to childcare on a daily basis. This registration is important for the purpose of more accurately planning the resources assigned to their training and to give them the infrastructure and materials relevant from the point of view of the children's development and learning, and of their ecological and cultural context.

By 1998, there were networks in at least 13 of the 24 states than make up the Republic. By the year 2000, despite the great lack of stability of Venezuelan political institutions during this time of re-foundation of the Republic, the networks are retained. The curriculum reform, now in its second stage, is directed towards the unification of the curriculum and instead of formal and informal preschools, the educational activity is directed at classrooms, family and community areas. This form of management means a great step forward for the programmes hitherto regarded as 'non-conventional', since the educational activity is approached from its human side, in its social and cultural context. *Thus the community modes would cease to be seen as an option which was unavoidable because of the shortage of classrooms, and begin to be regarded as a valid and desirable approach to early childhood care and education, with classroom models as simply one alternative.*

Another interesting element of the PIC is the real and effective inclusion of the children from birth until they go to Primary School. Since the network has its base in the family and the local arrangements for childcare, with the mothers and minders being responsible for direct contact with the children, the inclusion of children under 3 happens as a natural process. Registering these children in the education system's official statistics, adds a greater distributive power to the network and, at the same time, allows for more realistic planning on how to invest in the sector.

This is not a matter of increasing the registers artificially, but about recognising where and when the children are being looked after and then pointing out these facts to the education system in order that these children can benefit from teachers in neighbouring initial education units, as well as allowing them to have access to the welfare programmes that are administered through the education system.

Generally, it is almost impossible to find two identical PICs, since each community creates its own action model. Diversity is allowed within the limits of a few elements required by the Education Law, the International Convention on Children's Rights and, where applicable, the International Convention on Native Indian People's Rights.

PICs are not a new approach to preschool education, but a new strategy to join up the educational and daycare activity for children under 6 and their families, through community networks of solidarity and civic and governmental organisations.

The Teacher at Home (PEMEC): Development of Strategies to Organise Networks and Training in Management and Child Help

The Teacher at Home project started in 1998, with the participation of governmental and non-governmental organisations which develop child and family help programmes, and regional educational authorities (educational zones). The project is sponsored by the Bernard van Leer Foundation and is at present in a phase of expansion. There is a proposal to continue the cooperation for another three years (until the year 2002). The general administration of the funding for this cooperation is carried out by a civic organisation (AFIN) and operated in cooperation with the State.

Currently it is operating in eleven states, with the help of more than 30 public and private organisations. The project has a hired technical team, responsible for co-ordinating and advancing its development at a decentralised level, and for following its progress.

The project focuses on the identification of local initiatives directed in an integral way at children from 0 to 6 years old and their families, with the aim of giving them technical support and links to consolidate them and to learn about their achievements and difficulties.

Particular emphasis is placed on connecting together already existing programmes, like the Family Programme, Family and Child Centres, services from the Ministry of Education Special Education, Daycare Homes and Multi-homes from the Ministry for the Family, and dozens of other non-governmental experiences in the local sphere.

The Bernard van Leer Foundation's help has allowed the project to form a high quality coordination team, and to guarantee its mobility within the established area of activity. At present, it is felt necessary to expand cooperation with other official and multilateral bodies in order to widen the support network for PIC, paying particular attention to excluded sectors and children under 3.

To connect together disparate efforts was the key to giving credibility to the project. The contribution made by the American States Organisation and several loan administrative agencies from the World Bank, allowed for quality media material and relevant experiences of technical interchange between peers. Meanwhile, the contribution made by the United Nations Children's Fund helped to identify the successful characteristics of spontaneous local experiences of inter-sectoral agreement for initial care and education (Ramírez, 1996).

The focus of the regional meetings is to identify and consolidate local networks of child and family care; to highlight the importance of the cultural aspects of educational activity, and the importance of the participation of those parents and adults relevant in initial care and education. They also serve to present achievements and lessons drawn from local models.

The Teacher at Home scheme throws into sharp relief the confrontation between the needs identified by the governmental planners and the needs felt by the communities regarding childhood development. It allows for the clear identification of the strengths and advantages of local innovation and for the evaluation of the social benefits of each form of educational investment (Leiva & Dáger, 2000).

The Teacher at Home scheme has the following objectives:

(1) To provide training for those relevant adults that look after children aged 0 to 6, in order for them to apply innovative pedagogical strategies which stimulate child development.
(2) To identify, support and consolidate those early child raising practices which better stimulate children's development in quality surroundings, as much in the family as in the community.

(3) To offer information and guidance to the relevant adults to ensure the optimum use of available childcare centres in the community.
(4) To promote an efficient link between the different promoters and managers of child and family care and whole protection programmes.

ACHIEVED ACTIVITIES

Initially, an evaluation process, called 'Monitoring of the Significant Adult', started, made up of interviews and observations carried out by the same project facilitators (with previous training in the use of methodology and relevant research instruments). The results were presented during a one-day working session in May 1999 (Leiva & Dáger, 2000).

Subsequently the following measures were carried out:

(1) Systematic registering of statistics for the Teacher at Home scheme in each of the 11 participating states.
(2) Programming the termly monitoring of the situation in the states, and joint planning with the local coordination team.
(3) Technical presentations of the project to different organisations and institutions linked to the educational and social sector, in the different participant regions.
(4) Six months after it had started, adjustments were made to the project, taking into account the results of the Monitoring and the observations made during each visit to the regions.
(5) A promotional phase of the project was started using the written account of the most outstanding aspects found during the visits, aspects considered as successful factors to be shared with the rest of the participants.
(6) A periodical informative bulletin was designed called 'What happens with the Teacher at Home'.

What Makes the Teacher at Home Scheme a Successful Programme?

The success of the programme has been attributed to:

(1) Carrying out direct work in the house with the families' and communities' participation. As a result, there is an increase in self-sufficiency and greater involvement of the parents with their children's development, leading to a greater impact on the quality of the child's environment.

(2) The ability to learn about the needs and abilities of the communities and their institutions. In fact, there is greater participation from the family and the technicians from local institutions in the activities involving the facilitators.

(3) Existing local experiences lend validity and recognition to what has already been done and – without imposing a particular model – offer continuity, expansion and new targets.

(4) Although the project has some general guidelines, the specific practice is in agreement with local resources and specifications according to each community and the vision of each federal institution. In every level of decision-making, the practitioners were given the opportunity to participate.

(5) Consistent technical and systematic support and continuous evaluation by the supervisory team from the national and decentralised educational system.

(6) Trust among the central, state and local teams involved and identified with the project and its leadership.

(7) Immediate impact on the improvement in the lives of the families and the community, thanks to the visibility given to their needs at institutional level. Examples include:

   • In many homes the mothers (significant adults), previously aggressive and not very communicative, have started now to change their behaviour, talking more to their children, embracing them more and coping with conflicts with more patience and understanding.
   • Many mothers show themselves to be more alert with their children's cleanliness and to attend to their needs more quickly.

(8) Flexible funding for technical backup, independent of central governmental administration. This speeds up the expenditure and auditing processes, as well as giving a certain degree of stability, while retaining the State's technical supervision.

(9) Different organisations from the social area are integrated and participate, working together for a common aim.

(10) Permanent training of teachers and relevant adults.

(11) Development of community and family strategies within the network of Quality Integral Preschools (PIC), that join together the formal and informal system of initial education and day care.

(12) Strengthening of the help networks, that make possible access for the normal population to other programmes (nutrition, health, legal aid) and progressive self-sufficiency processes:

- In several communities where the project is working, neighbourhood associations have been organised (with the facilitators' support) in order to negotiate improvements in the community's surroundings (educational services, sewerage works, street tarmac, etcetera).

Four Illustrative Case Studies (Leiva & Dáger, 2000)

Bolivar State: An Alliance between the Ministry of Education (Educational Zone, Preschool Education Department) and a NGO – Fundacrensa
Fundacrensa is a nutritional recovery centre, sponsored by a member of a religious order and a group of businessmen from the mining region of the Orinoco river. It forms part of a community centre housing health, nutritional and assistance services for people with very little means.

The project started thanks to an alliance with the Ministry of Education, so that preschool teachers – belonging to the Family Programme (informal aiming at early stimulation) – support activities with children. Nonetheless, despite the efforts made in the centre and the talks given to the mothers and the families, the children, when they return home from the centre, go back to the same precarious state of health and early nutrition. The same effect is observed after every weekend or holiday period. In May 1998 Fundacrensa became part of the group of organisations that participated in The Teacher at Home project and began to expand their field of activity and to work directly with the families of the centre's children, actively involving them in the children's care in the centre and also visiting their homes to give guidance on childcare at home.

In January 2000, after the holidays, it was observed, among other achievements, that all the children came back in a good general condition and without the weight losses that had previously been noted, following gains through centre attendance.

One of the volunteer mothers and facilitator in her community, tells how her other two younger children do not suffer from malnutrition, since she is applying at home what she has learnt. Nowadays, she feels important because she helps and guides other mothers in her community.

Trujillo State: Casablanca Community
In June 1998, this community of very little means in the Trujillo educational zone, preschool department, decided to approach the Casablanca Community, in order to initiate a Teacher at Home scheme, using as the programme's base

a preschool centre from the Quality Integral Preschool, a place half an hour away. The travelling teacher Dalia visited six families, with whom she carried out activities within the home. She guided them in aspects related to daily routine, with the project's components. At the same time, she built links with the neighbours' association, parents and natural community leaders. This community (with tin and mud housing) did not have preschool education centres for five and six year old children. Neither did it have a primary school, and the few tuition hours for the 7 to 12 year olds were given in one of the community's shacks, in conditions of oppressive heat. As a result of the arrival of the project and the systematic work of the teacher (with help from her original centre and the educational zone), the community organised itself and made a block of buildings suitable for the 4, 5 and 6 year old children. Nowadays the Ministry of Education helps with a female teacher and there is a suitable classroom in good condition for classroom work. The work with the families continues and expands. The project is seen as an element that promotes quality of life in this community.

Sucre State: Alliances Between the Ministry of Education and Rotary –
Cumanagoto/Child Foundation
In June 98, actions to approach families started in two communities: Las Palomas (Ministry of Education/Child Foundation) and Campeche (Ministry of Education/Rotary). The Rotarians put into effect events of specific help but they had neither the experience nor knowledge of aspects related to education. They joined efforts with personnel from the Ministry of Education. In its turn, the Child Foundation appointed a female teacher for Las Palomas community. The three organisations, with guidance from the coordinating team, planned and combined human and logistical efforts.

Within a few months, they achieved acceptance by the programme and significant changes in the children's environment. For instance, in October of that year, hygiene and cleanliness in the children's homes improved (families cleaned, swept, and did not throw down fish entrails in the house or on the doorstep), the children were looked after (they were bathed, given clean clothes, breakfast and a meal timetable was organised, and food was served on a plate not the floor), parents played with their children, embraced them and showed them affection.

This is an example of how the synergy of the alliance favours the implementation of a social project, in an estate where traditionally other projects have failed due to continuous political instability. This experience is one of the highlights of the project.

Portuguesa, Acarigua Estate: Los Chagaramos Community

Librada Silva is a teacher from the Family Programme, with a wide experience in the promotion of breast feeding, childbirth tutoring and early stimulation. She is part of the PICEP project (towards Quality Preschool) through which 3 to 6 year old children are helped in one of the houses of the neighbourhood, in a community where there is no primary school.

Librada heard about the Teacher at Home Project, asked for information and, since the majority of the community does not have any aid, started direct action with the families on her own initiative. She went to project meetings invited by the technical group of Acarigua (a region of the central plains). Within the community she identified Judith (at that moment with no children of her own) as a natural leader; she trained and guided her on everything that helps child development. Judith started organising activities with families and children under 6 years old in her house, with help and assistance from Librada, who acted as judith's role model. At the same time Judith participated as a Significant Adult in a neighbouring region – Lara – and shared experiences with the training mothers of that locality. She had her own child and, on a voluntary basis, went on to implement activities with children and significant adults in her community.

Afterwards, two young educated women from that community became involved as facilitators. The three of them planned together, always under the guidance and coordination of Librada. They expanded the number of families involved. During these months, Judith grew up at a personal level, longing for learning and sharing her experiences. She stood out in the first focal workshop celebrated there in July 1999, with the help of teams from six estates. Contact was established with the local Council and a grant for salaries was obtained for these three voluntary facilitators.

These experiences exemplify the active and coordinating role of the teacher, in working directly with the families and the training of voluntary facilitators that enables expansion, increasing support to a community. They also exemplify the kind of human profile required in this project, among other characteristics a facilitator needs to be: committed, sensitive, able to show initiative, prepared for communal work and open to new experiences.

Still more importantly, these experiences show that a management which is built upon the base of existing social capabilities and which links them in a coordinated action network, can enhance the potential value of existing resources, make the children and their families' problems clear to the institutions with a mandate for social action and the social and business organisations. Such management also empowers parents, significant adults, and professional and paraprofessional personnel, to co-manage the negotiations in favour of the children.

Benefits and Synergies Obtained from these Alliances

(1) More effective use of human resources.
(2) Complementary participation of the organisations, where the single contribution of each one added together is translated into achievements in greater and more diverse fields of activity.
(3) In some cases, the field of activity that some organisations had, has been expanded. For example, the Rotarians (Rotary club) in the Sucre Estate at the moment tackle pedagogical activities with the coordination of the Ministry of Education, Culture and Sports; the non-governmental organisation *World in Colours* in the Portuguesa Estate has started activities to help families with children under 6 (its recreational-formative programme was originally directed to 5 to 12 year old children).
(4) Linking with the teacher training colleges of some of the local universities, through last year students' practices in the projects' activities.

An Opportune Moment to Change the Administrative Scheme for Preschool Education in Venezuela

When the project started, the country was going through a very favourable political and organisational phase. A number of events serendipitously coincided.

When the National Office for Preschool Educational lost its centralised role in implementing a budget, it also lost its power to organise the local educational system and to control the implementation of its local programmes. With only a minor and insignificant role in the process of decision-making regarding how to use the World Bank loan, its main activity was to update curriculum design and policies of that level.

With the help of UNICEF, studies were made into the available local capacity for achieving the targets relating to numerical levels of provision and the educational quality that was being offered by settings run by the states and their private and public partners. Additionally, the national policy for child support for children aged from birth to six years was redirected towards integration, aiming for holistic education and care in the spheres of classrooms, the families and communities. At the same time there was a call for integration with other governmental sectors and areas of civil society which were involved or affected by the challenges arising from children living in poverty.

The loan agreement with the World Bank for the strengthening of those sectors involved with childhood reached its end with more grief than glory. The performance of the programme was judged to have been very poor and the impact very low. But nonetheless, some aspects of the agreement, such as the strengthening of institutional and communication and information components, had been positive and this opened up some opportunities. Some of the established resources served as a basis for technical support to the incipient development of coordinated management of childcare based in the family and community.

UNICEF and OEA (Organisation of American States) offered modest but timely support for the initial activities of the then *National Office for Preschool Education* of the Ministry of Education. This financial assistance was invested into a study of successful experience of local administration by non-governmental organisation and regional and municipal governments, as well as in the publication of guidance materials directed towards the different participants of the proposal: parents, paraprofessionals, teachers and managers. The diverse strengths of the spontaneous local initiatives were explored and identified and the foundations were laid for the education sector to have an open administration.

The technical weakness of the government's coalition parties provided an opportunity for the different sectors involved (health, family, education, information systems and statistics) to demand the participation of non party managers. This had the favourable effect of opening up links and bonds between the various state agencies and society in the regions.

The Bernard van Leer Foundation's partnership with the project and its technical support took the form of first, a specific donation for the systematisation and promotion of collaborative development of provision set among families and communities and later, a two year grant for its introduction in eleven states of the Republic.

Current Challenges and Futures Prospects

- The project plays an active part in the educational policies concerned with children of preschool age and their families. Nevertheless, it is necessary to plan any national expansion of this type of strategy within the reform process that the country is undergoing.
- It is not a model for childcare, but a policy management model for child education.
- The budgetary base of the project must be consolidated.

- The next step is directed towards the creation and consolidation of regional and estate inter-institutional committees, where the organisations work, plan and perform jointly (with the network support) for the benefit of the project.

SOURCES OF RESISTANCE

There are certain prejudices and objections that are frequently directed against the educational modes centred in the community and family (informal programmes), raised by academics, trade unionists, planners and administrators from the formal education system.

Some of those objections which we most frequently face in Venezuela include:

(1) *The belief that the classroom mode is the only mode of excellence for Preschool Education.*

The reason for this seems to be the fact that the classroom model appears attractive for its image, its school regimen and its easy administration compared with the obvious informality and frequent lack of resources of the programmes based in the family and the community. Such stark differences and surface impressions reinforce this belief. However, the belief that a decorated classroom and a beautiful school infrastructure are synonymous with 'quality' (a value judgement in any case) has been challenged by different national and regional forums (Fujimoto, 1998). Even so, the State continues to spend large sums of money in this type of provision, despite the fact that access is quite limited for certain communities, owing to basic infrastructure and availability of public services. The poorest populations frequently live in places where is not possible to erect buildings for education, either because of land problems or because of obstacles relating to urban planning or property rights.

Until recently, the higher or further teacher training colleges only trained teachers for school-based preschools. Recently, some universities have expanded the curriculum to include the family and community models.

Generally, very few budgetary resources are assigned to informal preschool education programmes, demonstrating the lack of consistency between the discourse and the practice of governments participating in international forums on initial education centred in the family and the community. Despite this situation, informal programmes show great resilience.

Initially there was resistance from the teacher's unions about participation in the programmes, since they required teachers' mobility in the community. This resistance was understandable considering the lack of knowledge about the innovations, scarce resources and the uncomfortable conditions of work in those communities. The union leaders did not always have up-to-date pedagogical information, having themselves generally concentrated on policy and organisational skills. However, more recently the reputation of these programmes is changing and they now have more supporters among the teachers' ranks.

(2) The classroom model is easier to administer compared with the difficulties of control and dispersal relating to a community and family model.

In particular, when we are dealing with *centralised models* of education management, the tendency to generalise a model offers many advantages: in general, there is a clear definition of costs, uniform quality criteria, easily programmed actions and easy administration.

Due to the need to adapt to different contexts in a family and community model, it becomes impossible to establish a uniform model of administration. Frequently, the State keeps a feasible number of these projects, as demonstration models and pilot or experimental schemes, while the greatest part of the funding is invested in formal classrooms. In other cases, informal provision is allowed to survive due to public administration inertia, limited control and monitoring.

The traditional supervisory bodies are unfamiliar with these programmes and are inadequately briefed to follow and direct the experience. Therefore, the programme is usually coordinated by centralised technical teams, resulting in higher costs.

(3) Our national preschool curriculum design, based on the some of the most up-to-date international ideas about early childhood education and care, is limited to educational action in the classroom and, although it mentions the family and the community, it does not reflect at all the proactive role that these must have in planning and evaluation at this educational level.

In general, it is thought that children in informal provision are deprived of the benefits of the preschool classroom. Despite the evidence that children benefit more from the programmes centred around family and community, negligence in strengthening these programmes has helped justify the objections.

Classroom models are sometimes inappropriate when it comes to dealing with the needs of communities with massive rural populations of scarce means or ethnic diversity.

There is a double curriculum for Initial Education, a curriculum for formal education and a curriculum for informal education, one for the rich, one for the poor. Innovative and unconventional experiences are discussed in international forums but disappear in funding situations and in curriculum design projects.

(4) In Venezuela there is opposition to the privatisation of public education. The existence of an overly strict and obsolete law for the administration of private education, plus the hold of the trade unions and chronic fear of official teaching institutions towards the privatisation of education have led to an unjust generalisation which militates against the community sector. This has prevented pro-active participation of the populace in the decision-making process relating to their children's early childhood education. It is a serious mistake to believe that the non conventional models are only necessary as stop-gaps for more preschool classrooms. Although its cost per benefit might be smaller, research in Venezuela shows that a good quality family or community programme benefits children and their family group more than classroom arrangements do (Fujimoto, 1998; Ruesta, Yánez, Zarikian & Díaz, 1995).

Major Difficulties Encountered

We found that there are aspects of the programme which could be strengthened. For example we noted:

(1) *little experience and training* in organising and strengthening the local networks around projects, to make the most of available resources and to increase the capacity to put pressure on those authorities with political and budgetary decision power.

(2) *difficulties in developing relevant materials* that are easy to produce and use, low cost but high in pedagogical potential, to be used by children on their own or under the significant adult's supervision.

(3) *the frequent change of authorities*, typical of the Latin American region, affects the shaping and establishment of state teams in some federal entities and reduces the sustainability of solid support networks. The rotation of executives in the central and decentralised governments is undesirable, but it is out of the control of middle management.

(4) senior managers in the national executive are not capable of taking on board all the problems of the Education sector.

(5) *the economic situation, budget and allocations:*
   • the country's unstable economic situation affects the operational costs for projects (e.g. for rents, teacher mobility).
   • at practitioner level, the lack of a budget for teachers' mobility and materials for a non conventional programmes naturally reduces their activities.

- the precarious financial and organisational situation of many non-governmental organisations, prevents them from systematically collaborating in the execution of projects.
- because of the inadequate and out-dated communications and information technology resources, it proves difficult to communicate with the organisations.

(6) tension and mistrust among governmental and non-governmental organisations in some federal entities.

(7) *little training of teachers and members of the educational community* for participating in the processes of educational administration as well as little *training* by teachers of professionals and volunteers on theory and practice in early childhood education.

(8) the need to guarantee preschool coverage for the most vulnerable sector of the population contrasted with the impossibility of guaranteeing classroom-based education for all (which is reflected in the enrolment register, in the official records) is added to the arguments in favour of education based in the family and community.

(9) while the infant population increases at a level of approximately half a million children per year, the targets for expanding educational coverage are usually set at increasing the classroom sphere by hardly thirty thousand places. This situation makes the pressure on the current managers even more desperate.

(10) the investment made in training is unrelated to reality.
- despite the good management of the loan made to Fundapreescolar/Fndaescolar, the system adopted to train teachers was more in tune with the self financing needs of the universities than with the needs for the development of the sector, through family and community models.
- the country's universities were invited to compete with training proposals for teachers in service. The local coordination would be carried out by the regional authorities of the central government, with little or no participation by the regional governments. Sadly, most of these higher institutions' experience in early childhood education and care is either non-existent or highly limited. Meanwhile, the majority of experienced teachers, are already working full-time and could not participate as trainers within the project. Nevertheless, concerted efforts have been made to bring the teacher training curricula in the different higher education centres in the country up-to-date, but unfortunately this project did not precede or coincide with the disbursement of the World Bank Loan.

- the supervision of the fund, as required by the credit programme, was executed in an extremely centralised way, where the National Office had the technical responsibility and Fundapreescolar (a section created for the administration of the funds) the supervision. The absence of resources for this financial management prevented this supervision and the administrative records do not include information regarding who actually had access to the training programme. While the total number of hours and number of persons per course is known, it is not known who participated, whether some students repeated, etc. Records from the few supervisory visits which did take place show that rural teachers or those from poor sectors were excluded, and that the courses privileged teachers who were seeking promotion (often in order to be eligible for an enhanced retirement pension). Although it is not possible to generalise, due to the lack of evidence, the cases which have come to light show cracks in the training component. Cracks whose harm is incalculable.
- the training was evaluated through the perception of the workshops participants. But no follow-up of its impact on practice was undertaken. Such an evaluation should have been carried out by the Political Office of Preschool Education, but it has neither sufficient financial resources, nor the minimum supervisory personnel to follow-up even its regular programmes.
- the Venezuelan public administration is very similar to a relay race in which the next runner, without fail, would always drop the baton. To compensate for this failing, we are also very creative, as can be seen in the proliferation of ministries, institutes and programmes with each new administration. Instead of creating new models, it is preferable to learn how people solve their own problems and how to give them support to make their solutions as effective as possible.

Learning from our Mistakes: Sharing Some Lessons

In Venezuela we have many innovative programmes of non conventional care, almost all of them with an impeccable theoretical basis. But very few have gone beyond the pilot phase. Those taken to national level have reached the stage of a budget and infrastructure, but have had no impact on the overall quantity of provision. It is necessary to consolidate a new administrative mentality that will be open to a new, shared responsibility between the state and society.

This needs to take into account:

(1) the serious economic and social situation that most Venezuelan families live in, making it essential to promote educational processes in the home.

(2) families – although in extreme poverty, with social disadvantages and problematic family situations – have the capacity to improve children's development and to educate them holistically, given proper support, guidance and regular follow-up.

(3) a study made by UNICEF-Venezuela and Fundaici, reports that there are no children under 6 living on the streets. This fact implies that there are spontaneous solidarity networks to help children within the poorest communities. Subsequently, the assistance decreases progressively or the individual child develops skills that allow them to be independent from the family unit and to look for new alternatives in life. Often this is a way to escape abuse. The identification of these networks can reverse the negative effects and consolidate the positive ones (PEMEC).

(4) the strengthening of families must start with the certainty that parents and communities, when not living under stress, have the appropriate knowledge and skills to bring up their children. The strengthening of the family as a key factor for the children's development, in practice affects other important aspects, like the parents' self-esteem and ability to solve their children's care problems. This translates into activities which can lead to an improvement in the general quality of life (work, housing, motivation to complete courses of study) for the family and the community.

(5) the linking and coordination of efforts between the different local and regional organisations boosts inter-sectoral benefits. Social projects and programmes, in practice, go on linking and adding new elements that enrich the experience and make it possible to both expand and to be more accepted. In this sense, it has been advantageous to involve practitioners and beneficiaries of services and programmes linked to the network in the decision-making process.

(6) linking and co-ordinating efforts needs to be dealt with at local level. The government central authorities have, in practice, more difficulties in planning and carrying out activities in practice. Local capacities are better developed in those regions with greater local autonomy and among more open sectors that allow free local association between civic and decentralised governmental authorities.

(7) the use of radio and television provides access to a greater number of families and communities with difficult geographical access. It also

encourages the participation of multiple sectors in the management of early learning and childcare.

(8) the *family and community models* are better suited to the social and cultural context, as well as being better suited to the people that manage them and to the teachers and the community where the educational activity takes place.

(9) the *family and community models* have more capacity to capitalise on community strengths, taking advantage of the cultural repertoire, such as positive child raising practices, and facilitating dialogue between educators and the community through its promoters, travelling teachers, training mothers and any other community person acting as inter-mediaries.

(10) to assume that the problem of low coverage can be resolved with more infrastructure and money, sponsored by the investment projects of the multilateral Banks, instead of the conception of the communities' integral development idealised by the human development agencies, has created a very harmful distortion in the programmes of government debt.

(a) In fact the amount of resources with which the multilateral banking system has flooded investment in child education in our country, linked with its official and our governmental leaders' limited experience in this sector, has resulted in an enormous increase in public debt, with minimal impact and little sustainability in the sector.

(b) this is because, of the total investment in the sector, more than 80% was expended on infrastructure for preschool classrooms – the rest, in fitting out these classrooms and in training personnel for the formal classroom model. Little effort was made to modernise managerial capacity, either at a central or peripheral level, nor in the juridical or budgetary framework that limits and regulates it. With difficulty, a marginal investment was obtained for the family and community (informal) projects, towards the end of the negotiations.

(c) the technical means for tackling the issue of community participation in planning was borne by the regional staff of the central administration, with the effect that political and trade union considerations tainted the decisions. This in turn marginalised the population, and frequently also the municipal governments and parishes, and cut them off from participation and responsibility in the decision-making processes.

(d) as a condition for the loan, the largest part of the investment should be made available through public, and often international, bidding processes. Despite the enormous efforts made to allow participation of local enterprises, in the first instance, and national ones, in the second, it was very difficult for the small regional providers to compete. The tenders were won by those outside the country, with the effect that the sector associated locally with early childhood education and care did not develop at a national level and even less at a local level. The only exception to this was the building sector, in a purely marginal way. On this occasion, the loan speeded up inflation in the price of materials. Settings were equipped with beautiful materials which were pedagogically out of date, with no consideration for their cultural relevance. Aspects relating to sustainability and the need for consistency and integration among public policies, common in protocol declarations, were totally left out of the mechanisms for the implementation of the loan.

(e) frequently, the banking sector causes major problems to larger countries, since it does not have the integral and flexible structure required to tackle initial education with family and community participation. Consequently, the development of a strategy to be able to confront this situation has to take account of the multiple interests that affect decision-making regarding the administration of resources, policies and curriculum in the area of early childhood education and care. Despite the many difficulties, the circumstantial elements discussed above, could serve as points for reflection in the planning of new initiatives, for national and regional governments, as well as for multilateral organisations and banks.

Recommendations

- If their basic needs are covered, families are capable of looking appropriately after their children. We should not miss the opportunity of allying ourselves to local daycare systems, through institutionalised networks or solidarity with community networks.
- Propagating the achievements of these arrangements and incorporating lessons learnt, among communities, and not only among our immediate colleagues, has the effect of multiplying quality initiatives.
- Investing in information through mass or alternative media and through exchanges, is a good strategy to promote the permanent search for high levels of participation and quality.
- Investment in education cannot leave aside the importance of encouraging, sponsoring and facilitating the development of local infrastructures of

provision linked to existing education and care activities. Networks for the development and use of relevant, 'high quality' materials need to be generated for children and their families, to encourage economic activity that accompanies educational activities that have social relevance.
- It is necessary to put constant efforts into developing educational administration, through permanent training cycles. The rotation of management personnel in public posts is unavoidable.
- Cooperation between development agencies and organisations must include advice and assistance schemes for new managers, to deal with the challenges of multilateral negotiations.
- Early childhood education programmes based in the family and the community are the right path for quality care, but they cannot reach their ideals by decree, they must be supported and accompanied with dignity and respect. However, they are not the panacea – we must learn from them and retain a permanent attitude for exploration, negotiation, technical exchange and co-assessment.
- An adequate statistical system for education is required.
- It is necessary to re-think the curriculum, with the aim of finding common spaces that lead to relevant opportunities for all.
- Independently of the environment for ECEC – classroom, home or care centre – the child has the right to have high quality provision, the defining of which has involved parents and carers, educators and policy-makers.
- Instead of centralising supervision, control and technical support, it is necessary to train and build capabilities at a local level, with the participation of neighbours, paraprofessionals and personnel from the educational system available in each region.
- Those sectors linked politically or financially (health, day care, legal protection and nutrition) with ECEC need training and appropriate formal agreements articulating action at a local level, independently of of the circumstantial understandings among the different sectors and changes which occur in local senior management and at a national level.
- The development of an effective information system, with clear and non discriminatory criteria, with the aim of efficiently achieving higher levels of quality, is also important.

REFERENCES

Alvarado, S. (1997). Hacia el fortalecimiento de una base de conocimientos a favor de la niñez. *Report from the Second Encounter of the nets for the children in Latin America.* Cartagena, Colombia.

Colmenares, M. (1996). Programa Familia: Situación Actual y Perspectivas. Fundapreescolar, Dirección de Educación Preescolar. Caracas, Venezuela. Manuscrito no publicado.

Fundación del Niño, (1978). *Programa Hogares de Cuidado Diario: Estudio de Evaluación.* Caracas, Venezuela.

Fujimoto, G. (1998). La Educación Inicial no Escolarizada y su Capacidad de Respuesta a las Demandas de Cambio en la Atención Integral de la Población Infantil. In: *Jornadas sobre Nuevas Tendencias en Materiales Didácticos en la Educación Inicial. Currículo, Gestión y Producción.* Caracas, Venezuela.

González, N. (1998). 24 Años de Historia: Los Hogares y Multihogares de Cuidado Diario, 1974–1998. Caracas, Venezuela.

Hernández, W., Luis, J., & Adrian, S. (1998). *Sistematización de la Implementación del Proyecto Preescolares Integrales de Calidad: Hacia una nueva evaluación de impacto.* Ministerio de Educación – Fundación Escuela de Gerencia Social. Caracas, Venezuela.

Leiva, L. & Dáger, M. (2000). *Progress report on the advance of the Programme El Maestro en Casa.* Ministry of Education, Caracas, Venezuela.

Moreno, A. (2000). *Progress Report of the Peru Case.* Unpublished manuscript.

Ramírez, Y. (1996). *Hacia el preescolar integral de calidad, a través de la promoción, ampliación y consolidación de las redes de atención integral para los niños de 0 a 6 años y sus familias.* Documento Ejecutivo. Ministerio de Educación, UNICEF.

Ruesta, M. C., Yánez, J. L., Zarikian, A., & Díaz, A. (1995). *Environmental quality, culture and child development, Venezuela.* Final Report to Bernard van Leer Foundation.

Sánchez, O., & Yánez, J. L. (1996). *La Reorientación Político-Conceptual del Nivel Preescolar.* Ministerio de Educación. DEPE.Caracas, Venezuela.

Sánchez, O. (1997). *Primeros Aportes para la Fundamentación del Preescolar Integral de Calidad.* Ministerio de Educación. DEPE. Caracas, Venezuela.

Senifa, (1997). *El Programa Hogares y Multihogares de Cuidado Diario: Una experiencia replicable.* Caracas, Venezuela.

Torres, T. (1999). *Wawa Wasi: Experiencia Inédita del Altiplano Peruano, Puno, Perú.* Unpublished manuscript.

Yánez, J. L. (1994). *Logros y Avances del Programa "Centros del Niño y la Familia" C.N.F.* II Simposio Latinoamericano, Organización de Estados Americanos. Lima, Perú.

Yánez, J. L. (1996). *Algunas Ideas acerca del Preescolar Integral de Calidad.* Ministerio de Educación. DEPE. Unpublished manuscript.

Woodhead, M. (1996). In Search of the Rainbow: pathways to quality in large scale programmes for young disadvantaged children. The Hague: Van Leer Foundation.

Woodhead, M. (1998). 'Quality' in early childhood programmes – a contextually appropriate approach. *International Journal of Early Years Education, 6*(1), 5–18.

BIBLIOGRAPHY OF SUGGESTED FOLLOW-UP READING

Aizpúrua, J., Halpern, R., Fisk, D., & Ramírez, Y. (1978). Tomo II: El Contexto: El Niño y la Familia en las Comunidades Marginales de Venezuela y la Necesidad del Cuidado Diario. En: Fundación del Niño: *Programa Hogares de Cuidado Diario: Estudio de Evaluación.* Caracas, Venezuela.

Chaves, M. (1996). *Gestión de Instituciones educativas.* UCV.Centro De Estudios Del Desarrollo. Cendes. Caracas, Venezuela.

España, L. P. (1992). *Evaluación y Sistema de Seguimiento del Programa de Hogares de Cuidado Diario en su Modalidad Multihogar*, Caracas, Venezuela. Manuscrito no publicado.

Evans, J. (1996). Quality In ECCD: Everyone's Concern. *Coordinators' Notebook: An International Resource for Early Childhood Development*. Journal of the Consultative Group on Early Childhood Care and Development, No 18.

Evans, J., Myers, R., & Ilfeld, E. M. (2000). *Early Childhood Counts: A Programming Guide on Early Childhood Care for Development*. Washington, D.C., USA: The World Bank.

Gómez, G. (1994). *Planes Locales de Acción a Favor de la Infancia: Módulos de Información Técnica para Uso de Gobernaciones y Municipios*. Ministerio de la Familia. Dirección General Sectorial De Cooordinación de Programas de Desarrollo Social – (Unicef), Manuscrito no publicado, Caracas, Venezuela.

Herrera, M. & López, M. *Los Proyectos Pedagógicos de Plantel en el Plan de Acción del Ministerio de Educación*. Centro de Investigaciones Culturales y Educativas.- CICE, Caracas, Venezuela.

Iragorry, R., Apiolaza, L., & Rojas, L. (1978). Tomo VII: Determinación de los Requerimientos Financieros y de Personal del Programa Hogares de Cuidado Diario. *En:* Fundación del Niño: *Programa Hogares de Cuidado Diario: Estudio de Evaluación*. Caracas, Venezuela.

Jiménez, M. (1993). *Lineamientos para la Elaboración del Diseño de un Modelo Gerencial para la Administración de los Programas No Convencionales del Nivel de Educación Preescolar de las Zonas Educativas*. Universidad Pedagógica Libertador (UPEL) Instituto Universitario Manuel Siso Martínez, Caracas, Venezuela.

López, M., & Herrera, M. (1996). *De Actores y Autores: Manual Para Directores de Educación Básica*. CICE, Fundación Polar, Fundapreescolar. Ed. Arte. Caracas, Venezuela.

Ministerio de Educación. *Lineamientos Curriculares Programa Familia*. Dirección General de Docencia, Dirección de Educación Preescolar (DEPE), Unicef. Caracas, Venezuela.

Ministerio de Educación (1996). *Análisis de la Articulación entre el Nivel de Educación Preescolar y el Nivel de Educación Básica* (Informe Ejecutivo de Avance) OSPP, DEPE, Comisión para la Evaluacion del Nivel Preescolar. Caracas, Venezuela.

Ministerio de Educación (1996b). *Hacia el Preescolar Integral de Calidad a través de Redes de Atención a los Niños Menores de 6 Años y sus Familias* (Documento Ejecutivo). DEPE, Caracas, Venezuela.

Ministerio de Educación (1997). *Algunas Experiencias para Mejorar la Calidad e Incrementar la Cobertura del Nivel Preescolar. Un Enfoque Descriptivo* (preliminary report). DEPE y Unicef. Caracas, Venezuela.

Myers, R. (1992). *The Twelve who Survive: Strengthening Programmes of Early Childhood Development in the Third World*. London: Routledge.

Nunes, T. (1994). *El Ambiente del Niño*. Occasional Paper N° 6. Bernard van Leer Foundation, The Netherlands.

Peralta, M. V., & Fujimoto, G. (1998). *La Atención Integral de la Primera Infancia en América Latina: Ejes centrales y los desafíos para el Siglo XXI*. I.B.C., Santiago de Chile, Chile: American States Organisation.

Sánchez, O. *Preescolar Integral de Calidad* (Papel de Trabajo). Ministerio de Educación, DEPE, Caracas, Venezuela.

Yánez, J. L. (1995). *La Equidad en el Desarrollo de Programas para Sectores Vulnerables en Venezuela*. Ministerio de Educación. Caracas, Venezuela.

SECTION II:

THE WIDER CONTEXT: POLICY-MAKING AND ITS IMPACT

4. POLICIES AND PROVISIONS, POLITICS AND ETHICS

Peter Moss

> Our experience [of pre-school services in Reggio Emilia] is only one possibility out of many. Behind every solution and organisation is a choice, a choice of values and ethics, a social and political choice, and a responsibility for that choice. The identity of our schools is based on concepts and values. We do not offer a recipe, nor a method, our work is not to be copied because values can only be lived not copied . . . .What society hopes and expects of its children is a philosophical position underlying education . . . Who is a child? What is childhood? How does a child learn? I hope these questions never have a definite and final answer, for the answers are always contextual linked to a specific time and society (Rinaldi, 1999[1]).

The early years policies and provisions of the new Labour Government offer a dazzling display of managerial procedures and technical measures. From an array of audits and plans, targets and frameworks, regulations and inspection systems and so on, emerges an ideal of early years provision as a well managed enterprise producing products to meet the needs of consumers, and doing so to predictable and predetermined standards. Underpinning this is an ideal of order and control, summed up in the one question deemed worthy of asking – 'what works?' Depending on your position, this is either efficient, best value modern government, focused on outcomes and uncluttered by dogma and posturing – or else an example of what Cherryholmes describes as 'vulgar pragmatism' which

> holds that a conception is to be tested by its practical effects . . . what is true and valued is what works in terms of what exists. This is another face of instrumentalism in pursuit of production and efficiency . . . . This form of pragmatism is unreflective and dangerous . . . .

**Promoting Evidence-based Practice in Early Childhood Education:
Research and its Implications, Volume 1, pages 79–95.**
Copyright © 2001 by Elsevier Science Ltd.
All rights of reproduction in any form reserved.
ISBN: 0-7623-0753-6

> Vulgar pragmatism tests ideas and practices by comparing them to traditional and
> conventional norms with little or no sense of crisis or criticism . . . [and] promote[s] local
> ideologies as global and past ideologies as those of the present and future. (Cherryholmes,
> 1988: 151).

In this chapter, I want to suggest that early years policy and provision in Britain are the product of a particular political and economic context, which produces a particular ethical approach. However, despite the powerful effects of politics, economic and ethics, they are inaudible in the current public discourse of early childhood which instead is dominated by a technico-managerial vocabulary. I want to make politics, economics and ethics audible in the discourse. I want to argue that early childhood policy and provision is not about finding the one 'right' and sure answer, as government hopes and expects, but that it is a provisional, uncertain and contestable undertaking with many possible answers, that are 'always contextual, linked to a specific time and society'; and that it is not about looking to managers or scientists to tell us what must be done – rather, as Carlina Rinaldi so clearly states, we must make choices between many possibilities and take responsibility for those choices.

THE POLITICAL AND ECONOMIC CONTEXT

The work of Michel Foucault on power encourages us to ask why certain ideas and practices come to be viewed in a particular historical context as true, self-evident, inevitable. If we can begin to answer this question, we can begin to understand the forces working upon us and to develop some resistances to those forces through critical thinking. In this section, I will sketch three emergent conditions, all of which are closely connected: two at least of them are more fully developed in the Anglo-American world (in which I count Britain), but all are experienced to some extent in other countries. All contribute to a climate in which certain ways of talking about and practising early years policy and provision seem natural and inevitable: other early years experiences (two of which are touched on below) provide us not with a model to copy but with a lens through which to look at British policy and provision – and in so doing to question what seemed before natural and inevitable and make it instead contestable.

The (Re)Emergence of Liberalism as a Principle of Government

Liberalism first emerged as a principle of government in the 19th century, as a reaction to the idea of a totally administered state. Advanced liberalism has emerged in the last quarter of the 20th century. It is a reactivation of earlier liberal scepticism over political government, and a reaction against the social state which emerged at the end of the 19th century as a response to a demand for intervention to mitigate the adverse social consequences of capitalist economic arrangements (Rose, 1999a).

Liberalism professes suspicion of the state. It seeks to restrict state intervention in important areas of life, such as the family and the market. It emphasises freedom, liberty and the rights of the individual, and the individual governing herself – not needing to be governed. The advanced liberal state veers away from the social state, the state of social security, the state as service provider, in favour of an enabling state. The emphasis is on the autonomous and self-regulating subject, who assumes individual responsibility for the management of risks. The role of the state is to enable the individual to become this type of subject, to embody the necessary ways of thinking and being – and to control those who are unable or unwilling to conform to this ideal.

So, advanced liberalism values: promoting independence; privatisation of social insurance and security; markets in all sorts of services, from schools to pensions; consumer choice; social inclusion, meaning to bring people into this new form of citizenship. Great social and moral importance is attached to paid work: 'labour alone is the means by which the poor can acquire the status of citizen, a status increasingly a matter of consumption rights'. Other forms of human activity – such as care and play – are devalued and unrecognised. The ideal is enterprise and the entrepreneur – the entrepreneur in business, but also becoming an entrepreneur of oneself, conducting your life and your family as a kind of enterprise: 'the powers of the state are donated to empowering entrepreneurial subjects of choice in their quest for self-realisation'.

But one other feature of advanced liberalism should be noted. While the theory speaks of autonomy, freedom and choice, and the limitation of government – in practice liberalism does control, it does attempt to govern in the interests of morality and order. The state governs without governing 'society', by acting on the choices and self-steering properties of individuals. It does this by working through families, and other institutions such as schools, to create individuals who do not need to be governed by others but will govern themselves.

Advanced liberalism has a complex relationship with the family. On the one hand, it places the family in the private sphere, and suspects overt government interference. On the other hand, it realises that the family is a critical site for instilling properties, values, subjectivities: it is too important to be ignored. So the trick for liberal government has been to intervene without appearing to alter the centrality of the parent-child relationship or weaken 'parental responsibility'. The policy strategy, according to Nikolas Rose, has been to 'govern the soul' so that family members come to embody the dominant values and aims of the society.

> Our personalities, subjectivities, and 'relationships' are not private matters, if this implies they are not the objects of power. On the contrary they are intensively governed .... Government and parties of all political complexions have formulated policies, set up machinery, established bureaucracies, and promoted initiatives to regulate the conduct of citizens by acting upon their mental capacities and propensities. The most obvious manifestation has been the complex apparatus targeted upon the child: the child welfare system, the school, the juvenile justice system and the education and surveillance of parents ....
>
> Childhood is the most intensively governed sector of human existence. In different ways, at different times and by many different routes, the health, welfare and rearing of children has been linked in thought and practice to the destiny of the nation and the responsibilities of the state ....
>
> The modern private family remains intensively governed, it is linked in so many ways with social, economic and political objectives. But government here acts not through mechanisms of social control and subordination of the will, but through the promotion of subjectivities, the construction of pleasures and ambitions and the activation of guilt, anxiety, envy and disappointment (Rose, 1999b: 1; 123 & 211).

So we are confronted by an ideology and a style of government which speaks of freedom, choice and responsibility – yet acts to produce a certain subject, and does this not through overt coercion but through the action of various technologies and devices – which include social institutions, certain human sciences and disciplines, certain discourses. Through these means, liberal government seeks to 'govern the soul', through which process the individual constitutes his or her own subjectivity in conformity with liberal ideals.

The Increasing Dominance of Neo-Liberal/Anglo-Saxon Capitalism

By talking about 'capitalism' I do not mean to be polemical, but descriptive of a form of economic relations which has emerged as hegemonic from the collapse of Communism, the only economic show in town. This form actually has many variations, differing over time and between economies. But just now, a particular form is increasingly dominant: the recent and historic hostile take-over by the British Vodafone company of the Germany corporation Mannersman is a prime example of how aggressive Anglo-American capitalism appears to be making major inroads into what has been called 'Rhenish' capitalism, with its different set of relationships and values. What is distinctive about this Anglo-Saxon or neo-liberal capitalism? It places great value on markets and competition; social deregulation and contractual regulation – the rule of the lawyers over the rule of politicians; individualisation and choice; 'flexibility' and short-termism; the commodification of all activities and relationships – everything can be financially valued and traded, there is nothing that cannot be reduced to a number; and accountability solely to owners – shareholder value is the paramount value.

The increasing dominance of this form of capitalism has enormous consequences. I will single out just three areas. Employment practices are changing: flexible forms of work expand; there is an intensification of labour, not only longer hours but increasing productivity; insecurity becomes more widespread; workplace solidarity fragments and the employer exchanges social responsibilities for individualised packages of bonuses and occupational benefits targeted at key individual workers. Second, we are seeing the growth of welfare markets, in which businesses compete to provide private services which are traded for profit with consumers, employers and public agencies: for example, in both America and Britain, though nowhere else yet in Europe, most nurseries are run as business enterprises and increasingly as part of large companies with other interests in the service sector. Finally, neo-liberal capitalism increases inequality, which is viewed as part of a system of inducements and penalties to shape people's behaviour and make them more productive and competitive. In Britain, the number of children living in poverty trebled in the 1980s and 1990s, to reach 1 in 3: and while the New Labour Government is committed to reducing poverty, it appears to be comfortable with inequality.

Hollowing Out of the Nation State

There are a number of processes at work here. Powers are devolved to international bodies and to regional authorities. A unified national identity begins to fragment. Economic control is reduced due to the rise of deregulated global capital, which increasingly rejects any national identity or base: the multinational corporation is increasingly a law unto itself. Bill Readings describes this altered relationship between the nation state and capitalism:

> The decline of the nation state means that the economic is no longer subjugated to the political. Economy is increasingly the concern of transnational entities in search of profit without regard to national boundaries. The nation state becomes the bureaucratic apparatus of management. Under globalisation, the nation state does not disappear but becomes more and more managerial. The hollowing out of the nation state appears as 'depoliticization' (Readings, 1996: 46–47).

Increasingly, the role of the nation state is to attract roving and rootless global capital, scouring the world for the highest return, by offering inducements – such as a well educated and flexible labour force and a stable, risk free social environment.

The role of governments is to maintain order in their territories and package their populations into skilled, docile workforces with the correct attitudes in the hope that international finance may offer jobs through inward investment. Under the lash from capital seeking higher returns, big business abandons all pretence at patriotism and social responsibility and shops internationally for the most 'competitive and flexible' workers (Atkinson & Elliott, 1998).

NEW LABOUR, NEW MANAGERIALISM

New Labour's interest in early childhood policies and provisions is not, I would argue, motivated by an interest in or commitment to early childhood per se or to young children as a social group with entitlements. Rather it reflects a belief in early childhood as a means to the greater end of competitive labour markets. This rationality is vividly described in this American quotation, which I think applies well to Britain:

As the global economy takes hold, politicians and business leaders – heretofore largely uninterested in young children – are voicing concern and demonstrating readiness for action. Facing an increasingly competitive global economic market, they are worried about economic productivity . . . . Given this climate, quality early care and education services have been advocated as a cost-effective approach to maintaining a stable, well-prepared workforce today [through providing care for workers' children] – and preparing such a workforce for the future (Kagan et al., 1996: 12–13).

I would add that early childhood provisions are also seen as a means to achieving two other big projects: reduced welfare rolls ('welfare to work') and creating social stability through bringing order to the social chaos that 20 years of neo-liberal capitalism has caused in certain quarters. The production of the subject – the competitive, flexible and compliant worker, the autonomous, self-regulating adult who will assume responsibility for managing her own risks – is understood by politicians and business leaders as needing to start at earlier and earlier ages. So growing State interest in early childhood is not for young children *per se*, but as a means of preparation for school, for adulthood, for (paid) work.

The nation state may be hollowing out, losing power in major economic and political areas. We also hear a lot about the retreat or weakening of the 'welfare state'. But this process needs to be qualified. The state may have less control over some areas, for example control of capital flows, and be withdrawing from others, for example the provision of utilities such as electricity and water or the field of pensions. But where it does keep an interest and retains some influence, it is more powerful than it has ever been: early years policy and provision is a good example.

Everywhere we can see processes of decentralisation, devolution, individual-isation, the breakdown of old, monolithic structures, relationships and identities. Yet at the same time, new technologies are emerging that enable new forms of control to be applied to these processes of dispersal and fragmentation. By technologies I refer to what Rose calls 'human technologies' – 'technologies imbued with aspirations for the shaping of conduct in the hope of producing certain desired effects'. These control technologies may actually include electronic technologies, but they also involve a range of other procedures and methods. In particular, what has emerged in recent years has been 'new managerialism' which 'proclaims itself as the universally applicable solution to the problems of inefficiency, incompetence and chaos which characterise the old ways of providing public services ... [and] is an imperialist formation seeking 'the right to manage' (Clarke, 1998: 174).

The managerial state has taken over from the professional and bureaucratic states, subordinating professionals and bureaucrats to its authority, not destroying them but putting them to its own use. Managerialism is the perfect companion to this new nation state, since as already noted 'under globalisation, the nation state does not disappear but becomes more and more managerial'.

> The problems which the managerial state is intended to resolve derive from contradictions and conflicts in the political, economic and social realms. But what we have seen is the managerialisation of these contradictions: they are redefined as 'problems to be managed'. Terms such as 'efficiency' and 'effectiveness', 'performance' and 'quality' depoliticise a series of social issues (whose efficiency? Effectiveness for whom?) and thus displace real political and policy choices into a series of management imperatives (Ibid.: 179).

Managerialism is both an ideology and a battery of techniques and procedures for surveillance, control and mastery. Rose talks about an 'audit society': a society organised to observe itself through the mechanisms of audit in the service of programmes for control. In new rationalities of advanced liberal government, audit becomes an important mechanism for governing at a distance. Central to the audit society is the idea that everything can be reduced to quantitative values, to a profit and loss statement, as a means to control: 'if you can't count it, you haven't done it'. Elsewhere, I have talked about this as the age of quality (Dahlberg et al., 1999). By so doing I meant to problematise the concept of 'quality' as neither self-evident nor value-free, but as another managerial means of control, a technology for evaluating performance against quantifiable norms and targets, another example of trust in numbers.

So in Britain, a whole array of technologies are now deployed to the end of producing proper subjects for the advanced liberal state and neo-liberal capitalism. In early childhood, these technologies include: the application of normalizing sciences, in particular developmental psychology; early childhood audits and plans; targets set for EYDCPs and Sure Start areas; systems of regulation and standards; quality assurance schemes; a variety of funding mechanisms; learning goals; systems of baseline assessment; and the ever present search for effective programmes which can be generalized irrespective of context. A rhetoric of diversity and choice is matched by a practice of conformity and normalization; a belief in market solutions and consumerism sits alongside a need to regulate and control.

In every country, there are tendencies both towards children's rights and participation, on the one hand, and towards greater surveillance, control and regulation of children's everyday lives on the other. But there is, as Alan Prout (2000) points out, a striking difference between 'neo-liberal' societies like Britain and the U.S., where the tendency is towards greater surveillance, control and regulation is dominant in public policy; and societies like the Nordic states, which might be called 'social democratic', which show greater recognition of children's personhood and their participation in social life.

ETHICS OF EARLY CHILDHOOD

A Repersonalized Ethics

We can see the history of the last 200 years as a constant tussle between the economic and the social domains and their systems of values – or put more bluntly between production and reproduction, employment and care, private enterprise and social responsibility. At present, we might say that the 'business case' is well on top, riding on the coat tails of a dominating neo-liberal capitalism. Zygmunt Bauman argues that business has its own rationality and its own ethics:

> The instrumental rationality is what makes business tick . . . . Means are to be used to the greatest possible effect . . . . How much the available means may bring in is the only question one can ask about their available use. Other questions – moral questions prominent among them – are given short shrift.
>
> Business has its own special kind of morality, sometimes called 'business ethics'. The paramount value of that ethics is honesty – which is mostly concerned with keeping promises and abiding by contractual obligations . . . . The code spells out how far honesty must reach and when one can say that s/he was 'honest enough'. Everything stretching beyond this boundary is no concern for business ethics (Bauman, 1995: 263).

Business values focus on one question – 'what works'?', on solutions and answers, not critical questions. Following from Bauman, I would argue that a dominance of business values/ethics, in a society where everything can be commodified and traded, places great weight on the issue: how to realise, fully exploit, derive maximum return from assets, including children. Maximising returns requires that assets are predictable and their potential predetermined – else who will invest? If we know what the output should be, the only question is how to get it as efficiently as possible.

I want to problematise what might be called the business ethics approach, which is about instrumental rationality, keeping promises and contractual obligations – although I do not want to reject this entirely (it may have its place, the question being though 'what is that place?'). I also want to problematise another understanding of ethics: as a universal code that prescribes correct behaviour universally, that is for all people at all times, and which removes choice and responsibility from us, in favour of obedience to a rule. This is the ethics that informs ideals of norms and targets, technologies of quality assurance and developmental assessment. Rather I want to suggest and explore three other understandings of ethics, which might suggest another approach.

The first is Bauman's idea of ethics. In postmodern conditions ethics exists but without a universal code. We are our own moral agents. We recognise that we have to make choices between good and bad without seeking shelter in a universal code, and that we must take responsibility for the choices that we make. This, he says, is uncomfortable. Human reality is messy and ambiguous, so moral decisions are ambivalent:

> Confronting the choice between good and evil means finding oneself in a situation of ambivalence . . . . Dilemmas have no ready-made solutions; the necessity to choose comes without a foolproof recipe for proper choice; the attempt to do good is undertaken without guarantee of goodness of either the intention or the results (Bauman, 1995: 2).

Yet far from being pessimistic, Bauman is hopeful. People show moral competence – indeed, society is made possible by this competence. He welcomes a repersonalising of morality, and the release of morality from constructed ethical codes: 'personal responsibility is morality's last hope'.

What this says for me is that in life, including policy and provision for young children, we constantly confront choices that are ethical, which call on us to make decisions about what we think is good or bad, better or worse – and that we have to carry the responsibility for the decisions. We cannot look to some code, some standard, some certain foundation to tell us the right answer, to absolve us from responsibility, nor can we seek to convert this ethical choice into a managerial decision. As Carlina Rinaldi says, there is 'a choice of values and ethics, a social and political choice, and a responsibility for that choice'. Instead of 'vulgar pragmatism', we may decide to adopt a 'critical pragmatism' which

> continually involves making epistemological, ethical and aesthetic choices and translating them into discourses-practices. Criticisms and judgements about good and bad, beautiful

and ugly and truth and falsity are made in the context of our communities and our attempts
to build them anew. They are not decided by reference to universal norms that produce
'definitive' and 'objective' decisions (Cherryholmes, 1998: 151).

There are many implications of adopting this ethical understanding, not least in
what it implies for practice. There are many areas which call for ethical
choices, rather than seeking conformity to universal codes and norms. For
example, who do we think the young child is? What is our image of the child?
Adopting a social constructionist perspective, various understandings of the
child have been proposed, for example as knowledge reproducer, as nature, as
innocent, as redemptive agent and so on. Pat Petrie and I (1999) have argued
that the dominant discourse about the child in Britain produces the image of the
poor child, in the sense of the child who is lacking, deficient, passive,
incomplete, malleable, without agency – the child needing (in the words used
to describe various services or interventions in Britain) protection, support,
guidance and development. When they say in Reggio that they have chosen to
take the image of the 'rich' child, this seems to me a good example of making
an ethical decision, and taking responsibility for that decision through a
pedagogical practice which addresses the challenge of working with that
image.

What is interesting about Reggio is that they work quite explicitly with a
social constructionist perspective, which calls for an awareness of making
choices rather than a belief in uncovering the essential child. Similarly, the
recent major reforms in Sweden, which have seen early childhood and free-
time services (what we call in Britain school age child care) integrated into
education, have also been informed by this perspective, which has generated a
wide-ranging and radical rethinking running alongside restructuring. A
discussion paper, by Gunilla Dahlberg and her colleague Hellevi Lenz Taguchi
(1994), has been one important influence in this process. Titled *Pre-school and
school – two different traditions and the vision of a meeting place*, the paper
begins by identifying different pedagogical traditions in pre-school and school,
each produced by a different social construction of the child: 'the analysis
shows that the view of the child which we call the child as nature is, for the
most part, embodied in the pre-school, while the child as producer of culture
and knowledge is, for the most part, embodied in the school'. These different
constructions have had 'direct consequences on the content and working
methods of pedagogical activity, and in that way affected the view of the child's
learning and knowledge-building'. The paper goes on to suggest an alternative
construction of the child – the child as a constructor of culture and knowledge
– which could 'create a meeting place where both the pre-school teachers and

the primary school teachers are given the possibility to develop their pedagogical practices'.

> We do not wish to present a new pedagogical method or model, but a vision of a possible meeting place. This vision can be seen as a provisional, holistic picture of the educational institutions we need in a quickly changing society. The vision deals with a way of relating and a working process in relation to the child's creation of knowledge and everyday reality which is based upon continual discussions and common values which one wants to permeate the child's upbringing and education. This way of relating starts from the view of the child as a competent and capable child, a rich child, who participates in the creation of themselves and their knowledge – the child as a constructor of culture and knowledge. In this pedagogical approach, this way of relating is characterised by a researching, reflective and analytical approach at different levels (Dahlberg & Taguchi, 1994).

Sweden is moving from an industrial society into a post-industrial, information and knowledge society – a learning society. There is also recognition of a profound change – a paradigmatic shift – in how people understand and create meaning in their lives which has consequences for understandings of children and childhood. While many teachers retain the view of the child as 'the empty box', with question-and-answer as their most important pedagogical method, an alternative view is becoming increasingly common. This way of viewing the child

> builds on the notion of the child as an active and creative actor, as a subject and citizen with potentials, rights and responsibility. A child worth listening to and having a dialogue with, and who has the courage to think and act by himself . . . the child as an active actor, a constructor, in the construction of his own knowledge and his fellow beings' common culture . . . a child who in interaction with the world around is also active in the construction, in the creation of himself, his personality and his talents. This child is seen as having 'power over his own learning processes' and having the right to interpret the world (Dahlberg, 1997).

'Who is the child?' is only one of many critical questions. Another is what are the purposes of early childhood provisions or indeed other provisions for children such as schools? I have suggested that the implicit understanding of early years provisions in Britain is as processing plants, an idea captured by Lilian Katz (1993) when she says that 'early childhood programmes are increasingly in danger of being modeled on the corporate/industrial or factory model so pervasive in elementary and secondary levels of education . . . factories are designed to transform raw material into prespecified products by treating it as a sequence of prespecified industrial processes' (33–34). But there are other possibilities, for example the idea of early childhood services as 'children's spaces' where children and adults come together to engage in a variety of projects – pedagogical, cultural, social, moral, economic, political, physical, aesthetic – not just a place with a predetermined purpose, but a space or forum of many possibilities, a place of encounter and for childhood, a part of life not a preparation for life.

Once started, the questions flood out. What is a good childhood? What do we want for our children? What is the relationship between children, families and society? What is learning? Why education? Each critical questions challenges each of us to make a choice that is explicitly ethical and which demands we take responsibility for that choice.

But we can take this further. There may be no certainty about the ethical choices we make, but we need not be alone in making them. In a recent book, together with Gunilla Dahlberg and Alan Pence, I have explored the implications of this for early childhood through a critique of the concept of quality and its application, as a universal code, to evaluating pedagogical work (Dahlberg et al., 1997). Drawing on experience from Reggio, we suggest another way of conceptualising evaluation, as meaning making, which requires individuals to understand and judge pedagogical practice, in relationship with others but taking responsibility for that understanding and judgement.

We also find the perspective of Bill Readings very important. He recognises the importance of evaluation, but understands it as an act of judgement, embedded in a specific context that must be acknowledged. Evaluation is not just a judgement, it is a judgment of value, and since there is no single standard of value, there can be no single scale of evaluation. The evaluator as judge must take responsibility for his or her judgement 'rather than hide behind statistical pretenion to objectivity' and taking responsibility for a judgement 'invokes an accountability that is radically at odds with the determinate logic of accounting which only serves to prop up the logic of consumerism' (Readings, 1996: 134). Finally, Readings is at great pains to stress the provisionality of evaluation as judgement, the importance of 'keeping the question of meaning open as a locus for debate' rather than seeking foreclosure since 'the question of evaluation is finally both unanswerable and essential' (ibid.: 133) . . . with the logic of quantification (ibid.: 24).

> Measures of excellence raise questions that are philosophical in that they are fundamentally incapable of producing cognitive certainty or definitive answers. Such questions will necessarily give rise to further debate for they are radically at odds with the logic of quantification (Readings, 1996: 24).

The Ethics of an Encounter

I have just spoken about a repersonalised ethics, an ethics of uncertainty, ambivalence and responsibility. But it is also an ethics of relationships, in the sense that these decisions are better made in relation with others, rather than autonomously. But the ethical approach I want to suggest also involves relationships in another way. Emanuel Levinas talks of 'the ethics of an encounter', which addresses the issue of how we relate to the Other. This concept struggles with issues of difference and alterity: in particular how can we relate to the Other without trying to make the Other into the same as us? how can we move from grasping the other to respecting the Other? This is a major challenge since

> the concept of Totality has dominated Western philosophy in its long history of desire for unity and the One. In Western philosophy, when knowledge or theory comprehends the Other, the alterity of the Other vanishes as it becomes part of the same (Young, 1990: 13).

A question therefore is how to constitute forms of knowledge and types of relationships in early childhood settings that do not simply turn the Other into the same, which recognise the Other as unique and unexchanganeable, a relationship to a 'concrete Other', which foreground singularity and multi-plicity. Moreover how can we avoid a relationship that is instrumental, what Bauman refers to as 'the modern obsession with purposefulness and utility and a suspicion of things that claim to be their own end'.

In Reggio, the educators provide a good example of practice which seems to address the concept of an 'ethics of an encounter' and which struggles to respect the otherness of children and adults. We see this in their work with pedagogical documentation, which recognises subjectivity, uniqueness, inter-pretation and negotiation (for a fuller discussion, see Dahlberg et al., 1999), and their reluctance to use totalising concepts such as 'child development' and totalising methods such as standardised measures. We see it too in the ideas they have developed about a 'pedagogy of relationships' (Malaguzzi, 1993) and a 'pedagogy of listening' (Rinaldi, 1999), which recognises that learning is a process of co-constructing knowledge in relationship with others, that knowledge is therefore new and built, perspectival and provisional, and that listening is an active emotion, involving interpretation and therefore placing responsibility on the listener in relation to the Other. Carlina Rinaldi also speaks of a 'pedagogy of difference', which assumes the uniqueness of each of us and the importance of working with difference as a way to create something new.

Ethico-Politics

The third dimension of ethics concerns what Rose refers to as ethico-politics. Rose notes the injection of ethics into many spheres of activity in Britain, for example 'ethical business' or 'ethical foreign policy'. He welcomes this as an antidote to attempts to translate ethical judgements into more objective and scientific language. But he also sees a danger in that ethics can become yet another method of control, a means to manage through establishing yet more codes of universal good behaviour. This is an ethico-politics that 'attempts to technically manage the way in which each individual should conduct herself and her relations to others to produce politically desired ends . . . it seeks to inculcate a fixed and uncontestable code of conduct . . . to govern better'.

Rose proposes another idea of ethico-politics:

> which attempts to make forms of life open to explicit political debate . . . a politics whose ethos is a reluctance to govern too much, that minimizes codification and maximises debate, that seeks to increase the opportunities for each individual to construct and transform his or her own life forms, that validates diverse ethical criteria and encourages all to develop and refine their practical and experimental arts of existence (Rose, 1999a: 193).

This idea of ethico-politics connects to another concept used by Rose: 'minor' or 'minority' politics, a creative process arising from contestation between people engaged in particular activities and relations.

> These contestations are between diverse programmes, logics, dreams and ideals . . . . These minor engagements do not have the arrogance of programmatic politics . . . . They are cautious, modest, pragmatic, experimental, stuttering, tentative . . . . They frequently arise in 'cramped spaces . . . . And, in relation to these little territories of the everyday, they seek to engender a small reworking of their own spaces of action . . . . [But] such a molecular and minor engagement can connect up with a whole series of other circuits and cause them to fluctuate, waver and reconfigure in wholly unexpected ways (Ibid.: 279–280).

What Rose is emphasising is the importance of an ethics that is grounded in very concrete and local situations and practices and enables individuals and groups to think critically, to question commonplace assumptions and to contest dominant discourses and constructions – and by doing so to make the invisible visible, the familiar strange and, in Foucault's words, 'to show that things are not as self evident as one believed' (Foucault, 1988: 155). This carries the potential for change since 'as soon as one can no longer think things as one formerly thought them, transformation becomes both very urgent, very difficult and quite possible' (Ibid.). From an individual perspective it relates to Foucault's idea of 'care of the self', the possibility of having some agency over how we constitute ourselves – for as Foucault says 'the self is not given to us, we have to constitute ourselves as a work of art'. From the perspective of work with children, ethico-politics means that we may be governed less by dominant discourse about children and childhood, and can instead have the confidence and courage to construct new discourses and understandings.

THE DISCIPLINES OF EARLY CHILDHOOD

Underpinning early childhood policy and provision in Britain is the discipline of child development. In this respect, as so many others, policy and provision seems overly influenced by the United States, where, as Bloch (1992: 3) observes, 'one reason for the lack of recognition or acceptance of alternative theoretical and methodological perspectives in early childhood education is the century-long domination of psychological and child development perspectives in the field'. In a British context, Rose (1999b) has paid considerable attention to the role of the 'psy' sciences in 'governing the soul'.

Child development theories retain considerable resilience in policy and practice fields, despite being the subject of critiques from many quarters over the last 20 years (cf. Dahlberg et al., 1999). Developmental psychology can be seen as a powerful 'regime of truth', whose emergence 'was prompted by concerns to classify, measure and regulate ... [and which] is a paradigmatically modern discipline arising at a time of commitment to narratives of truth, objectivity, science and reason' (Burman, 1994: 14). Erica Burman continues:

> The project of developmental psychology as the presentation of a general model which depicts development as unitary, irrespective of culture, class, gender or history means that difference can be recognised only in terms of aberrations, deviations and relative progress on a linear scale .... The notion of 'progress', whether of societies or through the 'life span', implies linear movement across history and between cultures. Comparison within these terms is now being recognised as increasingly untenable. In particular, the implication that there is a detached, disinterested set of devices and techniques for this purpose, such as developmental psychology illustrates the extent to which we have come to believe in the abstract, disembodied psychological subject and dismiss all it fails to address as merely supplementary or inappropriate .... The issue is to bring to light and acknowledge the investment and hidden subjectivity that lie beneath the claims to disinterested and true knowledge (Ibid.).

It is not my intention however to reject developmental psychology, nor to ignore the work that is being undertaken to address some of the critiques. What is problematic is the way a rather crude developmentalism appears to leech into policy and provision, the idea of the universal child who follows biologically-determined ages and stages – and which then becomes part of a technology for producing predetermined and standardised outcomes, and acts as a universal code which obviates the need to examine what is actually happening and to take responsibility for pedagogical choices. What is also problematic is the absence of other disciplinary perspectives. Early childhood policy and practice, for example, seem to ignore the sociology of childhood, social constructionist theories, and many other disciplines and theories. Instead of being seen as offering one perspective and one type of knowledge out of many, developmental psychology can easily be seen as offering the truth, the one answer, the only way.

CONCLUSION

This short piece has had to gloss over many complexities. It could be argued, for example, that the New Labour Government's policies and provisions are also influenced by its inheritance of an extremely weak early childhood system, which could only be sustained and rapidly developed through strong normalising practices – that public policy having been indifferent for so long, the possibilities were extremely constrained. While I have some sympathy with this perspective, and appreciate the challenge facing the Government, it constitutes at best a contributory rather than a major influence. For what has been noticeably lacking from the start is any attempt to draw breath, make a considered analysis, search for critical questions, consider options and envisage a strategy both short-term and long-term. All this has been ignored in the interests of finding answers – quick fixes – for other agendas and projects, with a technico-managerial approach being offered as a short cut around the difficult terrain, with its ethical and political obstacles.

Where the discussions in this chapter lead me to is the possibility of questioning the dominance of a 'business case' or 'processing model' for early childhood provisions, which is about realising a known asset through correct management and technology. We can offer other possibilities, or cases, including early childhood provisions being 'children's spaces' or 'places of welfare', 'welfare' being understood as the possibility of producing solidarities, constructing social values and constituting the self. By putting forward these other possibilities, I am not rejecting other purposes and rationalities for early childhood provisions. For example, such provisions will make an important economic contribution by enabling parents to go out to work. They will also make an important contribution to a more traditional understanding of welfare, by protecting certain children. What I am arguing is that the purposes of these early childhood institutions, and the prioritising of these purposes, is not self evident, but is a contestable issue, involving political and ethical choices.

NOTE

1. Reggio Emilia is a city in the Emilia Romagna region of Northern Italy, whose early childhood services have become world famous for their pedagogical work. This

experience is discussed at greater length in Dahlberg et al. (1999) and Edwards et al. (1998).

REFERENCES

Atkinson, D., & Elliott, L. (1998). Anxious? Insecure? You'll get used to it. *The Guardian*, (6 June).

Bauman, Z. (1995). *Life in Fragments: Essays in Postmodern Morality*. Cambridge: Polity Press.

Bloch, M. (1992). Critical Perspectives on the Historical Relationship between Child Development and Early Childhood Education Research. In: S. Kessler & B. Swadener (Eds), *Reconceptualising the Early Childhood Curriculum*. New York: Teachers College Press.

Burman, E. (1994). *Deconstructing Developmental Psychology*. London: Routledge.

Cherrholmes, C. H. (1988). *Power and Criticism: Post-structural Investigations*. New York: Teachers College Press.

Clarke, J. (1998). Thriving on Chaos? Managerialisation and the Welfare State. In: J. Carter (Ed.), *Postmodernity and the Fragmentation of Welfare*. London: Routledge.

Dahlberg, G. (1997). Barnet och pedagogen som medkonstruktorer av kultur och kunskap ('the child and the pedagogue as co-constructors of culture and knowledge'), in *Roster om den svenska barnomsorgen. SoS-rapport 1997:23 (Voices about Swedish child care, SoS report 1997:23)*. Stockholm: Socialstyrelsen.

Dahlberg, G., & Lenz Taguchi, H. (1994). *Förskola och skola – om två skilda traditiner och om visionem om en mötesplats (Preschool and school – two different traditions and a vision of an encounter)*. Stockholm: HLS Förlag.

Dahlberg, G., Moss, P., & Pence, A. (1999). *Beyond Quality in Early Childhood Education and Care; Postmodern Perspectives*. London: Falmer Books.

Edwards, C., Gandini, L., & Forman, G. (Eds) (1998), *The Hundred Languages of Children: The Reggio-Emilia Approach – Advanced Reflections*. Norwood, NJ: Ablux.

Foucault, M. (1986, English ed.). *The Care of the Self*. New York: Pantheon.

Foucault, M. (1988). *Politics, Philosophy, Culture: Interviews and Other Writings, 1977–1984*. L. Kittzman (Ed.). New York: Routledge.

Kagan, S., Cohen, N., & Neuman, M. (1996). Introduction: The changing context of American early care and education'. In: S. Kagan & N. Cohen (Eds), *Reinventing Early Care and Education: A Vision for a Quality System*. San Francisco, Jossey-Bass.

Katz, L. (1993). What can we learn from Reggio-Emilia? In: G. Edwards, L. Gandini & G. Forman (Eds), *The Hundred Languages of Children*. Norwood, NJ: Ablex.

Moss, P., Dillon, J., & Statham, J. (2000). The 'child in need' and the 'rich child': discourses, constructions and practice'. *Critical Social Policy, 20*(2), 233–254.

Prout, A. (2000). Children's participation: control and self-realization in British late modernity. *Chidren and Society, 14*(4).

Readings, B. (1996). *The University in Ruins*. Cambridge, MA: Harvard University Press.

Rinaldi, C. (1999). Paper given during a British tour to Reggio-Emilia, April 1999.

Rose, N. (1999a). *The Practice of Freedom*. Cambridge: Cambridge University Press.

Rose, N. (1999b: 2nd ed.). *Governing the Soul: the Shaping of the Private Self*. London: Free Association Books.

Young, R. (1990). *White Mythologies: Writing History and the West*. London: Routledge.

5. DO POLITICAL PARTIES MATTER? DO SPANISH PARTIES MAKE A DIFFERENCE IN CHILD CARE POLICIES?

Celia Valiente

Do political parties make a difference is one of the biggest questions in social sciences and the extent to which parties do or do not make a difference has enormous implications for our appreciation of the democratic nature of our polities. Unsurprisingly, many studies have sought to estimate the extent to which political parties impact on policy outputs. Do the policy outputs of social democratic governments differ from the outputs of conservative governments?[1] To what extent does the ideological make up of the government determine the nature of government decision making in terms of measures taken? This is a huge question and the present chapter seeks to make a contribution to the ongoing debate. The chapter focuses on a single policy area (child care policy) and a single country (Spain). I ask: to what extent did the change in 1996 from socialist government to conservative government impact on child care policy outputs? Did the change in ideological disposition of the government make any difference on this policy matter? The chapter is organized as follows. First, I elaborate the main debates in studies of gender and politics and of political economy on the topic of 'do parties make a difference on policy matters?' The debate can be fairly crudely summarized using the following hypotheses 1 and 2: 1/Yes, parties do make a difference and 2/No, parties do not make a difference. Second, I justify the selection of the empirical case study and

Promoting Evidence-based Practice in Early Childhood Education:
Research and its Implications, Volume 1, pages 97–114.
2001 by Elsevier Science Ltd.
ISBN: 0-7623-0753-6

present the sources for research. Third, I describe the main central state child care policies in the post 1975 period in Spain. Drawing on analyses of statistics and policy documents, I argue that there are basic continuities in actual policy making in the area of child care regardless of the party in office. This appears to support, in a small (and with qualifications) but not insignificant way, hypothesis number 2. Fourth, I provide an interpretation of why child care policy outputs were not affected by the change of government from socialists to conservatives.

ANALYTICAL FRAMEWORK

Research on gender equality policy making in Western countries has argued that generally speaking conservative parties facilitate the elaboration of gender equality policies to a significantly lower extent than social democratic parties (Bashevkin, 1998; Beckwith, 1987; Gelb, 1989; Katzenstein, 1987; Lovenduski & Norris, 1993; Lovenduski, Norris & Burns, 1994; Mazur, 1995; among others). This is so at least for six reasons. First, feminist activism has been more intense within socialist parties than conservative parties. Social democratic parties have traditionally been much more concerned with class inequalities than with gender differences. Nevertheless, feminist leaders and activists of socialist parties have often succeeded in adding clauses involving women's issues to their party platforms. Feminists from social democratic parties have also become policy makers. In their role of state officials, these socialist feminists have advocated and contributed to the establishment of policies to advance the status of women.

Second, female politicians (more often than male politicians) at times try to direct the attention of the political class to issues that may interest women more than men such as child care or maternity leave (Lovenduski, 1993: 7). The proportion of women (whether self-declared feminists or not) among the political elite is often lower in conservative than in social democratic parties. Thus within conservative political elites, there are less people who would pay attention to issues of interest for women.[2]

Third, equality of opportunity and equality of outcome are present as aims to varying degrees in social democratic platforms. In contrast, when conservative parties pursue equality objectives, they tend to promote equality of opportunity. Thus socialist parties would in principle be more prone to establish policies in favor of disadvantaged groups of society, including affirmative action, in an attempt to achieve not only that people compete on the same terms but also that citizens obtain the same results (Lovenduski, Norris & Burness, 1994: 612; Squires, 1996: 75). The goal of some gender equality policies is that women and men have the same access to material and cultural rewards, which is an objective directed to equality of results.

Fourth, conservative parties usually defend that the state intervenes in the economy to a very limited extent, arguing that the free play of market forces is the only devise to achieve the best allocation of economic factors, high productivity and wealth. State intervention in society is not necessary either, since order and equilibrium in the economic sphere will translate into the social realm (Bosanquet, 1994; Gamble, 1986; Green, 1987; Krieger, 1986; Ruiz, 1997). Thus conservative parties would favor that the state sets basic anti-discriminatory guidelines, and allows the market and society to play freely.

Fifth, conservative policy makers are at times interested in the promotion of a traditional agenda regarding both sexes (Abbott & Wallace, 1992; David, 1986; Lovenduski, Norris & Burness, 1994: 611, 630–631). A mild variant of this agenda would emphasize that the family is the basic cell of the social fabric. Historically, the family has been the sphere where women dedicate more efforts than men. Some (or many) women may also want (or have to) work for wages. Nevertheless, society has to be organized in a way that permits women to fulfill their family and caring tasks. The main family function of most men (economic provision) and most women (the management of the intimate sphere in combination or not with bread-winning) are different but complementary and of equal worth for the development of society and its weakest members (children). Then, conservative governments would try to facilitate that women perform their family responsibilities. Conservative administrations would be less active making the labor market an equally attractive and rewarding place for women and men.

Sixth, conservative parties are supposed to avoid policies that increase public spending. Ultimately, public spending is financed by detracting wealth from citizens. Conservatives defend that this wealth belong to individuals, and that it is better allocated when citizens spend it in the solution of their problems or the satisfaction of their needs in the market. Many (although not all) gender equality programmes are measures that increase authorities' spending, since these programmes impose extra costs to the state.[3]

Studies on gender and politics have also acknowledged that conservative parties have at times responded to the demands of the women's movement (Byrne, 1996: 67; Lovenduski, 1993: 6–7, 13; 1996: 9; Lovenduski, Norris & Burns, 1994: 611–612; Skjeie, 1993). Thus conservative parties have to a limited extent converge towards socialist parties. Women within conservative parties have pressed claims to be fairly treated as party members, activists and leaders. Conservative parties have included women's issues in their agendas and made some efforts to present a higher number of female candidates in elections. Once in office, conservative parties have been more willing than in the past to appoint women to governing positions, establish some gender equality policies (especially those that do not contradict the free market logic), and set up or maintain institutions with the explicit purpose of advancing women's rights and status (the so-called 'state feminist institutions' – Stetson & Mazur, 1995). Nevertheless, the general conclusion of most pieces of the literature on gender and politics defend that parties matter and that social democratic parties are much more active than conservative parties in search for gender equality.

The comparative study of policy making by social democratic and conservative parties have been undertaken regarding other areas of public policy different than gender equality. This social science research has reached nuanced findings. To grasp the subtlety of these conclusions, it is useful to refer for instance to political economy studies. While many analyses of gender equality policy making tend to emphasize the differences between policy making by socialist and conservative governments, the conclusions of political economy research are more varied. Some of these studies have found mainly differences in economic policy making by socialist and conservative administrations. Studying the industrial world since World War II, scholarly research has argued that unemployment disproportionately affects workers, who are the main electoral constituency of social democratic parties. When in power, these parties tend to promote anti-unemployment policies. In contrast, more affluent social groups and the business community are chiefly concerned with inflation. Since these people are the principal constituency of conservative parties, while in office these parties usually develop anti-inflation policies (Alt, 1985; Hibbs, 1977, 1987a, b).

Other political economy studies have documented more similarities than differences between economic policies established by socialist and conservative governments, or have identified differences that are not very significant (Hicks, 1984; Williams, 1990). Deep changes in industrial economies have taken place since the oil crises of the 1970s such as high mobility of capital flows, fixed rates, and a pronounced degree of openness of some national economies to international trade. These dimensions of an increasing economic interdependence at the international level substantially reduce the room for manoeuvering in economic policy making at the national level. Thus economic policies undertaken by social democratic administrations tend to converge towards those defended by conservative parties. Economic policy makers from both types of parties have pursued a similar objective (price stability) and have attempted to reduce the degree of intervention of the state in the economy allowing market forces to play a bigger role (Moses, 1994; Notermans, 1993).

Still, other studies of political economy have documented some differences in policy making between socialist and conservative parties but not other divergences. Analyzing countries of the Organization for Economic Cooperation and Development since the 1970s, Rueda (2000) found that social democratic parties have tended to be more active maintaining the employment protection of workers with protected jobs. Nevertheless, Rueda did not identify significant disparities among the two types of governments regarding anti-inflation and anti-unemployment policies. On the other hand, it is commonly accepted that the globalization of the economy has produced the convergence of macroeconomic policies made by social democratic administrations towards those policies defended by conservative parties. Nevertheless, this has not been the case of supply-side economic policies. To increase fixed and human capital (factors of production), some socialist governments have extensively used the public sector, spending on infrastructure, education and, sometimes, creating or fostering a public business sector (Boix, 1998; Garrett & Lange, 1991).

In sum, an important part (but nonetheless a part) of the literature on political economy documents a pronounced erosion of the differences in actual policy making by social democratic and conservative parties. This conclusion is in line with studies on party change which propose that in democracies the requirements of political competition put pressure on parties to look alike rather than diverge. Political parties tend to converge on the center of the ideological spectrum in order to win elections by capturing the median voter (Downs, 1957). Conversely, a relevant part of the literature on gender equality policy making tends to highlight differences between conservative and socialist parties in this area of public policy. Putting the two literatures together, one can ask: has convergence between the two parties also taken place regarding gender equality? If so, why?

SELECTION OF THE EMPIRICAL CASE STUDY AND SOURCES

This chapter attempts to contribute to the knowledge of gender equality policy making by socialist and conservative parties with an empirical study on child care policies developed by the central state in Spain under socialist administrations (1982–1996) and conservative governments (from 1996 to date). In principle, child care may benefit fathers and mothers. Nevertheless, given the division of labor between men and women within most families, child care usually affects the availability of mothers for paid work much more than that of fathers (Randall, 1996: 178; Skjeie, 1993: 238). It can be argued that economic independence is a necessary ingredient for women's emancipation. Economic autonomy very often means participation in the labor market, since the majority of the population of active age acquires economic autonomy through paid work. Then, child care programmes can be considered a policy that promotes gender equality, since these services facilitate that mothers work for wages.

According to Arend Lijphart (1971: 691), the best research design to study social reality is the comparison of two or more cases. Therefore, I compare policies elaborated by conservative and socialist administrations. Nevertheless, a single case may also be useful. The strength of a single case study 'is that by focusing on a single case, that case can be intensively examined even when the research resources at the investigator's disposal are relatively limited'. Then, I study only Spain, although the comparison of Spain with other national cases would be highly advisable for future research. In addition, a single case can be chosen if it is interesting in itself. Spain is a case in point to analyze policy making by conservative governments, because it is the only European Union (EU) member state (together with Austria) governed by a conservative party. In landmark pieces of research, Ruiz (1999a, b: 449) has convincingly argued that most analyses on gender and conservative administrations examine the United States and the United Kingdom, where conservative parties were in office in the 1980s and early 1990s. Conclusions of research on these anglo-saxon conservative governments are then extended to other polities. This extension may be wrong, since conservative parties may or may not be similar in different countries. Therefore, it is imperative to analyze conservative governments in countries different than the United States and the United Kingdom.

It is important to note that in Spain, child care measures have been understood by policy makers mainly as a part of the education policy but not so much as a part of gender equality programmes (see below). In other countries some social and political actors (mainly feminists active in the women's movement, gender equality state institutions and trade unions) have advanced the demand for more extensive child care policies in order to help mothers to combine professional and family obligations. In Spain, the aforementioned three actors have scarcely advanced this demand (Valiente, 1995: 254–259). Nevertheless, Spanish child care policies are an adequate empirical case to test hypotheses generated by the literature on political parties and gender equality measures. This is true for two reasons. Child care policies de facto influence the degree of equality or inequality between women and men, irrespectively of whether political parties consider child care a gender equality programme or not. On the other hand, the literature on gender and politics to which this chapter refers is based on case studies on other countries different from Spain. Some of these case studies are on child care.

The sources for this chapter include published government documents, legislative pieces, political party documents, press articles, secondary bibliography, and personal interviews with social and political actors in the policy area of child care.

CENTRAL STATE CHILD CARE POLICIES

There have been mainly continuities in the policy area of child care at the central state level in the last two decades. Under both Socialist and Conservative governments parents have been receiving the following aid from the state for the care of children under six: a relatively generous supply of (free-of-charge) public pre-school services for three-, four- and five-year-old children; hardly any public child care service for children aged two or under; and (up till 1999) low tax exemptions for child care expenses.

In the last two decades, the main central state child care policy has been an ever increasing supply of public preschool programmes for children aged three or over administered chiefly by the Ministry of Education and Culture (*Ministerio de Educación y Cultura*, MEC; before 1996, it was called the Ministry of Education and Science – *Ministerio de Educación y Ciencia*). In academic year 1996–1997, the proportion of children who attended public preschool centers was: 70% of children aged 4 and 5, and 43% of those aged 3. The scope of these programmes is quite high in comparative terms. Since the private sector also provides pre-school places, school attendance rates of 3, 4 and 5 years old children are high in Spain in comparative terms (83%, 100%, and 100% respectively in academic year 1999–2000; provisional data). In contrast, the percentage of Spanish children aged 2 or under cared for in public centers (in academic year 1996–1997) is one of the lowest in the EU: 2.5%. The proportion of children aged 2 or under cared for in private centers is also very small: 3.5% – calculated by Celia Valiente from data contained in: Ministerio de Educación y Cultura (1999: 79, 132–134); and data available on 17 July 2000 at http://www.mec.es/estadistica/Cifras/NAC_04.html.[4]

The absolute number and proportion of children who attend pre-school programmes in public centers has been increasing since 1975. While this type of center was attended by 347,026 children younger than 6 in academic year 1975–1976, this figure was more than double (758,458 children) in academic year 1999–2000. Seen from another perspective, in academic year 1975–1976, above a third (38%) of children enrolled in pre-school education attended public centers. In academic year 1999–2000, this proportion was around two/thirds (68%). The expansion of the supply of places in public child care centers has happened in a context of a reduction of the supply of child care in private centers. In academic year 1975–1976, the number of children enrolled in pre-school education who attended private centers was 573,310, while in academic year 1999–2000 the figure was 361,282 – calculated by Celia Valiente from data contained in: Instituto Nacional de Estadística (1977: 101–103; 1981: 12); and data available on 17 July 2000 at http://www.mec.es/ estadistica/Cifras/NAS_01.html.

Public pre-school programmes cannot be used by mothers (or parents) as perfect substitutes for child care, since pre-school hours are shorter than working hours (and sometimes much shorter and interrupted by a break). Similarly, pre-school holidays in public centers are much longer than working holidays. It is important to note that even if the percentage of women in employment is lower in Spain than in most EU member states, most Spanish women who work for wages have full-time jobs. In 1998, the Spanish female employment rate (35%) was the lowest in the EU, and much lower than the EU average (51%).[5] However, 83% of female workers worked on a full-time basis in Spain. This figure (together with that of Portugal and Finland) was the third highest in the EU, after that of Greece (89%) and Italy (86%), and sixteen points above the EU average (67%) (Franco, 1999: 8–9).

Besides the pronounced expansion of the supply of public pre-school programmes, the other most important development in the policy area of child care under both socialist and conservative administrations has been territorial de-centralization. From the mid-1930s to 1975 Spain was governed by a right-wing authoritarian regime headed by General Francisco Franco. During the Francoist dictatorship, the state was highly centralized. During the transition to democracy, a broad process of devolution of powers from the central state to the regions (not so much to localities) was set in motion. Since the early 1980s, some regional governments have been acquiring responsibilities which had previously belonged to the central state (for instance, education). The process of devolution of full responsibilities on education to all regions was completed in year 2000.[6]

Other child care policies (such as state regulation of private centers, or tax exemptions for child care expenses) are much less important than the supply of preschool places in public centers. Regarding the regulation of private centers, the state established in 1990 that the minimum conditions required of public preschool centers (for instance, in terms of space per child or the number of children per carer) also apply to the private sector. Nevertheless, private centers opened before 1990 were given until year 2002 to adapt to this regulation. In contrast with other countries, paid care provided for children under six in private homes (by babysitters, child-minders, etc.) is not regulated by the state in Spain (regarding, for instance, the qualifications of carers, the maximum number of children who can be cared for by a person, or the characteristics of the home where care is provided).

With respect to tax reliefs, between 1991 and 1998, payers of the personal income tax could benefit from tax deductions for child care expenses (of the under-threes) of a maximum of 25,000 pesetas per year (around 93 Pounds Sterling) or the equivalent of 15% of the child care expenses. The income of the tax payer could not exceed a given level, and both parents had to work for wages outside the home. In fiscal year 1997 (corresponding to income generated in 1996), 116,371 tax payers benefitted from tax reliefs for child care. The average tax deduction for each tax payer was 12,073 pesetas (approximately 45 Pounds Sterling) (Ministerio de Economía y Hacienda, *Memoria de la Administración Tributaria 1997*, page 119; data from the whole Spain except the Basque country and Navarre; data available on 21 April 2000 at http://www.meh.es/INSPGRAL/MT97/cap2.pdf).

In brief, since 1975, under governments of different ideological colors, a substantial extension of the supply of public pre-school programmes (the main child care policy) has happened in Spain. This expansion has occurred in a context of continuously diminishing fertility rates (the synthetic index of fertility in Spain continuously decreased from 2.79 in 1975 to 1.15 in 1998; the data of 1998 is provisional – European Commission, 1999: 102). The process of devolution of powers to the regions has also taken place under both social democratic and conservative administrations. Thus basic continuities have characterized child care policies in the last two decades. The Conservative party has introduced only minor modifications in the policy area of child care. The conservative government increased (modestly) tax exemptions for child care expenses in 1998, but abolished them altogether in 1999, in a general and substantial reform of the personal income tax system.

SIMILAR POLICIES OF SOCIAL DEMOCRATIC AND CONSERVATIVE GOVERNMENTS: AN INTERPRETATION

This section shows that until year 2000 child care policies promoted by the conservative party have been similar to those implemented by the socialist party for two reasons: strong electoral competition between both parties; and in the late 1990s the successful mobilization of left-wing parties and organizations of civil society in defense of the status quo in the policy area of child care.

Studying party positions is a complex and difficult but a feasible task (Mair, 1999; Ramiro, 1999). Party points of view and commitments on specific issues are reflected in electoral programmes and in the resolutions of party congresses. Electoral programmes and resolutions of federal congresses of the social democratic party (*Partido Socialista Obrero Español*, PSOE) contain the commitment to develop programmes for the under-sixes, conceptualized as educational policies (Partido Socialista Obrero Español, 1979a: política sectorial 90, política municipal 8; 1981: 91, 277–279; 1982: 23–24; 1984: 66; 1986: 61, 63; 1988: 44; 1989: 29–30; 1990: 109; 1993: 29; 1996: 51–53). PSOE documents also include some references to child care in the sections related to 'gender equality' (although far fewer than in the sections on 'education') (Partido Socialista Obrero Español, 1976: 19; 1979a: política sectorial 19–20; 1979b: 22; 1981: 233; 1982: 29; 1989: 66; 1990: 61, 109; 1993: 59; 1996: 66–67; 2000: 17).

In its electoral programmes and party congress resolutions, the PSOE had proposed that preschool programmes can be used as tools to achieve a higher degree of class equality. According to this view, children from underprivileged social classes should be enrolled in public preschool programmes. This enrollment would provide them with the educational skills necessary to be successful students in elementary school. This enrollment would also diminish the cultural differences that exist among children of different socio-economic backgrounds. All these ideas reflect the PSOE leaders' opinion that the educational system might work as an efficient mechanism against social inequalities (Partido Socialista Obrero Español, 1979a: política sectorial 90, política municipal 8; 1981: 91, 277–279; 1982: 23–24; 1984: 66; 1986: 61, 63; 1988: 44; 1989: 29–30; 1990: 109; 1993: 29; 1996: 51–53).

While in office, the socialist party significantly increased the supply of places in public centers, in order to reverse the past trend of unequal access to pre-school educational services. In the 1970s and 1980s educational services for the under-sixes were mainly provided by the private sector. Therefore, chiefly families who could afford to pay the fees charged by private centers provided their children with preschool education. Proportionally less families from more modest socio-economic strata enrolled their children in these centers (De Puelles, 1986: 448–449; González-Anleo, 1985: 74; Medina, 1976: 123; Muñoz-Repiso et al., 1992: 21–22).

If preschool programmes are defined as an education service for pupils, one might ask: at what age should children start to attend education centers? Historically this age was fixed around 6 years (De Puelles, 1986: 447–448). Three decades ago, this age was supposed to be 4 or 5 years (Instituto de la Mujer, 1990; Medina, 1976: 115). Now, numerous political and social actors have agreed with the view that this age is approximately 3 years. In practice, this idea has been reflected in the provision of numerous places in public centers for children aged 3 or over, and hardly any for the under-threes. Significant sectors of the population have also agreed with these views about the advantages of the preschool experiences described above and the age at which children should start attending preschool activities (Instituto de la Mujer, 1990: 50–54; McNair, 1984: 41–42).

This is the background against which conservative policy makers had to clarify their positions in the area of child care while in opposition and promote policies while in office (since June 1996). In its electoral programmes, the conservative party (under the names of *Alianza Popular, Coalición Democrática, Coalición Popular* and *Partido Popular,* PP, the last one, the PP, being used in the rest of the chapter) has also understood preschool programmes chiefly as education policies (Alianza Popular, 1977: 31; 1982: 104–105; Coalición Democrática, 1979: 45; Coalición Popular, 1986: 9; Partido Popular, 1989: 10; 1993: 56–58; 1996: 98–99; 2000: 29), and to a much lesser extent as gender equality measures, and/or family policies (Coalición Democrática, 1979: 37; Alianza Popular, 1982: 135; Partido Popular, 1989: 29; 1993: 81; 1996: 181–182, 187–189; 2000: 18, 58).

Ruiz (1999a, b) has persuasively argued that it is reasonable to defend that since the late 1980s the conservative party changed its discourses regarding women's issues due to strong electoral competition against the PSOE. In the same line, I now defend that possibly the conservative party also changed its discourses on some topics related to social class (such as child care) while electorally competing with the socialist party. Moreover, once in office, the conservative party promoted public policy in line with these modified discourses.

In the 1970s and 1980s, the conservative party was identified by an important sector of the electorate as a party which defended the interests of affluent citizens (Montero, 1988: 154–157). This identification was extremely negative, since it impeded the PP to win the majority of the vote. After loosing several elections, the conservative party started to change its discourse regarding child care. It is an issue that the population and the political class could perceive as related to socio-economic inequalities. The PP electoral programmes between 1977 and 1986 insistently argued in favor of the private sector as provider of child care services. This idea was presented in terms of the freedom of families to choose the type of center that they prefer for their children (Alianza Popular, 1977: 31; 1982: 103–104; Coalición Democrática, 1979: 45–46; Coalición Popular, 1986: 8–10). This discourse resembles the discourses of conservative parties in other countries, for instance, that of the

United Kingdom (Peele, 1988: 27–28; Randall, 1996: 181–183, 190). However, since the 1989 electoral programme, the PP softened its pro-private sector position. Paragraphs on the matter started to appear less frequently in PP's electoral programmes. Electoral platforms began to contain (very few) lines on the importance of the public sector and the need to erode socio-economic inequalities in the access to education. The PP also committed itself to increase the quality of public education if in government (Partido Popular, 1989: 10–12; 1993: 56–58; 1996: 96–98; 2000, 28). Thus in the last decade there has been a convergence of positions by the PP and the PSOE (as reflected in electoral programmes) regarding education.

However, in spite of the aforementioned alteration of the discourse in PP electoral programmes since the late 1980s, in year 2000 the PP's position in education is still different from that of the PSOE. Generally speaking, PSOE electoral programmes have traditionally defended that the state should be the major actor in education, while the PP still defends (although less insistently than in the past) that the state has to play a subsidiary role in this policy area. PSOE programmes continuously refer to equality among social classes as an objective in the policy area of education, while PP programmes emphasize the freedom of individuals and organizations to set up education centers, and the freedom of parents to choose education centers for their children in a scenario of plural supply. Depending on the election, PP programmes also defend that the state provides generous subsidies to private child care centers and/or to families.

Since the conservative party reached government (June 1996), the socialist party, the electoral coalition the United Left (*Izquierda Unida* ideologically to the Left of the PSOE and the third electoral force in most national elections) and organizations of civil society (mainly associations of parents of pupils who attend public education centers, unions of teachers and workers of public centers, and students' organizations) have carefully watched governmental actions in the policy area of education. These left-wing parties and associations have mobilized endlessly against any governmental move in the direction of curtailing the public sector and fostering the private sector as provider of child care services, attempts to increase the tiny subsidies to private centers or to families who send their children there, and diminish the number of pre-school public places or public expenditure on public child care services. This mobilization by the left-wing parties and voluntary organizations has been amply covered by some mass media including *El País*, which is the main national newspaper.[7] Mobilizations in defense of the preservation of parts of the welfare state have also taken place in other areas of social policy (Guillén &

Matsaganis, 2000). This visible mobilization probably prevented that the PP elaborated more policies in favor of private child care provision.

CONCLUSION

Contrary to the predictions of an important part of the literature on political parties and gender equality policy, in Spain the conservative party in power since June 1996 has promoted central state child care policies similar to those put in place by previous socialist governments. In the last two decades the main child care policy has been the increasing supply of pre-school services in public centers for children aged 3 to 6. Possibly, this continuity in policy making can be explained in terms of the strong electoral competition between the socialist and the conservative parties and the successful mobilization of left-wing parties and organizations of civic society in favor of the preservation of the policies established before 1996.

This chapter confirms the conclusions reached by Ruiz (1999a, b) while studying the position of the Spanish conservative party regarding women's issues. Ruiz demonstrated that the ideas defended by the conservative party converged towards the position of the socialist party, probably because the conservative party is an electorally motivated party, which in the late 1980s attempted to convert itself into a catch-all party to reach power. Contrary to the conservative parties of the United Kingdom and the United States in office in the 1980s and early 1990s, the Spanish conservative party moderated its traditional views on women's roles. This chapter shows that since the late 1980s the Spanish conservative party has softened its defense of the private sector as the provider of education in general and pre-school programmes in particular. While Ruiz exhaustively analyzed party positions, this chapter also studies actual policy making. Once in power, the conservative party acted in accordance with the aforementioned renewed ideas in the policy area of child care.

From the conclusions of research made by Ruiz and this chapter, one can infer that more research is needed on electoral competition as a causal factor of changes in party positions and actual policy making. In the late 1980s the Spanish conservative party had lost several elections and started to modify its points of view in order to reach government. However, it is still unknown how the conservative party decided that the positions to be changed were those related to women's roles and child care (among others). Nor is it known which concrete mechanisms made possible the change in party positions (for instance, a modification of the party leadership, or the necessity to comply with the requirements of membership of supra-national institutions such as the European Union).

It is important to note that the socialist party was in power for fourteen years, while by the time of this writing the conservative party has been in office for four years. Thus the policy continuity regarding child care has to be interpreted with caution. This policy continuity may be a signal that party politics did not really matter in this policy area. Alternatively, it can be defended that the socialist party had been in power for a period long enough to set the agenda in government with respect to child care. Social democrats were able to set targets and values in government departments and civil service, and this remains in place despite a new and ideological different party arriving into power.

Since 1996, the Spanish conservative party continued to develop a part of the education policy (child care programmes) along the same lines of its predecessor in government, the socialist party. This policy continuity raises new questions. Why the socialist governments did not emphasize more the dimension of gender equality policy of child care programmes? Had the socialist party emphasized more the gender dimension of child care, would the conservative party have encountered more difficulties maintaining social democratic child care policies? These new questions go beyond the scope of this chapter but would require further research.

The policy continuity in the area of child care under socialist and conservative governments leads us to the question of policy innovation and preservation. Social democratic governments significantly expanded the supply of pre-school places in public centers and devolved education responsibilities to the regions. The conservative government preserved existing policies established by precedent administrations. Research in other measures different than child care may perhaps confirm that socialist governments innovate in the policy area of gender equality while conservative administrations maintain what is already in place without innovating further. Perhaps dismantling existing programmes requires too high an electoral cost for any party to pay.

Conservative parties are very different among each other. While some promote very traditional agendas regarding gender roles, others do not. Generally speaking, left-wing parties were historically the first to incorporate gender equality objectives in their platforms and actual policy making partly due to successful feminist activism within these parties. Afterwards, some conservative parties (in some cases with considerable delay) have followed suit preserving policies initiated by social democrats while others have not. More research is needed in the future in order to understand which conservative parties have converged towards social democratic positions, regarding which issues, and under what circumstances.

NOTES

1. In this chapter, the expressions 'social democratic' and 'socialist' are used as synonymous. The same applies to 'government/s' and 'administration/s'.

2. This argument has to be taken with caution, since the proportion of female members in conservative parties is usually higher than in socialist parties. Conservative female members can put pressure on activists and leaders of their party to include women's issues among their priorities. Nevertheless, it is not always the case that this pressure is exercised and that activists and leaders of (all) political parties know and bear in mind the demands of the rank-and-file.

3. It is important to note that economic costs are not the only or the most important costs that may preclude conservative parties from establishing gender equality policies. Perhaps the most costly policies for these parties are those which include not economic but ideological costs, such as the regulation of abortion or divorce, because of the moral and religious connotations of these issues.

4. For pre-school attendance rates in Spain and other industrial countries see: European Commission (1998: 76); and Organization for Economic Cooperation and Development (2000: 135).

5. The female employment rate is the proportion of employed women out of the female population of working age.

6. As a result of the process of devolution, programmes formulated by the MEC have affected a decreasing number of regions. Then, the data provided in this chapter for the 1990s (for example, the percentage of children younger than six who attended public pre-school programmes) are the result of public policies elaborated by the central state and regional governments with responsibility on education.

7. In order to document the coverage of this mobilization, I have exhaustively examined the daily edition of *El País* since June 1996 up to the writing of this chapter (Summer 2000).

ACKNOWLEDGMENTS

I would like to thank John Garry and Antonia M. Ruiz for priceless bibliographical advice and comments on an earlier draft of this chapter.

REFERENCES

Abbott, P., & Wallace, C. (1992). *The Family and the New Right.* London: Pluto Press.

Alianza Popular (1977). *Qué es Alianza Popular.* Madrid: Alianza Popular.

Alianza Popular (1982). General Elections: electoral program.

Alt, J. E. (1985). Political Parties, World Demand, and Unemployment: Domestic and International Sources of Economic Activity. *American Political Science Review, 79*(4), 1016–1040.

Bashevin, S. (1998). *Women on the Defensive: Living Through Conservative Times.* Chicago: University of Chicago Press.

Beckwith, K. (1987). Response to Feminism in the Italian Parliament: Divorce, Abortion, and Sexual Violence Legislation. In: M. F. Katzenstein & C. McClurg Mueller (Eds), *The*

Women's Movements of the United States and Western Europe (pp. 153–171). Philadelphia: Temple University Press.

Boix, C. (1998). *Political Parties, Growth and Equality: Conservative and Social Democratic Strategies in the World Economy.* New York: Cambridge University Press.

Bosanquet, N. (1994). *After the New Right.* Chippenham (Wiltshire): Dartmouth.

Byrne, P. (1996). The Politics of the Women's Movement. In: J. Lovenduski & P. Norris (Eds), *Women in Politics* (pp. 57–72). Oxford: Oxford University Press and The Hansard Society Series in Politics and Government.

Coalición Democrática (1979). General Elections: electoral program.

Coalición Popular (1986). General Elections: electoral program.

David, M. (1986). New Right in the USA and Britain: A New Antifeminist Moral Economy. *Critical Social Policy, 3*, 31–45.

De Puelles, M. (1986). *Educación e Ideología en la España Contemporánea.* Barcelona: Labor.

Downs, A. (1957). *An Economic Theory of Democracy.* New York: Harper & Row.

El País various years.

European Commission (1998). *Social Portrait of Europe.* Luxembourg: Office for Official Publications of the European Communities.

European Commission (1999). *Statistiques Démographiques: Données 1960–1999.* Luxembourg: Office for Official Publications of the European Communities.

Franco, A. (1999). Enquête sur les Forces de Travail: Principaux Résultats 1998. *Statistiques en Bref: Population et Conditions Sociales, 11.*

Gamble, A. (1986). The Political Economy of Freedom. In: R. Levitas (Ed.), *The Ideology of the New Right* (pp. 25–54). Cambridge: Polity Press.

Garrett, G., & Lange, P. (1991). Political Responses to Interdependence: What's 'Left' for the Left? *International Organization, 45*(4), 539–564.

Gelb, J. (1989). *Feminism and Politics: A Comparative Perspective.* Berkeley and Los Angeles: University of California Press.

Green, D. G. (1987). *The New Right: The Counter-Revolution in Political, Economic and Social Thought.* New York and London: Harvester and Wheatsheaf.

Guillén; A. M., & Matsaganis, M. (2000). Testing the 'Social Dumping' Hypothesis in Southern Europe: Welfare Policies in Spain and Greece during the Last Twenty Years. *Journal of European Social Policy*, (forthcoming).

González-Anleo, J. (1985). *El Sistema Educativo Español.* Madrid: Instituto de Estudios Económicos.

Hibbs, D. A. (1977). Political Parties and Macroeconomic Theory. *American Political Science Review, 71*, 1467–1487.

Hibbs, D. A. (1987a). *The American Political Economy: Macroeconomics and Electoral Politics.* Cambridge, Mass.: Harvard University Press.

Hibbs, D. A. (1987b). *The Political Economy of Industrial Democracies.* Cambridge, Mass.: Harvard University Press.

Hicks, A. (1984). Elections, Keynes, Bureaucracy and Class: Explaining U.S. Budget Deficits, 1961–1978. *American Sociological Review, 49*, 165–182.

Instituto de la Mujer (1990). *El Reparto de Responsabilidades Familiares: Análisis de la Demanda Femenina y sus Expectativas sobre Las Redes de Cuidados de Hijos.* Madrid: Instituto de la Mujer.

Instituto Nacional de Estadística (1977). *Estadística de la Enseñanza en España: Curso 1975–76.* Madrid: Instituto Nacional de Estadística.

Instituto Nacional de Estadística (1981). *Censo de Población, Tomo I, Volumen I, Resultados Nacionales, Características de la Población*. Madrid: Instituto Nacional de Estadística.

Katzenstein, M. F. (1987). Comparing the Feminist Movements of the United States and Western Europe: An Overview. In: M. F. Katzenstein & C. McClurg Mueller (Eds), *The Women's Movements of the United States and Western Europe: Consciousness, Political Opportunities, and Public Policy* (pp. 3–20). Philadelphia: Temple University Press.

Krieger, J. (1986). *Reagan, Thatcher, and the Politics of Decline*. Cambridge: Polity Press.

Lijphart, A. (1971). Comparative Politics and the Comparative Method. *American Political Science Review, 65*(3), 682–693.

Lovenduski, J. (1993). Introduction: The Dynamics of Gender and Party. In: J. Lovenduski & P. Norris (Eds), *Gender and Party Politics* (pp. 1–15). London: Sage.

Lovenduski, J. (1996). Sex, Gender and British Politics. In: J. Lovenduski & P. Norris (Eds), *Women in Politics* (pp. 3–18). Oxford: Oxford University Press and The Hansard Society for Parliamentary Government.

Lovenduski, J., & Norris, P. (Eds) (1993). *Gender and Party Politics*. London: Sage.

Lovenduski, J., Norris, P., & Burness, C. (1994). The Party and Women. In: A. Seldon & S. Ball (Eds), *Conservative Century: The Conservative Party Since 1900* (pp. 611–635). Oxford: Oxford University Press.

Mair, P. (1999). Searching for the Positions of Political Actors: A Review of Approaches and an Evaluation of Expert Surveys in Particular. Paper presented at the European Consortium for Political Research Joint Sessions of Workshops, Mannheim, 26–31 March.

Mazur, A. G. (1995). *Gender Bias and the State: Symbolic Reform at Work in Fifth Republic France*. Pittsburg and London: University of Pittsburg Press.

McNair, J. M. (1984). *Education for a Changing Spain*. Manchester: Manchester University Press.

Medina, A. (1976). Problemática de la Educación Preescolar en España. *Revista de Educación, 247*, 111–134.

Ministerio de Economía y Hacienda (1997). *Memoria de la Administración Tributaria*. Available on 21 April 2000 at http://www.meh.es/INSPGRAL/MT97/cap2.pdf.

Ministerio de Educación y Cultura (1999). *Estadística de la Enseñanza en España 1996/97: Resultados Detallados, Series e Indicadores*. Madrid: Ministerio de Educación y Cultura.

Montero, J. R. (1988). More Than Conservative, Less Than Neoconservative: Alianza Popular in Spain. In: B. Girvin (Ed.), *The Transformation of Contemporary Conservatism* (pp. 145–163). London: Sage.

Moses, J. W. (1994). Abdication from National Policy Autonomy: What's Left to Leave? *Politics & Society, 22*(2), 125–148.

Muñoz-Repiso, Mercedes et al. (1992). *Las Desigualdades en la Educación en España*. Madrid: Ministerio de Educación y Ciencia.

Notermans, T. (1993). The Abdication from National Policy Autonomy: Why the Macroeconomic Policy Regime Has Become So Unfavorable to Labor. *Politics & Society, 21*(2), 133–167.

Organization for Economic Cooperation and Development (2000). *Education at a Glance: OECD Indicators, 2000 Edition*. Paris: Organization for Economic Cooperation and Development.

Partido Popular (1989, 1993, 1996, 2000). General Elections: electoral programs.

Partido Socialista Obrero Español (1976, 1979a, 1981, 1984, 1988, 1990, 1994). 27–33 Federal congresses, resolutions.

Partido Socialista Obrero Español (1977, 1979b, 1982, 1986, 1989, 1993, 1996, 2000). General elections, electoral programs.

Peele, Gillian (1988). British Conservatism: Ideological Change and Electoral Uncertainty. In: B.Girvin (Ed.), *The Transformation of Contemporary Conservatism* (pp. 13–34). London: Sage.

Ramiro, L. (1999). Different Measures of the Ideological Positions of Political Parties: A Research Note from the Spanish Case. Paper presented at the European Consortium for Political Research Joint Sessions of Workshops, Mannheim, 26–31 March.

Randall, V. (1996). The Politics of Child Care. In: J. Lovenduski & P. Norris (Eds), *Women in Politics* (pp. 178–192). Oxford: Oxford University Press and The Hansard Society for Parliamentary Government.

Rueda, F. D. (2000). Political Parties and Economic Policy: An Analysis of Insider-Outsider Politics in the OECD. Paper Presented at the 12th International Conference of Europeanists, Chicago, March 30-April 2.

Ruiz, A. M. (1997). Reshaping the Welfare State: New Right's Moral Arguments in Southern European Conservative Parties, the Spanish *Partido Popular*. Unpublished paper written at the Instituto Juan March de Estudios e Investigaciones, Madrid, Spain.

Ruiz, A. M. (1999a). Cases That Do Not Fit? Paper Presented at the European Consortium for Political Research Joint Sessions of Workshops, Mannheim (Germany), 26–31 March.

Ruiz, A. M. (1999b). Evolución y Actitudes de AP-PP hacia la Participación Femenina en el Mercado de Trabajo: Discusión de Algunas Hipótesis Explicativas. In: M. Ortega, C. Sánchez & C. Valiente (Eds), *Género y Ciudadanía: Revisiones desde el Ámbito Privado* (pp. 449–468). Madrid: Universidad Autónoma de Madrid.

Skjeie, H. (1993). Ending the Male Political Hegemony: The Norwegian Experience. In: J. Lovenduski & P. Norris (Eds), *Gender and Party Politics* (pp. 231–262). London: Sage.

Squires, J. (1996). Quotas for Women: Fair Representation? In: J. Lovenduski & P. Norris (Eds), *Women and Politics* (pp. 73–90). Oxford: Oxford University Press and The Hansard Society Series in Politics and Government.

Stetson, D. McBride, & Mazur, A. G. (Eds) (1995). *Comparative State Feminism*. Thousand Oaks, Calif.: Sage.

Valiente, C. (1995). Children First: Central Government Child Care Policies in Post-authoritarian Spain (1975–1994). In: J. Brannen & M. O'Brien (Eds), *Childhood and Parenthood: Proceedings of ISA Committee for Family Research Conference on Children and Families, 1994* (pp. 249–266). London: Institute of Education (University of London).

Williams, J. T. (1990). The Political Manipulation of Macroeconomic Policy. *American Political Science Review, 84*(3), 767–795.

6. EARLY CHILDHOOD INTERVENTION PROGRAMMES IN NIGERIA: ISSUES, PROBLEMS AND CHALLENGES

Olusola Obisanya

INTRODUCTION

There are over 14.6 million children below the age of six years in Nigeria. The National Policy on Education (Federal Republic of Nigeria, 1981: 10) defined pre-primary education as 'the education given in an institution for children aged 3 to 5 plus prior to their entering primary school'. The provision of Early Childhood Education has not been given much attention in Nigeria by the government. For instance, 80% of the day care centres which are preschool institutions in the Situation And Policy Analysis of Basic Education in Nigeria (FGN/UNICEF, 1993) are owned by sole proprietors, the private sector, communities and religious organisations. Federal and State governments owned less than 10% of the day care centres. The policy states that to achieve the objectives of pre-primary education in Nigeria, government will 'encourage private efforts in the provision of pre-primary education' (FGN/UNICEF, 1993: 10) thereby leaving this crucial period of basic development and education to the private sector. Despite the fact that Nigeria has endorsed the recommendations of the Convention on the Rights of the Child with one of the strong recommendations stating that all children, without distinction of gender, race, language, religion or of any other kind, should have the opportunity to develop

Promoting Evidence-based Practice in Early Childhood Education:
Research and its Implications, Volume 1, pages 115–130.
Copyright © 2001 by Elsevier Science Ltd.
All rights of reproduction in any form reserved.
ISBN: 0-7623-0753-6

to their full potential, it is observed that pre-primary education is still not available to all Nigerian children especially those in the rural areas.

It is now widely agreed all over the world that learning begins at birth and that any shortcoming at this crucial stage is most likely to have a permanent effect on the child (Barker, 1987; World Conference on Education for All, 1990). Early childhood is also the critical period for the formation of personality and social behaviour. Research has documented that the most critical determinants of the learning capacity of children entering primary school are nutrition, health and the early social environment (Barker, 1987; World Conference on Education for All, 1990; King & Burgess, 1993). According to the World Conference on Education for All,

> a growing body of evidence demonstrates that health, nutrition, and psychosocial processes interact to affect survival and development in the early years of life. The outcomes of these interactions condition the readiness of the child for school and other learning opportunities, which in turn influences the child's chances of enrolment and success in basic education (World Conference on Education for All, 1990: 28).

The provision of preschool education in Nigeria is currently the preserve of the private enterprise, voluntary agencies and non-governmental organisations as observed by the SAPA survey. According to the SAPA report, access by children in Nigeria to daycare centres and pre-primary (nursery) schools is still rather low. Only a small proportion of children aged between 0–2 years and 2–5 years attended daycare centres and pre-primary (nursery) schools respectively, with the aim of accessing early educational stimulation. In 1986, only 4.7% of the estimated 19.3% children in the 2–5 year-age bracket were enrolled in nursery schools. Estimates from the SAPA study also showed that only 11% of the under-six children were given the benefit of some form of daycare/pre-primary education. When disaggregated, the SAPA data showed that the greater percentage (82.2%) of those children who gained access to daycare centres and nursery schools were in the urban areas. The issue of access was reported by Beckley (1994) who observed that 'data on education suggest that less than 5% of preschool age children in Nigeria benefited from early childhood care and stimulation opportunities and that the majority of children from rural and poor communities remain unreached by such services'.

Survey in five UNICEF assisted local government areas, where initial Early Childcare Development and Education (ECCDE) activities had taken placed showed that the preschool coverage was 2.0% in Urban areas and 0.7% for Rural areas. According to the FGN/UNICEF Master Plan of Operation, 'existing preschool and daycare programmes have paid little attention to health, nutrition, psychosocial and cognitive aspects of child development'. Many of the privately owned centres were ill organised, exploitative, predominantly urban-based and accessible only to families with incomes above the average (NERC, 1980; FGN/UNICEF Master Plan of Operation, 1991). A series of international events in the last ten years, notably the Convention on the Rights of the Child (1989), the 1990 Jomtien World Conference on Education for All (WCEFA) and the World Summit for Children (1990) have given added visibility and impetus to basic education. The basic message of these events was that developing countries and international agencies should confront the problem of illiteracy and decline by concentrating energies and investment in basic education.

According to the *'Framework for Action to meet Basic Learning Needs'* developed at the WCEFA; National Basic Education would be composed of four pillars:

- A four year concentrated, primary cycle for all children which would provide basic reading, writing, numeracy and life skills, both family and environmental;
- Non-formal education for children and adult not reached by schools, especially women;
- Expansion and improvement of early child development, care and educational services;
- Further teaching through the use of various communication channels (Bennett, 1994: 9).

From the above declaration of the WCEFA, the emphasis on early childcare, development and educational services presupposes that relevant facilities are in place. Article five (WCEFA, 1990: 159 & 160) of the Jomtien Declaration recognised the crucial importance of early childcare, development and education, recalling that 'learning begins at birth' and the need to involve families and communities in the provision of early childcare and stimulation opportunities (WCEFA, 1990).

The negligible involvement of the government in pre-primary education not only left this fundamental need for child development/care in the hands of the private sector but contributed in no small way to the problem of access and retention in the primary schools. At the same time, child survival with the resulting rapid population increase, was occurring at the time when more women had to join the labour force for economic survival. This trend led to increased migration, high mobility between urban and rural areas, disintegration of family cohesion and a decline in traditional family solidarity (UNICEF, 1996). All these problems brought about the UNICEF and Bernard van Leer Foundation (BvLF) initiative on Early Childcare Intervention. These bodies, with their focus on children, approached the Federal Government of Nigeria through the Nigerian Educational Research and Development Council (NERDC) using a multi-sectoral, multifaceted approach in 5 pilot UNICEF-assisted local government areas (LGAs) during the 1986–1990 Country Programme of Cooperation. Increasing recognition is given to the issue of Early Childcare, Development and Education in the 1986–1990 Country programme as a result of UNICEF'S advocacy for the Federal Government's interest in Child Survival and Development. Consequently, the Bernard van Leer Foundation (BvLF) entered into collaboration with the Federal Government of Nigeria and UNICEF to evolve the Early Childcare Development and Education Project in Nigeria (UNICEF, 1990).

In line with this collaboration, UNICEF worked in close collaboration with the government through the Nigerian Educational Research and Development Council (NERDC) to develop an alternative community based, low-cost approach to early childcare and development within a frame work of the primary health care programme, taking an integrated, multi sectoral approach, in five local government areas namely: Oyo, Calabar, Akko/Yamaltu Deba, Owo and Oyun between 1987 and 1990.

This paper sets out to report the findings of an evaluation study on the Early Childcare Development and Education Intervention project in Nigeria. The paper having reviewed the background to the intervention project will now present the project; the methodology used for the study and the findings of the study.

The Concept of Early Childhood Care and Education

It is generally agreed that the years of early childhood are the most influential in a child's life (Barker, 1987; Brierley, 1992; Pascal & Bertram, 1997). The importance of early stimulation, nutrition and an optimal interactional environment are widely recognised. The challenge of early childhood to practitioners therefore is to work out how development can best take place, and equally importantly, to judge what should be the role of parents, community, the state and the professionals, in determining and bringing about development.

There are major conflicts of opinions on these issues. Each society's cultures and sub-cultures demand the development of their children to match their social and cultural perspectives. Teachers, social workers, psychologists, economists, health workers and other professions present their special demands, backed by theories about how children ought to be developed without due attention to the voices and authority of parents and local communities to balance the outside demands on children and child-rearers, with the common senses views of those most intimately involved (Barker, 1987).

The term Early Childhood Care and Development and Education refers not only to what is happening within the child, but also to the care that child requires in order to thrive. For a child to develop and learn in a healthy way, it is important not only to meet the basic needs for protection, food and healthcare, but also to meet the basic needs for interaction and stimulation, affection, security, and learning through exploration and discovery (UNICEF: The Consultative Group on Early Childhood Care and Development, 1996).

ECCDE activities are those that support young children appropriately and seek to strengthen the environments in which they live. ECCDE includes working with parents to strengthen parental skills, working with siblings and other family members to recognise the specific developmental needs of younger children and working to provide or strengthen day care options. It involves developing preschools and other early years programmes that address the child's needs in holistic ways, as well as striving to bolster the community in its economic, physical and moral support of families and young children.

Internationally, Early Childhood Care and Development (ECCD) arose from the recognition that elements from the fields of early childhood education, infant stimulation, health and nutrition, community development and economics, interact within a young child's life. In order to support young children and help them to thrive, it is important to understand the many facets of their development, and also address the context in which they are living. Barker (1987: 3) ECCD 'is concerned with the linguistic, social, cognitive and educational growth of the child in its first five or six years. It includes nutrition and health care ... particularly dependent on the role of the parents and community surrounding the child'. Barker went on to state that if this human environment is one of poverty, apathy and low self-esteem, the child may be marked by the same characteristics unless the parents and community can be helped to achieve some measure of creative control over the child's microenvironment.

One of the pioneers of nursery education, particularly of this nature was Margaret McMillan (1860–1931). McMillan realised the importance of education to all children but was aware that many children living in poor communities did not have access to nursery education. She recognised that unhealthy and malnourished children found it difficult to learn and, therefore, focussed her efforts upon improving their health. Nursery education, she believed, compensated for the deficits in some children's lives (Neaum & Tallack, 1997).

McMillan was one of the firsts to appreciate the educational value of the home. She saw both the home and the community as contributors to the education of young children. She realised very early that if any progress was to be made, parents must be involved in their children's education. She noted that nursery schools alone could not overcome the ills of the society, but rather parents must be helped to improve their own child-rearing practices and to develop their potentialities. This visionary woman realised even at that time the importance of empowerment and the need for collaboration between the school, the home and the community. The concept of the nursery schools as an extension of and not a substitute for the home has long been an accepted principle of McMillan and her successors.

McMillan was convinced that specially devised preschool education would counteract the effect of a poor material environment. McMillan appreciated that little children cannot learn if they are unhealthy, she therefore specially designed all her efforts to improve their health. Her views were that once the children were restored to health, they were to be encouraged to respond to the instructive environment and the stimulating enrichment programme laid down for them. Margaret McMillan has left her mark on the current early childhood practice and many of her ideas on parental involvement, teacher education, continuity and progression are as relevant today as they were more than half a century ago (Curtis, 1986, 1998).

The ECCDE Project in Nigeria

The ECCDE interventions during the 1987–1990 pilot period were guided by the following objectives:

- Increase accessibility of childcare and preschool education for majority of pre-school children in Nigeria;
- Strengthen the role of parents and communities for the development and education of young children at home;
- Cater for the crucial developmental needs of children in the preschool phase;
- Develop a system based on early childhood centres, to address the wider needs of women at community level in preparing them for motherhood, improving their child rearing skills and their understanding of children's growth and development needs.

Promote, through the growth of alternative early childhood services, employment opportunities for young women, halting the drift to the city (UNICEF, 1993).

This pilot experience revealed the significance of community participation in planning meaningful interventions, which was necessary for programme sustainability. The project succeeded in establishing 45 centres which served a total of 10,250 children between birth and six years trained 170 ECCDE personnel including caregivers, mothers, older siblings, NGO leaders and preschool teachers (FGN/UNICEF MPO, 1991). Findings of the evaluation of the pilot project also revealed acceptability of the project and recognition of the positive effect of the intervention on the child and the community. UNICEF also reported that children from these centres who eventually got into the primary school were performing better academically than their peers who did not go through the ECCDE centres (UNICEF, 1993).

Based on the pilot experience and in line with the Jomtien framework for action on education for all, the ECCDE project formed the foundation of the Basic Education programme in the 1991–1995 FGN/UNICEF Programme of Cooperation. According to the Master Plan of Operation (FGN/UNICEF, 1991: 237), the major thrust of the ECCDE project was to:

- improve the overall development of children under the age of six years;
- strengthen the structure for appropriate ECCDE interventions;
- reduce the shortage of trained personnel and the lack of adequate facilities;
- strengthen the provision of informal, low-cost, community-based pre-primary care and education in selected communities of the 46 focus local government areas of the country.

OUTPUT OBJECTIVES OF THE PROJECT

The activities of the ECCDE project were to benefit 142,000 children of preschool age in Nigeria. The output objectives of the project were to:

- set up 920 low-cost, community-based ECCDE centres;
- provide early stimulation through non-formal learning opportunities to 92,000 children aged between 3 and 5 years;
- support and promote health and nutrition services to 50,000 children under two years;
- train 5,000 child care providers and 700 trainers and supervisors in improved ECCDE techniques and practices;
- orient 2,000 personnel from existing day care centres (FGN/UNICEF, 1991: 237).

APPROACH

The project used the following approaches:

(1) community-based, low-cost approaches to focus on the physical, psycho-
    social and social and cognitive development of children aged under six
    years;
(2) supported and assisted the revision of different curricula to include
    components and messages relevant to early child care and development;
(3) assisted in introducing appropriate, standardised and affordable teaching
    and learning materials;
(4) assisted the government to develop and introduce a comprehensive
    certificated training course for ECCDE personnel in Nigeria; and
(5) Promoted awareness of the need for ECCDE and Public participation in
    planning and delivery of services to children of preschool age. The project
    implementation strategies were Advocacy and Mobilisation, Training,
    Establishment of centres, Monitoring and Promoting Community Develop-
    ment, and the Pre-Primary/Primary School linkage (FGN/UNICEF, 1991:
    238).

RESEARCH METHODOLOGY

The research study sets out to determine the extent to which the ECCDE
project has achieved its output objectives and the effect the project had on the
target group. The ex-post facto research design was used as the study was
carried out in retrospect. An Evaluation Model, the CIPP was used to structure
the type of data collected and the type of questions asked.

Stufflebeam (1971) postulates an evaluation model, which focuses attention
on Context, Input, Process and Product (CIPP Model) to provide relevant
information, to decision-makers. The CIPP approach, according to Stufflebeam, is based on the view that the most important purpose of evaluation is
not to prove but to improve. He sees evaluation as a tool by which to help make
programmes work better for the people they are intended to serve. This position
is consistent with those presented by Patton (1978); and by Cronbach et al.
(1980). Stufflebeam states that Context Evaluation involves the identification of
needs statement or programme objectives and the development and selection of
criterion measures through interviews or expert opinion, research and surveys.

Input evaluation focuses on an examination of various input strategies and resources; evaluating their strengths and weaknesses to develop strategies for reaching proposed objectives.

Process evaluation involves an assessment of project outcomes as they relate to project objectives, context, input and process of the project. The CIPP model stresses the clarification of goals and objectives and advocates structured observation as a means of discovering whether these goals and objectives have been achieved or not. Calder (1994) also noted that the advantage of the CIPP approach is its comprehensiveness. Based on the CIPP model, the researcher developed a theoretical framework to structure the evaluation of the ECCDE project in Nigeria.

In the model, the context was indicated by the ECCDE project objectives, the input included the various project strategies vis-à-vis, establishment of ECCDE Centres, awareness/mobilization, capacity building, community development, supply of materials and monitoring.

Process indicators included the quality of interaction between the children and the caregivers, the children and the environment, the community and the ECCDE centres and interaction among the project participants.

POPULATION

The population of the study consisted of all the ECCDE centres in the ten UNICEF – assisted States in Nigeria.

The 1991–1995 ECCDE Project operated in 10 UNICEF assisted States in Four Zones as follows:

Table 1. Zonal/State Distribution of the ECCDE Centres.

A – Zone (Enugu)	B-Zone (Ibadan)	C – Zone (Kaduna)	D – Zone (Bauchi)
Benue State	Ondo State	Kaduna State	Adamawa State
Cross River State	Osun State	Niger State	Bauchi State
	Oyo State		Taraba State

SAMPLING

The samples for this study were drawn from the four UNICEF zones covering the ten States by sampling as follows:

- 4 ECCDE UNICEF Zonal Education Officers
- 10 States ECCDE Focal Persons
- 128 Caregivers (using purposive sampling)
- Observation of a centre in a State
- 3 Policy makers/implementers
- UNICEF ECCDE National Coordinator
- All the children in the centres observed
- 10 communities including members of the communities.

INSTRUMENTATION

The following six instruments were developed by the researcher for the study:

(1) Questionnaire for the implementers of the ECCDE Project (QIEP)
(2) Questionnnaire for ECCDE State Focal Persons (QEFP)
(3) Questionnaire for ECCDE Caregivers (QEC)
(4) Centre/Child Observation Form (COF)
(5) Structured Interview Questions (SIQ) for UNICEF Officers
(6) Focus Group Discussion Questions for Parents (FGDQP)

The six instruments (QIEP, QEFP, QEC, COF, SIQ and FGDQP) were given to research and evaluation experts for content analysis, clarity, language level and editing. The instruments were modified based on the comments received from the experts. Further empirical validation was conducted on the instruments through administration to selected samples not included in the main study. The instruments were modified until they were found to be appropriate and there were no ambiguities. The COF was used on some samples not included in the main study and it had a reliability index of 0.96, using Cronbach alpha.

DATA COLLECTION

The researcher visited the ten states involved in the project for the administration of the questionnaire. The researcher worked with the Planning, Research and Statistics Departments of all the Ministries of Education in the ten States since these departments in the States coordinated the project.

The questionnaires for the state ECCDE focal persons were administered by the researcher in the ten states. The researcher also administered the questionnaires for the implementers of the project. The researcher conducted the interview for the UNICEF zonal education officers in Ibadan, Enugu and Bauchi, while the National ECCDE coordinator's interview was conducted in Lagos.

The centre/child observation forms (COFs) were administered by the researcher in the ten states and the parents in the communities where these forms were administered served as discussants in the Focus Group Discussions. The discussions were recorded on audio tapes and later analysed. The focal persons served as interpreters in the states where the researcher did not understand the language of the environment.

The researcher briefed all the focal persons in the ten states on how to administer the questionnaires for the ECCDE caregivers in each of the states, and the researcher administered some of the distribution in the communities visited. The questionnaires were left with the focal persons who administered them and the focal persons later mailed the questionnaires to the researcher.

The data for this study were collected over a period of three months. The questionnaires were however taken to the states by the researcher.

STATISTICAL ANALYSIS

The Statistical Package for Social Sciences (SPSS) was used for the data analysis. Results obtained from the instruments for each of the research questions were subjected to descriptive statistical analysis such as the mean, standard deviation, percentages, ranking and frequencies. The Friedman's test ranks k variables from 1 to k for each case, calculates the mean rank for each variable over all the cases and then calculates a test statistic with approximately a chi-square distribution.

The converging line of enquiry was used as an interpretation procedure to ensure convergent validity of results through the collection of different kinds of data on the same question and validating information obtained through interviews, by checking information from the field and checking through programme documents/reports for comparative analysis.

RESULTS AND DISCUSSIONS

To determine the extent, to which the project achieved its output objectives, the results were obtained and are shown in Table 2.

Table 2 shows the achieved output objectives of the 1991–1995 ECCDE Project in Nigeria. From the Table, it could be observed that only objective one was fully achieved during the 1991–1995 ECCDE Project. More centres were established than the targeted number (108%). This situation was attributed to political instability in the country that led to frequent changes in administration especially at the local government level. This had a great influence on this project as all the chairmen wanted centres in their communities, not minding

Table 2. Achieved Output Objectives of the 1991–1995 ECCDE Project.

	Objectives	Targeted No	Achieved
1.	Set up 920 low cost, community based ECCDE centres	920	995 (108%)
2.	Provide early stimulation through non-formal learning opportunities to 92,000 children aged between 3 and 5 years	92,000	78,151 (84%)
3.	Support and promote health and nutrition services to 50,000 children aged under two years	50,000	No record
4.	Train 5,000 childcare providers in improved ECCDE techniques and practices	5,000	1,879 (37.5%)
4a.	Train 700 trainers and supervisors in improved ECCDE techniques and practices	700	221 (31.6%)
5.	Orient 2,000 personnel from existing daycare centres	2,000	205 (10.3%) (Figures from 5 states. Others had no records).

whether the community could sustain it or not. However, in spite of the surplus in the number of centres established during this period, the project was not able to meet the targeted number of children expected to have benefited from the project (84%).

The actual figure for objective number three could not be determined because all the ten states did not have separate records for children under three years. The researcher however found some children below three years, some centres had up to about fifty children below three years.

Less than half of the targets for trained caregivers and supervisors were achieved (37.6% and 31.6% respectively). This had been due to non-approval of planned activities and inadequate funds as reported by the implementing and the funding agencies respectively. The project also recorded a very low achievement in the number of trained personnel from existing daycare centres (10.3%) even though the figures used were collected from five states. Five states had no record for this objective.

At the end of the project, it was found that the project had succeeded in sensitising the communities in the selected states through the integrated approach adopted in the implementation of the project. Many of the communities in the focus states now have ECCDE centres. The project operated in 71 LGAs as against 46 stated in the MPO. Other achievements of the project are as follows:

- The project was also found to have increased enrolment in primary schools.
- Children are better prepared for formal schooling.
- Children socialise better and integrate better with people and their environment.
- Improved health of the children was also recorded.
- Parents have more time for their work, which was found to have increased family income and eventually led to improved standards of living.
- The communities had improved access to social amenities among others.

Some of the constraints to the project, according to the participants included lack of commitment on the part of the government, lack of counterpart funds, inadequate infrastructures, inadequate supply of stimulation materials, political instability in the country, inadequate monitoring and evaluation, poor system of fund disbursement and too much interference by the funding agency, inadequate record keeping procedure, lack of coordination between the states and the implementers due to lack of clearly defined role identification and improper communication flow among others (Obisanya, 1998). However in spite of the shortcoming, the ECCDE project was a laudable project. The communities were happy with the project and wanted it to continue.

CHALLENGES OF EARLY YEARS EDUCATION IN NIGERIA

Having achieved so much within five years in spite of all the obstacles, I think it is high time for us as a country to determine what we want for our children without necessarily relying on any agency to do it for us. We can seek support no doubt but I think we should first of all sit down and review our policies on early years services if we actually believe that these children are our future. We should remember that our goal should be to build children's capacities to become fully participating members of the society. We should therefore target their whole development; their nutrition and health status, their environmental supports, the love and nurturing they receive, their opportunities to play, explore, learn, interact with materials, solve problems and participate in their communities, knowing that life long capacity rests on the first several years.

The time is now ripe for us to review our policies with the aim of providing a comprehensive early years service that will cater for all children without distinction of gender, social class, religion or of any other kind. The idea of leaving early years services to the private sector cannot guarantee all of this. There should be equal opportunities to all children irrespective of where they live or who their parents are. Government should therefore invest money in early years education. The Jomtien declaration affirmed that learning begins at birth thus it is important to realise that education begins then too. While a focus on primary education is very important, six is too late to start paying attention to children's learning needs. Researches have shown that by the time a child reaches school age, most key brain wiring, language abilities, physical capabilities and cognitive foundations have been set in place (Brierley, 1987, 1993 and Evans, 1998. See also chapter 1 in this volume.).

In supporting young children, it is especially important to recognise that parents are the child's first teachers. Supporting and educating parents will be a very effective education strategy. Children live within a context; the family, community, cultures; their needs are most effectively addressed in relation to this context. Support to the family and community has a lot of advantages to children. The early years service should be responsive to particular local needs and demands (See chapter 4 of this volume).

While it is accepted that quality childcare programmes do positively affect development, a more complex concern is the potential for negative impacts of poor quality programmes on a child's development. It is particularly important to raise questions of quality in conjunction with increased demand for services. Government documents (NERC, 1980; FGN/UNICEF, 1991) had reported so many times that most of the existing preschools and daycare programmes had paid little attention to the health, nutrition, psycho-social and cognitive aspects of child development. Many of the privately owned centres were found to be ill-organised, exploitative, predominantly urban-based and accessible only to families with incomes above the average. Having noticed all these problems, what have they done about it? While quality is a complex, culturally defined, and relative concept, policy makers and practitioners must begin to generate standard categories and components of quality against which early years provisions can be measured.

In receiving the essential components of high quality care generated by the large body of existing data, several components have been consistently indicated and listed as follows:

- Developmentally appropriate curriculum that features child initiated learning activities within a supportive environment;
- Careful selection of staff with an ongoing strategy for in-service and on site training. Research has established that compared with formal education,

child-related training or experience is a strong predictor of caregivers' effectiveness;
- Attention to appropriate staff/child ratios;
- Ability of programmes to engage and establish partnership with parents and the community, empowering them with access information and an opportunity to internalise positive child-rearing practices;
- Strong administrative support with direct provision of or linkages to comprehensive services such as health and nutrition;
- Effective evaluation and monitoring procedures allowing staff to monitor and observe children's progress. Evaluation data should be available, providing feedback to strengthen operations, understand constraints, and foster the development of effective solutions (Schweinhart, 1987).

There is the need to have common objectives, based on societal values that all services must conform with and build into their definition of quality.

CONCLUSION

This paper has discussed the early years intervention project in Nigeria; the issues, progress, problems and challenges faced by early years services in Nigeria and the way forward. There is an urgent need to do something immediately to avert serious problems in future. We need to value our children and provide opportunities for their full development in an environment that reflects and respects their individual identity, culture and heritage. Even though these children are about 20% of Nigeria's population now, they are 100% of our future.

REFERENCES

Barker, W. (1987). *Early Childhood Care and Education: The Challenge*. The Hague: Bernard van Leer Foundation Occasional Paper no. 1, January.

Beckley, S. (1994). *The Nigerian Child in the Twenty-First Century – Problems and Prospects*. Keynote Address presented at the ECAN Conference, Lagos.

Brierley, J. (1987). *Give me a Child Until he is Seven*. Brain Studies & Early Childhood Education, London: The Falmer Press.

Brierley, J. (1993). *Growth In Children*. London: Cassell.

Calder, J. (1994). *Programme Evaluation and Quality: a comprehensive guide to setting up an evaluation system*. London: Kogan Page.

Curtis, A. M. (1986, 1998). *A Curriculum for the Pre-school Child: Learning to Learn*. Windsor: NFER/Nelson.

Evans, J. (1998). Effectiveness: the state of the art. In: *Early Childhood Matters*. The Bulletin of Bernard van Leer Foundation, February, No 88.

Federal Republic of Nigeria (1981). *National Policy on Education* (Revised). Lagos: FRN.

FGN/UNICEF (1991). *Master Plan of Operations for the 1991–1995 Programme of Cooperation.* Lagos: FRN.

FGN/UNICEF (1993). *National Report of the Situation and Policy Analysis of Basic Education in Nigeria.* Lagos: FRN.

King, F., & Burgess, A. (1993). *Nutrition for Developing Countries* (2nd ed.). Oxford: Oxford University Press.

Moss, P., & Penn, H. (1996). *Transforming Nursery Education.* London: Paul Chapman.

Neaum, S., & Tallack, J. (1997). *Good Practice in Implementing the Pre-school Curriculum.* Cheltenham: Stanley Thornes.

NERC (1980). Perspectives of Quantities and Qualities in Nigerian Education, A synthetic Report of the Bagauda Seminar.

Obisanya, O. (1998). An Evaluation of the Early Childcare Development and Education Project in Nigeria. An unpublished Ph.D. Thesis of the University of Ibadan.

Pascal, C., & Bertram, T. (Eds) (1997). *Effective Early Learning: Case Studies in Improvement.* London: Hodder/Paul Chapman.

Patton, M. Q. (1978). *Utilization-focused evaluation.* Beverly Hills: Sage.

Schweinhart, L. (1987). *When the Buck Stops Here: what it takes to run Good Early Childhood Programmes.* Ypsilanti, Michigan: High/Scope Educational Research Foundation.

Stufflebeam, D. L. (1971). *Educational evaluation and decision making.* New York: Phi Delta Kappa National Study Committee on Evaluation.

World Conference on Education for All (1990). *Meeting Basic Learning Needs: A vision for the 1990s.* Background Documents. New York: World Conference on Education for All/ United Nations.

UNICEF (1990). *Progress and Achievement in ECCDE in Nigeria.* New York: UNICEF.

UNICEF (1993). *Early Childhood Development: The Challenge and The Opportunity.* New York: UNICEF.

UNICEF (1996). *Situation Analysis on Basic Education in Nigeria.* New York: UNICEF.

7. EARLY CHILDHOOD CARE AND EDUCATION: STAFF TRAINING AND QUALIFICATIONS – MARKERS OF QUALITY?

Pamela Calder

INTRODUCTION

This chapter will argue that the training and education of those who look after our children is an essential aspect of the 'quality' of provision. But we need to explore this position in more detail.

SETTING THE CONTEXT

Definitions of what is meant by 'early childhood', by 'care' and by 'education' vary between countries and within countries. For the purposes of this chapter I shall be defining early childhood as the years from birth to the beginning of compulsory schooling. In Western Europe this varies from five years old in Britain to seven years old in Denmark, Finland and Sweden, with the majority starting compulsory education at six (Wintersberger, 1999).

Similarly there are differences between and within countries in the way in which early childhood care and education is conceptualised and relating to this, the ways in which provision is organised. These differences relate to both the purpose of provision and the ages of children. Often different groups may use the same terms but may have different understandings of their meanings. Thus

Promoting Evidence-based Practice in Early Childhood Education:
Research and its Implications, Volume 1, pages 131–148.
2001 by Elsevier Science Ltd.
ISBN: 0-7623-0753-6

where, historically, as in Britain, state nursery education has only been available for children over two, discussion of early childhood education is often interpreted as only applying to these older age groups, not to babies and toddlers, while care is seen as a parallel provision usually unrelated to education. Historically in Britain state provided care has only been available for children seen to be at risk, unlike much of the rest of Europe where it has been available for children of dual working parents.

Other major possibilities of misunderstanding arise because of unrecognised assumptions about the different structures of provision of care and education including: assumptions about the hours of opening and whether provision is provided part time or full time; the structure of the children's groups, that is whether they are organised into groups of similar or mixed ages; and the number of children in a group compared to the number of staff responsible for the group. The first of these differences, the number of hours available, is most likely to be related to the presumed purpose of the provision and whether it is seen as a short term or part time complement to the full time care of the mother, or, if educational, whether it is seen again as a part time complementary or compensatory addition to care being provided elsewhere, usually once again presumed to be by the mother.

Such difficulties, of understanding, arise because of the different histories of provision and the different conceptualisations and values underlying the purposes of provision, which can also be linked to differences in the training, and qualifications of staff. Examples of such differences can be drawn from Europe.

The U.K. is relatively unusual in having had parallel structures of care and education, such that where children are in state regulated provision (group care), children from three to compulsory school age at five could be cared for by staff with two year, further education qualifications gained after the age of 16; while alternatively, children of the same age could be receiving nursery education from nursery teachers with at least a four year higher education qualification (BEd or BA plus PGCE) taken after successfully completing secondary education (two or three A-levels) at the age of 18 plus.

This contrasts with much of the rest of Europe where the main divide occurs at the age of three, with children below this age more likely to be 'cared' for by less well trained staff, while children over three are usually in provision labelled as some version of nursery 'education' where the staff are better qualified and regarded as teachers.

The Scandinavian countries, Denmark, Sweden and Finland, provide an exception to both the U.K.'s situation of parallel systems and the rest of Europe's consecutive pattern, by providing integrated childcare provision of care and education from birth or soon after, till compulsory school at seven, six. And this integration is followed through in there being one, (in Denmark and Sweden), major training for qualified staff in the early childhood centres (Oberhuemer & Ulich, 1997). In Scandinavia this training takes place in higher education.

In Denmark the educators have a three and a half year higher education course equivalent to at least a bachelors degree. (Entry qualifications include successful completion of secondary education, and experience of childcare). They are described as social pedagogues, rather than teachers, (teachers being seen as having different aims (and currently different training, and regulated by a different government department) (Oberhuemer & Ulich, 1997). In Sweden they have a similar system of one major qualification for those working in childcare centres, in this case, a three-year university degree for nursery teachers, which is studied at the same university level institutions where primary school teachers are trained and which is a qualification for working with children from birth to compulsory school age. In Finland too, since 1995, initial training as early years educators is at university level (Oberhuemer & Ulich, 1997)

In terms of values these countries differ in the explicit ways in which the early childhood educators are trained and the government departments by which they are regulated, Social Services in Denmark and Finland, Education in Sweden, but they share a philosophy of comprehensive, integrated provision, They have seen the provision of early childhood care and education as an issue of gender equality. Finland has perhaps gone furthest in making it a right, since 1996, for all children from birth to have a place in a childcare centre, Biaudet (1999).

France has long had extensive free nursery education, École Maternelles, for children aged two and over, for which the staff have had teaching qualifications. The qualification is a two-year professional training following a three year university degree. Recent changes include more two year olds entering écoles maternelles and thus those working with younger children are increasingly expected to have the same qualifications as those working with three to five year olds. Since1991–1992 the qualifications have been upgraded. The courses are longer and take place in higher education institutions with university status. France values comprehensive free early childhood education for all, as citizens.

In Spain recent educational reforms have identified the years from birth to six as the first cycle of three cycles of education, placed early childhood care and education under the Department of Education and identified the main qualification, for staff working in centres for children between birth and six, as a specialist early childhood teaching qualification. The training of staff includes specialist consideration of the different curricula required for children as babies, toddlers, three year olds, four years olds and five year olds. The values underlying the changes stemmed from the democratic reforms after the death of Franco.

Thus many European countries already expect degree level qualifications or are in the process of upgrading the qualifications of their educarers.

However values differ. Kaufman, a sociologist, cited by Wintersberger (1999) in a report for the European Commission has identified, seven different motivations for family policies and thus the policies that influence a state's provision of early childhood care and education. These include: valuing the family in itself, for securing the birth-rate, for its economic contribution, for contribution to society, and for children's well being, or as policies to combat disadvantage, for example the financial disadvantages caused by child related expenses and lastly by feminist policies stemming from the argument that such economic and social disadvantages hit women only. He explicitly identifies only the last of these as a feminist rationale. Wintersberger (1999) sums up the differences in values between countries as "Some consider child day-care an educational institution; for others, it is a care service; and a third group defines it as a place where children can display their creative potential" (1999: 19).

In Britain, the major differences the state has expected in the tasks of different kinds of childhood services have historically been related to social welfare, (publicly funded daycare institutions, day nurseries), or compensatory education, (nursery schools). This is in strong contrast to the French view of early childhood education as a right for all French citizens and to the Scandinavian view of early childhood care and education as both a service to redress gender inequality and also as a service good in itself for children's enjoyment and development.

HAVING TRAINED AND QUALIFIED STAFF IN EARLY CHILDHOOD INSTITUTIONS HAS OFTEN NOT BEEN THOUGHT IMPORTANT. WHY?

As we have seen, countries have different motivations for family policies and these can stem from differing values and beliefs and discourses. One such discourse is that women are 'natural carers'. Then, if women are seen as natural carers, training and education for early childhood staff (who from this perspective are also presumed to be women) is seen to be unnecessary.

In Britain, we have a long history of allowing untrained and unqualified people to look after our children, as au pairs, as childminders/ family day carers and as unqualified or minimally trained staff in various forms of early childhood provision, including preschool playgroups/learning centres. (And we have not been alone.)

But what is striking, but so taken for granted that it is overlooked, is that this labour force is overwhelmingly female. It is also generally taken for granted that women themselves regard this as desirable, in that, if they are not going to look after their children entirely by themselves or be looked after, exceptionally, by their children's father, they prefer to have their children looked after by another woman or women. Thus in the New Year millennium edition of the Independent on Sunday, in a pictorial review of 100 of "Britain's most successful women" the author (Boam, 2000) points to lack of childcare still being the major issue affecting women's achievement. She mentions without further comment women's willingness to accept low wages and conditions but also their preference for other women to look after their children.

In unpacking some of the implicit assumptions here we may be better able to understand the history to women's low paid or unpaid participation in caring roles relating to young children. Two assumptions are perhaps intertwined. One is that females are 'naturally', biologically, more nurturing than males and the other is that girl children are more likely to be socialised into being patient, helpful, thoughtful and attentive to the feelings of others. The first is a highly controversial and speculative hypothesis, currently being given a new airing by the new evolutionary psychology (Cronin & Curry, 2000). However there is some evidence of the second. Several American studies have shown that parents' reactions to even their very young children differ, according to the children's gender (Fagot, Beverly, 1985; Fagot & Leinbach, 1989; Fagot et al., 1992). However, how children are socialised is an empirical matter, where there is ample possibility of change over time, and one that is open to current investigation.

There is still a pervasive societal view that women do have some special interest and natural expertise in looking after children and such discourses also have their effect on women themselves. Thus new mothers, who themselves may have little knowledge or previous experience of young children may share society's view, that other women will automatically know how to look after them. As inexperienced mothers themselves, they may not be aware of the skills, knowledge and attitudes needed. They too may share the prevailing view that childcare is easy, low skilled work. They may want someone who will 'love' their child, but again share the common presumption that this is something most women will provide.

Studies that have been carried out into childminding or baby sitting or au pairing indicate that it is not so simple. Many childminders in Britain do so for a short period while their own children are young. They may stop minding with little notice. Thus there is little evidence for 'love' for the child influencing the minder to carry on with a longer-term relationship with the minded child. In fact turnover is high, about a third of minders each year, and many children who are minded have a history of having several different minders in a relatively short period of time. Also recent court cases in America and the U.K. involving au pairs or untrained nannies in charges of child abuse suggest that there are many potential problems and that young women do not 'naturally' have either interest in, or the skills to work with, young children. But perhaps the mothers themselves do not recognise the issue as one for the need for training and qualifications any more than the society, at large, does. This may be because once mothers themselves have become experienced and begin to recognise what is involved, their own children have grown up and it is no longer an urgent issue for them.

Staff training and qualifications were not seen as particularly significant by mothers according to a recent U.S. based review by Pungello and Kurtz-Costes (1999) of research relating to why and how working women in the U.S. chose child care. The reviewers accepted that high quality child care was not widely available in the U.S., and aimed to build a theoretical model that related mothers child care choices to environmental contexts, mothers' beliefs, child factors and demographic characteristics of the mother and also to make recommendations for further research and public policy considerations. They argued that many studies showed that 'parents believe that having their children cared for by a warm, loving, and competent caregiver is important', (Pungello & Kurtz-Costes, 1999: 68). However having a caregiver with specialist education did not seem to be given much importance by mothers. The majority of the mothers in a study of 820 children carried out by Kontos et al. (1995),

> gave some attribute of the caregiver as their first reason for choosing their care arrangement
> . . . but caregiver's education or specialized training was mentioned by very few (only three mothers out of the entire sample' cited by (Pungello & Kurtz-Costes, 1999: 69).

Because of this continuing willingness to accept untrained unqualified women to look after our children we have not looked clearly at what would be necessary for agreement on good quality early childhood education and care. But if we begin to imagine young men rather than young women looking after our children, we might begin to be able to see more plainly, what training, qualities, experience and qualifications we would want them to have.

But where such discourses are pervasive, research into what counts as 'good quality provision also often overlooks issues related to staff qualifications. And perhaps it is because of such attitudes that British and American research has not often directly focused on the training and qualifications of staff as an aspect of high quality provision.

For example, although Boocock (1995) in a review of the effects of provision in 13 countries concluded that the most positive outcomes had been found in countries with "a national policy of providing preschool services to all children and a tradition of ensuring the quality of those services through enforceable regulations" (P14), she did not focus on staff education and qualifications, as one of the possible major aspects of those regulations. This is so even though two of the three countries services which she mentions as providing good provision, the French Ecole Maternelles (Oberhuemer & Ulich, 1997: 86) and the Japanese Yochien, (Yamamoto), have highly (higher education trained) qualified staff.

The third she mentions, Reggio Emilia in Italy, does not, but Malaguzzi, the educational pioneer who developed the programmes of Reggio and who was the founder and director of the services, recognised this as a major deficiency and set out to change it, arguing 'We have no alternatives but in-service training' (Malaguzzi, 1993: 67).

Malaguzzi was scathing about the Italian system he was working within, writing, 'the preparation of teachers to work with young children is, I believe, a sort of legally sanctioned farce, really unspeakable' (Malaguzzi, 1993: 65). Thus in Reggio Emilia the deliberate attempt to remedy this lack of education and training by in service training means that six hours a week of the working week of 36 hours is non-contact time and available for continuing training, (Penn, 1997: 31). And recently Reggio Emilia have begun developing their own degree courses for educators (Dahlberg).

SUMMARY

It is perhaps in the Anglo-American tradition, and particularly where provision is identified as 'care' that the discourses of mothers as natural carers is most pervasive, and perhaps least attention is given to the education and training of staff.

In some of the European countries, where, provision is identified as educational, the educators, are more likely to be regarded as professional civil servants, and to have graduate or post graduate qualifications, as for example in France. In the European tradition, where emphasis has been put on professional training, it is usually because provision has been identified as educational or because there has been an explicit attempt to instigate gender equality in the society. And the greater the value placed on either children themselves or gender equality then the higher the professional qualifications (degree level) expected of the staff. There is some evidence that staff who feel themselves to be valued by the society in terms of the resources that they and the children can access will have a more positive relationship with the children (Whitebook et al., 1989).

We will argue that early childhood educarers should have degree level education and training. Can such arguments be backed by research?

ANSWERS FROM RESEARCH

There is a, mostly American, tradition of research into 'quality'. Certain features of the provision are identified, and then related to particular child outcomes. Usually the criteria chosen have been easily measurable structural features, such as staff child ratios or size of group, for example. The research into 'quality' has varied in the extent to which staff training and qualifications have been explored as an aspect of 'good' provision, but such research has not been extensive. One often has to infer information on the background, training and qualifications of the staff, from such studies.

The evidence we have includes that gained from some longitudinal, both longer and shorter-term studies and some cross sectional studies. The identified child outcomes tell us what values the researchers have. Mostly they have looked for cognitive achievements as indications of 'positive' outcomes. For younger children they have often looked for the possibility of 'negative' effects and looked for emotional damage. This second research tradition, stemming from attachment theory, has seldom related differences of outcome to differences in staff training and qualifications.

The High Scope/Perry pre-school study (Schweinhart & Weikart, 1993) in the USA followed children through till the age of 27. It showed that those who had experienced the High Scope curriculum had better life outcomes, did better in high school, were more likely to go on to further education were more likely to earn more, more likely to own a house, less likely to have been arrested, and less likely to come into contact with social services. It may be significant that the staff in the original study had postgraduate qualifications, even though the authors did not mention this as important for replicating the High Scope findings.

In Sweden, Andersson (1989, 1992) followed children to the age of 13 and showed that those, who had entered daycare before the age of one were found to do better in school and had better emotional adjustment. It may be relevant that Swedish childcare-teachers in nurseries have higher education qualifications.

Some short-term longitudinal studies have looked at the different cognitive, educational outcomes, in reading, numeracy, and literacy, of children who went to different kinds of early childhood provision. Sylva, in a review for the Start Right Report (Ball, 1994) summarises:

> Jowett and Sylva found that the children who had attended LEA nursery engaged in more purposeful and complex activity in the reception class than did the children who attended playgroup; they chose more 'demanding' educational activities. Nursery children were more likely than the playgroup children to initiate contacts with the teacher that were 'learning orientated' while the play group children approached teachers for help (Sylva in Ball, 1994: 88, citing Jowett & Sylva, 1986).

and

> a more tightly controlled study, carried out by Shorrocks et al. (1992) found that 'nursery' attendance led to better performance in English, Science and Mathematics (Sylva in Ball, 1994: 88).

In these studies staff qualifications were not directly measured and can only be inferred from the nature of the provision. However a new three year longitudinal study entitled 'Effective Provision of Pre-School Education', which Kathy Sylva is currently undertaking for the DfEE, aimed at relating child outcomes to differences in settings and quality of settings will directly relate staff qualifications to child outcomes. One of the variables included will be the qualifications of the staff (described in Anning & Edwards, 1999: 34; also discussed by Angela Phillips in the Guardian, 30th March 2000).

CROSS SECTIONAL, CONTEMPORANEOUS STUDIES

Interactions

More research has used a combination of short term longitudinal and cross sectional designs to look at staff process/interactions and link them with child outcomes. They have measured aspects of interactions such as staff responsiveness, and sensitivity. Much of this research has once again focussed on structural variables such as staff child ratio or size of group, but some of these studies have explicitly related early childhood training to the quality of the staff child interactions.

Research which has specifically looked at staff qualifications and training and shown that this has effects in terms of 'quality', include those of, Arnett (1989), Berk (1985), Ruopp et al. (1979), Whitebook et al. (1989), Tietze et al. (1998) and Howes (1997). These studies have indicated that the amount of ECE training that a 'teacher' has received is related to 'positive' caregiver behaviour.

In reviewing this research Carollee Howes (1997) herself American, has commented on how much of it has been American. Tietze, for example, was the only non-American source cited in a recent review by Cryer (1999). Howes commented on the implications of this for research into quality, since she argues few researchers and reviewers have put much emphasis on staff training and qualifications, possibly because the majority of early childhood staff in the States have little professional, higher level education and training, The average/ median education is 'some college courses' (Howes, 1997). Writing about 'quality', a decade earlier in 1987, she had already argued for teacher training's importance in relation to infant toddler childcare but recognised that in an American context this was highly unusual. She writes:

> Teacher training as a quality indicator of infant toddler childcare is probably the most controversial of the criteria selected for this study [a study which looked at differences between different childcare settings judged as high and low quality on three indicators] (Howes in Phillips, 1987: 82).

There has been little research that has looked directly at *what* training and education staff have. For example does it matter whether staff are graduates? Does it matter what the content of such training is?

Howes (1997) was unusual in carrying out a study that began to answer these questions and which attempted to differentiate between confounding variables. Most previous research, she argued, had regarded staff qualifications as a linear variable; that is researchers had noted whether staff had more or less training but they did not specify what qualifications or level of qualifications staff had. Previous research had not discriminated for example, between staff having taken some specialised courses, and the staff levels of education. Thus she distinguished between five different teacher background categories. These were

> (a) high school education plus a few workshop trainings in child development; (b) Child Development Associate; (c) some college course in early childhood education (ECE); (d) a 2-year associate of arts degree in ECE; and (e) a bachelor or more advanced degree in ECE (Howes, 1997: 407).

A Child Development Associate (CDA) is a practitioner who has undertaken the national inservice training programme based on experiential learning. Howes selected this because there was little research data evaluating this programme although it was often seen as a policy solution to child-care staffing.

Her study indicated differences in child outcomes related to these categories. The child outcomes, in terms of the complexity of their play with objects or the complexity of their play with other children depended on the specific levels and kinds of education of the staff. Staff relationships with the children also varied in the extent of their 'sensitivity' and 'responsiveness'. Those with BA degrees in early childhood education showed the most 'positive' outcomes in all these respects. They were the most sensitive and responsive and children in their classrooms showed both the most complex play with other children and with objects. Those with CDA qualifications were not regarded as significantly more responsive or sensitive, nor did the children in their classrooms show more complex play with objects, but like those in classrooms with staff with Bachelor of Arts ECE degrees they did show more complex play with peers (Howes, 1997).

Thus the outcomes did vary, depending on the kinds of levels and thus also presumably the content of the training and education of the staff.

But we need more information about the level and content of such qualifications before we can apply such research to other situations, to other courses, BA's etc, in other countries.

Thus, to summarise, from the research we have reviewed it seems that there are strong arguments that the training and qualifications of workers do have effects. They do make a difference. It does matter. However depending on the outcomes that we value for our selves and for our children then we need to know more about the content of the training and qualifications that we might want to value as indicators of quality.

CAN WE SAY MORE ABOUT COURSE CONTENT?

In 1989 Jeffrey Arnett had asked for more evaluations of the effects of different training after a study that he carried out in Bermuda had shown that important aspects of the content of training were knowledge of child development and teaching behavioural management techniques. But the content of training is still under specified in much research. Although Howes' (1997) research pointed to differences relating to categories of qualifications, and thus to differences in the content of the qualifications, there has been little evaluation which examines the curriculum content of courses from other differences, of level, or of coherence and quantity of different course units.

However early childhood practitioners in the U.S. and Britain tend to agree that child development training matters – for example the publication in Britain of 'Quality in Diversity' by a group of early childhood organisations, (ECEF, 1998) – and that child development content is central to the idea of developmentally appropriate practice (Bredekamp, 1987).

However there are challenges to the assumption that there is necessarily universal agreement about what are considered 'positive' child development outcomes.

The critiques are (1) that child development theory is often seen as having universal validity where the evidence on which the theories are based may in effect be culturally specific and its universal validity is simply speculation and (2) that the implementation of particular kinds of working practices with children is justified by reference to child development theories as value free, neutral 'scientific' evidence without recognising the possible contextual basis to such theories or the different values that can be held with regard to what counts as appropriate development.

For example critics, such as Martin Woodhead (1999) argue that the hegemony of the United States as an economic world power has also meant that it has influence in other areas; that many countries in their childcare services mimic the practices of the U.S.; and that these practices are derived from 'theories of child development' and notions of 'developmentally appropriate practice', in circumstances which may not be appropriate for them. Thus the two critiques are embedded in such arguments. One concerns the status of supposedly value neutral theories of child development. The other concerns whether the concept of 'developmentally appropriate practice' can be generalised to different contexts.

The argument is that developmental psychology and child development can only provide theoretical perspectives, not 'proof', or incontrovertible 'facts'. The wider the cultural contexts in which research is undertaken, (rather than the U.S. or Britain) the greater the possibilities appear that there can be more than one route to 'development' or the concept of 'development' itself is challenged. For example research suggests that other societies can provide different 'developmental niches' (Super & Harkness, 1977, 1999) where parents behave quite differently from parents in the West; the Kaluli in the tropical rain forest of Papua New Guinea turn their babies to face outwards towards others and speak for them, rather than using 'motherese', 'babytalk', directed at the child, in the child centred way widely thought to be important for the development of language (Schieffelin & Ochs, 1999).

Different communities have different aspirations for their societies and their children. They can have different values concerning both adult and children's behaviour and different expectations for how their children should behave as part of that society. The Nso for example, place great importance on, children's respect for elders, on obedience and responsibility taking (Nsamenang & Lamb, 1999).

Closer to 'home', 'modern' industrialised nations can provide examples of different belief systems and values. A child's behaviour in a Japanese nursery school 'Yochien' can be given diametrically opposed interpretations by Japanese and American observers (Tobin Wu & Davidson, 1989). An American commentator on the world renowned nurseries in Reggio Emilia, described the different views of Italian and American practitioners concerning what counted as 'good' practice, in such aspects as organizational structure, teacher's role, and teaching strategies (New, 1993).

We can explore the example of Reggio Emilia. In terms of organisational structure there were differences over what counts as an appropriate staff child ratio: In Reggio, asked whether they would like more staff, the typical response was 'We'd rather have more space!'. New (1993) argued they strongly believed that "too many adults preclude opportunities for children to utilize and learn from each other". There are different beliefs concerning how long the same teachers should stay with children; teachers in Reggio are expected to stay together with the same children for three years. In contrast, U.S. professionals are advised to acquire age related experience (Bredekamp, 1987) and we are told that American parents express reservations about their child spending too much time with any one teacher (New, 1993).

There are major differences relating to concepts of the individual and the value of group membership. It is regarded as important in Reggio that children should gain a strong sense of group membership. They believe 'A child can't develop a good sense of self, isolated from other people. Children acquire an identity in the context of their group' (Sergio Spaggiari personal communication June 1986, cited in New, 1993: 219).

Lilian Katz, Malaguzzi, New, and Dahlberg have all commented on the teacher's role in Reggio. Teacher's have a concept of child as competent, the 'strong' child and the 'rich' child, Dahlberg et al. (1999). The curriculum is both child centred and (often) teacher directed – Vygotskian rather than Piagetian (Malaguzzi, 1993).

The emphasis is on the teachers being researchers alongside the children, more knowledgeable in some respects, but not in all. Katz (1993) comments:

> Comparing Reggio Emilia pre-primary schools and those I typically see in North America suggested to me that one way the quality of a preschool program can be evaluated is to examine the content of adult-child relationships. A program has intellectual vitality if the teacher's individual and group interactions are mainly about what the children are learning, planning, and thinking about their work, play, and each other, and only minimally about the rules and routines (Katz, 1993: 30).

There are different beliefs concerning teaching strategies. In Reggio one aspect of the importance given to group membership is that as group members, children can hear multiple points of view. They are encouraged to disagree, and debate.

New disagrees with the American view, citing Edwards et al. (1986), that American preschool teachers give a high priority to children's social relations and each child's social development. She argues that the American inter-pretation of promoting social development means that strategies are 'mostly aimed at promoting children's social competencies in ways that promote the individual rather than group. Thus there is little tolerance for arbitration once 'please' and 'thank-you' have been said.' (New, 1993: 219). She believes (citing Slavin, 1985; Whitworth, 1988) American educators are ambivalent about the value of the group, arguing they are particularly sceptical of co-operative strategies when they relate to academic performance.

Thus there is evidence to suggest that child development training can make a difference to the way in which educarers relate to children but there is also evidence that there can be differences between and probably within countries on the ways that different teaching strategies aims for children's development are evaluated. Thus training and qualifications do make a difference but the values we have will influence what implications we draw from it.

Only so much can be concluded from existing research. We need more research which starts from different premises: that training and qualifications are important and that we should be exploring the effects of change, improvement, not just researching the status quo. Thus we need action research that will help us evaluate our new innovations. This is the position that we would argue we are in, in Britain today.

THE POSITION IN BRITAIN?

As we argued earlier the different structure of training that exist in Britain stem from policies which divide care and education, and which implicitly assume that 'care' is women's business and 'naturally' so. Education has been regarded as more 'professional' in as much as it has been associated with older (school age) children and separated from care.

It was to try to change both the structures and content of training, from a feminist position which values children, that new early childhood studies degrees were pioneered in the 1990s. The values underlying these degrees included having a vision of an integrated early childhood service where workers would be educarers, (integrated teachers, caregivers, and play/leisure-workers) which would combine care and education for children from birth, which would be healthy, enjoyable and educative for children, and which would support the needs of all parents, and contribute towards increasing gender equity; providing an education and training for workers in such a service; providing a research base for the development of new knowledge and practice; and providing a base in the universities for greater knowledge of early childhood theories and practices and early childhood services to inform the wider society (politicians, lawyers, doctors and journalists and practitioners themselves).

The ECS degrees were envisaged as providing a reflective, critical, research led, approach to the study and practice of early childhood work. Even though they are not required in this country for child-face workers/practitioners, they were the kind of degree level training that we believed would ideally provide a good basis for practitioners.

As we have seen existing research can only go so far in supporting such a position. Because there can be different interpretations of what parents and societies consider important I would argue that this is a reason to make such conflict of meaning explicit as part of the content of a such a degree.

FINALLY: MARKERS OF QUALITY – A MATTER OF VALUES?

Thus to view training and qualifications as markers of quality is a matter of values. We have argued that staff should be trained, and that training and qualifications matter and that this argument can be linked to how we view our children and how we view women. For women it can be a matter of social justice. We can argue that staff should be graduates, as there is no reason why early childhood care and education is not a professional field of work. We should not have to defend this position. Instead one should have to answer a different question, why not? Why are young children not seen as needing permanent graduate staff when they are regarded as essential for older learners?

To specify what the content of such training and qualifications should be is also related to issues of values. What are our aspirations for our children as adults in a future society? What kind of life do we believe that they and their parents (mothers and fathers) should live now?

We need to be explicit about different values, since, as we have argued, the kind of content of training that we might consider an indicator of quality, depends on what outcomes we want for our children. Do we want an emphasis on: democratic children as in Reggio Emilia; the ability to relate to others, looking after the environment, as in Sweden; telling stories, acting, singing, skating and swimming as in Denmark; or counting, reading and writing as is currently promoted in Britain?

We can conclude that research is necessary but is not sufficient in helping us answer these questions.

REFERENCES

Andersson, B. E. (1989). Effects of public daycare; a longitudinal study. *Child Development, 60*, 857–866.

Andersson, B. E. (1992). Effects of daycare on cognitive and socioemotional competence of thirteen-year-old Swedish schoolchildren. *Child Development, 63*, 20–36.

Anning, A., & Edwards, A. (1999). *Promoting Children's Learning from Birth to Five*. Buckingham: Open University Press.

Arnett, J. (1989). Caregivers in Day-Care Centers: Does Training Matter? *Journal of Applied Developmental Psychology, 10*, 541–542.

Ball, C. (1994). *Start Right: The Importance of Early Learning*. London: R.S.A.

Biaudet, E. (1999). Conference Opening address at EECERA European Early Childhood Education Research conference, Minister of Health and social Services The Finnish government welcoming address 1 September Helsinki).

Boam, E. (2000). Women on Top: Success at last. *The Independent on Sunday, Sunday Review*, (2nd January), 4–16.

Boocock, S. S. (1995). *Early childhood Programs in Other Nations; Goals and Outcome the Future of Children, 5*(3, Winter) (http://www.futureofchildren.org/lto/05_lto.htm).

Bredekamp, S. (Ed.) (1987). *Developmentally appropriate Practice in Early Childhood Programs, serving children from birth through age 8*. Washington, D.C.: National Association for the Education of Young Children (NAEYC).

Cronin, H., & Curry, O. (2000). Pity Poor Men. *The Guardian*, (February), 24.

Cryer, D., Tietze, W., Burchinal, M., Leal, T., & Palacios, J. (1999). Predicting Process quality from Structural Quality in Preschool Programs: A Cross-Country comparison *Early Childhood Research Quarterly, 14*(3), 339–361.

Dahlberg, G., Moss P., & Pence, A. (1999). *Beyond Quality Early Childhood Education and Care: Postmodern Perspectives*. London: Falmer.

David, T. (Ed.) (1993). *Educational Provision for our Youngest Children: European Perspectives*. London: Paul Chapman.

Edwards, C., Gandini, L., & Forman, G. (Eds) (1993). *The Hundred Languages of Children*. New York: Ablex Publishing Corporation.

Fagot, B. L. (1978). The influence of sex of child on parental reactions to toddler children. *Child Development, 49*, 459–465.

Fagot, B. L. (1985). Changes in Thinking about Early Sex Role Development. *Developmental Review, 5*, 83–98.

Fagot B. I., & Leinbach M. D. (1989). The young child's gender schema. Environmental input internal organization. *Child Development, 60*, 63–67.

Fagot, B. I., Leinbach, M. D., & Boyle, C. (1992). Gender labeling, gender stereotyping, and parenting behaviors. *Developmental Psychology, 28*, 225–230.

Goutard, M. (1993). Preschool Education in France. In: T. David (Ed.), *Educational Provision for our Youngest Children: European Perspectives* (pp. 35–56). London: Paul Chapman.

Howes, C. (1997). Children's Experiences in Center-Based Child Care as a Function of Teacher Background and Adult: Child Ratio. *Merrill-Palmer Quarterly Journal of Developmental Psychology, 43*(3), 405–425.

Jowett, S., & Sylva, K. (1986). Does kind of pre-school matter? *Educational Research, 28*(1), 21–31.

Katz, L. (1993). What Can we Learn from Reggio Emilia? In: C. Edwards, L. Gandini & G. Forman (Eds), *The Hundred Languages of Children*. New York: Ablex Publishing Corporation.

Katz, L. (1996). Child Development Knowledge and Teacher Preparation: Confronting Assumptions. *Early Childhood Research Quarterly, 11*, 135–146.

Lubeck, S. (1996). Deconstructing 'child development knowledge' and 'teacher preparation'. *Early Childhood Research Quarterly, 11*, 147–167.

Lutz, W. (1999). Will Europe be Short of Children? Family Observer: Equality between women and men 10th Anniversary. Employment & social affairs series. Luxembourg: European Commission.

Mental Health Foundation (1999). *Bright Futures*. London: Peter Wilson.

Malaguzzi, L. (1993). History, ideas and basic philosophy. In: C. Edwards, L. Gandini & G. Forman (Eds), *The Hundred Language of Children* (pp. 41–90). Ablex Publishing Corporation.

Moss, P., & Pence, A. (1994). *Valuing Quality in Early Childhood Services: new approaches to defining quality*. London: Paul Chapman.

Moss, P., & Penn, H. (1996). *Transforming Nursery Education*. London: Paul Chapman.

Nsamenang, A. B., & Lamb, J. M. (1999). Socialisation of Nso children in the Bamenda Grassfields of Northwest Cameroon. In: M. Woodhead, D. Faulkner & K. Littleton (Eds), *Cultural Worlds of Early Childhood* (pp. 250–261). London: Routledge/Open University.

New, R. (1993). Cultural Variations of developmentally Appropriate Practice: Challenges to Theory and Practice. In: C. Edwards, L. Gandini & G. Forman (Eds), *The Hundred Languages of Children* (pp. 215–231). Ablex Publishing Corporation.

Oberhuemer, P., & Ulich, M. (1997). *Working with Young Children in Europe: Provision and Staff Training*. London: Paul Chapman.

Penn, H. (1997). *Comparing Nurseries Staff and Children in Italy, Spain and the U.K.* London: Paul Chapman.

Phillips, D. (1987). *Quality in childcare: What does research tell us?*. Washington, D.C.: National Association for the Education of Young Children.

Pungello, E. P., & Kurtz-Costes, B. (1999). Why and How Working Women Choose Child Care; A Review with a Focus on Infancy. *Developmental Review, 19*, 31–96. Online at httpp:/ www.idealibrary.com.

Rogoff, B. (1990). *Apprenticeship in Thinking: Cognitive Development in Social Context*. New York: Oxford University Press.

Rogoff, B., & Morelli, G. (1989). Perspectives on children's development from cultural psychology. *American Psychologist, 44*(20), 43–348.

Rogoff, B. (1993). *Guided participation in cultural activity by toddlers and caregivers*. Chicago, Illinois: University of Chicago Press, Monographs of the Society for Research in Child Development (Vol. 58).

Rogoff, B., Mosier, C., Mistry, J., & Goncu, A. (1999). Toddlers' guided participation with their caregivers in cultural activity. In: M. Woodhead, D. Faulkner & K. Littleton (Eds) *Cultural Worlds of Early Childhood* (pp. 225–250). London: Routledge/Open University.

Ruopp, R., Travers, J., Glantz, F., & Coelen, C. (1979). *Children at the center: Final results of the national day care study*. Cambridge, MA: Abt Associates.

Schieffelin, B. B., & Ochs, E. (1999). A cultural perspective on the transition from prelinguistic to linguistic communication. In: M. Woodhead, D. Faulkner & K. Littleton (Eds), *Cultural Worlds of Early Childhood* (pp. 48–64). London: Routledge/Open University.

Schweinhart, L. J., & Weikart, D. (1993). *A summary of significant benefits: The High Scope/Perry pre-school study through age 27*. Ypsilanti, Michigan: High Scope U.K.

Shorrocks, D., Daniels, S., Frobisher, L., Nelson, N., Waterson, A., & Bell, J. (1992). *ENCA 1 project: The Evaluation of National Curriculum Assessment at Key Stage 1*. Leeds: School of Education University of Leeds.

Super, C., & Harkness, S. (1986). The developmental niche; a conceptualisation at the interface of child and culture. *International Journal of Behavioural Development, 9*, 545–569.

Sylva, K. (1994). Appendix C The Impact of Early Learning on children's Later Development. In: C. Ball (Ed.), *Start Right: The Importance of Early Learning* (pp. 84–96). London: RSA.

Tietze, W., Bairrao, J., & Rossbach, H. (1998). Assessing quality characteristics of center-based early childhood environments in Germany and Portugal: A cross-national study. *European Journal of Psychology of Education, XIII*(2), 283–298.

Whitebook, M., Howes, C., & Phillips, D. (1990). *Who cares? Child care teachers and the quality of care in America. Final report of the National Child Care Staffing Study*. Oakland, CA: Child Care Employee Project.

Woodhead, M., Faulkner, D., & Littleton, K. (Eds) (1999). *Cultural Worlds of Early Childhood*. London: Routledge/Open University.

Woodhead, M. (1999). Towards a Global Paradigm for Research into Early Childhood Education. *European Early Childhood Education Research Journal, 7*(1), 5–22.

SECTION III:

CURRICULUM MATTERS

8. CONSTRUCTING THE EARLY CHILDHOOD CURRICULUM: THE EXAMPLE OF DENMARK

Stig Broström

In Denmark pedagogues (teachers in early childhood education) currently use the concept curriculum only with reservation. They have a strong feeling that early childhood education has to be something quite different from education in school. Early childhood education is rooted in a tradition going back to Rousseau, Pestalozzi, and Froebel (1826). Further, its foundations lie in a critical movement exemplified by work of the Danish priest and philosopher Grundtvig and in the general progressive wave early in the 20th century, expressed, among others, by *New Education Fellowship's congress in Denmark in 1929*. Together these approaches make up a background containing concepts as child-orientation, self-activity and self-development.

The concept *development* is related to this tradition of early childhood. Basing their work on humanistic psychology, Danish pedagogues generally believe that a rich environment will give the best opportunities for the child's comprehensive development, defined as an externalisation of the child's self. The realisation of the self is thought to come into effect through the child's self-governed activity. Consequently education in daycare centres/kindergartens is viewed as activity-based. Firstly *play*, but also *practical-aesthetic* activities (e.g. music, dance, drawing, painting) are seen as the most important activities through which individual children create themselves – and thus language, imagination, social and communicative skills will be developed. However, in order to develop the self, the child has also to interact with an

Promoting Evidence-based Practice in Early Childhood Education:
Research and its Implications, Volume 1, pages 151–170.
Copyright © 2001 by Elsevier Science Ltd.
All rights of reproduction in any form reserved.
ISBN: 0-7623-0753-6

adult, who is able to understand the child, to interpret the child's need, and in accordance with these, create the environment through which to act and develop oneself. That is to say an empathic adult to whom the child has a secure attachment (e.g. Howes & Hamilton, 1992). In other words, the relationship is to be an equal relationship, a subject-subject relation. Further, individual children construct themselves in a comprehensive and optimum way when the pedagogue creates a stimulating setting, and when he or she is available to the child and expresses a positive attitude.

The conclusion to such a view of early pedagogy might seem to be that there is no need to formulate a central curriculum. On the other hand the lack of a formulated policy on early childhood education could also be seen as disparaging the importance of the early years.

THE STATUS OF EARLY CHILDHOOD EDUCATION

In fact, during the whole of the 20th century in general there was very little interest in curriculum work relating to early childhood provision in Denmark. Neither the Ministry of Social Affairs, nor the local municipalities have taken initiatives in order to make work with young children in daycare centres, preschools and kindergartens visible. In comparison with public interest in school matters, there has been no public interest in aims, content or principles concerning early childhood education.

Instead of a central curriculum there have only been a few very general guidelines on which pedagogues and parents should base and create their own curriculum. So the *Circular of Day-offers for Children and Youth* from 1990 suggests 'In collaboration with parents, the daycare centre should create such conditions, that encourage the children's development, well-being, and independence'. A few additional educational guidelines stated that provision should include: 'Use of play and free space, where children can act on their own interests, in combination with planned activities and other shared actions in order to support the individual child's development and ability to function with others' (Ministry of Social Affairs, 1990).

These very loose formulations were developed a little in a revision of the law the *Act of Social Service* (1998), in which *a* few paragraphs on educational objectives are provided:

- to care the child and to support its appropriation of social and general abilities;
- to offer the child possibilities of experiences and activities, aiming at stimulating its imagination, creativity and linguistic development;

- to give possibilities for participation in decision making and joint responsibility in order to develop its autonomy and abilities to participate in binding social communities;
- to promote children's understanding of cultural values and interaction with nature.

Act of Social Service, Denmark par.

It is important to note that the Act made use of the term *learning*, which indicated a new idea in the thinking concerning early childhood in Denmark, where the term *development* is dominant:

> Many of the activities, the children are involved in, contain learning processes. By this the daycare centres have to be aware of those possible learning elements, which can be included in the different activities. And special awareness must be shown when a child is seeking learning opportunities, or to learn more or something new.
>
> Act of Social Service, Denmark par.

Though the wording is guarded, it has been seen by professionals as a step away from a 'pure' or extreme child-orientation towards an educational approach characterised by interaction between child and pedagogue in the context of conscious goals and a reflected educational content.

However, even the above formulations are relativity open and vague, rather than being overly prescriptive. On this basis, parents and educators in each centre formulate the educational goals, content and principles for their children.

On the one hand you might say the absence of a narrow policy, educational theories, goals and content, give opportunities for educators, parents and children to reflect on and create their own life, and individual educational style. Here individuals are able to act as a participant, and with that, pave the way for their own learning process. However, if parents and educators are not able to analyse, reflect and discuss, and to carry through an ongoing construction and re-construction of theory and practice, life in daycaresettings will lack reflective examination and be routine oriented, and will be reduced to a 'caring only' setting. More, there is a risk that an extreme child-orientation will be adopted and distance from children be dominant.

Research by Vejleskov (1997) seems to indicate, that pedagogues tend to hand over the initiative to the children, to instigate their own activity. Among other investigations this is illustrated through an analysis of 87 plans of activities. Pedagogues in Denmark must produce a curriculum planning document every year, describing and discussing their educational ideas and activities (Broström, 1996).

AN ANALYSIS OF EARLY CHILDHOOD CURRICULUM

In agreement with the Froebelian tradition of kindergarten 76% of the 87 plans give priority to *free flow play*. Here play is described as children's fundamental way of living. Play is seen as young children's way to learn and express themselves. Most of the plans mention how the pedagogues are able to make space for play and to 'feed' play. Moreover 43% of the plans describe how play influences the child's development according imagination, fantasy and creativity in general. However, the statements relating to *song, music, rhythmic, movement* and *artistic activities* in general are very limited. Only 30% of the plans mention song and music, 25% describe rhythmic and movement and only 22% of the plans mention artistic activities in general. Moreover these aspects are not mentioned at all in the objectives. Because the tradition of Nordic early childhood education is built on play and creative activities this low priority is surprising. Perhaps the educators understand aesthetic activities as an obvious content, and for that reason they think it is not necessary to mention it. Or perhaps the reverse is the case, maybe there is a general downgrading of aesthetic and artistic activities? This is indeed what some investigations seem to show (Vejleskov, 1997).

It is rare for plans to contain a clear description of content the children would be expected to encounter. However, in a few plans we see socially oriented -minded and critical ideas, such as developing of *conflict consciousness* (17%), *consciousness of culture and society* (11%) and *environmental consciousness* (26%). For example the following phrases are taken from different plans:

- *Developing the child's respect for and understanding of the nature*
- *create an ecological way of thinking*
- *responsibility for nature*
- *experiences with nature and environmental consciousness*
- *help the children to learn they are dependent on the nature.*

Because in Denmark environmental consciousness is increasing among the population, it is not surprising to find this dimension in the kindergarten. But with the exception of environmental consciousness, the objectives have a general character and only mention some types of activity, e.g. play and creative activities.

This reduction of educational content to mostly the forms of activity demonstrates that Danish early childhood education, as expressed through these 87 plans, lacks a conscientiousness of the underlying learning to be achieved. The problem can be described as 'form without substance', and some ethnographic studies characterise the educational practice in Danish early childhood education and care (ECEC) as laissez-faire (Broström, 1999).

However, as a result of the theoretical understanding on which children's autonomous participation and self-governance is based, many educators argue for not to have a shared content. In addition some academics in early childhood education argue for leaving the well-established theories in place in order to construct situation- or context-oriented theories, and are very reserved and critical about curricular work.

Here at least two problems are apparent. First, if neither parents nor educators interact with children in a reflective and goal-directed way, and understand the daycarecentre as an active learning setting, children will not be able to create competencies which the modern society (and the school) demand. Secondly, in accordance with the transition to school the child will experience a huge contradiction, or contrast, between the daycarecentre's care tradition and the school's teaching and learning tradition. This means children must change attitudes from day to day, and act in a fundamentally new way, and a number of children find this problematic. Thus it is important to 'bridge' education in the daycarecentre and the first year in school. Among other activities and initiatives the early childhood institutions have to develop educational practice, such that, at the same time, it is valuable in the present but also contributes to children's acquiring competencies for the future. That is a daycarecentre, which is consciously framing children's well-being, learning and development.

In a modern society where many parents exhibit insecurity related to issues about child raising, and the school calls for close interaction and cooperation, pedagogues and academics in early childhood education need to cooperate in order to make early childhood education visible. That means formulating educational aims, content, principles etc., in other words, to recognise and produce a curriculum.

DIDAKTIK AND/OR CURRICULUM

In the Nordic countries it is common to use the German word *didaktik* instead of curriculum. Didaktik is rooted in the Greek word *didaskein*, which means school, teaching and learning. In accordance with the German scholar Wolfgang Klafki the concept didaktik has both a narrow and broad definition, respectively 'a theory on the content and educational substance' and 'science of education'. In 1958 Klafki defined didaktik as:

the subsuming of all mental effort directed at aspects of content, at the "what" of
instruction and education (in contrast to the concentration on the "how" of methodology
(Klafki, 1958).

Here the content is seen as the core element of the concept didaktik. The theory
deals with reflections on the criteria for choice of content, its structure and
perspective. Though the content is very central, step by step Klafki widened the
definition. In the 1990s he wrote:

Didaktik may, in my opinion, justifiably be used as a comprehensive term for research in
educational science, for the elaboration of theories and concepts with regard to all forms
of intentional (directed), in any way reflective teaching and to the learning taking place in
connection with this teaching (Klafki, 1995: 188).

However, even the narrow definition contains the idea that decisions should be
made on more than just aims, content, and choice of educational principles.
Didaktik deals with the question of Utopian aims, the long-term perspective:
the future human in a future society. More, didaktik focuses on reflections
related to the choice of educational content. In other words, what kind of
subjects, themes, and challenges children need to be confronted with. And
finally how children's learning and development will happen, that is, an
analysis of their activity in order to reach the aims (Klafki, 1995: 191).

This seems little different from, for example, Ralph Tyler's definition of
curriculum

- What educational purposes should the school seek to attain?
- What educational experiences can be provided, that are likely to attain these
  purposes?
- How can these educational experiences be effectively organised?
- How can we determine whether these purposes are being attained?

                                                                (Tyler, 1949: 1).

Yet maybe there is a difference. There seems to be a tendency to use the
German word didaktik, when philosophical and theoretical reflections are
involved as an integral part of educational decision-making. Meanwhile, the
Anglo-Saxon use of the Latin word *curriculum* is often used in a narrow way,
based on empirical-psychological research, to provide a formulation of
educational goals and content for a *syllabus*. Thus in order to incorporate the
German dimension, one might widen the term curriculum to include
educational theory. A new international debate on this topic seems to be uniting
the two words (Hopmann & Riquarts, 1995; Gundem & Hopmann, 1998).
Wolfgang Klafki writes:

I have the impression that the views of many German-speaking didaktik specialists and a
number of English-speaking curriculum theorists have been converging over the last two

decades. In deference to this fact, it would often be more appropriate to speak of didaktik/ curriculum theory (Klafki, 1995: 188).

Regardless of a possible difference between didaktik and curriculum theory, many Danish pedagogues have a resistance planned and goal-directed practice in daycarecentres and kindergartens. This is rooted in a strong belief in seeing the child as an active and self-governed person, the *subject* in their own learning and development. They think goal-directed and reflective practice will reduce this anti-authoritarian approach, the child's own activity and rights, and turn the child-orientation into a teacher-directed and academic one, a 'scholastic practice'. Or, in other words, into *didactic practice,* where the term didactic is used in a traditional way to mean: 'inclined to teach or lecture others too much' or 'teaching or intending to teach a moral lesson' (Webster, 1989).

Of course this is an important point. When discussing didaktik/curriculum in relation to early childhood education, we have to stress the importance of being able to integrate the early years tradition. Among other things this includes: the individual child as *subject* of their own learning, and the use of play and practical-aesthetic activities. However, from my point of view the rational and progressive part of the tradition has to be integrated as part of a modern early childhood didaktik/curriculum theory, which also contains a formulation of aims, goals, objectives and also reflection on a binding content.

However, in order to agree a curriculum for the early years without omitting the tradition, one has to consciously articulate the core of that early childhood tradition.

CRITICAL APPROACH OR ADJUSTMENT

In Danish early childhood education one might say that a democratic endeavour is visible. That means the pedagogues want to give the child influence. The question might be asked: is it possible to formulate a curriculum and simultaneously allow children influence on their own lives. This cannot be answered simply with a yes or no.

Returning to the analysis of the 87 plans of activity. Though they can be criticised for their lack of any content, most of them do reflect an important educational understanding: education as *Bildung.* The word Bildung is German and is related to the humanities-oriented *Geistwissenschaft* (human science), and refers to the processes and products of personal development, guided by reason. It means each individual 'builds' themself. The word can be translated to general education, however, in order to stress the 'Bildungstheorie' it has been suggested that a better term would be *liberal education.*

Liberal education can be seen both as a product, and as a process, but first of all as a perspective, which can be maintained through the distinction liberal education versus adjustment. Adjustment is aimed at socialising people for their place in the social system, teaching them the rules. But it fails to acknowledge the factthat the social life can be discussed and changed. The Norwegian philosopher Jon Hellesnes argues:

> Adjustment reduces humans to objects for political processes which they do not recognise as political; an adjusted human being is thus more an object for direction and control than a thinking and acting subject. Liberal education means that people are socialised into the problem complexes pertaining to the preconditions for what occurs around them and with them. Liberal education emancipates humans to be political subjects Hellesnes (1976: 18).

From my point of view the term Bildung (liberal education) can be defined through three criteria:

- the child's own activity, and dialogue with others,
- a feeling of obligation and commitment,
- participation, action and democracy.

The Child's Own Activity

Liberal education does seek to transfer knowledge and norms without arguments. As opposed to persuading the child, the pedagogue tries to establish a dialogue, through which the child is supported to reflect and to draw his or her own conclusions in the search for a wider understanding. Here the child has to be an active person in his/her search for understanding the world. The educator and the child enter into a subject-subject relation through which they focus on a shared objective (Freire, 1972). The character of the dialogue can also be described in accordance with Habermas' concept of *non-controlling communication* and this includes four universal-pragmatic rules: a communication in which understanding; truth; correctness; and honesty are expressed (Habermas, 1984, 1987). Here the children are subjects in own learning processes in order to appropriate first-hand knowledge.

Obligation and Commitment

To appropriate knowledge through a practice like liberal education does not mean simply acquiring information. Here practice is not reduced to technique. Knowledge is closely connected to the individual's feelings and actions. The liberally educated person is bound to his or her knowledge. The Danish scholar Bent Nielsen:

> In liberal education, over and above insight in a sphere of knowledge, there lies the fact that a criterion has been established for utilisation of that knowledge, that one has accepted a responsibility for how, and for what one will use this knowledge (Nielsen, 1973, p. 40–41).

Liberal education is more than taking a conscious stand. On the basis of reflection and assessment the person *acts* in agreement with his or her understanding of the particular topic. Thus you might use the term *action competence*, which include the child's motive and feeling, his/her knowledge, and also the skills to transform the knowledge to practice.

Participation, Action, and Democracy

The distinction between *adjustment* and *liberal education* also contributes to maintaining the latter as a political *democratic* perspective. This is not about being treated like an object, but to be a thoughtful participant in the democracy, and not merely an adjusted (or indoctrinated) onlooker. First of all democracy is characterised through the possibility for people to participate in social action. Thus the intention of liberal education is that the children are listened to, and they have the possibility to influence their daily lives. The American scholar Giroux suggests a liberal education should:

> not only empower students by giving them the knowledge and skills they need to be able to function in the larger society as critical agents, but also educate them for transformative action in the interest of creating a truly democratic society Giroux (1988: xxxiii).

Looking at the objectives in the 87 Danish plans of activity, formulations like 'independence, social competence, fellowship, self-determination and democracy and conflict consciousness' indicate an underpinning by a kind of liberal education.

Although the everyday life of this education is democratic and in all probability will contribute to the development of a democratic view and competence, some problems arise. The objectives are rather diffuse, the educational content does not point to any particular subjects or substance, and the pedagogues give priority only to the child's self-governed activity. Applying Wolfgang Klafki's concept, the content does not have a *material* character. That means the pedagogues do not articulate a specific content, subject or problem or specific forms of knowledge, etc. Pedagogues believe that to do so would imply a *formal education* and that any activity the child is motivated and involved in, will contribute to development, so they deem advance articulation unnecessary. As mentioned earlier, one might define the practice linked to this belief as 'form without substance'.

In order to overcome such problems and maintain the aspect of emancipation and democracy, Klafki's category *liberal education* could be used as a starting point. This approach unifies formal and material liberal education, the personal subjective experience and the objective reality. The child acts as a subject, contemporary with his or her handling of the objective content. The objective or material aspect is the child's appropriation of concepts and knowledge. The subjective means the child is active, engaged and involved in his or her activity.

On the basis of this theory pedagogues (and children) have to select knowledge and categories through which the world will be available for the child, and at the same time the child is available for the world.

The selection of such categories are the pivot, which also is seen in Paulo Freire's (1972) theory, namely through the concept *themes of generative character.*

CONTENTS WHICH MIGHT HAVE A FUTURE

Children need to meet content, which points ahead and helps make the world transparent. When the child is grown up he or she will live in a future world and should be able to solve problems pertaining to that world. For that reason children have to experience some contemporary fundamental problems.

On the basis of an analysis of the modern society and a reflection on the future educational content could be established. The future needs to be seen through a double perspective. On the one hand it can be described through the threats posed by a high risk society (Giddens, 1990), and on the other hand it can be understood in the light of new visionary possibilities in a global world.

Giddens (1990) describes the threatening tendencies as a mutual relation between growth in the totality power, conflict on nuclear power, global war, ecological break down and a collapse in mechanisms of economic development. Corresponding Klafki (1994) discusses the relation between society and decisions about the content of education. He outlines six core problems, or *epoch typical problems*: question about war and peace; the problem of nationalism; ecological problems; socially manufactured disparities between groups; and finally the possibility and danger of new management-and-communications media.

This is often summarised and described in Danish didaktik/curriculum studies as three crises: an ecological, a democratic and, an economic crisis.

In Klafki's words '*such societal risks and possibilities set Education new and big problems and tasks*' (Klafki, 1994). On the basis of this crude model, one can outline some criteria for the kinds of problems and perspectives which could form part of the content of education.

Although such methodical thinking is not explicitly expressed in Danish plans of activity for ECEC, we do see some 'sprouts'. In 26% of the plans the objective 'environmental consciousness' is listed, and in 25% of plans 'nature and ecology' said to be the content of the programme, reflecting concern for the ecological crisis.

Because the Danish pedagogues' plans stress the development of environmental consciousness through subjects about nature and ecology, it should be possible to move from this position to formulate a didaktik/curriculum, which make use of Klafki's and Giddens' ideas of risk as starting points for making decisions of the educational contents.

TO CREATE A CURRICULUM

When the pedagogues and parents (and children?) in a single daycare centre formulate their plan of activities, or curriculum, they have to take their aims and a few guidelines from the Act of Social Service into consideration. This might seem a big challenge for pedagogues. First of all because in Denmark there is no tradition of seeing early childhood education from a didaktik/ curriculum perspective. But also because it calls for a reliable foundation in educational theory and an up-to-date knowledge about society. Of course, there is a risk that some pedagogues would not be able to undertake and realise such theoretical reflections, and that as a result their document will be weak and superficial, insufficiently robust to be used as a steering tool. On the other hand this decentralised practice forces pedagogues to analyse their observations and descriptions of their own practice with children, to reflect on and articulate their educational understanding. Once a year they have to analyse and report on their practice and educational reflections, and they must also demonstrate continuity as part of this evaluation by adding an outline of the educational profile for the following year. For example the pedagogues must make a case for their choice of a specific theme or activity during the ensuing year.

However there is often a gap between the guidelines and the ongoing development of the curriculum in a specific daycare centre. For this reason, a few municipalities have devised their own local curriculum. This initiative can be seen as a reaction to the vague educational practice found to be based on a misunderstanding of the tradition of the self-governed child, in which there is avoidance of close interaction between pedagogues and children.

A LOCAL CURRICULUM

In order to help parents and pedagogues carry through goal-directed discussions as a basis for creating their own curriculum, so far only two municipalities have taken the initiative and produced a local municipal curriculum. Such a document contains an interpretation and explication of aims and goals from the *Act of Social Service*, and also outlines educational content. Some theoretical analyses of modern society and possible future competencies could be added in order to inspire the pedagogues' discussions.

A municipality and even a single kindergarten can have several reasons for creating a local curriculum. Gundem (1997), a Norwegian curriculum researcher, points out the fact that very often some people have a *personal interest*. That means a few individuals think it important to have an explicit curriculum. For example the Lord Mayor of a municipality or the leader in a kindergarten might want to have their own curriculum, in order to gain status. More often the argument for the curriculum is based on a *practical interest*: the curriculum is a useful tool for governing educational practice. However, the leader of a kindergarten or a member of the local administration might also have an *organisational interest*, because the curriculum can help to establish stability and uniformity. Finally Gundem mentions *critical interest*, because the existence of a curriculum makes it possible to discuss, reflect, deconstruct and re-construct the theoretical basis, and also the formulation of a specific curriculum. Here groups of academics, members of educational organisations, some politicians and naturally a large group of pedagogues deal with this type of critical interest.

However, the construction of a curriculum can easily result in a series of issues concerning both the relation between theory and practice, and that between practitioners and theoreticians. Who should devise the curriculum – pedagogues in the field of practice, politicians represented by administrators, or a group of professional curriculum designers? The following four approaches provide different answers.

An *operational relation* between theory and practice is characterised by focusing on the functional or effectiveness. Here there is a risk of being too pragmatic, avoiding theoretical and ethical reflections. A trap into which it is easy to fall if the educators are formulating the curriculum, and also when professional curriculum designers must deliver a plan to politicians who want an easy and useful document.

Dominant of theoretical knowledge results in *logical relation*. This might be the expert's power, which can easily lead to resistance and theoretical distance from users.

The *dialectical relation* strives for dialectic between the producer of the curriculum, the politicians and the users. The problem here can arise if a specific educational theory or a political understanding is dominant. The idea is to ensure a dialectic relation between the politicians' visions, the parents' interests, the practitioners' experiences and the various educational approaches which are expressed by the theoreticians. As an example of a curriculum, which has been developed through such a complex process is *Te Whāriki* the national early years curriculum of New Zealand. Because practitioners have been involved in the process, and also because they have a distinct influence, in all probability this particular curriculum can be a useable tool.

Finally this curriculum work can have a research and problem-oriented character, where research on theory-practice and a prolonged cooperation between the partners involved will lead to a shared vision of the 'best society', which subsequently governs the curriculum work.

During 1999 *Gladsaxe,* a municipality close to Copenhagen, devised a local curriculum. Through very close cooperation between myself and the educational consultants from the social services department in Gladsaxe, and through continuous discussion and critical feed-back from a group of ten experienced kindergarten teachers, we devised a curriculum containing educational aims, goals, and content. Moreover a great deal of material describing the theoretical background was added as a supplement. The curriculum is based on didaktik/curriculum research, experiences from Sweden and Norway, written plans of activity from the 70 kindergartens in the municipality, a number of reports from local development work, and evidence from research projects focusing on education in a number of kindergartens. The endeavour was to avoid an *operational* relation between theory and practice, and to create a curriculum through a *dialectical* relation. In some way such a relation was visible. However, lack of time was an ongoing issue. It was difficult for the group of practitioners to take a very active part in the curriculum work, to use time to read, prepare critical responses, and to produce new, and better formulations. In addition, the politicians wanted the process to be undertaken speedily.

The written curriculum comprises a twelve-page document discussing and interpreting the text of *the Act of Social Service*, the formulation of aims, central competencies, goals and a binding content. This document is written for lay readers. This is because education in kindergartens (and schools) is a matter for everyone in a society. Nevertheless, it is necessary first that parents read and discuss the document, and then in cooperation with the pedagogues, the board of parents must interpret the curriculum and decide on an outline of next year's educational practice. However, neither the Gladsaxe curriculum nor the parents' educational sketches contained any descriptions of *how* and *when* pedagogues and children should work with content described. This is totally a matter for pedagogues and children to decide for themselves.

Two further documents connected to the curriculum and addressed to the pedagogues followed: the paper *Educational Thoughts behind a Curriculum* deals with critical reflections on children's lives in an institutionalised world, the institution as a learning setting, and theories on aims, content and educational principles. The paper *From Plan to Practice* deals with ideas about the relationship between theory and practice, and without giving narrow directions, some general principles are discussed.

THE GLADSAXE CURRICULUM

As an example here are some extracts from the curriculum document:

Aims

The kindergarten must create a safe setting with challenging possibilities, which make it possible for all children, through an active everyday life, to contribute to their own *comprehensive development*, and to experience and learn *democratic* attitudes, norms and behaviour. This means they will understand themselves as independent and autonomous persons, who can cooperate with other people, and by using their emotions and reason, they are able to change their social surroundings. Step by step, the children will be able to begin to take liberating action, based on shared democratic reflections, through which they create happiness and better conditions for themselves and others.

Basic Competencies

- Daily life in kindergarten gives rise to the development of the children's *personal and social competencies*:
  Through a close relation with pedagogues, and through an active life with peers, the child develops *self-reliance*, positive self-esteem, and self-worth. That is, they have confidence in their own ability, which form the basis for the development of social competence, defined as the child's wishes, knowledge and skills to interact and create social relations with other children.
- Daily life in kindergarten gives rise to the development of *language* and *communicative* competence.

Through meaningful dialogues with pedagogues, spontaneous and planned language activities, social activity, and play with peers, the children continuously develop language skills and communicative competence.

- Through daily life in kindergarten the children have to be familiar with, and also appropriate knowledge on *culture*.
  Through interactions with pedagogues children will appropriate Danish cultural norms and values, and acquire knowledge and experience joy related to cultural activities and results. However, they should also acquire knowledge about and a respectful attitude to other cultures.
- Through daily life in kindergarten the children should become familiar with, and also appropriate knowledge about *nature*.
  Through an active life in nature, children gain experience, they appropriate knowledge; they also grow fond of nature, and achieve ecological understanding.
- Through daily life in kindergarten the children should be familiar with, and also acquire skills in *practical-aesthetic* activities, and different forms of *movements* and body consciousness.
  The children should be involved in a variety of different forms of practical-aesthetic activities through which they achieve multi-facetted aesthetic expression. In addition, they should have opportunities to develop a healthy body and a comprehensive pattern of movement.

Content

The curriculum document includes ten themes of content, which are related to the aims and goals. In general the content should support the children:

- to be able to be a 'child of today'
- to 'conquer' the world
- to 'swim against the tide'
- to master and to gain added knowledge of their own life
- to develop new patterns of action and action competence
- to obtain a form of self-confidence in order to set free new energy for learning, and being able to handle new challenges.

The ten themes of content are as follows:
The child: me, my family, and my close surroundings
Play

Friendship and fellowship
The body and motor activities, for example dance, rhythmic, sport and games
Aesthetic activities, for example song, music, drawing, painting, modelling
Language, text and communication
Nature, technique and environment, ecology
Society and democratic processes
Globalisation and cultural diversity
Practical life – being self-reliant

Life in kindergarten provides many possibilities for incorporating the above forms of content. Both systematically planned activities and the daily routine will contribute to children's appropriation of skills and knowledge. The different forms of content are characterised by diversity, because we sought to encourage the comprehensive development of personality. However, there is one characteristic shared by the different areas, they all allow the possibility for children to be surprised, and to work on the surprises through varied forms of activities, such as creative work with visual art, or theatre and drama, or song, music and many forms of bodily expression which take a leading role.

The Gladsaxe curriculum concludes:
All these exploratory activities in childhood will be preserved by children, as strings of pearls, which they will be able to use later in life. The children have experienced wonder and surprised themselves.

EVALUATION AND ASSESSMENT

Thus, in Gladsaxe pedagogues have a local curriculum, which they use as one tool among many. The curriculum is not intended to be seen as a ready formula or straightjacket, but as a tool for helping pedagogues to carry through fundamental educational discussions in order to make 'didaktik analysis' (Klafki, 1998), interpreting aims, formulating goals, and pointing out educational content and principles. Moreover, the curriculum should also be a tool for carrying through the educational process, and conducting evaluation.

The pedagogues participate in an ongoing process starting with an evaluation of practice, followed by analysis and reflection. From that base planning which leads to new educational practice can begin. Practice which is observed and described, is followed by a new analysis and reflection, and with that new educational understanding, and the planning of innovatory elements. Such an ongoing circular process with 'planning-action-evaluation' is illustrated in below figure *the educational butterfly.*

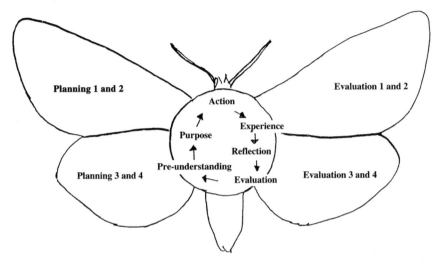

Planning, Action and Evaluation.

The body of the 'butterfly' is the central part. This represents the meeting between pedagogue and child. Here there is a meeting, on the one hand, between the pedagogues' existing understanding, purposes, actions experiences, reflections and evaluations, and on the other, the children's interests, purposes and activities. The pedagogues have to be able to make this meeting fruitful for the children, which demands a balance between the pedagogues' and the children's interests and intentions. From the 'body' we move to the 'wings' of the 'butterfly'. First the 'wings' of planning:

P1: *The political level of planning.* Here the official documents are dominant. The board of parents and the pedagogues will interpret the Act of Social Service and, in some municipalities, a local curriculum.

P2: *The public local level of planning*: The board of the parents and the pedagogues evaluate the past year, and from that starting point they decide goals and objectives, some educational principles, and general ideas related to the content for the coming year. This planning is made in a general way, without discussion of *how* and *when.*

P3: *The institutional level of planning*: The group of pedagogues continue with general educational discussions through which they bring the general overall from the level of P2 towards a more specific level. However, the planning is dynamic, allowing space for the children's interests and spontaneous ideas.

P4: *The personal level of planning*: Building on the general educational planning, each team of pedagogues carries through more specific planning. At this point the children become involved.

Parallel to the 'wing' of planning there is a corresponding 'wing' for evaluation. Thus P4 corresponds with E4 *the personal level of evaluation*. On this level each individual pedagogue carries through a situated evaluation. Here the pedagogue reflects on specific activities and this evaluation impacts on ongoing and subsequent activity.

E3: *The institutional level of evaluation:* By reviewing the many and varied activities during the previous year, the team of pedagogues are able to carry out their evaluation. Their documentation contains, for example, written observations and videotapes of some activities, transcribed interviews about some of the children's experiences, and sometimes parents' voices too.

E2: *The public level of evaluation*: Here the board of the parents are invited to evaluate the educational practice and theory at the kindergarten. The documentation mentioned above is presented to the board, and related to both theoretical foundations and the general planning. Through this stage of the evaluation, parents and pedagogues have the possibility to change practice during the subsequent year.

E1: *The political level of the evaluation*: Currently, national evaluation or municipal evaluation of all kindergartens in an area is very rare. In some municipalities, consultants who are very close to the settings read through all the plans of activity from the kindergartens, and give professional feedback and a critique. However, because such a process is very time consuming, some adopt a formal quantitative evaluation with a kind of tick-list instead. From our evidence, however, it appears that the approach where an educational consultant and the pedagogues discuss the educational practice and theory together is preferable.

Pedagogues are also responsible for the *assessment* of the children's learning and development. This is rarely systematic, and it is organised and carried out very differently from one kindergarten to another. Thus there is no common tool for assessment, neither at national level, nor in a particular municipality. In general the local authorities leave this aspect to the pedagogues, and make them responsible for carrying out some sort of assessment. As a result, the pedagogues make use of a range of different instruments, and they also have varied understanding of both what to assess, and how to assess and find themselves sharing ideas about *school readiness*.

CONCLUSION

Early childhood education and care in Denmark seems to be at a crossroads. One road leads to child-oriented practice, where the pedagogues are visible and available without taking over or directing children's activity. The pedagogues stress the child's own choice, free-flow play, and spontaneous practice rather than a planned curriculum. Devotees of this approach also want to keep kindergarten and school apart, and reject the idea of kindergarten as a learning environment. For them, kindergarten provides the possibility for children to have a few years where the children are allowed to 'be children and not learners'. The other road leads toward a more consciously planned, activity-oriented practice. In this model, both children and pedagogues have a high level of activity and engagement. The pedagogues reflect on their aims, and formulate goals and objectives, and they also discuss and select content, which is intended to embrace the children's chosen activities. They strive for a practice, where the content and the children's activity will achieve the character of 'Bildung' and with that not only contribute to the acquisition of skills and knowledge, but also form the basis for the development of the future citizen of the future society.

The danger is that both the child-oriented and the Bildung-oriented approaches will be subsumed under a technologically oriented kindergarten movement. The latter would strive for a close connection between kindergarten and school, one which could result in a 'push down' effect, in which content and methods from the school would replace traditional kindergarten approaches and the most important goal would be to produce 'school ready' pupils. The lack of a national or local curriculum and the tendency to a laissez-faire approach could provoke this development, as can be seen in the narrow Anglo-Saxon curriculum tradition.

Hopefully we will see in the future in Denmark, a process characterised by dialectical cooperation bringing together an open national curriculum framework, local municipal educational documents and curriculum, and the thousands of plans of activity from the individual kindergartens. Such a dynamic process will avert an end-means curriculum model, and support the ongoing lively educational debate.

REFERENCES

Broström, S. (1996). Early Childhood Education in Denmark. A critical-democratic education? *Journal of International Early Childhood Education, 28*(2), 7–14. London: OMEP.
Broström, S. (1999). Kulturen i børnehave og børnehaveklasse. [An ethnographical analyses of everyday life in kindergarten and kindergarten class]. Rapport. Copenhagen: DLH.

Freire, P. (1972). *Pedagogy of the Oppressed.* Harmondsworth: Penguin Books.

Fröbel, F. (1826). *Menschenerziehung.* Kielhau.

Giddens, A. (1990). *The Consequences of Modernity.* Cornwall: Polity Press.

Giroux, H. A. (1988). *Teachers as Intellectuals: Towards a Critical Pedagogy of Learning.* South Hadey, Mass.: Bergin and Garvey.

Gundem, B. B. (1997). Läroplansarbete som didaktisk virksomhet. [Curriculum work as didaktik activity]. In: Michael Uljens (Red.), *Didaktik.* Stockholm: Studentlitteratur.

Gundem, B. B., & Hopmann, S. (1998). *Didaktik and/or Curriculum. An International Dialogue.* New York: American University Studies/Peter Lang.

Habermas, J. (1984 & 1987). *The Theory of Communicative Action* (Vol. 1 and 2). Boston: Beacon Press.

Hellesnes, J. (1976). *Socialisering og teknokrati.* [Socialisation and technocracy]. Copenhagen: Gyldendal.

Hopmann, S., & Riquarts (Eds) (1995). *Didaktik and/or Curriculum.* Kiel: IPN.

Howes, C., & Hamilton, C. E. (1992). Children's Relationships with caregivers: Mothers and Child care teachers. *Child Development, 63,* 895–866.

Klafki, W. (1958, 1974). *Studien zur Bildungstheorie und Didaktik.* Fünfte Studie. Weinheim und Basel: Beltz Verlag.

Klafki, W. (1994). Neuen Studien zur Bildungstheorie und Didaktik. Weinheim/Basel.

Klafki, W. (1995). On the problem of teaching and learning contents from the standpoint of critical constructive didaktik. In: Hopmann & Riquarts (Eds), *Didaktik and/or Curriculum.* Kiel: IPN.

Klafki, W. (1998). Characteristics of Critical-Constructive Didaktik. In: B. B. Gundem & S. Hopmann (Eds), *Didaktik and/or Curriculum. An International Dialogue.* New York: American University Studies/Peter Lang.

Ministry of Social Affairs (1990). *The Circular of Day-offers for Children and Youth.* Copenhagen: Ministry of Social Affairs.

Ministry of Social Affairs (1992). *Report on Governing Body of the Parents from the Social department of the Parliament.* Copenhagen: Ministry of Social Affairs.

Nielsen, B. (1973). *Praksis og kritik* [Practice and Criticism]. Copenhagen: Ejlers Forlag.

Tylor, R. W. (1949). *Basic Principles of Curriculum and Instruction.* Chicago: University of Chicago Press.

Vejleskov, H. (Ed.) (1997). *Den danske børnehave. Studier om myter, meninger og muligheder* [The Danish Kindergarten. Studies on myths, meanings and possibilities]. Skrifter fra Center fra Småbørnsforskning Nr. 8. Danmarks Lærerhøjskole.

9. EARLY LEARNING AND EARLY LITERACY

Bridie Raban

In this chapter, evidence from earlier in Section 1 of this collection will be located alongside evidence from research on literacy learning during the early childhood years. Principles for early learning and development will be identified and the implications for practice will be highlighted.

It is understandable if early childhood professionals are at best confused and in some instances even intimidated by the volume of conflicting evidence concerning children's literacy development. Theorists and practitioners from many disciplines continue to put forward their views and contribute to the debate concerning skills and abilities involved in learning to read. Indeed almost everyone in a literate culture like ours will have an opinion, and these are frequently, and emphatically, expressed in the media; newspapers, television and the like. Each person putting forward a point of view will be coloured by a particular perspective along with research and theorising paradigms associated with their discipline and with their understandings and experience (Goodman, 1998). For instance, one paediatrician argues strongly that babies should not be given book experiences before nine months of age. When asked why, he advised parents that their baby would need to be able to hold their head up independently first!

What we put forward as a position on early literacy, therefore, is clearly coloured by our particular world view. Literacy 'experts' will be similarly influenced, although privileged, in their opportunities to dictate the early literacy 'agenda'. However, much research evidence has been misinterpreted, misrepresented, left unreported and misunderstood. There are clear signs that

Promoting Evidence-based Practice in Early Childhood Education:
Research and its Implications, Volume 1, pages 171–184.
Copyright © 2001 by Elsevier Science Ltd.
All rights of reproduction in any form reserved.
ISBN: 0-7623-0753-6

practitioners have lost confidence in the wealth of knowledge built up over time of how children learn about literacy and how they learn to read and write, and this is because a vacuum has been created between theory and practice. More recently we have found ourselves less able to fully articulate real, evidence-based alternatives to centrally imposed curricula decisions while feeling some disquiet with simple solutions to what we acknowledge as complex educational issues. Simple answers to basic questions are unlikely to account for the diversity of children's literacy behaviours.

With the development of brain imaging technology and other neuro-scientific advances, many theoretical hypotheses, including the important role of early experience in development, are being confirmed. Evidence is converging from a number of different scientific fields that enable a more certain account of early learning and development to inform policy and practice. The key finding from this wide range of evidence (Brandsford et al., 1999) is the significance of early experiences in contributing to the architecture of the brain. Development is clearly not solely the unfolding of pre-programmed patterns. Rather, experience actually modifies the structure of the brain and the complexities of the linkages necessary for later learning.

One traditional view of learning and development was that young children know and can do little, but with age (maturation) and experience (of any kind) they become increasingly competent. However, a substantial body of evidence about the remarkable abilities that young children possess now stands in contrast to this older emphasis on what they lacked. It is now known that very young children are competent active agents of their own development (Gelman & Brown, 1986). This view challenges the notion of "readiness", and waiting for children show interest in, for instance, literacy before engaging them in appropriate activities. It is now understood that there is a corresponding relationship between experience in a complex environment and structural change in the brain.

- Development is an active process that derives essential information from experience.
- Learning changes the physical structure of the brain and organises and reorganises the linkages within the brain.
- Structural changes alter the functional organisation of the brain.
- Different parts of the brain will be critical for specific learning at different times.
- Some experiences have the most powerful effects during sensitive periods, while others can effect the brain over a much longer period.

There is, therefore, a set of principles that underpin learning, development and progression for all children. This is not to suggest that all children follow the same developmental pathways, either at school or during the preschool years (Clay, 1998). Hill et al.'s (1998) research highlights how the children in their study demonstrated greater within group differences than between group differences, indicating the diversity of developmental pathways among young children. Because of this, the mismatch between an imposed curriculum and what individual children can do is not overcome by gathering together from research reports some averaged description of sequences of acquisition. Such research-base sequences can drive the expectations of teachers while individual children are working their way along various different paths.

In this respect equity is not served by providing unequals with equal provision. What is required is a clear understanding of the principles for learning and how best to implement these effectively in a variety of settings for diverse populations of young children. These principles include first, respecting what children already know and using this knowledge as the basis for acquiring new knowledge; second, taking account of the transformations which take place as a result of learning and experience; and third, distinguishing between concepts essential to, for instance, literacy development and contexts within which literacy is embedded, while clearly articulating the links between the two.

FROM THE KNOWN TO THE NEW

Research (e.g. Anderson et al., 1977) reveals that children identified as 'low achievers' in school have limitations in their 'prior knowledge' and understandings rather than any limitations in their ability to learn. It becomes important, therefore, to ask the question; 'Where do these prior understandings come from?' Not from systematic and specific instruction because that in turn requires an amount of understanding. Prior understandings come from more general experience and a wide variety of contexts in which the learning takes place. Young children actively engage in making sense of their world. They may lack knowledge and experience, but not reasoning ability. Although young children are inexperienced, they reason with facility using the knowledge and understandings they do have. Indeed, because of limited experience and undeveloped systems of logical thinking, young children's knowledge base may well contain misconceptions, and lead to errors of both judgement and behaviour.

Students learn about new processes or new information in the light of what they already know and understand (Smith, 1986). The problem for students who fail to learn in school is not one of not being able to learn, but rather not being able to make sense of what they are trying to learn. Argument here is supportive of the culturally inclusive curriculum coupled with strong family and community partnerships. It is also important to remember that children can hold both unconventional *and* conventional notions about literacy at the same time. Therefore, early behaviours predicting later ones become problematic. When children move from where they are to new conceptualisations, account must be taken of what they already know and think about the activity.

TRANSFORMATIONS

Through the dual processes of *accommodation* and *assimilation* (Piaget, 1985), new knowledge is not joined to previous knowledge in any additive sense. Rather, new knowledge transforms the already existing knowledge base and restructures what comes to be known. This process of transformation is fundamental to the changing architecture of the brain, changes that are rapid during the early years of life (Shore, 1997). It is now known that during these early years there are 'critical periods' which can be identified as a time span when a particular part of the brain is most apt to change and most vulnerable to environmental influences. But how critical are these critical periods? As windows of opportunity pass, for instance, for language learning, binocular vision, emotional control etc., are they closed forever? In some areas of development this is the case, for instance, very young children discriminate many more phonemic boundaries than adults, but they lose their discriminatory powers when certain boundaries are no longer supported by their experience of the language spoken around them (Kuhl, 1993). However, Chugani (1997) argues that 'prime times' stretch for quite extended periods. In addition, Werner and Smith (1992) point out that children who grow up in disadvantaged or deprived settings can adjust well to the demands of school and become successful learners. Clearly, evidence for 'critical periods' needs to be interpreted with caution.

Nevertheless, the brain is not a given, static organism. It has the potential for enormous plasticity, and experience is the driver and the shaper in the dynamic process of what comes to be known and understood. This implies that a curriculum that takes account of what children already know and understand is essential to necessary transformations, as thinking is modified over time within the light of previous experiences and past knowledge and understandings. The suggestion from research (see Yaden et al., 1999) is that those children who already have an incipient foundation of knowledge, experience, and under-standings to build upon will make good progress with learning to read and write when they enter school. However, the later this foundation is built, the slower the growth.

CONCEPTS AND CONTEXTS

In view of what is becoming referred to as 'dynamic' development (Hill & Louden, 1999), concepts appropriate for school learning and progression are accrued through a wide range of contexts. It is these changing contexts which provide the variety and necessary repetition for students whose experiences are far from the assumptions made by the requirements of formal schooling. Essentially, participation in social practice is a fundamental form of learning because it leads to understandings. This initial learning involves becoming attuned to the constraints and resources, the limits and the possibilities, that are involved in the practices of a community.

The important role of caregivers involves efforts to help children connect new situations to more familiar ones. Skills and knowledge need to be extended beyond the narrow contexts in which they are initially learned. Learners are helped in their independent learning attempts if they are able to develop conceptual knowledge in this way. Studies of children's concept formation and conceptual development show the essential role of learners' mental representations of problems, including how one problem is similar to and different from others, and understanding the part-whole relationships of the components in the overall structure of a problem.

In addition, learning is promoted by social and cultural norms that value the search for understanding. Early learning is assisted by the supportive context of the family and the social environment, through the kinds of activities in which caregivers engage with children. These activities have the effect of providing toddlers with the structure and interpretation of the culture's norms and rules, and these processes occur long before children enter school. Through numerous interactions, caregivers help children make connections between new situations and familiar ones. Children's curiosity and persistence are supported by those who direct their attention, structure experiences, support learning attempts, and regulate the complexity and difficulty levels of information.

In these ways, children exhibit capacities that are shaped by their understandings, environmental experiences and interactions with the individuals who care for them. Developmental processes, therefore, involve interactions between children's early competences and the environmental supports, thereby strengthening relevant capacities and pruning the early abilities that are less relevant to the child's community. Learning is promoted and regulated by both the biology and the ecology of the child, and in this sense learning produces development rather than the reverse. It is worth remembering that economic levels alone do not determine school success.

Along with children's natural curiosity and their persistence as self-motivated learners, what they learn during their first four or five years is not learned in isolation. Infants' activities are complemented by relationships that encourage the gradual involvement of children in the skilled and valued activities of their family and the society in which they live. In addition to the research showing how caregivers arrange the environment to promote children's learning (Schaffer, 1977: 73), a great deal of research has also been conducted on how they guide children's understanding of how to act in new situations through their emotional cues regarding the nature of the situation, non-verbal models of how to behave, verbal and non-verbal interpretations of events, and verbal labels to classify objects and events (Rogoff, 1990; Walden & Ogan, 1988).

Successful caregivers make efforts to build on what children know and extend their competencies by providing supporting structures (or scaffolds) for the child's performance (Wood et al., 1976). Scaffolding includes several activities and tasks:

- Supporting children in interpreting different forms of meaning through modelling and demonstration,
- Supporting children to make sense of an activity by suggesting strategies that will help govern the number of steps required to solve the problem,
- Engaging children in learning by making it meaningful, and keeping their attention in this way through motivation and direction of the activity,
- Encouraging and providing support for problem solving using scaffolding techniques that minimise frustation and risk in problem solving by telling and revealing,
- Providing examples and sharing ideas to reinforce the processes of problem solving and demonstrating the solution by revisiting the process as a whole.

Along with these aspects of cognitive growth, social opportunities influence learning. Feeling that one is contributing something to others appears to be especially motivating (Schwartz & Brandsford, 1999). For example, young learners are highly motivated to write stories of their own and draw pictures that they can share with others. Indeed, learners of all ages are more motivated when they can see the usefulness of what they are learning and when they can use that information to do something that has an impact on others (Pintrich & Schunk, 1996). Yaden et al. (1999) indicate that effective mediation appears to require adults to match their strategies to the child's intentions, knowledge and understandings, and to phase in and out of more or less directive roles. The importance of adult support in children's learning can be demonstrated by considering the question; How is it that children, born with no language, can develop most of the rudiments of story telling during the first three years of life? (Engle, 1995). A variety of literacy experiences prepare children for this prowess and the importance of story reading and retelling connected to personal experience has recently been scientifically validated (Snow et al., 1998).

LEARNING ABOUT LITERACY

Increasing expertise in a domain helps people develop a sensitivity to patterns of meaningful information, patterns that are not available to a novice (see de Groot, 1965 for an example from chess). However, seeing a pattern or relationship that has personal meaning cannot be explained or treated in terms of a 'trait' or an 'ability' (Olson, 1999), but rather in terms of what the perceiver knows, believes, wants and tries, and these characteristics are framed by experience. The fact that experts' knowledge is organised around ideas and concepts that are important to them suggests that curriculum during the early stages of learning should be organised in ways that lead to conceptual understandings first and only later leading to detailed knowledge.

Given our understanding that literacy is constructed by individuals and groups as part of everyday life (Luke, 1993: 4), speaking, listening, reading, viewing, writing and drawing are social practices that occur in a range of daily situations. Children learn what can be said or written, how it can be said or written, and to whom under what circumstances, through a myriad of experiences in a wide range of contexts. Long before formal lessons in reading and writing, for instance, children will be building up their own understandings of the purposes and functions of these activities in the literate lives of others. Indeed, it will be from insights into these purposes and functions that curiosity will be aroused, awareness fostered, and concepts formed. This rich seed-bed has been shown to provide students during their first year in school with an accelerated trajectory on a number of spoken and written language measures (Raban et al., 1999).

Socio-cultural studies (Dyson, 1992, 1993; Purcell-Gates, 1995) provide an additional perspective for understanding the nature of early literacy. They show how interactions and strategies are tied, explicitly or implicitly, to culturally held definitions of literacy, power relationships and values. These studies raise a number of issues concerning societal values and definitions of literacy, clashes of culture between home, other prior to school contexts and school itself, and the differential valuing of the experiences, knowledge and understandings that children bring with them to school.

In a study reported by Vukelich (1994), print was incorporated into children's preschool environment and experience, without disturbing the ecology of that context. This incorporation of print increased the children's contact with literacy materials and their engagements with literacy behaviours. In this study the adult interactional style was like that which is experienced in the world outside the preschool, a style where the print-meaning associations are woven naturally into activities and accompanying conversations. Children in this context were found to learn significantly more words in context than their peers who experienced a print enriched environment without adult interactions. What is being indicated by this research and that of others (e.g. Neuman & Roskos, 1997; Raban et al., 1999), is that a combination of exposure to environmental and other print are known to result in young children making significant meaning-making connections, associations known to be important precursors to conventional reading.

Neuman and Roskos' study (1997) strongly suggests that long before formal instruction takes place, young children use reading and writing behaviours as an integral part of their everyday lives if encouraged to do so. As a legitimate part of early literacy, participation in authentic writing and reading practices represents an important phase of early literacy learning. These experiences engage children in practicing not only what written language is for, but also how it works. Preschool children also need a variety of experiences and interactions that stimulate conceptual and factual knowledge about literacy. Lesiak (1997) gives a fuller review of this research literature.

However, in a study of U.K. preschool teachers, Hannon and James (1990) report that these teachers did not see literacy as a central concern of the preschool curriculum. They were aware of parents' interest in their children's literacy development but they were worried about parents using inappropriate 'methods' teaching their children to read, and about parents putting too much pressure on children. In an Australian study (van Moorst & Graham, 1995) 82% of parents said they sent their children to preschool to get them 'ready' for primary school while only 57% of the preschool teachers saw this as an important reason. However twice as many primary school teachers than parents expressed anxiety concerning children's 'readiness' for school when asked this question directly in a study reported by Raban and Ure (1999). Clearly, preschool educators do not agree about preparing children for school, either as an overall aim or with respect to developing their awareness of literacy which surrounds their daily lives. Clay (1998: 42) points out that some are committed to having children learn their letters, while others leave children unaware of such things prior to entry into school. Personal experience of inviting 156 preschool centres to join a literacy project in Victoria, Australia resulted in 40 agreeing to take part (Ure & Raban, in press). Many of these centres saw literacy development as the domain of schooling and of no concern to them.

In a U.S. study of 3–4 year olds and their access to literacy within prior to school contexts in Philadelphia, Neuman (1999) also reports centres who refused to participate in her book-flood program. Of the 100 rooms she included in her research and reported on, prior to the intervention, an inventory of the physical resources sketched a brief backdrop for the literacy experiences available for these children. 21 rooms had book corners, 25 had bookshelves, the books themselves appeared tattered and worn. 84 rooms showed print in the form of signs, alphabet letters, numbers, colour names and the like. Some of these signs were at the children's eye-level but most were not. 30 rooms had TV and video, 20 had record and audio cassette players, and 2 had writing centres. However, Neuman reports impressive transformations as a result of the book flood intervention. Interactions between the teachers and the children increased; reading aloud increased in both amount and variety, to whole group, small groups and individual children. Lasting effects were reported in contrast to children in other centres. Neuman concluded that young children need rich and diverse reading materials shared with more knowledgeable others, to acquire the complex set of attitudes, skills and behaviours associated with literacy development.

When there is a paucity of high quality children's books in economically disadvantaged communities in particular, then we see a dramatic impact from interventions of this kind which place high-quality books into child care centres and preschools. The staff became engaged in using books frequently, interactively, and developmentally appropriately with young children. Changes were observed in both the physical and social environments. The physical placement of books in close proximity to the children was seen as critical for early literacy activity. Nevertheless, this is not sufficient in itself. Children need an excellent interactional environment as well. The physical proximity of books, especially high quality attractive books within the children's eye-line, seemed to have a coercive effect in instigating these interactions.

In such play enriched environments, however, young children were not merely passive recipients bombarded with stimuli. Rather, they appeared to be active agents in their own development; exploring, discovering, and using the physical environment as an important medium for transactions. Numerous observations often indicated that it was the children, even more than the adults, who generated the reading activity. Earlier studies also claim similar findings (Neuman & Roskos, 1990; Vukelich, 1990; Noble & Foster, 1993). The inclusion of literacy-enriched play centres increases, often dramatically, the amount of literacy-related activities in which children engage during play. When materials only, and materials coupled with adult scaffolding were compared (Pickett, 1998), children engaged in significantly more literacy-related play when adults were present and involved.

Descriptive studies of children's early experiences of literacy and literacy learning offer critical insights into their rich and complex processes of making sense of their world as it is mediated by their experiences with print and other's attitudes towards it (Heath, 1983; Purcell-Gates, 1996). Nevertheless, even print rich environments provide fewer opportunities for literacy growth if children do not know how to interact with the print artefacts around them. This will be achieved by the modelling and demonstrations provided by surrounding adults. From a different perspective, Heibert and colleagues (1998) from the Centre for the Improvement of Early Reading Achievement (CIERA) and other reviewers (e.g. Adams, 1990) indicate that powerful predictors of reading achievement are letter-name knowledge and phonemic awareness. However, in order to apply this knowledge in learning to read, children need to understand first the purposes and conventions of reading and writing. Merely teaching letter-name and sound knowledge will not of itself make the difference.

Predictors of this kind reduce the complexity of children's learning to misleading and meaningless prescriptions for teaching. As Clay (1975) observed;

> children ... do not learn about language on any one level of organisation before they manipulate units at a higher level .... As children learn to read and write there is a rich intermingling of language learning across levels, which probably accounts in some ways for the fast progress which the best children can make. A simplification achieved by dealing firstly with letters, then words, and finally with groups of words, may be easy for teachers to understand, but children learn on all levels at once (Clay, 1975: 19).

What children bring with them in learning to read is their skill as users of language. They already know that language makes sense and they have a powerful tacit understanding of the way in which language is structured. They know the syntactic probabilities of their language and giving them opportunities and support to use this knowledge will help them through the early stages towards fluency. Bishop and Adams (1990) argue that phonological proficiency is not the main determinant of reading development, rather it is a result of using these syntactic and semantic abilities which are responsible for the major part of the variation in reading ability. They are here pointing out the role of semantic and syntactic cuing systems which both support and focus the need for the use of grapho-phonemic cues as children learn to read both fluently and accurately.

The complexity of this intermingling of language levels that reinforce and support spoken and written language development indicate that there will be more than a single route to successful reading achievement (Konold et al., 1999). This will be true for the early years of childhood before school and during the first years of formal schooling. For instance, with struggling readers, teachers may be tempted to postpone the advanced and independent aspects of comprehension skills until 'lower order' skills and strategies such as fluency and accuracy are fully in place. Nothing can be more damaging to the comprehension growth of struggling readers. Indeed, Gray's work (1999) demonstrates clearly that young children and older struggling readers benefit from explicit strategies which reveal the links across levels of language with the meanings embedded in text, benefits also accrue with this style of pedagogy towards increased fluency, accuracy and comprehension of what is being read.

Research in the future needs to acknowledge these layers of information and their interrelationships. The clash of paradigms and methodologies with different messages for practice has been unhelpful in the literacy education of our youngest children. For instance, longitudinal research in New Zealand in the 1970s showed a strong relationship between writing in the first year in school and early reading progress (Robinson, 1973), whereas in Britain (Raban, 1988) and the United States (Juel, 1988) longitudinal research showed little relationship between these two activities. Clay (1998: 90) interprets these reports to mean that there are different paths to achievement related to different educational practices in timing, emphasis, and expectations. In NZ, writing forms a significant part of the early reading program, where this has not been the case in the U.K. or USA. Clay reminds us all that the evidence of research is strengthened by replication studies, and those research communities that can sustain large research and development budgets and activities will provide many confirmations of *their* paths to successful literacy development, while communities with little opportunities for research and replication studies will have little voice in the discourse concerning evidence and whose evidence counts.

REFERENCES

Adams, M. J. (1990). *Beginning to Read: Thinking and learning about print.* Mass: MIT Press.
Anderson, R. C., Rand, J. S., & Montague, W. E. (1977). *School and the Acquisition of Knowledge.* Hillsdale, NJ: Erlbaum.
Bishop, D., & Adams, C. (1990). A prospective study of the relationship between specific language impairment, phonological disorders and reading retardation. *Journal of Child Psychology and Psychiatry, 31*(7), 1027–1050.

Brandsford, J. D., Brown, A. L., & Cocking, R. R. (1999). *How People learn: Brain, mind, experience and school.* Washington, D.C.: National Academy Press.

Chugani, H. T. (1997). Neuroimaging of developmental non-linearity and developmental pathologies. In: R. W. Thatcher, G. R. Lyon, J. Rumsey & N. Krasnegor (Eds), *Developmental Neuroimaging: Mapping the development of the brain and behaviour.* San Diego, CA: Academic Press.

Clay, M. M. (1975). *What Did I Write?* Auckland, NZ: Heinemann.

Clay, M. M. (1991). *Becoming Literate: The construction of inner control.* Auckland, NZ: Heinemann.

Clay, M. M. (1998). *By Different Paths to Common Outcomes.* York, Maine: Stenhouse.

De Groot, A. D. (1965). *Thought and Choice in Chess.* The Hague: Netherlands: Mouton.

Department of Education and Community Services (1996). *Early Years Literacy Profile.* Hobart, TAS: DECS.

Dyson, A. H. (1992). Whistle for Willie, lost puppies and cartoon dogs: The sociocultural dimensions of young children's composing. *Journal of Reading Behaviour, 24,* 433–462.

Dyson, A. H. (1993). From invention to social action in early childhood literacy: A reconceptualisation through dialogue about difference. *Early Childhood research Quarterly, 8,* 409–425.

Engle, S. (1995). *The Stories Children tell: Making sense of the narratives of Childhood.* NY: Freeman.

Gelman, R., & Brown, A. L. (1986). Changing views of cognitive competence in the young. In: N. Smelser & D. Gerstein (Eds), *Discoveries and Trends in behavioural and Social Sciences* (pp. 175–207). Washington, D.C.: National Academy Press.

Goodman, K. S. (1998). The reading process. In: V. Edwards & D. Corson (Eds), *Encyclopedia of Language and Education, 2,* 1–8.

Gray, B. (1999). Scaffolding Literacy with indigenous children in school. *SRP News,* (June), 3. Australian Curriculum Studies Association, DETYA Canberra: Commonwealth Government of Australia.

Hannon, P., & James, S. (1990). Parents' and teachers' perspectives on preschool literacy development. *British Educational Research Journal, 16*(3), 259–272.

Heath, S. B. (1983). *Ways With Words: Language, life and work in communities and classrooms.* Cambridge: Cambridge University Press.

Heibert, E. H. (1998). *Text Matters in Learning to Read.* CIERA Report #1–001. Ann Arbor: University of Michigan.

Heibert, E. H., Pearson, P. D., Taylor, B., Richardson, V., & Paris, S. G. (1998). *Every Child a Reader.* CIERA Ann Arbor: University of Michigan.

Hill, S., Comber, B., Louden, W., Rivalland, J., & Reid, J. (1998). *100 Children go to School.* DETYA, Canberra: Commonwealth of Australia.

Hill, S., & Louden, W. (1999). Literacy development during the first year of schooling. Paper presented at ACER Conference. *Improving Literacy Learning: What does the research tell us?* Adelaide, SA.

Juel, C. (1988). Learning to read and write: A longitudinal study of 54 children from first through fourth grade. *Journal of Educational Psychology, 80*(4), 437–447.

Konold, T. R., Juel, C., & McKinnon, M. (1999). *Building an Integrated Model of early Reading Acquisition.* CIERA. Ann Arbor: University of Michigan.

Kuhl, P. K. (1993). Innate predispositions and the effects of experience in speech perception: The native language magnet theory. In: B. de Boysson-Bardies, S. de Schonen, P. Juscyzyk,

P. McNeilage & J. Morton (Eds), *Developmental Neurocognition: Speech and face processing in the first year of life* (pp. 259–274). Dordrecht, NL: Kluwer.

Lesick, J. L. (1997). Research-based answers to questions about emergent literacy in the kindergarten. *Psychology in Schools, 34*(2), 143–160.

Luke, A. (1993). The social construction of literacy in the primary school. In: L. Unsworth (Ed.), *Literacy Learning and Teaching: Language as a social practice in the primary school.* Melbourne, VIC: MacMillan.

Neuman, S. (1999). Books make a difference: A study of access to literacy. *Reading Research Quarterly, 34*(3), 286–311.

Neuman, S., & Roskos, K. (1990). Print, play and purpose: Enriching play environments for literacy development. *Reading Teacher, 44*(3), 214–221.

Neuman, S., & Roskos, K. (1997). Literacy knowledge in practice: Contexts of participation for young writers and readers. *Reading Research Quarterly, 32*(1), 10–32.

Noble, E., & Foster, J. E. (1993). Play centres that encourage literacy development. *Day Care and Early Education, 21*(2), 22–26.

Olson, D. (1999). There are x kinds of learners in a single class: Diversity without individual differences. In: J. S. Gaffney & B. J. Askew (Eds), *Stirring the Waters: The influence of Marie Clay.* Portsmouth, NH: Heinemann.

Piaget, J. (1985). *The Equilibrium of Cognitive Structures: The central problem of intellectual development.* Chicago IL: University of Chicago Press.

Pickett, L. (1998). Literacy learning during block play. *Journal of Research in Childhood Education, 12*(2), 225–230.

Pintrich, P. R., & Schunk, D. (1996). *Motivation in Education: Theory, research and application.* Columbus, OH: Merrill, Prentice Hall.

Purcell-Gates, V. (1995). *Other People's Worlds: The cycle of low literacy.* Cambridge, MA: Harvard University Press.

Purcell-Gates, V. (1996). Stories, coupons and the TV guide: Relationships between home literacy experiences and emergent literacy knowledge. *Reading Research Quarterly, 31,* 406–429.

Raban, B. (1988). Language and literacy relationships: Some reflections. *British Journal of Educational Research, 14*(3), 12–25.

Raban, B. (1997). Reading skills: Emergent literacy. In: V. Edwards & D. Corson (Eds), *Encyclopedia of Language and Education* (Vol 2, pp. 19–26).

Raban, B. (2000). Reading: Literacy and beyond. In: B. Moon et al. (Eds), *International Companion to Education* (pp. 799–806). London; Routledge.

Raban, B., & Ure, C. (1997). Systemic issues in preschool teachers' practice. *Melbourne Studies in Education, 38*(2), 85–99.

Raban, B., Ure, C., & Smith, G. (1999). Accelerating literacy progress for new school entrants. Paper presented at the *Australian Association for Educational Research* Conference, Melbourne.

Raban, B., & Ure, C. (1999).Continuity for socially disadvantaged school entrants: Perspectives of parents and teachers. *Journal of Australian Research in Early Childhood Education, 7*(1), 54–65.

Robinson, S. E. (1973). *Predicting Early Reading Progress.* Master's thesis. University of Auckland.

Rogoff, B. (1990). *Apprenticeship in Thinking: Cognitive development in social context.* NY: Oxford University Press.

Schaffer, H. R. (1977). *Studies in Infant-Mother Interaction.* London: Academic Press.

Schwartz, D., & Brandsford, J. D. (1999). A time for telling. *Cognition and Instruction.*

Shore, R. (1997). *Rethinking the Brain: New insights into early development*. New York, NY: Family and Work Institute.

Smith, F. (1986). Insult to Intelligence: The bureaucratic invasion of our classrooms. Portsmouth NH: Heinemann.

Snow, C. E., Burns, M. S., & Griffin, P. (1998). *Preventing Reading Difficulties in Young Children*. Washington, D.C.: National Academy Press.

Ure, C., & Raban, B. (in press). Teachers' beliefs and understandings of literacy in the preschool: Preschool literacy project Stage 1. *Contemporary Issues in Early Childhood Education*.

Van Moorst, H., & Graham, S. (1995). *Kindergarten at the Crossroads: The Werribee Kindergarten Study*. Werribee, Vic: Victoria University of Technology Press.

Vukelich, C. (1990). Where's the paper? Literacy during dramatic play. *Childhood Education*, *66*(4), 205–209.

Vukelich, C. (1994). Effects of play interventions on young children's reading of environmental print. *Early Childhood Research Quarterly*, *9*, 153–170.

Walden, T. A., & Ogan, T. A. (1988). The development of social referencing. *Child Development*, *59*, 1230–1240.

Werner, E. E., & Smith, R. S. (1992). *Overcoming the Odds: High-risk children from birth to adulthood*. Ithaca: Cornell University Press.

Wood, D., Bruner, J. S., & Ross, G. (1976). The role of tutoring in problem-solving. *Journal of Child Psychology and Psychiatry*, *17*, 89–100.

Yaden, D. B., Rowe, D. W., & MacGillivray, L. (1999) *Emergent literacy: A polyphony of perspectives*. CIERA Report #1–005. Ann Arbor: University of Michigan.

10. EARLY MATHEMATICS

Carol Aubrey

> Between 'situated cognition' on the one hand, and cognitive neuro-psychology on the other, there may be scant common ground! But acceptance of the complementarity of different perspectives may be essential for progress towards a shared goal.
>
> (Donlan, 1998, *Preface, xiii*)

This chapter on early years mathematics education will adopt the position that traditionally research by cognitive psychologists on young children's early mathematical development has been experimental in design which, by excluding the context of learning as a source of knowledge, may have underplayed the extent to which mathematics is a socially-defined activity. How children approach mathematics depends upon the way in which they define and respond to the social situation in which it is presented. The challenge, as Nunes and Bryant (1996) have argued, is to help children form a view of mathematics that will enable them to bring their understanding from everyday life into the classroom. This, as they noted, may require the revision of 'our notion of what mathematics knowledge is and of how it is to be acquired' (Nunes & Bryant, 1996: 112). It requires a shift away from the view of 'conventional school maths learning as the all too mechanical transmission of a collection of facts to be learned by rote' (Lave, 1990: 309) towards a view of 'doing mathematics' as 'situated practice'. 'Doing mathematics', then, is always embedded in a context and situationally accomplished, so the question of *how* children learn mathematics, constructed through ethnomethodology and conversation analysis, becomes as important as *what* they know, accessed through the clinical investigation of children's existing knowledge and understanding. In other words, changing theoretical views of learning mathematics lead to corresponding shifts in the research methodologies being

Promoting Evidence-based Practice in Early Childhood Education:
Research and its Implications, Volume 1, pages 185–210.
2001 by Elsevier Science Ltd.
ISBN: 0-7623-0753-6

employed, as well as broader explanations of the way children learn mathematics.

From this discussion it can be seen that new theoretical orientations eschew the individualistic bias of traditional, experimental methods and stress instead the importance of documenting the social processes collectively produced by children and adults in the many interwoven local cultures that make up their lives (Corsaro & Molinari, 2000: 180). Ideally, longitudinal ethnography is best suited to the investigation of children's evolving experiences of learning and behaving in respect of mathematical activities and especially at key times of transition.

RESEARCH QUESTIONS

In order to examine the evidence we have concerning pedagogy in respect of early mathematics from these new theoretical perspectives, a set of questions springs to mind:

- how do young children engage in mathematical experiences in pre-school and home settings and how, if at all, is their learning being enhanced?
- how do adults support children's access to mathematical knowledge in different kinds of learning environments?
- what are the features of mathematical learning environments for children under three, under five and under eight?

These questions provide a structure for the examination of early childhood mathematics which will focus on:

- the home;
- the pre-school setting;
- the early years classroom (for five- to seven-year-olds).

Moreover the answers to such questions are likely to be reached through very detailed observations of children and the contexts in which they interact, including speech, activity and specific resources. Whilst broadly ethnographic in approach and likely to generate qualitative field data, both qualitative and quantitative methods may be utilised and analysed in a wide range of ways. In general such studies are small-scale, yet time-consuming. They can demand a time-scale which occupies months and sometimes years of working within the contexts being examined. They may demand data collection from different sources and perspectives in order to take account of the complexity of foci, described by Aubrey et al. (2000: 113) as 'the study of text(s) in context(s)'.

THE ORIGINS OF MATHEMATICAL COGNITION

As Donlan (1997) has suggested, arguments about innate mathematical cognition which serve as a foundation for mathematical development have been advanced alongside competing but, perhaps, complementary empiricist accounts. These hold that children's simple mathematical knowledge is grounded in their activities and interactions with adult authorities and that they learn about mathematical structure within their social and material world.

Wynn (1998) has generated a substantial body of evidence to support her view that human infants come into the world already equipped with number concepts and that they have the ability to represent number across a range of different kinds of entities – physical objects and patterns, regardless of colour, size or configuration – perceived through visual or auditory modalities. Using the so-called 'habituation method' she observed that infants 'habituate' to a given property, for example, a repeated display of two or three items, and will look longer at novel stimuli, that is, they will examine more persistently a *change* to that display which does not have the same property. Moreover, at five months an infant will look longer at the enactment with Mickey Mouse puppets of $1 + 1 = 1$ than $1 + 1 = 2$ or $2 - 1 = 2$ than $2 - 1 = 1$, when the first quantity is displayed, then hidden whilst the quantity is being manipulated, and finally revealed in order that the outcome can be disclosed. This, she has suggested, indicates that infants can not only represent number but engage in processes of numerical reasoning to determine the numerical relationship that holds between different numbers. At this age, infants manage numbers no greater than two to three though, sometimes, they can deal with three to four. Some time between eight to thirteen months, however, this expands to four to five. To account for this, Wynn uses the model of an 'accumulator' to represent an inborn mechanism that can determine discrete numbers of individual entities. Sophian (1998), on the other hand, does not accept the preverbal 'counting' of the accumulator model and has argued instead for a perceptual processing or 'subitizing' model which works faster than counting and can be inferred from the speed and accuracy with which adults and children are observed to enumerate small arrays of one to three objects, as compared with larger numerosities. Furthermore she has cited the work of Cooper (1984) who proposes that whilst ten- to twelve-month-old babies are sensitive to equal and unequal sets, it is not until fourteen to sixteen months that they respond to 'greater than' and 'less than' relations in respect of pairs of slides presented in rapid succession. The main thrust of Sophian's work, however, has been to consider the relation between infant numerical abilities and the development of verbal counting over the pre-school period and beyond. In this respect children's early awareness of Gelman and Gallistel's (1978; 1992) three 'how-to-count' principles – the one-to-one correspondence principle; the stable-order of counting principle; and the cardinality principle, attached to the last number in a count which quantifies the whole set – has provided an influential hypothesis which, again, holds that early on infants display innate knowledge of numerical properties. In fact, in addition to these three principles, they posited a further two – the order irrelevance principle which allows that items can be counted in any order and the abstraction principle, which indicates that all kinds of objects can be counted. Taking the notion of Wynn's accumulator in relation to Gelman and Gallistel's how-to-count principles, Sophian has suggested that the 'accumulator' may constitute an innate structure which *facilitates* children's attention to salient features of the counting process. Emphasis on innate structures, however, directs attention away from the influence of social activities and interactions in which children participate and which are directed to specific, socially-defined goals, as Sophian has emphasised. The important goal of early visual processing appears, thus, to help the infant to identify distinct objects within the visual field and discriminate changes in numerosity. The goal of quantification, in turn, engenders an interest in number words which is used to describe these quantities. This suggests a dynamic relation between goals and activities established through social interaction and children's developing mathematical knowledge. Sophian has favoured the notion of a dynamic relationship relation between children's conceptual knowledge about numbers and their goal-based numerical activities which, again, underlines the importance of paying close attention to the kinds of social interactions within which children engage in number.

YOUNG CHILDREN LEARNING WITH PARENTS

Durkin et al. (1986) made a longitudinal study of an opportunistic sample of ten infants' spontaneous reference to numbers and very early counting, in interactive and linguistic contexts of parental pedagogical strategies in conversational turn-taking, at monthly intervals from nine to twenty-four months, and at three-monthly intervals thereafter until thirty-six months. Below two years, number words were used either singly in conversation or as part of standard expressions, such as, 'one, two, three, go . . .'. Between twenty-one and thirty months recitation of the number sequence in the context of turn-taking was observed to constitute a substantial proportion of number-word utterances. Overall, in the second and third year, young children used number words incidentally or in conversation rather than in the context of generating the number string. Counting then blossomed but only one set of objects at a time.

At the time this study was carried out, it was not known how frequently children encountered number in parental speech, which numbers were used, or the distributions of particular numbers in children's early number productions. Nor was it known how clear were parental strategies in matching the number lexicon and other aspects of language to number experiences and behaviour. The most frequently produced words were 'one', 'two', 'three' and 'four' and mothers used these more often than children so that they had many opportunities for exposure to the first four numbers and, spasmodically, to larger numbers. Numbers were used in nursery rhymes, stories and songs, 'sequential complements' such as the example provided above . . . 'ready, one, two, three . . .', recitation of number strings . . . 'count them, look, one, two, three, four . . .', repetition and clarification of cardinality with simple counts, alternating strings between mother and child . . . 'one, your turn . . . two, three, . . . your turn . . . four,' and incidental uses . . . 'where do you live?' and 'how old are you?' In the early stages, children encountered numbers in a variety of ways though, interestingly, these routines declined considerably in the child's third year. At the same time, the number of words used by the child increased with age, just as the mother's declined. This study showed that children encounter numbers and counting in the course of interactions with their parents from before the emergence of language and throughout the period of early linguistic development. The relationship between parental strategies and the child's advancement in number and counting skills, however, is by no means clear and, as noted by Wood et al. (1978) not all parental strategies are equally effective. As Durkin et al. (1986) concluded, it is only by examining social-interactive contexts in which children acquire their number words that we can envisage the complexity of the knowledge and processes children bring to bear to make sense of their early experience. Since the recordings were made in a studio, with four cameras, two overhead microphones and with minimal materials, the context for learning as a source of knowledge was somewhat artificial, and this study highlights the need for closer attention to 'doing mathematics' in natural settings.

Hughes (1986) examined a large number of recorded conversations between young children of three to four years and their mothers, collected in a previous study (Tizard & Hughes, 1984) during their everyday interactions in the home. He concluded that there were relatively few conversations in the transcripts where the children's mothers were explicitly using the language of arithmetic. Walkerdine (1982: 1988) also drew upon the Tizard corpus to identify mathematical activities. She proposed that such learning could be understood as taking place within the social and discursive practices of the home or preschool setting and, in fact, she noted a remarkable similarity in mothers' and teachers' pedagogic discourse. She described certain sorts of tasks in relation to mathematics in the home suggesting that mother-child exchanges, in relation to practices involving number, could be classified using two typifications: *instrumental* and *pedagogic*. In instrumental tasks the mother's main focus or goal was the practical accomplishment of a task in which the numbers were used as an incidental feature whereas, in pedagogic tasks, numbers would be the explicit focus of a purposeful activity, that is, the teaching and practice of counting. Furthermore these practices could be distinquished from the more formal teaching situations by the participative role taken on by the mother. In the home mothers, to some extent, took on the role of playmate and equal participant, with the child as helpmate. Although in this play the adult and child were equal participants, the adult both joined in and extended the child's knowledge, recognising the pedagogic importance of the activities. Matthews and Matthews (1978), moreover, had emphasised that such practices were embedded in activities involving active manipulation of objects which provided opportunities, to take a different example, for classification, using such terms as 'big', 'little', 'small', 'bigger', 'smaller' or 'biggest'. This observation serves as a timely reminder that too close a focus on the discourse practices in isolation may result in a lack of attention to the social practices themselves and the materials or 'tools' which embody them. Meanwhile, Walkerdine also recognised that mothers engaged in pedagogic discourse which involved size relations but, as was the case for number, she stressed that discrimination of size might not be the main objective but simply the focus for imparting information relating to size. Furthermore, she noted that such discourse practices in the home were not always adult-initiated. Children themselves also initiated counting sequences quite spontaneously.

Another study of mother-child conversations in the home by Gordon Wells (1982) *Language at Home and at School*, 1972–1982, had not been examined from the mathematical perspective, according to recent correspondence with the writer. This work had involved a representative sample of one hundred and twenty-eight children who were followed from eighteen months to four years, at three-monthly intervals, in order to chart language development. It provided a natural data set for the present writer and colleagues (Aubrey, Godfrey & Godfrey, 2000) to exploit for evidence of home influences on the course of numerical development. An initial scrutiny of a set of transcripts for thirty-nine-month-old toddlers in conversation with their mothers was sufficient to reveal mothers supporting children's counting of objects, pictures and playing cards, most commonly one to four, but sometimes to six, seven and eight. There was one example of a child being supported to rote count to twelve and above, and one or two references to shape and position. As previous studies had shown, there were instances of children counting by themselves, though usually only from one to three. Ten full sets of transcripts were purchased from a researcher associated with the original project, which included five girls and five boys, who represented as wide a social spread as possible. Discourse covering important aspects of mathematical ideas and numeracy understanding were extracted from the transcripts. This included mathematical language such as 'in front of', 'bigger/smaller than', 'less' and 'more' to describe shape, position, size and quantity. It encompassed comparing, sorting, matching, ordering and sequencing activities, as well as counting familiar objects, recognising and recreating patterns, nursery rhymes, songs, counting games and activities. Recognition and use of numbers, practical problem-solving, indication of an awareness of number operations, such as addition and subtraction and the language involved, were also sought.

After identifying the number of ninety-second samples where reference was made to mathematics in recordings of approximately thirty-six minutes, it was possible to use the sample as a unit of account for the purpose of quantitative modelling. This served as a framework for the qualitative analysis which was carried out. Overall, 2.1% of samples made reference to mathematics. There was some variance between children and some indication of a slight increase with age. Most of the relevant references were made to number and counting, and only two references were made in field notes to shape and block-fitting activities, unaccompanied by speech. In terms of frequency, reference to shape and measure was second only to number and counting. Moreover, the most frequently-occurring utterance was the single utterance, where a mathematical reference made by the mother or child did not receive any response. In fact, the majority of these utterances arose from target children themselves. The most frequently-occurring exchange was two utterances which comprised, most often, a short comment, request or question and response. Adult-led exchanges revealed a pedagogic style which reinforced number words and counting objects in a didactic manner, as well as a more supportive and discursive style in which children might be tutored and guided, for example, in an activity which involved sorting cars by colour. Children practised counting by themselves, from one to three, and also talked aloud about size relations, predominantly 'big' and little'. This study goes some way to answering some of the questions which the Durkin et al. (1986) study posed, though what significance can be attached to the finding that 2.1% of samples contained reference to mathematics or, on average, one reference was made every thirty-six minutes? The evidence being largely verbal in nature may not, however, have provided as complete a picture of other activities in the home which contributed to children's developing mathematical understanding as might be hoped.

More recently Donlan (1997), on the basis of an unpublished diary record, summed up early achievements by noting that from as young as two years children are developing the skills to allow them to share with others, both their awareness of numerical attributes of objects or events and their grasp of written numerical symbols. Whilst it is interesting to note here the first reference to very young children's attention being drawn to *written* symbols the parent, in this case, as cognitive scientist with a primary interest in the development of early mathematical skills, may not be the most naive of research participants!

Bottle (1999) has reported an on-going study of mathematics in the home over children's pre-school years, using observation, interview and diary records. Of the six families to figure in her first report of this study, all described mathematical tasks carried out by their young children though only one half seemed aware of the mathematical significance of these or their possible relationship to later educational achievement. Again, number and counting activities predominated. All children were observed by the researcher to experience mathematical tasks initiated by adults in which they were actively involved. Five of the six children also observed adult-initiated, as well as engaged in child-initiated tasks on their own. Activities varied in length from less than one minute, which was most common, to one observed activity which lasted for over fifteen minutes. Overall the range, quality and extent of mathematical experience varied from child to child.

Young (1995), in an unpublished Ph.D. thesis, maintained a personal diary record over a twenty-month period of home mathematical experiences, as well as collecting diaries from six other families from two to four years. Home as well as playgroup or nursery video-recordings were made, six nursery nurse/ teacher interviews were also carried out, as well as forty parent interviews. Hour for hour, the average pre-school setting recorded a higher number of numerical mediations with adults, although the nature of home and pre-school experiences was similar. Being able to recite numbers to twenty, count in one-to-one correspondence to ten, recognise small quantities and, possibly, recognise the first ten digits was thought to be all the young child needed or would be expected to know. Once these expectations were met, mathematical support appeared to subside. No real need or use was seen by adults for large numbers, number recognition or sums, which were unnecessary for children's play and daily routines. Numerical mediation always took place in the context of the adult's involvement in a child's activities, such as counting buttons whilst dressing or when a play situation was developed to mediate aspects of number, such as playing dominoes. Parental interviews indicated, as did those in the Bottle study, that varying rates in the quality and quantity of number-mediated interaction were probably widespread, and young children's accomplishments with number seemed to be linked to the quantity and quality of mediated interactions with the caregiver. Moreover, all nursery teachers interviewed indicated that young children entered nursery school with a wide range of already-developed number skills and this supported the conclusion that there was a discernible relationship between children's spontaneous use of number, and the quality and quantity of mediated support.

LEARNING AND TEACHING IN THE PRE-SCHOOL SETTING

Munn and Schaffer (1993) in a study of ten Scottish nurseries and two- to three-year-old children, noted the scarcity of numerical experiences relative to literacy experiences in all nurseries. Very few activities explicitly dealt with quantity or comparison and very little talk specifically focused on number and quantity. In fact, just 5% of time for two-year-olds and three-year-olds was recorded. This is considerably more than the recorded 1.6% incidence of mathematical and numerical experiences in New Zealand kindergartens by Young-Loveridge et al. (1995).

Munn (1995) examined the role of organised pre-school learning in literacy and numeracy development, and observation confirmed a relationship between levels of staff reflectiveness and the quality of children's literacy and numeracy experiences. In Scottish nurseries, moreover, it appeared that progress in literacy and numeracy as communication systems was related to children's development in symbol understanding. Clearly concepts of early mathematics and numeracy change over context and over time. As Nunes and Bryant (1996) noted, to think mathematically about situations children need mathematical systems of representation and these systems need to have meaning. That is, they can be related to the situations in which they are used. The question still remains about which tools we may need to be numerate in today's world, as noted by Nunes and Bryant, and whether, in our present case of a Scottish nursery, numeracy as a formal system related to symbol understanding best maps onto young children's own existing, quantitiative knowledge.

In this context, Munn (1997) was able to show that pre-school children's numerical goals might not be the same as their adult partners where, for them, early counting was essentially imitative of the social practices and playful in intent rather than quantitative, with little sense of adult definitions. For her, shifts towards a greater self-consciousness occurred around school age and these might be accounted for in terms of changes in children's social environments which increasingly emphasised the importance of symbolic function. Munn (1998) identified children's growing awareness of the function of numerical symbols as a foundation for subsequent development of arithmetic skills. Maturing use of symbols when integrated with the development of number concepts was seen to 'bootstrap' numeracy development in ways far superior to concrete number experience.

Nunes and Bryant (1996: 20) have argued more broadly that conceptual development in mathematics proceeds through understanding of logical principles, learning new forms of mathematical representation, and connecting old forms to new situations in order to enrich them with meaning. This takes us right back to the origins of mathematical thinking discussed above. From this perspective, children may be observed to count well, yet neither understand the significance of counting in order to deploy it effectively, nor appreciate the variety of situations in which counting can serve as an effective strategy for problem-solving. Moreover, whilst Piaget has become a controversial figures in respect of his claims about logic and children's mathematics, as noted by Nunes and Bryant (1996: 6) 'there is no disagreement at all, so far as we know, about the other aspect of Piaget's theory, that *children must grasp certain logical principles in order to understand mathematics*'. The best-known of these principles, or 'invariants', was conservation, which holds that the number of a set of objects can only be changed by addition or subtraction: all other changes are irrelevant. This notion has already been introduced above in the context of the counting principles. Similarly, all quantities (number, size, weight, temperature) can be arranged in order from smaller to larger according to a basic logical rule of 'transitivity'. So, for example, if one quantity X, is greater than another quantity Y, which itself is greater than a third quantity Z, then it follows that X is also greater than Z. Young children who have an incomplete idea of this rule will not have full understanding of the relationship between different numbers or measures. It also follows that not only do children need to understanding that increasing or decreasing a set size changes the quantity but that these changes have *inverse* effects. To take the early illustration from Wynn's work with infants, $2 - 1 = 1$ and $1 + 1 = 2$, or $2 + 1 - 1 = 2$. These are very basic principles but, nevertheless, are being established gradually through the period of early mathematics development which this chapter covers and, moreover, underpin children's early mathematical understanding. To revisit Sophian's (1998) description of mathematical learning as 'progressing from special cases to more general ones', it can now be better appreciated that this may include cognitive constraints, understood as beliefs, expectations or goals, age-related changes in the kinds of socially-mediated activities within which children engage with numbers, as well as developmental constraints which may be biological, as well as social and cultural, and which limit the effectiveness of children's numerical strategy use.

THE PROCESSES OF INSTRUCTION IN EARLY YEARS CLASSES

Given the above description of children's mathematical development, the findings from ten years of this writer's own empirical research into four- and five-year-olds' mathematical knowledge and abilities, before and during the early stages of schooling (Aubrey, 1993, 1994, 1995, 1996; Suggate, Aubrey & Pettitt, 1997) should come as no surprise.

Work with these children showed not only that children brought into school a rich informal knowledge of counting, recognition of numerals, skill in simple addition, subtraction and social sharing, but that this matured considerably over the children's first year in school. Most striking of all was the sheer range of knowledge and competence possessed by children at the beginning of schooling and, indeed, the diversity of this knowledge was in no way diminished by the end of the first year. Improvement in some was observed in counting reliably, reading and writing numbers and problem-solving. A few others still showed little knowledge of counting, number skills or arithmetic by the end of the year. Characteristics of the observed curriculum, however, were an emphasis on play, flexibility and choice, as well as teacher-focused group work, which emphasised areas in which children had already demonstrated competence. Significant was the fact that whilst many children entered school with competence in solving simple concrete word problems, the introduction of calculation in school was determined by its position in the published school scheme of work. In fact, of seven teachers observed during one year of the project, four were observed to introduce no simple calculation at all and the others did, in between only one and three lessons. Overall, there was little evidence of four-year-olds carrying out addition and subtraction in simple problem-solving situations. It was concluded that 'empirical investigation of young children's construction of mathematical knowledge provides both a starting point for designing an appropriate curriculum and a means of critical analysis of existing curricula .... It remains now for us to consider the development of instruction by the creation of a curriculum content and sequence that both reflects and advances the structure of children's existing forms of representation, problem solving and knowledge' (Aubrey, 1997: 88).

More recently Hughes, Desforges and Mitchell (1999, 2000) have investigated different approaches to applications of mathematics for children five- to seven-years-of-age which, they observed, reflected teachers different theories about how children can be helped, as well as their immediate perceptions of what was appropriate at that stage of their learning. Children, for their part, found difficulty in using and applying knowledge outside school to novel problem situations. The writers concluded that in the context of recent changes to the English mathematics curriculum with its prescribed content, emphasis on number knowledge and calculation skills, such work had a low priority. As Brown et al. (2000) have noted, in the longer term this curriculum shift, while in an appropriate direction may well be shown to have gone too far, and necessitate eventually a counter-movement towards the synthesis and meaning needed for creative application, problem-solving and investigation.

Designing and implementing a research-based, early years mathematics curriculum is in itself a formidable task, as noted by Fuson (1997). This demands consideration of:

- knowledge of mathematics as a subject;
- learning trajectories in young children's thinking and how to move children through those learning trajectories;
- the structure of particular domains within early mathematics, for instance, early counting and its relationship to later calculation strategies; as well as
- the challenge of building on the existing knowledge children bring into the setting.

It also raises fundamental questions about the nature of that knowledge and the assumptions underlying its applications, which carry implications for both programme design and for teaching. Typically such interventions, which have been designed to raise young children's mathematical understanding, have placed central emphasis on children's informal knowledge. Peterson et al. (1989), for instance, have argued for a better appreciation and use to be made of children's informal knowledge in school instruction. Their argument rests upon four related constructs that represent fundamental assumptions underlying much contemporary cognitive research into children's learning:

- children construct their own mathematical knowledge;
- maths teaching should be organised to facilitate children's construction of knowledge;
- children's development of mathematical ideas should provide the basis for sequencing topics for instruction;
- mathematics skills should be taught in relation to understanding and problem-solving.

Over the last decade, a number of researchers have turned their attention to this rich body of knowledge in order to develop programmes that involve learning and teaching mathematics in the early years of schooling (for example, Cobb, Wood, Yackel, Nicholls, Wheatley, Trigatti & Perlwitz, 1991; Fennema, Carpenter & Peterson, 1989; Griffin & Case, 1997, in the United States). Comparable work which draws on a similar knowledge base has been carried out by Young-Loveridge et al. (1993, 1994, 1995, 1999) in New Zealand and Wright et al. (1993 and 1997) in Australia, and more recently, Wright, Martland and Stafford (2000) in England. Some, notably Griffin et al., have argued that low achievement for mathematics has its origins in the variability in levels of mathematical understanding which can be detected as early as four- to five-years-of-age. It has been shown that variability in mathematics achievement at school entry increases as children proceed through school, getting further behind. The programmes of Griffin and Case and Young-Loveridge have, in fact, been designed specifically to change the long-term outcomes for children in lower-achieving groups.

Whilst the underlying models and theories of children's early numerical conceptions have differed, as well as the nature of the social context and role of supporting adults, there are commonalities in number 'recovery' programmes such as those designed by Griffin and Case and Young-Loveridge. Such interventions which, in each case, have used number-based board and card games to develop the early numerical cognition of four- and five-year-olds, have been successful in demonstrating significant gains which appear to be sustained, at least in the short-term. These programmes represent comprehensive models of intervention which focus, as noted above, on low-achieving groups and include assessment material, curriculum resources and teacher education. Also in common has been the shared belief in the effectiveness of game-like formats in providing motivation, reinforcement and practice of relevant skills, acquisition of concepts and real-life problem-solving, benefits identified by Ernest (1986). Kamii (1985, 1989), too, was a notable advocate of the use of number games to foster mathematical development and, in the England, Sugarman (1997) has made a significant contribution to the recognition that pupils' developing awareness of the ways in which the number system operates can be promoted through the use of games.

Whilst aware of the problems and pitfalls, Ainley (1988, 1990) also recognised that mathematical games were rich in their potential for providing real and enjoyable contexts, applying newly-acquired skills and concepts, and the means for informal assessment through observation and questioning. Perhaps most important, she recognised the fundamental role of the adult in

demonstrating and modelling, observing and monitoring, helping and supporting games in which children of all levels of achievement engaged.

In summary, those children who enter school unable to count, compare
quantities of different amounts and construct mental representations of these,
are likely to fail in school mathematics. Programmes such as those of Griffin
and Case (1997) capitalise upon the knowledge-base concerning young
children's early informal mathematical cognitions and attribute later failure to
the variability of basic school entry skills. Intervention programmes designed
to improve basic number skills through games have been found to be effective
in providing children with a great deal of practice in basic mathematical
concepts, in a motivating and meaningful social context. Such programmes are
thought to offer general ideas for conceptualising children's learning and
showing how assessment can inform teachers' theories of children's learning.

As noted above, however, comprehensive curriculum design which takes
account of mathematics as a subject, children's learning and construction of
that subject, as well as teaching which facilitates children's movement through
the domains of early mathematics, is a challenge indeed. In the case of the
interventions described here, their function has been to supplement an existing
curriculum rather than replace it – to provide 'catch-up' of essential early
concepts and skills in the course of on-going, regular curriculum experiences.
The extent and duration of interventions has varied, and additional support
tends to have been provided for the class teacher by other educational
professionals or parents. Perhaps their most important characteristic is that they
provide examples of 'doing mathematics as situated practice' which shifts
away from the conventional school mathematics transmission model. Ueno
(1998) has attempted to formulate the 'situated practice' view in terms of
context. In the situated view:

- first of all, the context is not a static given but situatedly organized by
  participants of an activity with various resources in an ongoing activity;
- secondly, the meaning of speech, action and use of tools are always
  dependent upon context at the same time that speech, action and use of
  artefacts reflexively constitutes the context of *other* speech, actions and tool
  use in a sequence of interaction;
- thirdly, while talk, action and use of tools or participants become some of the
  resources for organising a context, they simultaneously socially display
  participants' ways of understanding the context;
- fourthly, context is interactively organised, understood and formulated by
  participants in an activity.

In these programme familiar artefacts and procedures of calculation have been organised to serve specific game-like practices and these have been utilised for organising specific courses of actions and mathematical procedures, within these practices. In contrast to the formal curriculum, decontextualised skills and knowledge have no place. Learning skills and knowledge cannot be separated from learning to organise a context.

It seems, so far, that attempts to address low mathematics achievement in the English-speaking world have lead to earlier and earlier interventions. Moss (1999) has suggested that the young child has become an item on the agenda of two major and related projects: improved educational standards in schools and increasing economic competitiveness. Ball (1999), moreover, has argued that the over-riding emphasis on education's role in contributing to economic competitiveness rests on a set of pedagogical strategies the effects of which are antithetical to the needs of a 'high skills' economy. The acquisition of skills and dispositions in current policy terms is stripped of social and psychological meaning to serve 'performativity'. The current pressures for performance act back on pedagogy and the curriculum, both narrowing the classroom experience and shaping it to maximise test scores. This is in some contrast to learning theory of, for instance, Lave (1988) or Rogoff (1990) or, indeed, mathematics as conceived by the original English National Curriculum group which emphasised investigations, open-ended problem-solving and real world applications.

DUTCH REALISTIC APPROACHES

By contrast, to take an example from outside the English-speaking world, a new approach to mathematics education has been developed at the Freudenthal Institute, in the Netherlands, termed 'realistic mathematics'. Instead of simply taking the knowledge base of children's early mathematical thinking as a starting point, realistic curriculum development is embedded within a broad theoretical framework which provides a basis for the curriculum and a tool for constructing teaching and learning approaches. It may be easiest to demonstrate how the instructional-theoretical framework works by providing an example from the primary mathematics curriculum, namely, the introduction of 'the bus' model (Van Brink, 1991).

In realistic mathematics instruction, as Gravemeijer (1994: 85) noted a 'standard procedure is taught by letting it evolve from informal ones, in a learning process which starts in a situation where a mathematical model offers itself in a natural manner'. The bus context is introduced in relation to counting skills and the on-going changes in passengers getting on and off a bus. This provides a realistic situation in which addition and subtraction can emerge as well as a description of these quantitative changes in terms of an informal written language. Children are introduced to a context which can be developed into a 'maths drama' based on passengers getting on and off a bus, with role-play of a situation to 'realise' their own ideas and experiences. Turns are taken in play-acting as passengers, bus driver or 'storyteller' who decides how many passengers get on or off the bus and, in this way, children help to determine what takes place. A special arrow language is introduced together with drawings of buses on the chalk-board to form a 'bus chain'. A number is written on the side of the bus showing how many passengers are on the bus. The arrow linking the buses indicates direction and the sign at the bus stop shows how many people get on or off.

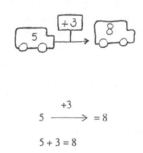

$$5 \xrightarrow{+3} = 8$$

$$5 + 3 = 8$$

Fig. 1. Progressive fading of arrow language.

From: Brink, F. J. van den (1991). Realistic arithmetic education for yound children. In L. Streefland (Ed.) *Realistic mathematics education in primary school. On the occasion of the opening of the Freudenthal Institute.* Utrecht University: CD-β Press.

Meanwhile the arrow language in the bus context can be generalised to other situations which children generate in 'free productions', such as queueing in the post office, without the arrows losing their meaning. Gradually the arrow language is replaced by standard forms of notation and 'bare sums'. Although children may operate with formal language symbols, their knowledge of number relations remains connected to the original bus context. This is consistent with Freudenthal's view of children's 'mathematizations' as activities in which they can move back and to between the real world context and the world of symbols which represent it. An everyday problem is recast in mathematical terms The gradual fading of meaning of the symbols supports the idea that mathematics. can be carried out at different levels and a lower level can itself be the object of analysis at a higher level.

At the ground level, mathematics – as in bus transportation problems – is attached to objective quantities and actions. At the first level, relations between numbers and quantities become the objective of investigation, as a relational field is being created, for example, two passengers on a bus and one descends at ground level becomes 'two minus one' or $2 - 1 = 1$. At the second level, the relations themselves, are under investigation, for instance, the inverse relation $a - b = c$ is equivalent to $c + b = a$, or $2 - 1 = 1$ and $1 + 1 = 2$. Connections are made which allow the creation of a logical system. The gradual fading of the meaning of the symbols supports the idea of 'vertical mathematization', that is, the transfer of the bus context to the context of 'bare' arithmetic sums. This is achieved by means of the bare arrows which were already contextually embedded in the material. The reinvention principle is illustrated in the decorated arrow language which describes quantitative changes. As the decoration is faded the arrow language becomes more central and increasingly detached from reality. This also illustrates the notion of formalization, as everyday language is exchanged for the formal language of mathematics. Meaning to arithmetic problems is thus achieved and can be extended, for instance, with a double-decker bus, illustrating the commutative property (four passengers upstairs and two downstairs being the same as two upstairs and four downstairs) as well as the relationship between 'doubles' (four upstairs and four downstairs) and 'near doubles' (four upstairs and five downstairs). See Fig. 2 (top of next page).

Following the idea of guided reinvention, children explore number relations, properties and notation by way of real-life contexts which allow these relations, properties and notations to be reinvented in the bus.

A key idea of realistic instruction theory has been for children to 'reinvent' mathematics under the guidance of the teacher, who builds upon their existing ideas in a highly interactive manner. This has resulted in theory-formation at different levels – from domain-specific instructional theory, through teaching particular topics or courses, to micro theories located in specific teaching activities. It has also resulted in the creation of relevant instructional material.

Freudenthal (1983), thus, expressed structure in the number curriculum in two dimensions. The first dimension distinguished basic number concepts and the second dimension formed the developmental stages of a relational framework. The relational framework was dependent upon the formation of relationships at ground level between counting and 'numerosity' number. He distinguished among many number concepts, differing in content and form, and informed by different methodological, developmental and didactical perspectives. Fundamental to this analysis was the question of different forms of access to the concept of number for children. In other words, how numbers

The double-decker bus representation is also used to illustrate properties

and connections between 'doubles' and near-doubles:

Whilst children are using real-life problems, they are also being inducted into the logical properties of number.

Fig. 2. Double decker bus problems.

From: Aubrey, C. (1999). *A Developmental Approach to Early Numeracy.* Birmingham Questions.

emerged, and how their domains and operations are extended – or restricted. Five uses of number were distinguished:

- *reference number,* which refers simply to learning numerals;
- *counting number,* which is learning the number sequence, including counting forwards and backwards;
- *numerosity number,* which refers to the notion of cardinal number or amount, and the recognition of equivalence or non-equivalence between sets with the same number of elements (this implies one-to-one correspondence but not necessarily counting);
- *measuring* or '*proportional*' number, which is commonly used in real-life to express a relation, for example, a child might think 3 small chocolates for 2p is better value than one chocolate bar for 10p, where cost expresses a relation;
- *reckoning number,* which is really a different entity, since arithmetic involves working with numbers within a system of conventions and rules, hence, it appears at level one of the relational framework, when children are exploring at ground level.

The first dimension of analysis is described as phenomenological as it connects number to real-life and fits with the notion of reinvention. The second dimension, developmental stages of a relational framework, as noted above, takes as its starting point exploration of different aspects of the concept of number at ground level and was integrated in reckoning number at the first level of thinking.

The construction of a framework is made possible by restricting it to small areas, for example, numbers zero to six. Here various number relations can be explored which lead to structuring (splitting or re-ordering into two equal and unequal groups), which precedes addition and subtraction, and forms the basis for exploring the larger area of zero to twelve and later, zero to twenty. Exploration at each successive stage, will incorporate previously formed relations. At first, a child may be able to say that two bricks added to an existing three, already hidden under the adult's hand, will make five altogether, but not recognise that three bricks taken away from the eight bricks, already hidden under the adult's hand, leaves five bricks. Later it will be recognised that buying five, one-penny toffees from a purse of nine pence will leave four pence but not necessarily known that buying a seven pence ticket will leave eight pence in a purse containing fifteen pence.

In respect of simple arithmetic, two aspects of number concept can be explored:

- *counting number*, with addition and subtraction related to counting-on and back;
- *numerosity number*, where structuring number is central.

Whilst these are described separately they are, in fact, closely integrated in:

- *resultative counting*, which requires that countable objects are mapped one-by-one onto the number-word sequence and the last number represents the cardinal number, in other words, the counting principles.

From the Dutch perspective, the relational framework is dependent upon the formation of relationships at ground level between counting and numerosity number. Treffers (1991) identified various forms and functions of counting in terms of:

- *acoustic counting*, or reciting the counting sequence;
- *synchronous* (or asynchronous) *counting*, counting in unison with rhythmic movements;
- *resultative counting*, counting or otherwise determining amounts;

- *abbreviated counting*, by taking structured amounts of differing sizes, with ordered and unordered, or visible and partly visible, sets of objects. The ability to count acoustically and synchronously is prerequisite to resultative counting, that is, it is necessary but not sufficient. Children who have mastered these skills, in the case of resultative counting, will need to deploy them efficiently to determine amounts. Commonly, however, children find difficulty in co-ordinating reciting the counting words and rhythmical, one-to-one touching of objects to be counted. Typically children who can recite the counting sequence and yet fail in resultative counting tasks, either do not count everything or count some things twice in response to 'how many?' questions, particularly if arrays of objects are not set out in a line.

Bearing in mind the popularity of board games for developing early number concepts in recovery programmes, noted in an earlier section of this chapter, it is interesting to note that board games which involve counting and rolling a die are also regarded by Dutch educators, as presenting a context for practising the subskills together in a meaningful context. Here modelling, demonstration and coaching by the adult, and gradual appropriation by the child, occur in a natural game-like situation. Counting the dots of the die throw, or instantly recognising an amount, is related to the number of synchronous moves on a board and children quickly learn the configuration of dots up to six. Counting number and numerosity number are combined and counting-on is related to working with quantities.

In fact, counting on the number line can also be abbreviated to allow for counting in smaller or larger structured amounts. Questions like, 'who threw the biggest/smallest number (most/least) stimulate comparison of amounts and once two dice are introduced, the possibilities for counting and combining two numbers, as well as recognising doubles up to twelve, are increased. First, counting the separate numbers one after the other and recounting takes place, later 'successive' counting of only the second number occurs, for example, five and two more quickly becomes . . . five, six, seven.

This procedure also links counting number to numerosity number and, hence, supports the development of resultative counting. The most elementary form of addition – recounting – is linked first to counting of quantities, which, through a process of 'shortening and internationalization' of the action, becomes increasingly detached from concrete objects. The objects to be counted disappear from the foreground to be replaced by counting-on (in jumps). The same process can be used for counting back within the number sequence, for instance, in the game of Snakes and Ladders, which leads progressively to subtraction. Counting games can be seen not only as the basis for resultative counting but remain significant as the foundation for addition and subtraction. In other words, the number line serves both as a *working* model, which allows for a mental image of a number word sequence to be constructed as a series of ordered numbers, and as a starting point for reflecting on the relationship between addition and subtraction by means of visualizing the number line, that is, a *reflection* model for building a relational number framework.

Two examples from learning strands have now been examined – calculation through the 'bus' context and early counting concepts. Each illustrate five major learning and teaching principles that lie at the heart of realistic mathematics. The first learning principle is that learning mathematics is a constructive activity. Children discover successive counting or calculation for themselves. This is possible because at the start of a learning strand a concrete basis for the skill to be learned is laid. The second learning principle is that learning of a mathematical concept or skills is a process which is often stretched over a long term and which moves at various levels of abstraction. Early counting and calculation, for instance, spans the years of birth to eight years and shifts from physical manipulation of objects to mental manipulation of symbols. In order to cross from informal, context-bound arithmetic to formal arithmetic the child must have at his or her disposal the tools to bridge the gap between concrete and abstract.

Materials, visual models, model situations, schemes, diagrams and symbols serve this purpose and, in fact, schematising with a 'mental' number line, can also provide the basis for a bridge between concrete and abstract. Raising the level of the learning process is promoted through reflection on thought processes, as seen above, and leads to the third instruction principle, that pupils must continuously have the opportunity – and be stimulated to – reflect on what has been encountered and what may lie ahead. Learning is, thus, not merely a solo activity but one which is located in society and directed by that socio-cultural context – the fourth principle of learning. Free productions and solution methods are discussed and evaluated in the group and in the case of counting board games, a sense of fairness gives the stimulus and purpose to accurate counting and co-operative turn-taking. The fourth instruction principle says that mathematics education should by nature be interactive. Besides individual work, there is opportunity for exchange of ideas, evaluating arguments and discussion of short cuts. The fifth learning principle is that learning mathematics is the construction of knowledge and skills in a structured process. For the fifth instruction principle, learning strands must, where possible, be intertwined with each other.

CONCLUSIONS

Dutch realistic mathematics provides an early years curriculum in which:

- formal knowledge can be developed from children's informal strategies;
- teaching in school is not isolated from the real world but related to that world by using the knowledge and experience children already have;
- a process which is as natural as possible allows children to contribute to the teaching/learning process;
- mathematization is important in developing knowledge from children's own thinking;
- 'horizontal' mathematization allows children to come up with mathematical tools to help organise and solve a problem located in a real-life situation – leading from the perceived world to the world of symbols; and
- 'vertical' mathematization enables children to operate within the mathematical system itself through a process of reorganisations and operations, that is, with a world of symbols.

Gradually as children become more proficient they 'graduate' to number positioning on a bead string as an introduction to a semi-structured number line up to 20 and then to 100. Again, the beads are faded away as children are left with an empty number line upon which can be mapped their existing informal knowledge. This allows mental calculation with smaller numbers under 20 and larger number up to 100. In turn, mental arithmetic is a stepping stone to written addition and subtraction on the one hand, as well as a natural bridge back to the informal strategies children bring into school.

This image of teaching is entirely consistent with the models and approaches proposed by Griffin and Case (1997) in the U.S. and Young-Loveridge (1991, 1994 and 1995) in New Zealand all of whom were aware of realistic methods. Bearing in mind the relatively low incidence of mathematical experiences in home and preschool setting, improving children's number knowledge through the use of mathematical games is an obvious target for development. Whilst preparing this chapter a leading mathematics teacher, in discussion with the writer attributed the lack of numerosity knowledge in her reception class to the reduction in children's use of mathematical games. This echoed the view of a teacher involved in research carried out by this writer some eight years ago:

> I've watched children play . . . make their own games up . . . they don't seem to have the form of games that we did. I can remember when I was little as soon as you could sit on the carpet you played games – board games . . . . That's right, and dominoes and cards, especially with grandparents and with my mother and father . . . . They would play for fun with pennies and so they learned a terrific lot even before school.

Indeed, it seems the case that not only do young English-speaking children live in social and physical contexts which offer relatively few opportunities for developing early mathematical problem-solving and numerical concepts, but that they may be losing a cultural tradition of number games which has provided a real-life context for the development of such skills. This chapter has explored how children engage in learning experiences in home, preschool and school setting and how learning can be enhanced through the use of numerical games. A theoretical model from Dutch realistic mathematics has been described in order to show key features of appropriate practice for three- to five-year-olds and its rich potential to inform early years pedagogy by providing children with access to mathematical knowledge which builds upon and extends their previous knowledge gained in diverse social and cultural settings Moreover the provision of key model situations, such as the transportation context, provides a bridge between their own, real world experience and the more abstract world of mathematics. In the end it is practitioners themselves who are best placed to make sensible links and imaginative leaps between researcher's knowledge and real life classroom contexts.

REFERENCES

Ainley, J. (1988). Playing games and real mathematics. In: D. Pimm (Ed.), *Mathematics, Teachers and Children*. London: Hodder and Stoughton.

Ainley, J. (1990). Playing games and learning mathematics. In: L. P. Steffe & T. Wood (Eds), *Transforming Children's Mathematics Education: International Perspectives*. Hillsdale, NJ: Erlbaum.

Aubrey, C. (1993). An investigation of the mathematical knowledge and competencies which young children bring into school. *British Educational Research Journal, 19*(1), 19–37.

Aubrey, C. (1994). An investigation of children's knowledge of mathematics at school entry and the knowledge their teachers hold about teaching and learning mathematics, about young learners and mathematical subject knowledge. *British Educational Research Journal, 20*(1), 105–120.

Aubrey, C. (1995). Teacher and pupil interaction and the processes of mathematical instruction in four reception classrooms over children's first year in school. *British Educational Research Journal, 21*(1), 31–47.

Aubrey, C. (1996). An investigation of teachers' mathematical subject knowledge and the processes of instruction in reception classes. *British Educational Research Journal, 22*(2), 181–197.

Aubrey, C. (1997). *Mathematics Teaching in the Early Years. An Investigation of Teachers' Subject Knowledge*. London: The Falmer Press.

Aubrey, C., Godfrey, R., & Godfrey, J. (2000). Children's early numeracy experiences in the home. *Primary Practice, 26*, 36–42.

Bottle, G. (1999). A study of children's mathematical experiences at home. *Early Years, 20*(1), 53–64.

Brink, van den (1991). Realistic arithmetic education for young children. In: L. Streefland (Ed.), *Realistic Mathematics Education in Primary School* (pp. 77–92). Utrecht, CD-β Press.

Brown, M., Millett, A., Bibby, T., & Johnson, D. C. (2000). Turning our attention from the what to the how: the National Numeracy Strategy. *British Educational Research Journal, 26*(4), 455–471.

Cobb, P., Wood, T., Yackel, E., & McNeal, B. (1992). Characteristics of classroom mathematics traditions: An interactional analysis. *American Educational Research Journal, 29*(3), 573–604.

Cobb, P., Wood, T., Yackel, E., Nicholls, J., Wheatley, G., Trigatti, B., & Perlwitz, M. (1991). Assessment of a problem-centred second-grade mathematics project. *Journal for Research in Mathematics Education, 22*(1), 3–29.

Corsaro, W. A., & Molinari, L. (2000). Entering and observing children's worlds. In: P. Christensen & A. James, (Eds), *Research with Children. Perspectives and Practices*. London: The Falmer Press.

Donlan, C. (1997). Unpublished diary study. In: C. Donland (Ed.), *The Development of Mathematical Skills*. Hove: Psychology Press.

Durkin, K., Shire, B., Riem, R., Crowther, R. D., & Rutter, D. R. (1986). The social and linguistic context of early number word use. *British Journal of Developmental Psychology, 4*, 269–299.

Ernest, P. (1986). Games: A rationale for their use in the teaching of mathematics in school. *Mathematics in School, 15*, 2–5.

Fennema, E., Carpenter, T. P., & Peterson, P. L. (1989). Learning mathematics with understanding: Cognitively guided instruction. In: J. Brophy (Ed.), *Advances in Research on Teaching* (Vol. 1). Greenwich, CT: JAI Press.

Freudenthal, H. (1973). *Mathematics as an Educational Task*. Dordrecht: Reidel.

Freudenthal, H. (1983). *Didactical Phenomenology of Mathematical Structures*. Dordrecht: Reidel.

Fuson, K. C. (1997). Research-based mathematics curricula: New foundational goals require programs of four interacting levels of research. *Issues in Education, 3*(1), 67–80.

Gallimore, R. (1996). Classrooms are just another cultural activity. In: D. L. Speece & B. K. Keogh (Eds), *Research on Classroom Ecologies: Implications for Inclusion of Children with Learning Disabilities* (pp. 229–250). Mahwah, NJ: Erlbaum.

Gelman, R., & Meck, E. (1992). Early principles aid initial but not later conceptions of number. In: J. Bideaud, C. Meljac & J. P. Fischer (Eds), *Pathways to Number: Children's Developing Numerical Abilities* (pp. 29–57). Hillsdale, NJ: Erlbaum.

Gravemeijer, K. P. E. (1994). *Developing Realistic Mathematics Education*. Utrecht University: CD-β Press.

Griffin, S., & Case, R. (1997). Re-thinking the primary school math curriculum: An approach based on cognitive science. *Issues in Education. Contributions from Educational Psychology, 3*(1), 1–50.

Hughes, M. (1986). *Children and Number. Difficulties in Learning Mathematics*. Oxford: Blackwell.

Hughes, M., Desforges, C., & Mitchell, C. (1999). Using and applying mathematics at Key Stage. In: I. Thompson (Ed.), *Teaching Numeracy in Primary Schools* (Vol. 1, pp. 67–77). Backingham: Open University Press.

Kamii, C. (1985). *Young Children Reinvent Arithmetic*. New York: Teachers College Press.

Kamii, C. (1989). *Young Children Continue to Reinvent Arithmetic*. New York: Teachers College Press.

Lave, J. (1990). The culture of acquisition and the practice of understanding. In: J. W. Stigler, R. A. Schweder & G. Herdt (Eds), *Cultural Psychology: Essays on Comparative Human Development* (pp. 309–327). Cambridge: Cambridge University Press.

Moss, P. (1999). Renewed hopes and lost opportunities: early childhood in the early years of the Labour Government. *Camrbridge Journal of Education, 29*(2), 229–238.

Munn, P., & Schaffer, H. R. (1993). Literacy and Numeracy Events in Social Interactive Contexts. *International Journal of Early Years Education, 1*(3), 61–80.

Munn, P. (1995). The role of organized preschool learning environments in literacy and numeracy development. *Research Papers in Education, 10*(2), 217–252.

Munn, P. (1997). Children's beliefs about counting. In: I. Thompson (Ed.), *Teaching and Learning Early Number* (pp. 9–20). Buckingham: Open University Press.

Munn, P. (1998). Symbolic function in pre-schoolers. In: C. Donlan (Ed.), *The Development of Mathematical Skills* (pp. 47–71). Hove: Psychology Press.

Nunes, T., & Bryant, P. (1996). *Children Doing Mathematics*. Oxford: Blackwell.

Peterson, P. L., Fennema, E., Carpenter, T. P., & Loef, M. (1989). Teachers' pedagogical content beliefs in mathematics. *Cognition and Instruction, 6*(1), 1–40.

Rogoff, B. (1990). *Apprenticeship in Thinking: Cognitive Development in Social Context*. New York: Oxford University Press.

Sophian, C. (1998). A developmental perspective on children's counting. In: C. Donlan (Ed.), *The Development of Mathematical Skills* (pp. 27–46). Hove: Psychology Press.

Sugarman, I. (1997). Teaching for strategies. In: I. Thompson (Ed.), *Teaching and learning Early Number*. Buckingham: Open University Press.

Aubrey, C., David, T., Godfrey, R., & Thompson, L. (2000). *Early Childhood Educational Research: Issues in Methodology and Ethics*. London: Falmer Press.

Tizard, B., & Hughes, M. (1984). *Young Children Learning. Talking and Thinking at Home and at School*. London: Fontana.

Treffers, A. (1987). *Three Dimensions. A Model of Goal and Theory Description in Mathematics Education: The Wiskobas Project*. Dordrecht: Kluwer Academic Publishers.

Ueno, N. (1998). Doing mathematics as situated cognition. In: C. Donlan (Ed.), *The Development of Mathematical Skills* (pp. 111–128). Hove: Psychology Press.

Walkerdine, V. (1982). From context to text: a psycho-semiotic account of abstract thought. In: M. Beveridge (Ed.), *Children's Thinking through Language* (pp. 129–155). London: Edward Arnold.

Walkerdine, V. (1988). *The Mastery of Reason. Cognitive Development and the Production of Rationality*. London: Routledge.

Wells, G. (1982). Language at Home and School. *Newsletter of the Child Development Society, 30*.

Wright, B., Stanger, G., Cowper, M., & Dyson, R. (1993). First-graders' progress in an experimental maths recovery program. Paper presented at Sixteenth Annual Conference of the Mathematical Education Research Group, Brisbane, Australasia, 9–13 July.

Wright, B. et al. (1997). *Mathematics Recovery. Teachers' Handbook 32*. New South Wales, Australia: Southern Cross University.

Wright, R. J., Martland, J., & Stafford, A. K. (2000). *Early Numeracy Assessment for Teaching and Intervention*. London: Sage.

Wynn, K. (1998). Numerical competence in infants. In: C. Donlan (Ed.), *The Development of Mathematical Skills* (pp. 3–26). Hove: Psychology Press.

Young, J. (1995). *Young Children's Apprenticeship in Number*. Unpublished Ph.D. University of North London.

Young-Loveridge, J. M. (1989). The relationship between children's home experiences and their mathematical skills on entry to school. *Early Child Development and Care, 43*, 43–59.

Young-Loveridge, J. M. (1991). *The Development of Children's Number Concepts from Ages Five to Nine. Early Mathematics Learning Project: Phase ll. Vol.1 : Report of Findings.* Hamilton, New Zealand: Education Department, University of Waikato.

Young-Loveridge, J. M. (1993). *The Effects of Early Mathematics Intervention. The EMI-5s Study. Vol. 1: Report of Findings.* Hamilton, New Zealand: Department of Education Studies, University of Waikato.

Young-Loveridge, J. M., & Peters, S. A. (1994). *A Handbook of Number Books and Games. From the EMI-5s Study.* Hamilton, New Zealand: Department of Education Studies, University of Waikato.

Young-Loveridge, J. M., Carr, M., & Peters, S. (1995). *Enhancing the Mathematics of Four-Year-Olds. Vol. 1: Report of Findings.* Hamilton, New Zealand: School of Education, University of Waikato.

11. EQUAL OPPORTUNITIES: UNSETTLING MYTHS

Glenda MacNaughton

Since the early 1960s researchers have known that young children know about and act on gender differences and that their knowledge and actions are often stereotyped (e.g. Silcock, 1965; Flerx et al., 1976). Using this research early years researchers and practitioners have argued for pedagogies to challenge sexism and promote gender equity. Despite these arguments, gender equity is not a reality in many early years classrooms (Alloway, 1995). In this chapter, I argue that our poor progress in realising gender equity in early years education derives from the power-knowledge politics that are embedded in equal opportunities approaches to gender equity. I draw on my own research with early years staff in Australia and on recent feminist theory to unsettle a forty-year old myth that gender equity in early years can be realised through creating equal opportunities in early years classrooms. I begin by tracing the emergence of the equal opportunities myth.

THE MYTH OF EQUAL OPPORTUNITIES: ITS BEGINNINGS AND ITS EVOLUTION

> What I understand by 'Equal Opportunities' is that girls can do everything like boys. But only if they get a chance (Angela quoted in Shamaris, 1990: 55).

Angela's 1990s view that 'girls can do everything like boys if they get a chance' has its roots in the early demands of the 1960s–1970s women's movement for greater women's equality and equal educational opportunities for girls. More specifically, it has its roots in the liberal feminist theories of change that produced those demands.

Promoting Evidence-based Practice in Early Childhood Education:
Research and its Implications, Volume 1, pages 211–226.
2001 by Elsevier Science Ltd.
ISBN: 0-7623-0753-6

Broadly speaking, liberal feminist approaches to women's equality centre on ensuring that women had the same life 'chances' as men. These 'chances' became known as 'equal opportunities'. Liberal feminists argued that women's equality required equal access to the experiences, positions and pay of men. They argued for equal pay, equal work rights, equality before the law and equality in education and relationships. As Friedan explained, 'In the first stage, our aim was full participation [of women], power and voice in the mainstream' (Friedan, 1981: 27).

The liberal feminist demand for women's right to equal participation in all aspects of society rested on the argument that women can do anything that men can do, given the chance. This argument challenged the idea prevalent in the 1960s that sex predestined behaviour and it generated enormous research interest in the relationships between sex and behaviour. Such was the interest in sex differences at that time that in 1974, Maccoby and Jacklin (1974) were able to review over 1400 studies about differences between girls and boys. These studies continued to amass during the late 1970s exploring sex-role stereotyping young children (e.g. Holman & Williamson, 1979) and how sex-role stereotypes operated in young children's lives (e.g. Flerx et al., 1976; Wangman & Wagner, 1977).

The liberal feminist emphasis on equality through 'participation, power and voice in the mainstream' combined with the growing research evidence that sex-role stereotypes developed in early years to directly influence approaches to gender in early years education. Classroom teachers learnt that sex-role stereotypes were formed in early childhood and that it was their responsibility to challenge these stereotypes. Teachers were told to institute equal opportunities policies so that girls had equal access to teacher time, resources, educational experiences, playspaces and play materials (e.g. Cuffaro, 1975; Cohen & Martin, 1976; Guttenberg & Bray, 1976; Davis, 1979; Robinson & Hobson, 1978). An early guide to non-sexist education produced in the United Kingdom in the mid-1970s contained exemplifies this approach. It suggested reading non-sexist stories, developing non-sexist plays, encouraging role-reversal and modeling non-sexist behaviour would give girls the chance to be non-sexist. For instance:

> I would like to put together a few ideas for playgroup activities which lend themselves to developing non-sexist play situations. We obviously do a lot of things similar to other playgroups, but we try to approach them differently. When we do woodwork, we especially encourage girls to learn how to use tools as well as boys, and try to make sure that women help with this (Playgroup Pamphlet Group, 1975: 27).

These and similar strategies for increasing girls' chances at being non-sexist appeared and reappeared during the next fifteen years. In the U.K. (e.g.

Aspinwall, 1984; Shameris, 1990), Australia (e.g. Davis, 1979; Elliot, 1984) and the USA (e.g. Cuffaro, 1975; Cohen & Martin, 1976) it became standard advice in any early years literature tackling gender equity. For instance, in Australia, Elliot (1984) advised early years staff that children's sex-role stereotypes should be challenged and that:

> In order to provide positive role models for young children we must be seen by children as performing a wide variety of roles (Elliot, 1984: 20).

> Always be cautious when choosing curriculum materials to ensure they depict an approximately equal quantitative representation of male and female characters (Elliot, 1984: 21).

This advice was fundamentally liberal feminist – given the right environment and the chance to be non-sexist, young children would be. This premise was tested in the 1980s and early 1990s when researchers studied the impact of the specific equal opportunities strategies on children's sex-role behaviours. Specifically they studied the effects on children's sex-role behaviours of teachers:

- modeling non-traditional behaviours for children (Butterworth, 1991)
- reinforcing non-traditional sex-role behaviours (Koblinsky & Sugawara, 1984; Butterworth, 1991)
- reading non-traditional and traditional stories to children (Flerx et al., 1976; De Lisi & Johns, 1984; Pardeck & Pardeck, 1985; Ayers & Ayers, 1989)
- changing the arrangement of equipment in the room (Kinsman & Berk, 1987).

The results were less than decisive. Some researchers found a short-term reduction in children's stereotyped play (De Lisi & Johns, 1984; Pardeck & Pardeck, 1985; Ayers & Ayers, 1989). One of the few long-term studies reported (Koblinsky & Sugawara, 1984) found it took six months presentation of non-sexist stories to children to create less stereotyped views, and activity preferences. A second long-term twelve-month study of two centres (Swadener, 1986) found that teachers' use of non-sexist language, materials, and teachers' did prevent gender stereotyping and reduce children's stereotyping. However, alongside this research reports of gender inequities in early years classrooms persisted. One U.K. study (Dunn & Morgan, 1987) provided strong evidence of persistent differences in how boys and girls played, including gender-based differences in their choice of friends, choice of materials and use of toys. Similar results emerged from other studies of children's play patterns, play styles and use of play materials in early years classrooms (Beeson & Williams, 1982; Thomas, 1986; Logan, 1988). Giving girls the chance to be non-sexist didn't seem to be sufficient.

By the mid 1980s a formidable array of information had been generated about how young children can and do play, think, and react in gender-stereotyped ways in early years education (e.g. Silva, 1980; Meade, 1982; Rickwood & Bussey, 1983; Smith & Grimwood, 1983; Kaarby, 1986). During the 1990s we added to this again showing that young children were highly gendered and often traditionally so (MacNaughton, 2000).

Throughout this time advice to early staff about how to work for gender equity remained firmly embedded in liberal feminist principles of gender change through equal opportunities (e.g. MacNaughton, 2001). Give girls the chance to play with blocks, ride bicycles, climb, etc. and they will and they will become non-sexist. The persistence and consistency of this approach to gender equity is most powerfully illustrated by the fact that Cohen and Martin (1976) has remained on the book list of Association for Childhood Education International (ACEI) for 25 years. To date, AECI has no other publication on its list that tackles gender equity in early years education.

After nearly forty years of concern about sex-role stereotyping in early years and twenty-five years of liberal feminist advice about how to tackle it gender inequality in classrooms persists. Why is this? Some would argue that classroom teachers have not practiced equal opportunities consistently or persistently enough. However, in my own research where teachers were both consistent and persistent in embracing equal opportunities in their classrooms the children were equally consistent and persistent in not doing so.

To explore this conundrum and the knowledge-power politics of equal opportunities strategies in early years classrooms I draw on a gender equity research project I conducted with twelve Australian early years teachers and the preschool children attending their services (see MacNaughton, 2000 for detailed discussion of the research project). The Gender Equity Research Group (GERG) involved classroom research with teachers over an eighteen-month period. In this research I talked with children about their relationships with each other, their play preferences and their likes and dislikes. In these conversations the children revealed much about how gender is understood, lived and practiced in early years classrooms and much about why gender equity requires more than giving girls a chance to be realised.

RESEARCHING GENDER, RETHINKING EQUAL OPPORTUNITIES

Sandra was four years old when I first talked with her about why she didn't play with any of the boys in her classroom. The conversation unfolded as follows.

Equal opportunities and pinched bottoms

Glenda: I noticed in all the pictures I have taken of you playing in the sandpit you never seem to play with any of the boys. Why is that?

Sandra: Shrugs her shoulders, grimaces and then laughs. Her laughter indicated I should know why.

Sandra then said: 'Cos they are mean.

Glenda: How are they mean?

Sandra: They pinch your bottom, they pull your hair. (Thinks for a bit) They knock your blocks over. Daryl knocks sand over.

Glenda: What do you think you can do about that?

Sandra: I don't like boys, they are not my friends.

Glenda: When does Daryl upset you?

Sandra: When Miss M. (the teacher) doesn't see.

Sandra's preschool teacher, Edna, actively implemented an equal opportunities policy in her classroom. Edna believed passionately in providing equal access to all classroom areas for boys and for girls, in modeling non-sexist behaviour and in reading children non-sexist stories. Her book collection of non-sexist stories was better than most and she actively sought out images, songs, poems and experiences that promoted non-sexism. Edna was a model equal opportunities teacher.

Despite this, Sandra had developed a series of 'no-go' areas in the classroom. They included the block area and the sandpit, especially if the boys were present. Sandra also had very strong and clear ideas about gender. She chose her friends and her activities on the basis of gender. She knew why she made the choices that she did and gender was central to them.

As a teacher committed to equal opportunities Edna believed that she could change the girls' view of block play and of boys by providing equal access to block play, modeling playing with blocks and providing images in the area of girls enjoying block play. However, these strategies failed Edna. As she explained:

> ... I've given them [the girls] space, I've given them encouragement, I've given them reinforcement, I've given them everything, but they [Sandra included] are not perceiving those blocks as being relevant to them.

Why did Edna's strategies fail her and the other GERG teachers who followed them? Returning to the Sandra's conversation with me about 'pinched bottoms' offers some beginning insights. Sandra avoided block play and other play spaces dominated by the boys because of what had happened when she had played with boys. They not only 'knock your blocks over' but boys also physically intimidate you by pinching your bottom and pulling your hair. In Sandra's experience, boys generally do this when the teacher is absent. For

Sandra taking the chance offered to her by Edna to play with blocks meant exposure to physical harassment.

Sandra was not the only girl in Edna's centre to resist the chance offered to her to play with blocks. Most of the girls in Edna's centre avoided play with blocks and they avoided play with boys. In fact, most of the girls in each of the twelve centres participating in the study avoided playing with blocks and with boys (and vice versa). In conversations I had with the children about these decisions the reasons they gave were simple – the girls and boys didn't like each other and they knew that they didn't like each other. The two conversations that follow capture these feelings and knowings.

> *They're not interested in me*
> Glenda: Do you play with the girls?
> Hugh: I play with the boys.
> Glenda: Why is it you play with boys?
> Hugh: Because I like them.
> Glenda: You don't like the girls?
> Hugh: I don't like the girls either.
> Glenda: Can you tell me why? I'm interested.
> Hugh: Because. They are not interested in me either.
>
> *He won't listen*
> Glenda: Do you ever play with Simon?
> Pippa: No.
> Sharne: No way.
> Glenda: Why not?
> Pippa: We don't like him. He's not our friend.
> Sharne: 'Cos he always blocks his ears when we try to talk to him.

Equal opportunities – the chance to play with the other gender – was unattractive for Pippa, Sharne and Hugh. For these three children, the chance to play with the other gender meant playing with children you didn't like or who didn't like you. The girls and the boys didn't want to play with each other because each gender assumed the other wasn't interested and each gender disliked each other.

Sandra, Pippa and Sharne were not the only girls in the research project to experience opportunities to play with boys as problematic. In fact, their wary responses to opportunities to play with boys and in spaces traditionally inhabited by the boys were the rule rather than the exception. Girls in each of the twelve GERG early years centres regularly avoided playing where the boys played. They were incredibly adept at doing this using several strategies that meant that the girls avoided boys' 'meanness'. They were watchful of where the boys were, listened hard for boys' noisy outbursts and regularly sidestepped playing with the boys. The girls' watchfulness increased as their proximity to the boys increased. A flavour of how this worked is evident in a moment of Maria's play. She had decided to play in the block area when some boys were present:

Eyeing the boys
Maria spent some time building a very complex and intricate building. She was on the edge of some very active 'boys' block play. Some of the boys had been watching her and seemed to want to enter her play. They brought a block over and put it by her building, just touching. She then walked around and took it away. Then one of the boys leant a block against her building. There was eye contact then he went away. When he did she went around and took it away. She constantly had her eye on the boys and on the teacher. The moment the teacher left to answer the telephone Maria left blocks. The boys then moved in and started adding to her building. She watched from a safe distance and then moved into the home-corner area and started feeding the dolls.

Maria, like many of the girls, was especially watchful when she was near boys and quickly sought the safety of girls' spaces in the teacher's absence. Maria wouldn't chance playing with the boys without the teacher as a safety net.

Other girls resisted the chance to play with boys because boys and girls were not the same. They played in different ways and they liked different things. Four and a half year-old Sheralyn put this difference very clearly during a conversation about what girls and boys do and can do:

Girls can't do anything
Glenda: Can girls do anything that boys can do?
Sheralyn (four years old): No.
Glenda: Can you tell me what they can't do?
Sheralyn: Bad games.

The other differences girls identified between boys and girls included boys 'liking getting dirty', 'throwing mud', 'messing up the play' and 'not asking if they can play'. Carla and Carol were particularly annoyed at the boys for not asking if they could play with the girls and very clear that this was a problematic male characteristic:

They don't ask if they can play
Glenda: Do they? What sort of things do they do to mess up your game?
Carol: Well they come in straight away.
Carla: And then they . . .
Carol: And then they don't ask if they can play.
Glenda: They don't ask and what did you say Carla?
Carla: Even when I told them to ask, they just said well we don't have to ask, we can play wherever we like.

The girls' determination to avoid contact with the boys, their 'bad games' and their 'meanness' was most apparent in dramatic play. In this play they developed their games using storylines that many boys found 'boring' and that made boys irrelevant to the game. The girls' storylines, based on the domestic world of 'having babies', 'cleaning the house', 'preparing for parties', 'getting dinner', etc. made the boys effectively irrelevant and made 'mums' the most powerful people (MacNaughton, 1995).

The 'mum's power was evident in three ways. Firstly, having a 'mum' was essential for the play to begin. If a 'mum' could not be agreed upon the girls often dispersed quickly. When 'mum' had been decided, they often played for twenty minutes or more. Secondly, once the play began it was clear why it had been so important to find a 'mum'. For the girls' play 'Mum' was the director, producer and writer of the dramatic play. 'Mum' also maintained the play by adding to it, reminding other children what to do and changing the play as needed, for example, when someone new entered. Thirdly, 'mum's' power was evident in how other girls regularly deferred to her such as in the conversation below.

> *Mum, are we going out now?*
> Sarah (to Patricia): Mum, are you the mum?
> Patricia: We're going out now.
> (Sarah makes a move to the door).
> Patricia: Hang on, I've gotta get my shoes on (she repeats this three times).
> Sarah (to Patricia): Are we going out now?
> Patricia: You need your shoes and your hat on.
> (Patricia continued to direct the play for the next twenty minutes.)

The girls found power and pleasure in their domestic storylines. In them they also found safety from the boys' meanness and bad games. Efforts by the boys to enter the girls' play were consistently met with attempts to 'side step' or 'quieten' the boys by suggesting that they be 'dad' or a 'pet'. 'Dad' was sent to work – and thus away from the girls – or told to sit at a table and wait for his dinner. He was then ignored. One boy sat for nearly twenty minutes waiting for dinner whilst the girls busily got on with 'being mums' and ignored his presence. 'Pets' were often taken for a walk, fed or sent to their kennels. In both instances, the girls attempted to ensure that the boys were minimal trouble in their dramatic play.

The boys' responses to being 'dads' and 'pets' suggested that the girls' strategies were extremely effective at blocking play with the boys. The boys regularly told me that playing 'mums' with the girls 'was boring' and 'not fun' and that they didn't like to do it. For this reason, girls rarely had to play for long with the boys in the safety of their home-corner space (MacNaughton, 1995). As Hugh said, they are just not interested in boys so why should the boys be interested in them?

So, in the GERG classrooms equal opportunities strategies floundered. They floundered, not because the teachers were ineffective but simply because the girls just didn't want to play with the boys. They didn't want to do this because:

- Boys pinch your bottom
- Boys knock your blocks over
- Boys are mean
- Boys don't like you
- Boys don't listen to you
- Boys don't ask you if they can play
- Boys play bad games
- Boys mess up your play.

Under these conditions, equal opportunities for the girls was a liability rather than a liberatory experience. The liability arose from the differential ways in which boys and girls experienced and exercised gendered power in their classrooms and from the silence in equal opportunities strategies on how to tackle this issue.

RETHINKING THEORIES OF GENDER, RETHINKING EQUAL OPPORTUNITIES

Sandra and the other girls in GERG lived in their classroom with 'the asymmetrical power relationships that underlie gender' (Alloway, 1993: 4). They also lived with the inequitable cultural values associated with male and female roles. Equal opportunities approaches to gender equity fail to come to terms with each of these aspects of gender relations and consequently fail to tackle the pleasures and risks of children taking up the chances teachers offer them to be differently gendered. Alloway (1995) summarised these failings thus:

> ... the proponents of equal opportunity have, for the most part, unwittingly maintained the social valuing of male over female ... the equal opportunity model offers minimal contestation of what it means to be male, no questioning of whether incursion into the male world is a worthy path to travel ... (Alloway, 1995: 30).

Furthermore, Alloway (1995) and others have argued that the equal opportunities strategies espoused by liberal feminists and used by Edna ignore the asymmetrical power relationships underlie gender and how children live, understand, practice and produce these relationships in their daily lives. They rely instead on simplistic accounts of how sex roles are produced in young children's lives. Such accounts assume that gender differences in our society are created and maintained through a process similar to osmosis (Davies, 1988) and assume that children and adults absorb gender messages automatically and uncritically (Davies, 1988; MacNaughton, 1996). Hence, young girls who participate in block play or other traditionally male activities automatically and uncritically become non-sexist. Likewise, boys who play in gender-tagged areas such as blocks automatically and uncritically absorb the sexist gender messages in these areas. As Garrett (1987) explained the social learning theory that underpins sex-role socialisation theory:

> . . . argues that the learning of gender roles takes place first through observation, then by imitation (p. 22).

Intersecting with these theories, liberal feminist theories of change simplistically assume that the reasons girls don't do things is because they are not given the opportunity to do them. So, if you tell or show girls that they can play with blocks, etc. by modelling these behaviours or telling them about them in stories then they will change their behaviours. As Sandra and other girls in GERG showed, the reasons why they don't do things is more complex than that. They don't play with boys or in traditionally male classroom spaces because boys are more powerful in those spaces than are the girls. Girls gain and maintain power over their play by staying in their own places of safety well away from the boys.

Davies (1988) and others (e.g. Connell, 1987; Weiler, 1988) believed that social learning theories were simplistic and flawed because of their silences about an individual's ability to resist attempts to 're-socialise' them and their capacity to remake dominant practices, meanings and understandings. They argued for pedagogies based on understandings of gender and gender politics that acknowledged power relations and acknowledged children's capacity to resist. Davies (1989, 1993) and others (Alloway, 1995; MacNaughton, 2000) argued for theories of gendering that acknowledged the differential ways in which boys and girls lived, practiced and experienced power, desire and pleasure.

In her pioneering work on identity construction in early years, Davies (1988, 1989) argued that social learning theories of the relationships between the individual and the social are inadequate because they cannot answer four general questions about how children understand the world. To explain, I have 'translated' each of Davies's general questions into a specific question concerning equal opportunities in the classroom:

- How does the child handle contradictory understandings about gender? (How does the a girl handle contradictory understandings, such as "block play is good for you" and "boys knock your blocks over"?)

- How does the child choose between dominant and alternative gender understandings? (How does a girl choose between dominant and alternative understandings of gender around blocks are for boys, blocks are for everyone?)
- How does the child resist or reject dominant understandings of gender? (How does a girl resist or reject dominant understandings of gender constructed by boys and by teachers?)
- What influences the child to reject dominant or alternative understandings? (What influences a girl to reject dominant or alternative understandings of blocks are for boys, blocks are for everyone?)

Feminist poststructuralist theorists such as Davies (1993) emphasised that identity formation is not just an abstract, cognitive exercise but is inherently emotional. Emotion and desire are core in creating identities and we need to recognise the pleasures associated with different identities. She argued that developing identities involves learning to:

> ... read and interpret the landscape of the social world, and to embody, to live, to experience, to know, to desire as one's own, to take pleasure in the world, as it is made knowable through the available discourses, social structures and practices (Davies, 1993: 17).

In other words, as children construct their identities, they encounter various meanings and must 'actively':

- read, interpret and understand those meanings
- desire or reject them
- live, embody and express the meanings s/he desires by taking them up as her/ his own and, through this . . .
- gain pleasure from them.

However, this does not mean that children can freely choose who they want to be, or how they want to act. For instance, girls cannot and do not freely choose to be non-sexist just because they are given the chance or the opportunity to play with blocks in an early years classroom. Their choices are constrained by their understandings of what is pleasurable to them and by how power operates in and through their choices. Their choices are constructed and constrained by emotion, desire and power. As Hughes and MacNaughton explain:

> This is not to say that the child is free to construct any meanings or construct any identities s/he wishes. The meanings and identities that a child can construct may be many and variable *but* they are restricted to the alternatives to which they have access. This is more than just a truism. Children do not enter a 'free market' of ideas but a 'market' in which some meanings are more available, more desirable, more recognizable, more pleasurable and, therefore, more powerful than others (Hughes & MacNaughton, 2001: 128).

For the majority of the girls in the GERG research the meanings of being a girl that were more desirable, more recognizable and more pleasurable than others were those in their 'safe spaces' and those that they could practice away from boys. Being different from boys and doing different things to the boys was the meaning of being a girl that had most power for girls like Sandra, Pippa and Carla. Against this power merely providing girls with the chance to play in particular spaces is destined to fail. Against the emotion, power and desire that constructs the girls' choices equal opportunities policies are destined to flounder.

Feminist poststructuralist views of how emotion, power and desire produce gendered practices have clear pedagogical implications for teachers who are seeking gender equity in their classrooms. In overview:

> They suggest that teachers need to do more than just role-model desirable gender behaviours or provide environments that present alternative gender images and messages to young children. Instead, teachers need to actively engage in the complex processes through which young children negotiate and produce gendered cultural meanings, so that teachers' understandings of gender identity become part of young children's experience in their classroom (Hughes & MacNaughton, 2001).

The majority of girls in the research project were traditionally gendered and for these girls avoiding harassment and seeking safe places was part of the daily negotiation of the classroom's gendered terrain. In this negotiation the girls faced clear choices: to play in blocks or with the boys meant danger and experiencing their power to be mean, play bad games, not listen to you and knock blocks over. To play away from the boys meant pleasure, safety and exercising their power as 'mums' and as resisters to boys' meanness. It also meant playing with people who liked you and 'didn't cover their ears' when you talked to them.

So in the GERG project, the girls' chances to play with boys and in boys' spaces came at a cost and at considerable risk to their pleasures and safety in girls' places and spaces. The girls regularly choose the safety of girls' places, spaces and ways of being and they regularly resisted the chances teachers offered them to play with boys and in boys' places, spaces and ways of being.

In doing so, the girls actively resisted the chances they were given by their teachers to be like the boys, do what the boys did or play with what the boys played with. According to Davies (1989) such resistance to adult desires and expectations is a key aspect of how we negotiate our social world:

> Children do not accept what adults tell them as having application to every aspect of their lives .... It is not possible for children simply and straightforwardly to accept the world as it is told to them, not least because the difference between the 'real' and the 'ideal' world is often quite marked in adult-child discourse (Davies, 1989: 6).

Sandra certainly did not accept what the adult world told her about playing in blocks. Blocks were not for everyone they were for the 'mean' boys. She knew that taking up the opportunities to play in blocks meant living in the real world of boys' meanness not the ideal world of equal opportunities.

Feminist poststructuralist theories of gender suggest that teachers working with girls such as Sandra and the boys she met need to be able to:

- explore what cultural meanings they are giving to gender
- study how they have come to these meanings
- recognise why they are emotionally invested in these meanings
- reflect on how these investments intersect with children's resistances to teaching for gender equity
- look for how the gendered exercise of power and desire in the classroom might constrain the possibilities that they explores for themselves
- talk with them about gender, their meanings of it, their desires and their power
- engage with them and help them to remake their gendered subjectivities, desires and practices
- ensure that there is the possibility for power and pleasure in the alternative meanings of gender that are offered to children.

RESEARCHING FOR GENDER EQUITY: FUTURE DIRECTIONS

The questions researchers in the past forty years have asked about sex-role stereotyping and their explanations of it have relied heavily on sex-role socialisation theory. In doing so, the research that has guided gender equity pedagogies in early years have expressed a set of assumptions about gender relations and about how children learnt gender that paralleled those of liberal feminists. This brief review of research and gender equity in early years education since the 1960s shows that the politics of liberal feminism and the knowledge of young children's learning that informed liberal feminist approaches to gender equity to be flawed. They rest on a myth that equal opportunities are both possible and desirable.

We still have much to learn and to share about working in the early years for a world in which children's gender does not limit their sense of who they are, who they can be and who they want to be. We still need to debate, explore and learn about how we work with gender issues in early years and research can help us in this process. Many questions and issues have yet to surface and need to. Such questions worthy of further research include:

- How can we create new ways of working with young children that seriously engage with and help them to remake their gendered subjectivities, desires and practices?
- Can we learn to reject simplistic understandings of gendering in early years and embrace complexity in our theories and our practices?
- What mix of theoretical concepts might be of most use in designing gender equity pedagogies with young children in the 21st century?
- How do gender, 'race' and class intersect in children's lives and how do and should these intersections impact on how gender pedagogies?
- How can we work with parents, with colleagues (women & men) and with government to create greater gender equity for young children?

(MacNaughton, 2000)

These research questions are only some of those possible. However, whatever the questions are that are generated by the next wave of gender equity researchers it is important that they continue to expand how we understand and practice gender equity in the early years and that we move beyond equal opportunities approaches to change.

REFERENCES

Alloway, N. (1995). *Foundation Stones: The Construction of Gender in Early Childhood*. Carlton: Curriculum Corporation.

Aspinwall, K. (1984). *What Are Little Girls Made Of? What Are Little Boys Made Of?* London: National Nursery Nurses Educational Board.

Ayers, M., & Ayers, M. (1989). Effects of traditional and reversed sex-typed characters and family relationships on children's gender role perceptions. Paper presents at the *International Conference on Early Childhood Education and Development*. Hong Kong, August.

Beeson & Williams (1982).

Bruce, W. (1985). The implications of sex role stereotyping in the first years of school. *Australian Journal of Early Childhood*, *10*(2), 48–52.

Butterworth, D. (1991). Gender equity in early childhood: the state of play. *Australian Journal of Early Childhood*, *16*(4), 3–9.

Cohen, M., & Martin, L. (1976). *Growing Free: Ways to Help Children Overcome Sex-Role Stereotypes*. Washington, D.C.: ACEI.

Connell, R. (1987). *Gender and Power*. Sydney: Allen and Unwin.

Cuffaro, H. (1975). Reevaluating basic premises: curricula free of sexism. *Young Children*, (Sept.), 469–478.

Davies, B. (1988). *Gender Equity and Early Childhood*. Canberra: Commonwealth Schools Commission.

Davies, B. (1989). *Frogs and Snails and Feminist Tales: Preschool Children and Gender*. Sydney: Allen & Unwin.

Davies, B. (1993). *Shards of Glass*. Sydney: Allen and Unwin.

Davis, W. (1979). *Towards a Non-sexist Classroom*. South Australia: Education Department, Women's Advisory Unit.

De Lisi, R., & Johns, M. (1984). The effects of books and gender constancy development on kindergarten children's sex-role attitudes. *Journal of Applied Developmental Psychology, 5,* 173–184.

Dunn, S., & Morgan, V. (1987). Nursery and infant school play patterns: sex-related differences. *British Educational Research Journal, 13*(3), 271–281.

Ebbeck, M. (1985). Pre-school teachers interactions with boys as compared with girls. A report of an observation study. *Australian Journal of Early Childhood, 10*(2), 26–30.

Elliot, A. (1984). Creating non-sexist day care environments. *Australian Journal of Early Childhood, 9*(2), 18–23.

Flerx, V., Fidler, D., & Rogers, R. (1976). Sex role stereotypes: developmental aspects and early intervention. *Child Development, 47*(4), 998–1007.

Friedan, B. (1981). *The Second Stage.* New York: Summit Books.

Garrett, S. (1987). *Gender.* London: Social Science Paperback.

Guttenberg, M., & Bray, H. (1976). *Undoing Sex Stereotypes.* McGraw-Hill.

Holman, J., & Williamson, A. (1979). Sex labelling: adult perceptions of the child. *Australian Journal of Early Childhood, 4*(1), 41.

Hughes, P., & MacNaughton, G. (2000). Identity-formation and popular culture: learning lessons from Barbie. *Journal of Curriculum Theorizing* (Accepted May 2000).

Karrby, G. (1986). Time structure and sex differences in Swedish preschools. Paper presented at XVIII World Congress of OMEP (World Organisation of Early Childhood Education), Jerusalem, Israel, July 13–17.

Kilman, D. (1978). Avoiding sexism in early childhood education. *Day Care and Early Education,* (Fall), 19–21.

Kinsman, C., & Berk, L. (1987). Joining the block and housekeeping areas. In: J. Brown (Ed.), *Curriculum Planning for Young Children* (pp. 28–37). Washington, D.C.: NAEYC.

Koblinsky, S., & Sugawara, A. (1984). Nonsexist curricula, sex of teacher, and children's sex-role learning. *Sex Roles, 10*(5/6), 357–367.

Logan (1988).

Maccoby, E., & Jacklin, C. (1974). *The Psychology of Sex Differences.* California: Stanford University Press.

MacNaughton, G. (1995). A post-structuralist analysis of learning in early childhood settings. In: M. Fleer (Ed.), *DAPcentrism: Challenging Developmentally Appropriate Practice* (pp.35–54). Watson, ACT: Australian Early Childhood Association.

MacNaughton, G. (1996). Is Barbie to blame: reconsidering how children learn gender. *Australian Journal of Early Childhood, 21*(4), 18–22.

MacNaughton, G. (2000). *Rethinking Gender in Early Childhood Education.* Sydney: Allen & Unwin.

MacNaughton, G. (2001). Silences, sex-roles and subjectivities: 40 years of gender in the Australian Journal of Early Childhood. *Australian Journal of Early Childhood, 26*(1), 21–25.

MacNaughton, G., & Hughes, P. (2001). Fractured or Manufactured: Gendered Identity and Culture in the Early Years. In: S. Grieshaber & G. Cannella (Eds), *Embracing Identities in Early Childhood Education: Diversity and Possibilities* (pp. 114–132). New York: Teachers College Press.

Meade, A. (1982). Don't take that dress off James! *Australian Journal of Early Childhood, 7*(3), 37–42.

Millard, C. (1995). Free choice writing in the early years. *Australian Journal of Early Childhood, 20*(1), 33–37.

Mortimer, M. (1979). Sex stereotyping in children's books. *Australian Journal of Early Childhood*, 4(4), 4–8.

Pardeck, J., & Pardeck, J. (1985). Using Bibliotherapy to Help Children Adjust to Changing Role Models. ED265946.

Playgroup Pamphlet Group (1975). *Out of the Pumpkin Shell: Running a Women's Liberation Playgroup*. Birmingham: Playgroup Pamphlet Group, Birmingham Women's Liberation.

Plummer, S., Braithwaite, V., & Holman, J. (1983). Anything they want to be? Sex-role stereotypes in commercials during children's viewing time. *Australian Journal of Early Childhood*, 8(2), 39.

Rickwook, D., & Bussey, K. (1983). Sex differences in gender schema processing. *Australian Journal of Early Childhood*, 8(2), 40–41.

Robinson, B., & Hobson, C. (1978). Beyond sex-role stereotyping. *Day Care and Education*, (Fall), 16–18.

Shameris, C. (1990). Deepa's story: writing non-sexist stories for a reception class. In: E. Tutchell (Ed.), *Dolls and Dungarees: Gender Issues in the Primary School Curriculum* (pp. 52–61). Milton Keynes: Open University Press.

Silock, A. (1965). Sex role. *Australian Pre-school Quarterly*, (August), 23–26.

Silva, P. (1980). Experiences, activities and the preschool child: a report from the Dunedin multidisciplinary study. *Australian Journal of Early Childhood*, 5(2), 13–18.

Smith, A., & Grimwood, S. (1983). Sex role stereotyping and children's concepts of teachers and principals. *Australian Journal of Early Childhood*, 8(2), 23–28.

Wangman, N., & Wagner, S. (1977). *Choices: Learning about Sex Roles*. Minneapolis: Jenny Publishing Co.

Weiler, K. (1988). *Women Teaching for Change: Gender, Class and Power*. Massachusetts: Bergin and Garvey Publishers, Inc.

Willis, S. (1990). Some beliefs about girls, mathematics and the early childhood years. *Australian Journal of Early Childhood*, 15(1), 47–48.

12. GLOBALISATION AND ITS IMPACT ON EARLY YEARS FUNDING AND CURRICULUM: REFORM INITIATIVES IN ENGLAND AND THE UNITED STATES

Sally Lubeck and Patricia Jessup

> There is a dialectic at work by which . . . global processes interact with national and local actors and contexts to be modified and, in some cases, transformed. There is a process of give-and-take, an exchange by which international trends are reshaped to local ends (Arnove, 1999: 2–3).

The latter half of the 20th century has witnessed dramatic changes in the global political economy. As a result, governments in the English-speaking West have begun to influence more directly how young children are being educated. The purpose of this chapter is to explore how England and the United States are responding to the challenges of globalisation.[1] The next section surveys some of the economic, political and cultural consequences of globalisation and describes ideological shifts that are beginning to affect how young children are educated. We then provide brief overviews of early years care and education in England and the United States (U.S.)[2] and compare current funding and curricular initiatives.

Promoting Evidence-based Practice in Early Childhood Education:
Research and its Implications, Volume 1, pages 227–249.
Copyright © 2001 by Elsevier Science Ltd.
All rights of reproduction in any form reserved.
ISBN: 0-7623-0753-6

Although we acknowledge the strong press of globalisation in contemporary policymaking, we argue that it is important to interrogate the seeming inevitability of 'greater forces [that] leave the nation-state 'no choice' but to play by a set of global rules not of its own making' (Burbules & Torres, 2000: 2). Governments support a wide diversity of policies and practices in relation to the care and education of young children, and, within nations, there are always competing definitions of what should be done. Comparing policies and practices cross-nationally thus becomes one way of ensuring that a greater range of options and approaches will be considered.

GLOBALISATION

Globalisation has been defined in various ways. Most specifically, it is a phenomenon that, in real time, connects what happens locally with the far reaches of the globe. Major social, political, and economic shifts have resulted in a dramatically altered international landscape. Stock exchanges around the world are almost instantaneously affected by what happens elsewhere. Technological advances have made it possible for people even in repressive societies to communicate with others via the Internet, cellular phones, and fax machines. And goods can be adapted to changing styles and preferences and rapidly transported from distant lands. Harvey (1990) has described this as a 'time-space compression' in which 'the time horizons of both private and public decision-making have shrunk, while satellite communication and declining transport costs have made it increasingly possible to spread those decisions immediately over an ever wider and variegated space' (Harvey, 1990: 147).

This 'time-space compression' can be seen in the economic, political and cultural realms, with considerable overlap and interplay between them. The economic impact of globalisation is seen in the interdependence and integration of work on a global basis (Carnoy, 1999). The service sector is growing in importance. Industry has shifted from Fordist to post-Fordist flexible production, and the new high-tech 'information society' (Bell, 1987) is primarily concerned with the production and distribution of information. These changes create a need for literate workers who are able to adapt to change, learn quickly, work collaboratively, interpret information, and solve problems (Harvey, 1990; Kumar, 1995). There is considerable disagreement as to the impact of such changes on the work force. On one hand, there are those (Wolf, 2000; Martin, 2000) who see economic benefits from a global economy, while others (Cassen, 2000) see a growing gap between the rich and poor, with the less skilled and less educated being increasingly disadvantaged.

In the political arena, discussion focuses on the perceived decrease in the power of the nation-state (Morrow & Torres, 2000) and the rise of neoliberalism and neoconservativism. The former finds expression in a weak nation-state, economic rationality, explicit connections between education and business, and decreases in public sector spending (Apple, 2000). Public spending on education with the goal of increasing productivity, however, can be viewed as warranted. By contrast, neoconservativism affirms a strong state, a national curriculum and national testing, a 'return' to standards, and increased state control of teachers and teaching (Apple, 2000). While neoliberals believe that the market, left to its own devices, will solve economic and social ills (and thus support policies like vouchers and tax credits), neoconservatives believe in the efficacy of a strong state. These seemingly opposing tendencies meet and mingle in contemporary centrist politics. Finally, while some predict the decline of nation-states, others argue that they 'will survive as the only viable sites of political representation and accountability, and as the building blocks of cultural governance' (Green, 1997: 4).

Culturally there are those who bemoan the homogenisation of culture while others are excited by the increased contact among people from diverse backgrounds (Lechner & Boli, 2000). Globalisation, however, cannot simply be reduced to these dichotomous positions but must be seen as 'a conflicted situation of sustained tensions and difficult choices' (Burbules & Torres, 2000: 14). Education is one of these conflicted areas.

The effects of globalisation on education have become a recent topic of inquiry (e.g. Burbules & Torres, 2000; Carnoy, 1999; Popkewitz, 2000). As Carnoy writes:

> Globalisation is having a profound effect on education at many different levels, and will have even greater effect in the future, as nations, regions, and localities fully comprehend the fundamental role educational institutions have, not only in transmitting skills needed in the global economy, but in reintegrating individuals into new communities built around information and knowledge (Carnoy, 1999: 14).

Apple (2000) lays stress on the fact that 'education is a site of struggle and compromise':

> It serves also as a proxy for larger battles over what our institutions should do, who they should serve, and who should makes these decisions. And yet, by itself it is one of the major arenas through which are worked resources, power, and ideology specific to policy, finance, curriculum, pedagogy, and evaluation in education. Thus, education is both cause and effect, determining and determined (Apple, 2000: 58).

Within the field of early childhood education in both England and the United States, there is now a heightened emphasis on laying a foundation for later learning, in preparation for participation in the workforce of tomorrow.

Dahlberg et al. (1999: 44) have called attention to an emerging construction of the young child 'as knowledge, identity, and culture reproducer', a child who must be ready to take her place as a future worker in a globalised economy.

Yet, as the writers cited above indicate, the implications of globalisation are not self-evident, and there is no one way in which institutions such as education are affected. Thus, there is a need to explore 'the diversity of such responses to globalisation, across varied national contexts, and the diversity of state-education relationships that generated educational principles, policies, and practices in light of these new conditions' (Burbules & Torres, 2000: 16). England and the U.S. currently are taking strikingly different approaches to funding early childhood education and care (ECEC) services and to changing the early years curriculum. They also have two of the most diverse 'systems' of care and education in the world.[3]

CURRENT FORMS OF ECEC PROVISION IN ENGLAND AND THE UNITED STATES

England

The Blair Government has made a substantial investment of resources to expand and improve childcare in the United Kingdom, but care arrangements for children under the age of three are still in high demand and short supply. In most cases, the cost of childcare is incurred by parents. Parents working at least 16 hours a week may take a childcare tax credit, but children 0–3 (and school age children) are generally not eligible for direct services unless they qualify for special services or are considered to be 'at risk'. Historically, services for children birth to age three were the province of the Department for Health, while the Department for Education and Employment (DfEE) governed programmes for children 3–5. The Government recently consolidated 'care' and 'education' giving the DfEE (Education) primary responsibility for the early years.

A Children's Unit at cabinet level was recently established. Table 1 describes the types of childcare provision for children birth to five and extended day care options for school-age children.

Several factors mediate discussions of the provision of childcare services in England. First, the U.K. has the second highest rate of part-time female employment in the European Union. As a consequence, many children are in part-time care. Increasing numbers of parents also work hours outside the Monday to Friday, 9–5 work week (Bertram & Pascal, 1999). Secondly, childminders and nannies constitute 56% of the childcare workforce, with

Table 1.   Forms of Childcare Provision for Children Birth to Age 5 in England.

Types Childcare	Description
Local Authority Day Nursery	Locally-funded day nursery for children birth to five years of age who are considered to be at risk for educational failure.
Private Day Nursery	A nursury run by employers (workplace nursery) or private companies, providing part time, full-day, or extended day care to children birth to five years of age.
Full-day Preschool/Playgroup	A preschool or playgroup run by parents or a non-profit organisation
Childminder	A caregiver who offers full-day and/or wrap around care in her own home.
Nanny/au pair	A caregiver who provides full- or part-time care for children in the family home.
Friend/neighbor	Someone who will care for a child in their own home or the child's home, usually for pay.
Relative	Someone who will care for a child in their own home or the child's home with or without remuneration.
Parent-toddler Group	Informal group for parents and children birth to five.
Before/after School Club	Club that provides wrap around care for children three and older.
Holiday Club	Club that provides care when school is not in session.

nursery workers constituting only 15% (HERA 2 Report, 1999: 3). The number of women working as childminders is on the decline, however, and the Government, in May 1998, launched a National Childcare Strategy, with the expressed intention of creating places for up to one million children. Because of the high rate of part-time employment, each 'place' statistically serves three children. The new Early Years Development and Childcare Partnerships (EYDCP) function in local authorities as the primary mechanism by which the provision of universal preschool education and the Childcare Strategy will be realised. Consisting of representatives from all sectors, local education, health, and social services, and others, the local Parnerships are responsible for assessing current provision and devising plans for expansion.

As described in Table 2, local education authorities and social services departments now sponsor centres that provide both care and education, and, in the case of the Early Excellence Centres, comprehensive services as well.

Table 2.   Forms of Care and Education Provision in England.

Combined Nursery/Family Centre	Centre offering both early education and day care for children birth to five, sometimes with extended day and full year options.
Early Excellence Centre	Centre that offer full-day care for children birth to five, drop-in facilities, outreach, family support, health care, adult education, and practitioner training. Designated by the Government as models of exemplary practice.
Opportunity Group	Group that provides additional support for children with special needs aged three to five and their families.

Recent reforms have dramatically altered the picture of provision for children aged three to five in the United Kingdom. Since September 1998, free part-time early education (a 2–2.5-hour session, five times a week during the school-term) has been available to *all* four year olds, and targets have been established to ensure provision for all three-year olds by 2004. In England, the current priority is to expand provision for three year olds in need in 1999. The primary providers of early education for three- and four-year olds were the local education authorities (about 59%), the private sector (about 30%), and the community and voluntary sector (about 9%) (Prior et al., 1999). The various options are listed in Table 3.

Types of provision operating outside the maintained sector are run by community or voluntary groups, private, for-profit businesses, and employers. All providers are entitled to government funding, if it can be shown through inspection that curricular goals are being adequately met. In recent years, there has been a noticeable decline in enrolments in preschools and playgroups sponsored by the voluntary sector as increasing numbers of children enroll in school-based classes. Reception classes have essentially become the new entry point into state-funded education. Admission to formal compulsory schooling occurs at age 5 in England, Scotland and Wales, and at age 4 in Northern Ireland, the earliest starting age in Europe.

The United States

Although there are fewer recognizably distinct forms of care and education in the United States, there has been no effort, comparable to that in the United Kingdom, to bring coherence to the ECEC field. The OECD review team, which visited the United States in the Fall of 1999, stated the point succinctly:

Table 3. Forms of Early Education in England.

Nursery School	A state-funded school normally providing 2 to 2/5 hours of pre-school education for 3s and 4s during the regular school year. Some full-time.
Nursery Class	A class located in a state-funded primary or infant school, serving children 3–4 years of age.
Early Years Unit	A class for children 3–5 within a state-funded primary and infant school on a part- or full-time basis during school terms.
Reception Class/Class R	The first class (for children 4–5 +) of a state-funded primary, first or infant school. Children attend from 9–3:30 during school terms. Scotland does not have Reception classes.
Special School	A school serving children with special needs aged 3 and older. The school may be a day or boarding school operating during school terms.
Opportunity Group	A service offered by Local Education Authorities (LEAs) that provides free education/care to children with special needs. Service may also be offered by Social Service Departments (SSD) or Health Departments.
Private Nursery School Pre-Preparatory school	A school run by a company or trust and serving children 3–5 + on a fee-paying basis.
Independent School	A school run by private company or trust, and serving children from age three and upwards.
Preschool/playgroup	Occasional or sessional preschool or playgroup serving children 2–5, and run by parents, a non-profit organisation or by a for-profit business.

Source: compiled from Bertram & Pascal, 1999.

> An important starting point for trying to understand the U.S. system of early childhood education and care is to realise that there is no 'system'. There is no national co-ordinated policy framework, and none of the 50 states across the country has as yet established a coherent within-state approach concerning early services for children under compulsory school age (OECD U.S. Country Note, 2000: 18).

As in the United Kingdom, there has been an historical division between care and education, although, as the rate of maternal employment has increased, this distinction is somewhat less marked. Nonetheless, care and education continue to be governed by different departments at both national and state levels. The Department of Health and Human Services at the federal level is responsible for childcare, Head Start and Early Head Start. Childcare is administered at the state level by departments of human resources or social services. These departments are also responsible for programmes for children 0–3 with special needs. Federal funds for intervention services for children 3–5 are funnelled through state departments of education. Head Start funds do not go through state departments but rather are allocated directly to more than 1400 grantee agencies.

Although early childhood professionals have criticised the care-education distinction on the grounds that all young children need both, the terms are used in Tables 4 and 5, in order to distinguish between programmes that provide full-day/full-year childcare and education and those that provide a (part-time) programme. As suggested below, there is some overlap in these categories.

Table 4 describes common types of childcare provision within the U.S. As is the case in the United Kingdom, most American parents incur the lion's share of the cost of childcare, although tax credits help to defray the expense.

Table 4. Forms of Childcare Provision for Children 0–5 in the United States.

Types	Description
Day Care Centre	Run by individuals, private companies, agencies and employers, a centre may be 'for-profit' or 'not-for-profit''. Provides part-time, full-time, or extended day care to children from birth to five years of age.
Family Daycare Home/Group Home (the term *childminder* is not used in the United States)	A home that provides part-time, full-time, or extended day care. Some states allow home providers to serve up to 12 children when they are supervised by an additional adult.
Early Head Start/Head Start	A programme for low-income parents and their infants and toddlers and 3–4 year olds respectively. Currently efforts are underway to expand full-day/full-year enrolments through partnerships with other early childhood programmes.
Nanny/babysitter/au pair	A caregiver who provides full- or part-time care for children in the family home.
Friend/neighbor	Someone who will care for a child in their own home or the child's home, usually for pay.
Relative	Relative who will care for a child in his or her own home or the child's home with or without remuneration.
Family support programme	Programme aimed at families living in poverty. Services include drop-in childcare, information and referral services, home visits, and instruction on parenting. Usually for families with children under 3.

Table 5.   Forms of Early Education for Children 0–5 in the United States.

Nursery School/ Preschool	Full or part-time early education programme, usually for children 3–5 with some programmes serving twos. May operate 2–5 mornings per week or 5 days/week on a fee-paying basis and be sponsored by churches or other voluntary organisations or by the private sector.
Early Intervention services	State and federally funded education and other services for children birth to age 3 with special needs. Services provided in child's home or in a centre.
Early Head Start	Federally funded programme for low-income families with infants and toddlers. Focuses on child development and family development.
Head Start	Federally funded comprehensive programme providing education, health and other services to children from families living in poverty. Centre- based programme primarily for children 4 years of age but also serve 3s. Most are half day, four days a week for the school year but many are expanding to full time/full year provision. Programme also has a home-based component in some areas for threes and children living in rural areas.
Pre-kindergarten programme/ state-funded Pre-K	Programmes that currently operate in 41 states. Most are part time and targeted at children ages 3 and 4 considered to be at risk for later school failure.
Special education	A programme operated by the LEA and funded by local, state, and federal funds. Aimed at children ages 3–5 with special needs. Provides education and related services as needed by the child. Most are centre based.
Kindergarten	State and locally funded part- and full-day (school day) programme, usually for 5s, operated by the LEA. Typically located in primary school buildings and nearly universally available at no cost to parents. Parents may choose to pay for a private kindergarten placement.
Private Kindergarten	Part- or full-day (usually 6 hours) programme for children five years of age operated on a fee-paying basis.

Additional financial assistance is available due to low income or special circumstance (see the discussion of funding below). More than 60% of American preschool-age children are now in some form of out-of-home care (National Center for Education Statistics, 1996). Table 5 describes common forms of early education provision in the U.S.

In contrast to England where universal provision has been established for four year olds and will soon be available for three year olds, the U.S. continues to provide public funds only for children 3–4 with special needs and those considered to be at risk for school failure. Efforts have been made in a few states (notably Georgia and New York) to provide early education for all four year olds. Kindergarten, usually for children five years of age, is almost universally available and, although not mandatory, is increasingly seen as the first year of primary school. In the United States, compulsory schooling begins at age 6.

REFORM INITIATIVES IN ENGLAND AND THE UNITED STATES

Reform initiatives in England are being advanced at a particular historical moment. The Tory Government had endeavored to decentralise decision making and decrease public spending on education. The new Labour Government, which came into power in 1997, has adopted a dramatically different approach. Early years reforms feature prominently in the Government's plans to eliminate child poverty, to make it possible and desirable for people (especially mothers) to work, and to ensure that children are being prepared to take their place in the workforce of tomorrow. To achieve these ends, the Government has mounted a comprehensive plan of action in a remarkably short period of time.

Prompted by concerns that the early years' system was diverse and fragmented (e.g. Oberhuemer & Ulich, 1997), the Government has spearheaded sweeping reforms to extend and enhance the delivery of services. There has been unprecedented attention and resources devoted to bringing people into the workforce and to expanding and improving early childhood services. Since 1997, the Blair Government has established *statutory maternity and parental leave* (40 weeks of maternity leave with payment at 90% of earnings for six weeks and a flat rate for an additional 12 weeks), *parental leave* (parents are also entitled to 13 weeks unpaid leave from the time a child is born until she turns 5), a *Childcare Tax Credit*, a *minimum wage, universal preschooling for fours*, a *National Childcare Strategy, Early Years Development and Childcare Partnerships (EYDCP), the Sure Start Programme, the Early Excellence Centres Programme, Education Action Zones (EAZ)*, and *Health Action Zones (HAZ)*. The Early Years National Training Organisation (NTO) was constituted in November 1998 as one of 75 NTOs set up to improve the knowledge and skill of workers in each sector. The Early Years NTO includes everyone except teachers working in the early years (0–8) field. It is currently working with the

Qualifications and Curriculum Authority (QCA) to develop a 'climbing frame' that will link care and education training schemes nationally (QCAa, 1999). The Government has also increased funds for training childcare workers.

Funding for childcare and for training has also increased in the U.S., and there are more children in Head Start than ever before. However, the United States' approach lacks coordination and an overall plan. Proponents of decentralisation argue that the United States is so geographically, economically, and culturally diverse that it is better to allow states and local communities to make decisions about how public monies will be dispersed. Currently, federal monies are dispersed to states in the form of Block Grants, but decisions about how programmes will be regulated and how public programmes (with the exception of Head Start) will be funded are largely the province of state and local authorities (see the discussion below).

A federal policy of unpaid parental leave pertains to those employees who work in firms with 50 employees or more. There is also a national minimum wage, and, as is now the case in England, this has consequences for the lowest paid workers in childcare. Two forms of tax credit help to subsidise childcare expenses, although these forms of public assistance do not help to build infrastructure. Parents simply purchase a place that is currently available. Head Start is the only national programme that provides for young children 3–5. There has also been increased state and federal funding for childcare and education, but these monies primarily target children considered to be 'at risk' because of poverty and other factors.

In summary, the U.K. has crafted a comprehensive plan of action to address ECEC issues, with the Government playing a strong role in the planning, funding, and implementation of programmes. Universal preschooling for fours – with universal preschooling for threes soon to be achieved – is a hallmark of this plan, as is the National Childcare Strategy. By contrast, the United States has increased funding, while maintaining a highly decentralised approach in which significant decision making occurs at the state and local levels and public funding remains focused on children in need. In the next section we examine how public funds are being expended in support of the early years and how the early years curriculum in each nation is in the process of change.

FUNDING

Childcare

Childcare costs are primarily incurred by parents in both England and the United States. In 1997, it was estimated that parents paid 93% of costs in the

U.K. (Daycare Trust, 1997). Fees for childcare in England vary by the age of the child, by type of provision, and by locale. On average, a place per week for an infant cost £125, a toddler £120, a child 2–3 £110, and a child 3–5 £108 in 1999. Fees are generally higher in London and in the south and lower in the north (Daycare Trust, 1999).

With the new Childcare Tax Credit, parents will receive tax relief for childcare expenses. It has been estimated that as many as two-thirds of parents will be able to get some tax relief for childcare expenses. Moreover, the Childcare Strategy includes plans to invest as much as £8 billion to expand and improve services for young children and after school care for school-age children, although the Government will not itself operate programmes (Daycare Trust, 1999).

The Early Years Development and Childcare Partnerships (EYDCP) within each local authority is responsible for doing a Childcare Audit and developing a plan for expansion in the area. The audit and plan are then submitted to the Government, which, in turn, provides a grant that may be used to support new places, to run a Childcare Information Service, and/or to fund training. A grant may also be given to ensure that a provider stays in business (Bertram & Pascal, 1999). National Childcare Strategy funds are expected to be supplemented by monies available through the New Opportunities Fund (NOF). Under NOF, £170 million from the National Lottery will be used between 1999 and 2003 to create childcare places for 865,000 children throughout the United Kingdom (DfEE, 1999).

In the United States also, parents are primarily responsible for financing childcare. According to a recent report published by the Children's Defense Fund, the average cost for childcare for a four year old living in an urban areas was $3,000/year in most states and more than $5,000 per year per child in 17 states (Adams & Schulman, 1998).

Parents are eligible for tax relief from two programmes: the Dependent Care Tax Credit and the Dependent Care Assistance Plan. With the former, parents can claim up to $2400 for one child and $4800 for two or more children under 13 years of age. With the latter, taxpayers are permitted to exclude from taxable income up to $5000 incurred for childcare expenses for children birth to 14 (OECD U.S. Country Note, 2000, p. 23).

Federal and state support targets children with disabilities (Part C of the Individuals with Disabilities Education Act), children from low-income families, and children considered to be 'at risk' for academic failure. Early Head Start (for children 0–3 from low-income families) and Head Start (for children 3–5) are federally funded programmes that provide grants directly to hundreds of grantees (school districts, community action programmes, non-profit organisations) throughout the nation. There is currently discussion about – and opposition to – the proposition that these funds also be funneled through the states (Ripple et al., 1999).

Head Start grantees may fund delegate agencies which operate centres, or they may operate centres directly. Increasing numbers of Head Start centres offer full-day childcare for children three to five whose parents are working (See the discussion below). Low-income families also can receive subsidies to purchase childcare from a licensed provider on a sliding fee scale. Federal monies are allocated to states through the Childcare and Development Fund and the Social Services Block Grants and then dispersed locally. A recent effort aims to combine federal funds, including Title One monies, with state and local funds, in order to develop partnerships that will serve a broader range of children.

States have also begun to play a much more active role in supporting early care and education, but priorities vary. Some states elect to supplement federal funding for Head Start so that the programme can serve more children. Others have established state-funded pre-kindergarten programmes, while others subsidise federal spending on childcare, provide tax credits on state taxes, increase subsidies to accredited programmes or do some combination of the above.

Early Education for Children Three to Five

Free part-time preschool for all children four years of age is now state supported throughout the United Kingdom, and universal provision for threes is expected to be reached in England and Scotland between 2002 and 2004. As described above, this means that each four year old is entitled to a 2.5 hour session five times a week during the school term. The funds for three year olds are currently being distributed first to local education authorities that serve the most economically disadvantaged children. In England a Reception class for children 4–5 + provides full-time places (9–3: 30) during the school term in a state-funded primary, first or infant school. Scotland does not have reception classes.

In the United States, both Presidential candidates voiced support for universal preschooling during the 2000 campaign, but it is unlikely that this will become a reality in the forseeable future. Two states, Georgia and New York, now offer universal preschooling for fours at the state level. With these exceptions, public support for early education is confined to children with diagnosed disabilities, those living in poverty, or those considered to be 'at risk' for educational failure. Programmes for 3–5-year-old children with disabilities are funded under Part B of the Individuals with Disabilities Education Act (IDEA). Federal funds are allocated to states that, in turn, establish guidelines for funding. It is usually school districts that submit a plan to the state. Programmes vary from district to district, but some districts have begun collaborations with local Head Starts or state-funded prekindergarten programmes.

Head Start is a federal programme that offers (free) comprehensive services to children and families. These include part- or full-time education and care, nutrition (2–3 meals per day), health and social services, and additional educational services (e.g. speech and language) as needed. With funding at $4.7 billion, 826,000 children were served in 1999 (Administration for Children, Youth, and Families, 2000). Funding increased to $5.27 billion in 2000. Children eligible for Head Start live in families below the official poverty line (roughly $17,000 for a family of four) or are eligible because they have disabilities (approximately 13%) (Administration for Children, Youth, and Families, 2000). The programme serves 36% of children who qualify (OECD U.S. Country Note, 2000, p. 18). Other federally-funded programmes that target children from low-income families are Even Start, which focuses on literacy, and Title I, which provides funding to schools. These funds are also dispersed to the states, which have discretion over how the monies are used.

State-funded pre-kindergarten programmes have expanded in recent years (Schulman et al., 1999). They differ from one state to another, but, in most cases, programmes serve 4-year-old children considered to be at-risk for school failure (Adams & Sandfort, 1994; Schulman et al., 1999).

CURRICULUM

England

In both England and the United States, concerns about globalisation are beginning to affect what and how young children learn, and literacy and numeracy have a newfound importance. The two nations differ, however, in regard to how this is happening. In England, the Government is playing a strong role in planning, funding, and implementing change. There is a national curriculum for children 6–16, and efforts have been made to delineate more clearly what and how young children should be taught. Care has been taken not to use the language of a national curriculum for the early years, but goals were published in 1999 (QCA, 1999) and guidance for teachers (QCA, 2000) in 2000.

The statement of *Early Learning Goals* (QCA, 1999), commissioned by the Department for Education and Employment (DfEE), establishes expectations for children to reach by age 5/5 +. The Goals are subdivided into six areas of learning, with play still considered to be important. However, the goals for literacy and numeracy are ambitious for children of this age, and one might anticipate that the preschool experience will be considerably altered as teachers adapt to heightened expectations. Regarding literacy, for example, it is expected that most five year olds will be able to

(1) Hear and say initial and final sounds in words, and short vowel sounds within words;
(2) Link sounds to letters, naming and sounding the letters of the alphabet;
(3) Read a range of familiar and common words and simple sentences independently;
(4) Write their own names and other things such as labels and captions and begin to form simple sentences sometimes using punctuation;
(5) Use their phonics knowledge to write simple regular words and make phonetically plausible attempts at more complex words (QCA, 1999: 27).

The goals for mathematical development include the ability to:

(1) Say and use number names in order in familiar contexts;
(2) Count reliably up to 10 everyday objects;
(3) Recognise numerals 1 to 9;
(4) Find one more or one less than a number from 1 to 10;
(5) Begin to relate addition to combining groups of objects, and subtraction to 'taking away' (QCA, 1999: 31).

These goals are consonant with the targets that have been set through the National Literacy and Numeracy Strategy. By 2002, the Government expects 75% of all children 11 years of age to reach standards for their age in mathematics and 80% to achieve the standards for literacy (Bertram & Pascal, 1999).

The United States

There are no government-sponsored goals or guidance regarding either the content or approach for educating young children in the United States. That is to say, neither the federal government nor any state government has established curriculum guidelines for young children. Nonetheless, there are signs that policy makers want literacy and numeracy instruction included in the early years curriculum. For example, the 1998 Reauthorization of Head Start mandated that all Head Start children learn 10 letters of the alphabet (Administration for Children, Youth, and Families, 1998). And, in 1999, the Head Start Bureau announced a grant competition to fund four Head Start Quality Centres to study curriculum models and their outcomes over the next five years (see the discussion below).

While the Government in the United Kingdom has directly sponsored curricular change initiatives, government involvement in the U.S. has been more indirect. Professional organisations and national commissions have been instrumental in promoting literacy and numeracy in the United States. A selection of recent reports appears in Table 6.

In 1987, the National Association for the Education of Young Children (NAEYC) established *Guidelines for Developmentally Appropriate Practice* (Bredekamp, 1987). The guidelines strongly supported the importance of play for young children and represented academic instruction of any kind as 'developmentally inappropriate'. More recent documents, however, while still supporting play, have begun to lay stress on aligning the curriculum with subject areas (Bredekamp & Rosegrant, 1995) and gaining foundational skills during the preschool years. For example, *Learning to Read and Write* emphasises that 'It is vital to teach reading and writing to children; literacy does not just emerge naturally' (Neuman et al., 1999: vii).

Another report, *Curriculum and Mathematics in the Early Years*, has been published by the National Council of Teachers of Mathematics (1999). It

Table 6.   Recent Literacy and Numeracy Reports in the United States.

Sponsoring Organisation	Publication
National Research Council	*Preventing Reading Difficulties in Young Children* (1998a) *Starting Out Right* (1998b) *Eager to Learn* (in press)
National Association for The Education of Young Children (NAEYC) and the International Reading Assn.	*Learning to Read and Write: Developmentally Appropriate Practices for Young Children* (2000)
NAEYC	*Reaching Potentials: Transforming Early Childhood Curriculum and Assessment* (1995)
National Council of Teachers Mathematics (NCTM)	*Curriculum and Mathematics in the Early of Years* (1999)
NCTM & NAEYC	*The Young Child and Mathematics* (Copley, 2000)

outlines the content needed for mathematical understanding and presents examples of exemplary programmes for young children. The National Association for the Education of Young Children and the National Council of Teachers of Mathematics also recently released a monograph on mathematics instruction in the early years (Copley, 2000).

The federal government asked the National Academy of Sciences to convene national committees on reading (National Research Council, 1998a, b) and early childhood curriculum (Committee on Early Childhood Pedagogy, 2000). *Preventing Reading Difficulties in Young Children* (National Research Council, 1998a) was the result of the work of the committee established by the National Academy and commissioned by the U.S. Department of Education and the U.S. Department of Health and Human Services. It reviews research on typical reading development and instruction, surveys factors that place children at risk for reading failure, and offers recommendations for effective prevention and intervention, in order to foster positive child outcomes. A follow-up book (National Research Council, 1998b) aims to show parents, teachers, and childcare providers how to help young children become successful readers.

The report by the Committee on Early Childhood Pedagogy (in press) has yet to be published, but the Executive Summary states the following:

> The striking feature of modern research is that it describes unexpected competencies in young children, key features of which appear to be universal. These data focus attention on the child's exposure to learning opportunities, calling into question simplistic conceptualizations of developmentally appropriate practice that do not recognise the newly understood competencies of very young children. Techniques that provide a window into the developing brain allow us to see that stimulation from the environment changes the very physiology of the brain, interlocking nature and nurture (Committee on Early Childhood Pedagogy, in press: 4).

References such as these herald an emerging discourse within the United States. Children are represented as much smarter than was realised; the DAP guidelines, if not themselves simplistic, can be 'simplistically conceptualised', and brain research is being used to argue that early childhood is a 'critical period' for development, one that has lasting effects. According to this logic, it is important to do more – and sooner – to ensure that children will develop the skills and resources needed to participate in a new 'information age' (Bell, 1987).

SUMMARY AND CONCLUSIONS

In this chapter, we have described ways in which globalisaton is beginning to affect early education practice in England and the United States. After a survey of some of the economic, political, and cultural consequences of globalisation, we described how care and education are organised in each country, and then turned to a discussion of recent reform initiatives, specifically focusing on current approaches to funding and curriculum. It was suggested that a new kind of worker will be needed in the global economy that is emerging. This is a worker who is literate, technologically savvy, able to solve problems, and adapt easily to change. As a consequence of these changes, the early years thus has a newfound importance as the foundation for later learning.

This comparison of changing policies and practices in England and the United States occurs at a particular historical moment. Current educational policies in England can be seen to have retained the previous Government's policies of a national curriculum and national assessments, while abandoning that Government's voucher approach to the provision of nursery education. This approach had been supported under the assumption that market forces would drive quality and meet demand. The Blair Government has instead re-asserted a strong role for government and sought explicitly to encourage employment, decrease child poverty, and ensure that children will be adequately prepared for employment in a drastically different work environment. To that end, a large financial investment is being made to expand and improve childcare services and to bring coherence to the existing array of services and types of provision.

The Department for Education and Employment has been given primary responsibility for the early years in England. The local EYDC Partnerships are responsible for submitting plans that link national standards with local improvement initiatives. Self evaluation and action planning have been prominent features of local initiatives, although the Government retains the right to approve the plans before funding is forthcoming. The Early Years National Training Organisation (NTO) is working with the Qualifications and Curriculum Authority to develop a 'climbing frame' that will link care and education training schemes nationally. And a new arm of the Office of Standards in Education (OFSTED) has been made responsible for the regulation of early years care and education settings. Previously OFSTED had only inspected providers of early education. Finally, in the early years' curriculum arena, goals and guidance for achieving these goals have been established (QCA, 1999, 2000).

As these examples suggest, the Blair Government is attempting to forge a coherent plan of action that establishes common standards, goals and procedures and promotes what is referred to as 'joined up' thinking (Bertram & Pascal, 1999). The United Kingdom is now more diverse than at any time in its history, and rates of child poverty have escalated in recent years. This agenda supports coherence and fosters common goals. Yet debate continues within the U.K. regarding whether it is sufficiently comprehensive (Moss, 1999), attuned to the rights of children (Alderson, 2000; David, 2000), and reflective of an ethical and moral stance that values diversity in children, families, and services (Moss & Penn, 1996; Moss, 1999).

When the Clinton Administration came into power in the United States in 1993, there was expectation that the Democrats would forefront children's issues, especially in education and health.[4] Republicans continued to control Congress, however, and Clinton's plan for a national health care system was criticised and ultimately defeated. The tradition of decentralised (state and local) control in the United States also makes it difficult to assert federal authority in education. And the dominant economic ideology – that the market, rather than the government, should function to set prices and drive quality – has made policies such as tax credits and subsidies more politically viable than building infrastructure. As a consequence, the Administration has been successful in funneling more money into childcare, but the lack of a 'system' is still apparent. Rather than taking the lead and forging a plan of action, the federal government instead disperses monies to states that, in turn, have wide discretion regarding how funds will be allocated and programmes regulated. Moreover, both federal and state monies are primarily used to fund childcare and education for children with special needs, children living in poverty, and children otherwise considered to be at 'risk'. Here critics argue that this approach segregates and stigmatises, and fledgling efforts have been made to establish universal provision in two states.[5]

Given the difficulty of legislating change, the Administration has requested that national commissions of experts be convened to distill research and provide guidance for standards and 'best practice'. Professional associations such as the National Association for the Education of Young Children, the International Reading Association, and the National Council for Teachers of Mathematics have also assumed a role in responding to the demands of globalisation. For example, the NAEYC has not only begun to emphasise the importance of literacy and numeracy instruction in the early years but also endeavored to create a coherent training structure (e.g. Bredekamp & Willer, 1992), as well as set standards for curriculum (Bredekamp & Rosegrant, 1995) and teacher training (NAEYC, 2000). Overall, one might say that the approach to the early years in the United States is characterised by a lack of an overall strategy, more indirect government influence, and continuing struggles between neoliberal and neoconservative interests.

Comparing policies and practices cross-nationally provides a framework for understanding how concerns about globalisation are being used to effect educational change and how the field of early childhood education is being reconstituted in the process. There have been suggestions that early childhood professionals need to become more responsive to context and to the ways in which people 'make meaning' in specific locales (e.g. Woodhead, 1999), more critical of knowledge and power relations (Bloch, 2000), and more willing to move beyond utilitarian concern with 'what works' to consider questions of value (Dahlberg et al., 1999). A critical and comparative approach, what Arnove (1999: 7) terms 'educational borrowing and lending', provides one way to open discussions to new possibilities. Much more work is needed to suggest how such information might be made useful to policymakers and practitioners. This chapter has been one small step in that direction.

NOTES

1. The United Kingdom of Great Britain and Northern Ireland is comprised of four countries: England, Wales, Scotland, and the counties of Northern Ireland. Since devolution, there are differences in the ways in which each country has responded to early education reform initiatives. The discussion here focuses primarily on England.

2. The sise of the U.K. population (59 million) is less than one-fourth that of the United States (nearly 274 million in 1999); the U.K. land mass is approximately twice the sise of the state of New York.

3. This paper compares the English and American approaches to ECEC along several dimensions. Due to space constraints, we are unable to describe these approaches within their temporal and cultural contexts. Such contextualising is crucial to understanding why and how particular values and practices prevail at this moment in time.

4. The U.S. basically has a two-party system, although two other parties with (currently) small followings have been trying to capture national attention. The Democrats are considered to be liberal and the Republicans conservative, although critics maintain that politics has shifted so much to the centre that their agendas are, in many ways, indistinguishable.

5. In the case of Head Start, the issues are more complex than this, since this large federal programme is organised to meet the needs of the 'whole child' and her family. Thus, educational services, health services, social services, nutrition, services to children with disabilities, etc. are all included in the Head Start mandate.

REFERENCES

Adams, G., & Sandfort, J. (1994). *First steps, promising futures: State prekindergarten initiatives in the early 1990s*. Washington, D.C.: Children's Defense Fund.

Adams, G., & Schulman, K. (1998). *Childcare challenges*. Washington, D.C.: Children's Defense Fund.

Administration on Children Youth & Families (1998). *Head Start Act*. Washington, D.C.: Department of Health & Human Services.

Administration on Children Youth & Families (2000). *Head Start statistical fact sheet*. Washington, D.C.: Department of Health & Human Services.

Alderson, P. (2000). The rights of young children. In: H. Penn (Ed.), *Early Childhood Services: Theory, Policy and Practice* (pp. 158–169). Buckingham: Open University Press.

Apple, M. W. (2000). Between neoliberalism and neoconservatism: Education and conservatism in a global context. In: N. C. Burbules & C. A. Torres (Eds), *Globalisation and Education: Critical Perspectives* (pp. 57–77). New York: Routledge.

Arnove, R. F. (1999). Reframing comparative education: The dialectic of the global and the local. In: R. F. Arnove & C. A. Torres (Eds), *Comparative Education: The Dialectic of the Global and the Local* (pp. 1–23). Lanham, MD: Rowman & Littlefield.

Bell, D. (1987). The world and the United States in 2013. *Daedalus, 116*, 1–31.

Bertram, T., & Pascal, C. (1999). *The OECD thematic review of early childhood education and care: Background report for the United Kingdom*. Worcester: Worcester University College of HE, Centre for Research in Early Childhood.

Bloch, M. (2000). Governing teachers, parents and children through child development knowledge, *Human Development, 43*(4–5), 257–265.

Boyden, J. (1990). Childhood and the policy makers: A comparative perspective on the globalisation of childhood. In: A. James & A. Prout (Eds), *Constructing and Reconstructing Childhood: Contemporary Issues in the Sociological Study of Childhood* (pp. 190–229). London: Falmer Press.

Bredekamp, S. (1987). *Guidelines for developmentally appropriate practice*. Washington, D.C.: NAEYC.

Bredekamp, S., & Rosegrant, T. (1995). *Reaching potentials: Transforming early childhood curriculum and assessment* (Vol. 2). Washington, D.C.: NAEYC.

Bredekamp, S., & Willer, B. (1992). Of ladders and lattices, cores and cones: Conceptualizing an early childhood professional development system. *Young Children*, 47–50.

Burbules, N. C., & Torres, C. A. (2000). Globalisation and education: An introduction. In: N. C. Burbules & C. A. Torres (Eds), *Globalisation and Education: Critical perspectives* (pp. 1–26). New York: Routledge.

Carnoy, M. (1999). *Globalisation and educational reform: What planners need to know* (Vol. 63). Paris: UNESCO: International Institute of Educational Planning.

Cassen, B. (2000). To save society. In: F. J. Lechner & J. Boli (Eds), *The globalisation reader* (pp. 14–16). Malden, MA: Blackwell.

Committee on Early Childhood Pedagogy (2000). *Eager to learn: Executive summary* (http://www.nap.edu/openbook/030968363/html).

Copley, J. V. (2000). *The young child and mathematics*. Washington, D.C.: NAEYC.

Dahlberg, G., Moss, P., & Pence, A. (1999). *Beyond quality in early childhood education and care: Postmodern perspectives*. New York: Teachers College Press.

David, T. (2000). Valuing young children. In: L. Abbott & H. Moylett (Eds), *Early Education Transformed* (pp. 82–92). London: Falmer Press.

Daycare Trust (1997). *Working wonders: Quality staff, quality services*. London: Daycare Trust.

Daycare Trust (1999). *Making the most of the National Childcare Strategy*. London: Daycare Trust.

DfEE (1999). *Developing DfEE's research strategy consultation paper*. London: DfEE.

Glauser, B. (1990). Street children: Deconstructing a construct. In: A. James & A. Prout (Eds), *Constructing and Reconstructing Childhood: Contemporary Issues in the Sociological Study of Childhood*. London: Falmer Press.

Green, A. (1997). *Education, globalisation and the nation state*. New York: St. Martin's Press.

Harvey, D. (1990). *The condition of postmodernity: An inquiry into the origins of cultural change*. Cambridge, MA: Blackwell Publishers.

HERA 2 (1999). *Final report: Childcare training in the U.K.* Suffolk: Suffolk County Council.

Kumar, K. (1995). *From post-industrial to post-modern society: New theories of the contemporary world.* Oxford: Blackwell.

Lechner, F. J., & Boli, J. (Eds) (2000). *The globalisation reader.* Malden, MA: Blackwell Publishers.

Martin, P. (2000). The moral case for globalisation. In: F. J. Lechner & J. Boli (Eds), *The Globalisation Reader* (pp. 12–13). Malden, MA: Blackwell Publishers.

McNeil, L. (2000). Creating new inequalities. *Phi Delta Kappan, 81*(10), 728–734.

Mitchell, A., Stoney, L., & Dichter, H. (2000). The good news: Innovations in childcare financing. *Young Children, 55*(4), 88–91.

Morrow, R. A., & Torres, C. A. (2000). The state, globalisation, and educational policy. In: N. C. Burbules & C. A. Torres (Eds), *Globalisation and Education: Critical Perspectives* (pp. 27–56). New York: Routledge.

Moss, P. (1999). Renewed hopes and lost opportunities: Early childhood in the early years of the Labour Government. *Cambridge Journal of Education, 29*(2), 229–238.

Moss, P., & Penn, H. (1996). *Transforming nursery education.* London: Paul Chapman.

National Association for the Education of Young Children (1996). *Guidelines for the preparation of early childhood professionals.* Washington, D.C.: NAEYC.

National Association for the Education of Young Children (2000). *NCATE programme standards: Initial and advanced programmes in early childhood education.* Washington, D.C.

National Centre for Educational Statistics (1996). *The condition of education 1996.* Washington, D.C.: U.S. Department of Education.

National Council of Teachers of Mathematics (1999). *Mathematics in the early years.* Reston, VA: NCTM.

National Research Council (1998a). *Preventing reading difficulties in young children.* Washington, D.C.: National Academy Press.

National Research Council (1998b). *Starting out right: A guide to promoting children's reading success.* Washington, D.C.: National Academy Press.

National Research Council (in press). *Eager to learn.* Washington, D.C.: National Academy Press.

Neuman, S., Copple, C., & Bredekamp, S. (1999). *Learning to read and write: Developmentally appropriate practices for young children.* Washington, D.C.: NAEYC.

Oberhuemer, P., & Ulich, M. (1997). *Working with young children in Europe: Provision and staff training.* London: Paul Chapman.

OECD Country Note. (2000). *Early childhood education and care policy in the United States of America.* Paris: OECD.

Popkewitz, T. (Ed.) (2000). *Educational knowledge: Changing relationships between the state, civil society, and the educational community.* Albany, N.Y.: SUNY Press.

Prior, G., Courtney, G., & Charkin, E. (1999). *2nd survey of parents of three and four year old children and their use of early years services* (Research RR120). London: Division for Education and Employment.

Prout, A., & James, A. (1990). A new paradigm for the sociology of childhood? Provenance, promise and problems. In: A. James & A. Prout (Eds), *Constructing and Reconstructing Childhood: Contemporary Issues in the Sociological Study of Childhood* (pp. 7–33). London: Falmer Press.

Qualifications and Curriculum Authority (QCA) (1999). *Early learning goals.* London: Department of Education and Employment.

Qualifications and Curriculum Authority (QCA) (1999a). *Early years education, childcare and playwork: A framework of nationally accredited qualifications.* London: QCA.

Qualifications and Curriculum Authority (QCA) (2000). *Curriculum guidance for the foundation stage.* London: QCA.

Ripple, C., Gillam, W., Chanana, N., & Zigler, E. (1999). Will fifty cooks spoil the broth? The debate over entrusting Head Start to the states. *American Psychologist, 54*(5), 327–353.

Schulman, K., Blank, H., & Ewen, D. (1999). State prekindergarten initiatives: A varied picture of states' decisions affecting availability, quality, and access. *Young Children, 54*(6), 38–41.

Wolf, M. (2000). Why this hatred of the market? In: F. J. Lechner & J. Boli (Eds), *The Globalisation Reader* (pp. 9–11). Malden, MA: Blackwell Publishers.

Woodhead, M. (1999). Towards a global paradigm for research into early childhood education. *European Early Childhood Education Research Journal, 7*(1), 5–22.

SECTION IV:

RESEARCHING EARLY CHILDHOOD EDUCATION AND CARE

13. RESEARCH INVOLVING YOUNG CHILDREN

Ann Lewis

The research process, if done well, forces us to frame, ask, evaluate and respond to important developmental and educational questions about young children. The unexamined practice, I would argue, is not worth doing. Research methodology provides a well-established cluster of ways to examine that practice. The scope of research and methodologies involving young children is very wide encompassing the three broad research strategies summarised by Robson (1993): case studies, surveys and experiments. Cutting across these research strategies will be a bias by the researcher towards either interpretive or 'scientific' approaches. This highlights at the outset the notion that research cannot be value-free. Every researcher brings to the research, value judgements both about the focus of the research and the nature of enquiry. It is beyond the scope of one chapter to review the full range of research involving young children (see Aubrey et al., 2000; Grieg & Taylor, 1999, for very clear overviews) and I am narrowing this to a discussion about research that involves eliciting the young child's perspective, attitudes and/or (particularly linguistic) behaviour. The chapter is organised around key aspects of eliciting these: the research context, ethical considerations, setting including group size, form of response by the child and adult language to the child (the latter linking with various issues pertaining to suggestibility).

Promoting Evidence-based Practice in Early Childhood Education:
Research and its Implications, Volume 1, pages 253–271.
Copyright © 2001 by Elsevier Science Ltd.
All rights of reproduction in any form reserved.
ISBN: 0-7623-0753-6

1. THE RESEARCH CONTEXT

Adult: (pointing to oil slick on the road)
    Look, what's that?
Child: It's a dead rainbow

If that incident was taken from a research project one might examine the meaning of the exchange in various ways. We might ask – what was the wider situation and how might it have affected the child's response? What was it about the child and the situation that made the adult ask this question at this time and in that way? Was this perhaps a well-worn family joke? What was the adult seeking from the child – scientific understanding, any communication, and reference to something other than the oil slick? Did the adult phrase the question in an appropriate way? Did the child hear the question correctly? Did she have the linguistic skills to understand what was said (receptive language) and the skills to articulate a response (expressive language)? Was she sufficiently motivated to give a considered response? These kinds of questions raise two central issues relating to research involving children. The first relates to the reasons why the research is undertaken (the research question) and the second relates to fundamental methodological issues about the trustworthiness (reliability and validity) of the information (data) collected.

Research involving young children now usually recognizes the multiple and two-way nature of influences. For example, children's behaviour in classrooms is interpreted not simply as reactions to the teacher, but rather as transactions, with the child's behaviour influencing and hence modifying the teacher's behaviour as well as the teacher's behaviour affecting that of the child. Children's behaviour is also affected by their biological characteristics but these may also be influenced by environmental factors. For example, the young child with high levels of distractibility may be influenced by change of diet, medication, modified classroom arrangements and teaching approaches, or a combination of these. Hence the focus has shifted from single one-way relationships to a broader view of the wide range of bi-directional influences on children.

There are direct implications for research. For example, when observing children's behaviour in classrooms, it is necessary not only to have a construct such as distractibility as a variable, but also the teacher's behaviour, the nature of the learning tasks and the setting. Further, it is important to view the child as interpreting what is happening, not simply responding to the researcher. In summary, there are many influences operating between and around the rescarcher and the child; thus all research results need to be considered in the light of the context in which they were collected, whether this context refers to a particular task or a wider social system.

2. ETHICAL CONSIDERATIONS

Ethical issues in research involving young children have, rightly, been given increasing recognition in recent years. For example, it is now usual for students writing a field-based thesis for a higher degree in the U.K. to include a substantial section on the ethical issues associated with the conduct of the study. Hood et al. (1999) link the growing concerns about ethical issues in research involving children with critiques of developmental psychology. They note the shift away from a view of children as victims, threats, vulnerable incompetents or deviants. In that model adults' role in relation to children was to protect and control. In their work, drawing on the sociology of childhood (see also Lloyd Smith & Tarr, 2000), they stress that research should not be on children but with them and for them. From a similar perspective, Mahon et al. (1996) argue that researchers involving children should addresss seriously issues about how involvement in the research affects the children.

Many writers in this field stress the importance of rapport with children involved in research. This is a particularly sensitive issue when the research is being conducted by adults (or older children) not known to the child (see Aldridge & Wood, 1998). The building of rapport links with concerns about the importance of researchers not placing undue stress on the children involved.

Ethical issues concerning researching children's perspectives have been examined extensively in Lewis and Lindsay (2000). In summary, key aspects include the roles of gatekeepers, confidentiality, informed consent/assent (and the distinction between these two) and the nature of various codes of ethical conduct in this context. At the root of this issue is the importance of approaching research involving young children from a position of respect for the individual child. Lindsay (2000) extrapolates the principles embodied in various ethical codes (APA, 1992; BERA, 1992; BPS, 1996; CPA, 1992) and adds notions of competence, responsibility and integrity as well as the researcher's responsibility to society.

3. SETTING INCLUDING GROUP SIZE

Children can be studied in either their natural environment or a formal research setting. Either choice has limitations as well as strengths. For example, working with children in schools means that although the children are in a familiar setting, the vagaries of the school timetable, unexpected special events, classroom dramas and staff absence may limit the researcher's work. Moreover, children may be concerned that information revealed will be fed back to teachers, parents or peers. In contrast, laboratories while supplying a degree of experimental control may also add artificiality and unfamiliarity thus limiting the generalisability of the findings. The advantage of such settings is that they provide a basis for making clear changes to test specific hypotheses. For example, the considerable advances in our understanding of children's suggestibility would not have been possible without the control allowed by experimental procedures (Ceci & Bruck, 1993).

Related to choice of setting and method of data collection are questions about group size. Group size can be particularly significant where interviews are used as a method of data collection. Group interviews have been used with young children and in that context consideration needs to be given to matters such as group size, selection of group members, physical arrangements, recording and transcription, seating of group members and contamination of ideas between groups (discussed further in Dockrell et al., 2000; Lewis, 1992). Group interviews allow the possibility that the discussions between individuals will spark off new ideas, criticism or developments. Other potential strengths of group interviews include the probing of consensus beliefs, the provision of social support in the context of 'risky' topics and a natural style of interaction. Group interviews may also be particularly valuable at the exploratory stage of research (see Lewis, 1992, 1995).

On the other hand, a serious problem with group interviews involving young children is that some participants may dominate by either restricting the topics for discussion or dominating the discussion themselves. Some members of the group may be hesitant to offer a different or alternative perspective. Other potential disadvantages include difficulties for the interviewer in following through an individual's line of argument, inadvertent 'tidying up' of talk in the transcription process and group order effects.

4. FORM OF RESPONSE BY THE CHILD

Behaviour

When we collect data from children we can only ever measure their overt behaviour. We use this behaviour as an indicator of a child's competence. There are special problems with studying children that can lead us either to under- or over- estimate their abilities. Children's behaviour as research participants will be determined both by their developmental levels in relevant domains, and also by the nature of the task. It is often difficult to disentangle which of these factors is leading to success or failure for the child.

The child's behaviour is not always an accurate indication of her competence – this may lead to incorrect conclusions being drawn. In the research context we may make judgements about, for example, the child's beliefs, based on what she chooses to reveal to the researcher. We can make errors that occur because we underestimate a child's competence (a 'type 1 error') and errors that occur because we overestimate a child's competence (a 'type 2 error'). In summary, several features may lead to an under-estimation of children: linguistic (children may fail a task because they do not understand the language that is being used or the meanings of specific vocabulary items); cognitive (the task may rely on higher order factors so that the child is unable to work out the task demands); memory (a child may fail a task not because they do not understand the nature of the task but rather because additional demands are placed on the child's memory system or information processing resources); and/or the balance between text and context (See Dockrell et al., 2000 for a fuller discussion of these issues).

Drawings

Researchers in child development have often turned to children's drawings as a means of understanding their views of situations and cognitive levels. The status of children's drawings for addressing these two foci is rather different. Using drawings to make inferences about a child's personality or emotional state is a highly suspect process. As Thomas and Jolley (1998) conclude 'children's drawings on their own are too complexly determined and inherently ambiguous to be reliable as sole indicators of the emotional experiences of the children who drew them'. Thus the use of drawings for such purposes is likely to be unreliable and lead to erroneous conclusions. They may however be used effectively when combined with interview techniques or specific assessment activities.

The use of drawings to reflect the child's cognitive changes, although fraught with methodological problems, is quite promising. As we know by looking at children's drawings their pictorial notations develop across the years (Thomas & Silk, 1990). A number of authors have argued that investigations of children's early drawings and notations for numbers and words indicate that there are representational principles underlying early spontaneous notations. Such early notations are thought to provide clues to how the child's representation meshes with the environmental input, resulting in a creative and flexible system (Karmiloff-Smith, 1992).

Questionnaires

A critical issue when planning research is considering the child's ability to respond to the, behavioural, oral or written language demands of the task. It is probably developmentally inappropriate to require five-year-olds to complete a conventional questionnaire. However the approach need not be dismissed out of hand. Interesting work by teacher researchers, for example, has involved children using simple pictorial questionnaires similar to school-based work-sheet activities. Currently, work in progress is using internet-based pictorial questionnaires with young children. This is still an undeveloped area but, given technological advances, is likely to grow and to generate a new set of methodological issues.

We can also use a scaled response to investigate children's views such as 'How much do you like working on your own?' with a rating of 1 (not at all) to 6 (very much). Such questions could be used with a visual scale in which the child manipulated materials to reveal the 1–6 position of her response. Ingenious devices based on rolling up or unrolling a 'toothpaste tube', drawing miniature curtains across the scale or rolling out a piece of fabric over the scale have all been used successfully with young children. This type of structured response forms a bridge between questionnaires and structured interviews.

Diary Studies

Methods of data collection in natural settings include observation and diary studies. Diary studies have been a principal source of information about early childhood for a long time. For example, Piaget (1929) used the diary method to collect much of his data. For researchers in child language (e.g. Brown, 1973) diaries of children's early utterances form most of the data collected, especially in the early stages of acquisition, more recently diaries have been used to investigate such topics as children's homework. A diary acts as a self-administered questionnaire. It is convenient, cost-effective and a relatively easy means of recording behaviours in naturalistic environments. Diaries can range from being totally unstructured to a set of responses to specific questions. They can also serve as a proxy for observing situations that are not amenable to the presence of observers, e.g. night time waking. Parents have several advantages as observers above outside researchers – they may interpret the child's speech or actions better as they know the child; and they can observe without disturbing the child or other members of the household. There are however some disadvantages – parents may over-interpret their children's behaviour, training may be required to use the technique and diaries can be time consuming both to complete and to analyse.

Observational Studies

When we ask parents or teachers to complete diaries we are asking them to report on their observations about particular behaviours or situations. Equally the investigator can carry out the observations. In research contexts we are interested in a sample of the child's behaviour (for example, temper tantrums during a specified series of time intervals, parental records of a child's sleep disorders over a four week monitoring period, attainments on a slice of mathematical learning or a child's recall of best friends). Observations are time-consuming both in terms of planning and execution.

The initial step is to decide which behaviours to observe. If we were interested in whether a child was happy we would need to consider which of the various indicators of happiness (e.g. smiles, laugh, verbal expressions of pleasure, open eyes, hand clapping and so forth) we were going to measure. Secondly, we would need to decide whether we were going to measure every occurrence of the behaviour (event sampling) such as the number of requests during free play. Alternatively we can measure whether the behaviour occurs at preset intervals (time-sampling) such as every 10 minutes, or every 30 seconds. Further, the intervals for sampling may be fixed or random. The sampling basis chosen may be highly significant as particular behaviours may typically occur in a pattern that the sampling overlooks or exaggerates. For example, classroom misbehaviour typically occurs more frequently around lesson changes than during the main body of lessons; consequently classroom observation at these different times would give very different impressions of the 'typical' frequency of misbehaviour. How we measure is intimately linked to the behaviours that are measured and the context of measurement. Investigators are not immune to over-interpretation or misinterpretation of behaviour and often investigators will also require training with the particular measurement tools.

Interviews

Interviews are another form of data collection that can take place in a natural environment such as the child's school but within that the setting may be more or less structured. Some researchers have used children to interview other children so aiming to increase the naturalness of the setting. Children can also be used to interview adults so that we can tap the child's views of the critical dimensions surrounding a particular topic such as a job or holiday. Other work (e.g. Gross, 1993) entails an external researcher not known to the children interviewing them in the school in a room set aside for the purpose. Here the context is clearly much more formal. The interview format is particularly important with vulnerable or disempowered groups, such as children. There is a particular need to be sensitive to the kinds of questions asked so as not to lead the children's responses. Thus is discussed further below, in relation to suggestibility.

A key issue is to ask how 'truthful' are verbal reports provided in interviews? Do the depth and subtlety that they provide allow for a reflection of the beliefs of the children? Some cognitive psychologists have argued that verbal reports are not good indicators of actual thought processes (Nisbitt & Wilson, 1977). It is argued that the reports are a biased, generalised reconstruction. However, more detailed examination has shown that verbal reports can be accurate reflections of the process under investigation if the individual is recounting a specific event or set of events (Ericsson & Simon, 1980). A parallel argument has been made by some social psychologists. Billig (1987) proposes that both the general and the specific levels of verbal data are useful since they investigate social interpretations and actual situations respectively. So a researcher might be interested in a child's general view of playing with friends and their specific view about a particular game. Accordingly the data that are collected serve different kinds of purposes.

For example, questions about the child's family may be interpreted very differently depending on whether the situation is settled, and neutral to positive, compared with the case of a child in fear (e.g. a child subject to abuse), or where the subcultural 'rule' is to give nothing away 'to authority'. These response tendencies will interact with the subject matter of the questions, but may also be more pervasive tendencies. Furthermore, the language used must be understood, an issue not only of vocabulary and sentence complexity but also of accent and rapport.

We must be very wary of using our adult stereotypes to investigate children's views. A good example of an accident, for an adult, might be a car crash but this might not be a child's prototypical response. Equally a picture of a child with Down syndrome might be used to investigate views of special need but this might artificially limit the child's responses. So the use of non-verbal materials need to be considered as carefully as verbal ones to minimise the occurrence of error of commission and omission.

The impact of expectations on young children's responses in interviews is illustrated by Ceci in work involving a character (Harry) whose 'clumsiness' was described (over a 2 month period) (reported in Ceci & Bruck, 1993). 'Harry' then visited the children's nursery. Children were later told that three toys had been broken and asked about what happened when Harry visited. Only 10% of the children alleged that it was Harry who had broken the toys. When asked presumptive questions (e.g. 'How many toys did Harry break?') young children reported more (inaccurate) clumsiness than had occurred. This highlights both the importance of the way in which expectations about people with learning difficulties are presented to children and the danger of leading questions.

The language the child thinks the interviewer would use may also shape the young child's responses. This is illustrated well in Eleanor Nesbitt's work (Nesbitt, 2000). She interviewed a wide range of children, of different ethnic origins, about their views concerning religion. Eleanor noted that, for example, some children used, when talking to her, terms like 'vicar' to describe the person who took the service even though this would not be the child's natural choice for that person (e.g. for a Baptist child, it would be 'minister'; for a Catholic, 'father' etc). The child was not picking up a word Eleanor had used but seems to have used a word that the child thought would be Eleanor's preferred term. The issue is the same but less obvious when a child uses particular terms to describe classmates, for example 'having difficulties'/ 'trying hard'.

5. ADULT LANGUAGE TO THE CHILD (LINKING WITH VARIOUS ISSUES PERTAINING TO SUGGESTIBILITY)

Difficulties particular to interviewing young children (c 3–6 years) include a tendency for the child to agree with the interviewer or to feel compelled to provide an answer even to 'nonsense' questions. Hughes and Grieve (1980) reported work in which 4-year-olds were asked to decide whether red was bigger than yellow, or milk was bigger than water, for example. The children gave a reply and did not say that the question was nonsensical. So, there is clear evidence that children will respond to questions even if they do not know what they mean.

Young children will also tend to interpret questions very literally (see examples in Lewis, 1995), be distracted by events outside the interview and want to find out about the interviewer. If the interviews take place in a school then the conventions of teacher-child dialogue, such as that a repeated question is indicative of an incorrect answer, may also invalidate responses (Rose & Blank, 1974). Further the child's understanding of particular terms may not match the adults'. For example, young children questioned about the nature of severe learning difficulties appeared to confuse this with hearing difficulties. It is unclear whether this was a conceptual confusion or whether these children understood the concept but lacked the language with which to express their understanding (Lewis, 1995).

A fascinating range of research, stemming largely from the context of ascertaining possible child abuse, has produced important findings about the dangers of suggestibility when talking with. young children. Young children have been found to be more suggestible than older children or adults and they tend to be less full in their recall of events. There is some evidence (reviewed by Ceci & Bruck, 1993) that young children are less suggestible in matters relating to direct, personal experiences.

Effect of Prompts

If a particular level of question is more effective than other levels then it is useful for all researchers to recognise this, whether they are approaching the interview through highly structured questioning or a more open style. In general, questions that require only yes/no or very precise answers are to be avoided. The optimum degree of verbal prompting has been examined in seminal work by Dent (1986) and reviewed by Ceci and Bruck (1993: 'The focus has [thus] shifted from examining whether children are susceptible to determining under what conditions they are suggestible' p. 16). A distinction was found between normally developing children and children with learning difficulties (8–11-year-olds from an MLD school). For the former, unprompted recall was the most accurate (but the least full) while for the learning difficulties group, general but not leading questions were most effective in terms of accuracy plus fullness). Specific questions were unhelpful for both groups and produced more information but this tended to be inaccurate. Similarly, Ceci has reported research in which children, having witnessed a classroom incident, were questioned about this. The more they were asked for elaboration (for example, 'Who came in?' (a lady), 'What was she wearing' (a hat), 'What did the hat look like?' (it had feathers), 'How many feathers?') the more children supplied (incorrect) detail.

Dent concluded that if accuracy of recall is desired then specific questions should not be used at all with children aged 8–14. General open-ended questions appeared to be best with children with mild or moderate learning difficulties. There has been debate since (see Bull, 1995) about whether the rejection of specific questions in this context was justified and a suggestion that clarification is needed about the types of specific questions which are associated with greater/ lesser accuracy.

A different type of prompt used with children with young children is pictorial cues, either as a prompt card (e.g. 'The girl in this picture is happy, but in this picture she is sad. Which one shows how you would look when . . .'). Pictorial cues may also be used as part of a vignette depicting a series of events about which the child being interviewed is asked to comment. Some work (e.g. Begley, 2000) has used standard scales using pictorial cues about which the child's response is rated. In other work with children, innovative techniques such as ecomaps or outline faces have been used (Hill et al., 1996).

These approaches have intuitive appeal but they may be more open to bias even though the most obvious e.g. using pictures of a same sex/ race/ age child can be avoided by using parallel sets of cards so that children depicted are from the same groups as the interviewee.

Use of Statements Rather Than a Question, as a Prompt

A range of work with children has shown the value of making statements that prompt a response, rather than a direct question, to elicit views. The tendency for adults, particularly teachers, to use question-answer-feedback routines has been described by some writers as reflecting power relationships (Edwards & Mercer, 1993). Through the use of questions, the adult keeps the 'upper hand'. Thus in the research context, the use of statements rather than questions also reflects an implied power relationship. The use of statements as prompts in research interviews can occur naturally in small group interviews with children. Here one child's comment may trigger a response from another child in the group. This is shown well in the following example in which children from a primary school were discussing likely work in adulthood for pupils from a special (SLD) school who visited the class regularly.

Kay	Kirsty's quite good at . . . [pause]
	at um . . . stencilling;
	she can find the letters really quickly
Jo	Jeremy's quite good at jigsaws mainly
Stevie	Yeh.. Kirsty's good at jigsaws
Kay	Yeh but there's no JOB to do with jigsaws
Jo	They could check all the pieces

Free Narrative as a Response Format

The value of free narrative has been demonstrated in interviews with children. Saywitz (1995) notes that the main purpose in encouraging free narrative is to encourage children to elaborate their account, without compromising accuracy through the interjection of potentially leading questions by the interviewer. In line with this, Saywitz and Snyder (1996) trained 7–8 and 10–11-year-olds, using pictorial cue cards (representing, for example, 'feelings', 'place'), to build a mental script to represent a series of events. The cue cards reminded the children to consider including particular categories of detail without explicitly leading them in a particular direction. It is clearly important to make these cue cards as neutral as possible otherwise children will be 'led' by the pictorial cues.

Current work (Lewis, in preparation) has developed this approach with young children. While the strategy showed considerable promise and did encourage more elaborated accounts than were generated through unprompted narratives, there were potential difficulties associated with cue cards and young children, particularly those with learning difficulties. For example, some children perseverated and once a particular cue card had been linked with a particular response, that response recurred across successive showings of that cue card in relation to other events. For example, in one account of what had happened during an incident on his holiday Chris (a 7-year-old with learning difficulties) on being shown the 'feeling' cue card recalled that he had felt happy because he received a gift. Then in other contexts, such as recalling what had happened on a particular day at school, Chris when shown that cue card again 'recalled' receiving a gift. This example highlights the particular difficulties when interviewing children with learning difficulties. Yet, because of their disproportionately high representation among victims of child abuse, it is especially important that effective interview strategies which produce valid and reliable responses are developed with that group of children (Lewis, in press).

Providing a Resumé

Providing a group of statements in the form of a brief resumé can be particularly valuable with young children who have short attention spans. However doing so may inadvertently distort what was being said, as may have been the case in this example in which mainstream children were being asked about the inclusion of children with learning difficulties into their school:

Wayne	Cos their playground, their playground is big
David	But there's not many children in it
Wayne	And some of them don't like the loud noises and cos
	Cos I mean our playgrounds *a lot* noisier than theirs
Tracey	Yeh and their playground hasn't got many people in it
Interviewer	You think the noise [in primary school playground] would upset some of them so they wouldn't like it.

On reading this transcript extract, it is apparent the interviewer's summary comment introduced the notion of being 'upset' and this may have biased subsequent responses from the children. This may also have repercussions for coding when the resumé is consciously or otherwise used to aid interpretation of the sequence of dialogue.

Another type of resumé occurs in the legal context when the questioner may be trying to confirm a series of facts leading up to an event (e.g. 'So you were downstairs, there was knock at the door, the man came in, then what happened . . .?'). Saywitz (1995) reviews work suggesting that such long compound sentences with embedded clauses are beyond the linguistic comprehension and memory skills of many children under about 8-years-old.

Value of Pause

Some researchers (Bull, 1995) have argued that in all interviews, but particularly those involving children or people with learning difficulties, it is valuable to allow long pauses (up to 3 seconds) in order to encourage a response. Julie Barsby gives a good illustration of this in her research involving children with learning difficulties evaluating their work in collaboration with a friend.

1st interview
Interviewer Could you make your writing better
Child [nods]   How could you do that
Child Don't know
Interviewer You don't know
Child No
Interviewer What could you do to make your writing more interesting. How could you make your story better?
Child Write little
Interviewer Pardon? Write small?
Child Yes
Interviewer What about the story itself?
Child [long pause]

This can be contrasted with Julie's 3rd interview with this child, 3 weeks later.

3rd interview
Interviewer Could you make your writing better? How do you feel about your work?
Child It's not bad for me. I could've done a bit better but I did my best because I had a late night
Interviewer How could you make your writing better?
Child I could have a little think about it and tell the truth why they were enjoying themselves

Interviewer Mm
Child   Well I know you wouldn't tell me off cos you giggle too. I've seen you with
              Mrs C [long pause . . . . . .] I could say that the kids have a good laugh and
              think it's well funny when teachers run and fall over and look through their
              glasses over their noses. If I put that then I'd really 've painted a picture of the
              best sort of teacher in the world. All the er kids 'd know then.

Multiple Questions

Multiple questions disguised as one question are a notorious trap in interviews.
Even experienced interviewers may make this mistake, for example:

> If you could change anything you wanted about your present class or school, or the work
> you do at school, what changes would you make?
>
> (from Gross, 1993)

This multiple questioning may be problematic for young children if they do not
seek clarification. One strategy to help deal with this is to permit and explicitly
to encourage 'don't know' responses and clarification requests (cf Hughes,
1986). This has emerged as important in legal contexts but has applicability for
more general research situations. Saywitz (1995) notes that children with
learning difficulties may be particularly liable to say 'don't know' (and/or not
to ask for clarification). If they have had unsuccessful school or assessment
experiences in which they have come to expect that they will not fully
understand what is being asked they may have learned that they can 'get away
with' avoiding answering. The same may be true of young children without
learning difficulties.

Permitting/Encouraging 'Don't Know' Response

Understanding of complex abstract concepts, such as those associated with
religion, may prompt a high proportion of non-responses. Ursula McKenna's
work (1998), on primary age children's views about understanding of Christian
symbols involved, posed many of the children with difficulties. In this extract
one suspects that the child needed to give a genuine 'don't know' answer, or to
ask for clarification. Instead he and Ursula struggled on, endeavouring to
communicate:

Interviewer What work d'you like best in RE
Danny . . . The Celtics
Interviewer The Celtics. . . What did you do in that topic
Danny . . . The Roman Celtics
Interviewer What did you do when you were doing about them?

Danny	They go and kill the Romans
Interviewer	What activities did you do?
Danny	Well . . . the Romans kill Julius Caesar
Interviewer	Was that RE work?
Danny	Yeh
Interviewer	Was it?
Danny	It was this [showing mosaic picture]

Effect of Repeating Questions

There is a variety of evidence that repeating a question to young children tends to lead them to change the first response. This is done on the assumption that the first response was an incorrect answer. Moston (1987) tested this hypothesis with 6, 8 and 10-year-olds. He found that repeating a question did lead to fewer correct responses but not to more incorrect answers i.e. there were more 'don't know' type of responses.

It would be interesting to know whether this also occurs with child, rather than adult, interviewers. In natural conversation among peers it is unusual for a question to be repeated unless the speaker believes that the listener has not heard the comment.

Modifying Terms (Used by the Interviewer)

Many aspects of specific question wording will influence responses. One category leading to potential bias is the use of modifying terms. Ceci and Bruck (1993) report work in which children's responses reflected a developmental shift in their understanding of marked and unmarked modifiers. Modifiers are adjectives or adverbs e.g. fast/slow; clever/stupid. Marked modifiers have a definite zero, so slow is marked, it contains a possible zero i.e. not moving; but fast is unmarked, and it is limitless. Children generally acquire unmarked forms, for example fast before marked forms e.g. slow.

There are also cultural connotations to modifiers which influence response. When asked the question 'How slow/fast was the car going when it hit/smashed into the wall' the version with 'fast' elicited higher speeds than did 'slow' for all ages from 6 to 14. For 12–14-year-olds (but not the younger age groups) there were also faster estimates when 'smashed' not 'hit' was used. So some aspects of wording and hence suggestibility may affect older but not younger children. This is contrary to the usual stereotype that it is young children who will be the more suggestible. These differential effects may, in a similar way, vary with developmental level so that a 14-year-old with very limited receptive and expressive vocabularies may not give faster estimates for the 'smashed' rather than the 'hit' version of the above question.

These two sets of issues concerning the use of modifiers in questions to children have implications for interviews with children in which they are asked to choose (verbally or non-verbally) between polar opposites. For example, a range of research in the integration/ inclusion field has asked children to rate peers (or photographs/video clips of unknown children) on scales such as 'slow worker' – 'quick worker'. The developmental work summarised above would suggest that younger children might favour the latter ('fast worker') because it had been acquired while understanding of the former ('slow worker') had not.

Order Effects Within the Question

The above examples may be compounded by order effects as it has been shown that children and adults with learning difficulties were particularly prone to acquiescence (saying yes to yes/no questions) (Sigeleman et al., 1981, cited in Bull, 1995) they, like very young children, showed a tendency to prefer the last of two or a series of options. Sigelman proposed that picture alternatives be used as appropriate as an alternative to verbal questions only. The preference for the 2nd of two alternatives was much less marked when pictorial cues were used (see above concerning prompts).

Use of Pronouns and Referents

Another feature of specific question wording that can inadvertently direct children's responses concerns the use of pronouns and referents. 'Did you see THE car;' produced, in both adults and 4–5-year-olds, more affirmatives than did the question 'Did you see A car' (reviewed in Ceci & Bruck, 1993). In an informal context the interviewer may unguardedly switch pronouns in this way, unwittingly leading to a bias in the way the child 'reads' the question:

'Did you like playing THOSE games?'
'Do you like working with THESE other children?'
 (> 'yes' response tendency)
'Did you like playing games?'
'Do you like working with other children?'
 (> 'no' response tendency)

Further, Saywitz (1995) notes that young children often misunderstand referents such as that, they, them, those, here, there. This may be particularly problematic if the researcher is trying to standardise interview questions by using referents, so that the identical question is applicable across respondents, and avoiding use of proper nouns (e.g. not naming the types of game or children in the above examples). If teachers and researchers work with children with, and children without, learning difficulties then the need for more specificity with children with learning difficulties may easily be overlooked.

6. CONCLUSION

This chapter has reviewed a range of work relating to conducting research involving young children. Various matters concerning ethical issues and the planning of the research have been explored including the choice of setting, size of group and choice of method of data collection. Particular attention has been given to the adult's language as this is relevant across a range of research methods but is particularly pertinent in relation to interviewing children, a very common approach with young children. Various ways in which adults may inadvertently suggest a response to the young child were examined.

This is undoubtedly an exciting and innovative period in the development of research involving children. We are well-placed, having made the underlying ethical and sociological leaps required, to explore and foster diverse ways of involving young children in research.

REFERENCES

Aldridge, M., & Wood, J. (1998). *Interviewing Children: A guide for child care and forensic practitioners*. Chichester: Wiley.

American Psychological Association (APA) (1992). Ethical principles of psychologists and code of conduct. *American Psychologist, 47*, 1597–1611.

Aubrey, C., David, T., Godfrey, R., & Thompson, L. (2000). *Early Childhood Educational Research*. London: Routledge.

Barsby, J. (1990). *Self-evaluation by 7 year old children*. MA dissertation, University of Warwick.

Begley, A. (2000). The educational self-perceptions of children with Down syndrome. In: A. Lewis & G. Lindsay (Eds), *Researching Children's Perspectives* (pp. 98–111). Buckingham: Open University Press.

British Educational Research Association (BERA) (1992). *Ethical Guidelines for Educational Research*. Edinburgh: BERA and Scottish Council for Research in Education.

Billig, M. (1987). *Arguing and thinking: A Rhetorical Approach to Psychology*. Cambridge: Cambridge University Press.

British Psychological Society (BPS) (1996). *Code of Conduct, Ethical Principles and Guidelines*. Leicester: BPS.

Brown, R. (1973). *A First Language: The Early Stages*. London: Allen & Urwin.

Bull. R. (1995). Innovative techniques for the questioning of child witnesses, especially those who are young and those with learning disability. In: M. S. Zaragoza (Ed.), *Memory and Testimony in the Child Witness* (pp. 179–194). Thousand Oaks: Sage.

Ceci, S. J., & Bruck, M. (1993). The suggestibility of the child witness: An historical review and synthesis. *Psychological Bulletin, 113*, 349–403.

Canadian Psychological Association (CPA) (1992). *Companion Manual to the Canadian Code of Ethics for Psychologists, 1991.* Quibec: CPA.

Dent, H. R. (1986). An experimental study of the effectiveness of different techniques of questioning mentally handicapped child witnesses. *British Journal of Clinical Psychology, 25,* 13–17.

Department for Education/Welsh Office (DfE/WO) (1994). *Code of Practice for the Identification and Assessment of Children with Special Educational Needs.* London: HMSO.

Department for Education and Employment (DfEE) (2000). *SEN Code of Practice on the Identification and Assessment of Pupils with Special Educational Needs.* Consultation Document London: DfEE.

Dockrell, J., Lewis, A., & Lindsay, G. (2000). Researching children's perspectives: a psychological dimension. In: A. Lewis & G. Lindsay (Eds), *Researching Children's Perspectives* (pp. 46–58). Buckingham: Open University Press.

Edwards, D., & Mercer, N. (1993). *Common Knowledge.* Buckingham: Open University Press (2nd ed.).

Ericsson, K. A., & Simon, H. A. (1980). Verbal reports as data. *Psychological Review, 87,* 215–51.

Grieg, A., & Taylor, J. (1999). *Doing Research with Children.* London: Sage.

Gross, M. (1993). *Exceptionally Gifted Children.* London: Routledge.

Hill, M., Layborn, A., & Borland, M. (1996). Researching Children: Methods and Ethics. *Children and Society, 10*(2), 129–144.

Hood, S., Mayall, B., & Oliver, S. (Eds) (1999). *Critical Issues in Social Research.* Buckingham: Open University Press.

Hughes, M. (1986). *Children and Number.* Oxford: Blackwell.

Hughes, M., & Grieve, R. (1980). On asking children bizarre questions. *First Language, 1,* 149–60.

Karmiloff-Smith, A. (1992). *Beyond Modularity: A Developmental Perspective on Cognitive Science.* London: MIT Press.

Lewis, A. (1992). Group children interviews as a reseach tool. *British Educational Research Journal, 18*(4), 413–421.

Lewis, A. (1995). *Children's Understanding of Disability.* London: Routledge.

Lewis, A., & Lindsay, G. (Eds) (2000). *Researching Children's Perspectives.* Buckingham: Open University Press.

Lewis, A. (in press). Interviewing children and young people as a method of enquiry in the context of educational inclusion. *Journal of Research in Special Educational Needs.*

Lewis, A. (in preparation). The use of cue cards to elicit elaborated narratives from young children with learning difficulties.

Lindsay, G. (2000). Researching children's perspectives: ethical issues. In: A. Lewis & G. Lindsay (Eds). *Researching Children's Perspectives* (pp. 3–20). Buckingham: Open University Press.

Lloyd Smith, M., & Tarr, J. (2000). Researching Children's Perspectives: A Sociological Dimension. In: A. Lewis & G. Lindsay (Eds), *Researching Children's Perspectives* (pp. 59–68). Buckingham: Open University Press.

McTear, M. (1985). *Children's Conversation.* Oxford: Blackwell.

McKenna, U. (1998). Religious understanding in primary age children with learning difficulties. MA thesis, University of Warwick.

Masson, J. (2000). Researching children's perspectives: legal issues. In: A. Lewis & G. Lindsay (Eds), *Researching Children's Perspectives* (pp. 34–45). Buckingham: Open University Press.

Moston, S. (1987). The suggestibility of children in interview studies. *First Language, 7*, 67–78.

Nesbitt, E. (2000). Researching 8–13 year olds' experience of religion. In: A. Lewis & G. Lindsay (Eds), *Researching Children's Perspectives* (pp. 135–149). Buckingham: Open University Press.

Nisbitt, R. E., & Wilson, T. D. (1977). Telling more than we can know: verbal reports on mental processes. *Psychological Review, 84*, 231–59.

Piaget, J. (1929). *The Child's Conception of the World*. New York: Harcourt Brace.

Robson, C. (1993). *Real World Research*. Oxford: Blackwell.

Rose, S. A., & Blank, M. (1974). The potency of context in children's cognition: an illustration through conservation. *Child Development, 45*, 499–502.

Saywitz, K. J. (1995). Improving Children's Testimony: The question, the answer and the environmen. In: M. S. Zaragoza (Ed), *Memory and Testimony in the Child Witness* (pp. 113–140). Thousand Oaks: Sage.

Saywitz, K., & Snyder, L. (1996) Narrative elaboration: Test of a new procedure for interviewing children. *Journal of Counselling and Clinical Psychology, 64*(6), 1347–1357.

Thomas, G., & Jolley, R. (1998). Drawing conclusions: a re-examination of empirical and conceptual bases for psychological evaluation of children from their drawings. *British Journal of Clinical Psychology, 37*, 127–39.

Thomas, G., & Silk, A. (1990). *An Introduction to the Psychology of Children's Drawings*. London: Harvester Wheatsheaf.

14. QUESTIONING COMPARATIVE APPROACHES: CONTEXT AND THE ROLE OF INTERNATIONAL COMPARISON IN POLICY-MAKING

Carol Aubrey

On 14 January, 2000 the English newspaper, *The Times*, carried a news item entitled – International tests show English pupils 'lagging' (O'Leary, 2000). This article featured yet the latest re-analysis of international achievement testing surveys conducted in the 1990s, commissioned by the, then Chief Inspector of Schools, Chris Woodhead. Attention already devoted to the recent Third International Mathematics and Science Study (TIMSS), Harris *et al* 1997, by policy-makers and the media alike, has been huge. This can best be exemplified by a leaked story to *The Sunday Times* (3 July, 1996: 1) on the comparative low ranking of England in mathematics. This was marked by a front-page headline, 'English pupils plummet in world maths league,' at a time when, according to Brown (1998: 17), an embargo had been placed on release of the findings until November, 1996. It was rumoured that the leak was occasioned by ministers' need of a legitimate reason for introducing both mental arithmetic and a calculation-free paper into national mathematics tests, without unduly upsetting teachers. What this represents is a *misuse* of the results of international comparison.

Promoting Evidence-based Practice in Early Childhood Education:
Research and its Implications, Volume 1, pages 273–287.
2001 by Elsevier Science Ltd.
ISBN: 0-7623-0753-6

In fact, the commissioned study cited above is just a further indication of the continuing dissatisfaction about standards and practice in primary mathematics of The Office for Standards in Education (see, for instance, OSTED 1994; 1995 and 1996), particularly for children of seven to eleven years, following the introduction of school inspections with the *Education (Schools) Act*, 1992. Moreover, an earlier review of international surveys of educational achievement involving England (Reynolds & Farrell, 1996) also commissioned by OFSTED, indicated that English children had a very wide range of achievements and a 'trailing edge' of low-performing pupils. This, it concluded, interacted with an educational system which attempted to respond to the range of initial achievement by the use of a complex pedagogy involving differentiation practices serving merely to accentuate the difference. The National Curriculum system carries no requirement that children reach a certain level in order to proceed to the next class. Few children study mathematics beyond sixteen years-of-age as advanced mathematics is not required for higher education or, indeed, for prospective primary school teachers. The recent Third International Mathematics and Science Study (TIMSS) moreover confirmed that English pupils *had* slipped from a 'middling' position to one below the international mean. The important role in high achievement of whole-class teaching, as well as individualisation, with use made of homework which this study emphasised, fuelled an existing concern about teaching methods which had been highlighted by an influential report of Alexander, Rose and Woodhead (1992). In fact, this echoed concerns expressed in classroom research which pre-date the introduction of the National Curriculum.

Suffice it to say that both previous and current governments in the U.K. have used international studies to justify their emphasis on raising levels of numeracy in primary schools and a 'back-to-basics' approach in arithmetic with whole-class teaching methods. Whether there *is* such a things as a 'national teaching style' is, at least, open to debate since large-scale international comparisons of mathematics attainment do not include direct observation of classroom processes. Even if they did, the possibility of 'transferring' such a thing as a teaching style from one nation to another is even more questionable. When one takes account of the benefits presumed by governments in terms of economic improvement and social advancement to follow from emulating the educational practices of high- achieving countries such as those of the Pacific Rim, the enterprise seems vain indeed.

One could be forgiven for wondering why the most recent study, *Comparing Standards* (2000), was commissioned in the first place – at a time when the Government must be reviewing its pledge to raise standards of literacy and numeracy by the year 2002? Crossley and Broadfoot (1992) have referred to the more sinister phenomenon of 'a deliberate manipulation of research activity to support a particular national or international agenda' and concluded that it is indeed the responsibility of all educationalists to draw attention to the misuse of comparative international data.

Comparative education can, of course, serve a variety of functions, most significantly, it can deepen and enrich our understanding of our own society and educational system. More specifically, it can describe teaching in cultures with different social conditions and different value systems which is of interest to policy-makers, practitioners, parents and the public, alike. On the other hand, more serious questions are raised with respect to the political dimension of comparative education. What control do international researchers have over the way their results are used, and what influence does the scientific community have in the ensuing debate, which typically focuses on national ranking lists?

On the one hand, international comparison has high potential for examining differences and similarities in pedagogical practices elsewhere, as well as interpreting why these exist, in order to help to improve the home system of education. On the other hand, one should not under-estimate the methodological problems associated with attempts to measure educational outcomes in terms of achievement testing, quantifying the intended curriculum and identifying significant pedagogical variables in the implemented curriculum, never mind estimating relationships *between* the curricula and social and educational contexts in question.

At the most fundamental level, one needs to consider whether selected achievement test items *can* cover adequately the curricula of many different countries and whether it is justifiable to assume that scores so obtained can represent some notion of a discrete 'mathematical ability' which is independent of cultural valuation of mathematics and opportunities to learn mathematics at home and at school. Moreover, the challenges raised by attempting to quantify pedagogical phenomena and, at the same time, to justify the representativeness of observed processes in international terms, may support the argument for carrying out small-scale, qualitative case studies restricted to a smaller number of countries, similar in socio-cultural and economical terms. This, of course, TIMSS *did* also carry out. As Postlethwaite (1988) has noted, the aim is 'estimating the relative effects of variables (thought to be determinants) on outcomes (both within and between systems of education)'. Perhaps, most significant in public debate concerning international comparison, however, is the absence of a proper consideration of the problems and limitations of such studies, which serves merely to *diminish* the pedagogical merits of such endeavours.

The last decade has seen a growing interest in comparative education and the purpose of this chapter is to consider both the potential pedagogical and policy-related benefits, as well as the pitfalls associated with comparative studies. Accordingly, the next section will set the scene by providing a background to and critical analysis of such studies. The succeeding section will then look at the public concern about standards in the English context, highlighting the potential role of comparative education in this climate, in serving to interrogate policy-makers' decision-making. This will pave the way for a critical examination of the assumption of successive U.K. governments that providing specifically-focused numeracy and literacy teaching from an ever-earlier age will lead to the raising of standards, to be judged in national and international terms. It will also lead to the examination of such comparative education studies as we have which actually focus on early childhood educational achievement, instead of extrapolating back from pupil ranking in international achievement terms at age nine years. The final section will then discuss both the strengths and the problems raised by established, tradition comparative research.

BACKGROUND TO COMPARATIVE EDUCATION

To start with a working definition, discussion so far would suggest that comparative education refers to a field of study dealing with comparison of current theory and practice in the education of pupils in their respective countries, cultures and localities. An obvious benefit is that it places our own everyday professional policies and practices within a broader perspectives. Bereday (1964) suggested that it was a young sub-field in the very old discipline of pedagogy which indicates that comparing educational ideas and practices goes back a long way. It was probably not until the nineteenth century, however, that attempts were made to develop a more systematic approach to the comparison.

Over three thousand years ago BC, Plato made numerous comparisons between Athenian and Spartan educational ideas and practices which Noah and Eckstein (1969) described as 'travellers tales' but the history of comparative as a scholarly discipline is generally regarded as beginning in the eighteenth century with Marc-Antoine Jullien's so-called 'borrowing' phase. He was one of the first people to visit other countries, carry out systematic observation and attempt to identify both the philosophical base and its influence on the systems observed. In fact, one significant achievement of the 'borrowing' phase was its recognition of the danger inherent in the uncritical transplanting of educational ideas or practices. Overlapping with this phase and identified as the third phase was 'international co-operation', associated with the names of both Jullien and Sir Michael Sadler, who was working at the turn of the twentieth century. Sadler's sensitive accounts of foreign systems showed an interest in how and why educational phenomena occurred, rather than in trying to apply 'detachable details'. In fact, as early comparative research moved increasingly towards interpretive or 'national character' approaches, which recognized the two-way relationship between society and education, more sophisticated predictions of the likely success of one educational system on the basis of observed precedents elsewhere, could be made. This fourth phase, which attempted to identify influences on the development of educational systems or specific elements of a system, was most closely associated with the name of Sadler. The fifth phase, which flourished in the nineteen sixties and seventies, was marked by the adoption and application of social science methods, which relied on complex and multilevel techniques to examine the relative effects of various factors which were inter-correlated and which were presumed to influence educational achievement. Inevitably these empirical approaches introduced their own set of methodological problems, related to sampling and measurement error, as well as constraints associated with the particular statistical techniques being applied.

This period coincided with the First International Mathematics Study (FIMS) which was carried out in 1964. This served as a stimulus to the later, and more sophisticated Second International Mathematics Study (SIMS) carried out in the early eighties and reported in the late eighties and early nineties. By this time, Noah (1988) had identified major methodological concerns associated with the construction of scales which fairly represented national curicula, as well as establishing valid and reliable data collection, administration and analysis which did *not* reflect ethnocentric bias in data interpretation, inference and policy recommendations. More fundamental methodological concerns were raised by Eckstein (1988: 9) who challenged the positivist assumptions underlying the very methods being used which:

> represent the view that educational and social phenomena are results of multiple causes, that there are regularities or tentative laws of input and outcomes (cause and effect), and that these are discoverable through systematic collection and analysis of the relevant facts (Eckstein, 1988: 9).

Crossley and Vulliamy (1984) argued, meanwhile, that comparative education *should* display a greater balance by the infusion of micro-level, case study approaches. In fact, they averred, the case study was not inimical to positivism if the objective was to employ findings about particular instances in order to explicate larger patterns of social relations whereby *complementing* positivist findings. Broadfoot noted that large-scale studies provided one aspect, one side of the picture, of a nation's educational achievements.

> They cannot reveal what goes on in an individual classroom or uncover the assumptions that are taken for granted in the educational system which lend it its idiosyncratic nature (Broadfoot, 1977: 135).

Postlethwaite (1988) would argue, more fundamentally, that this is more a question of selecting the most appropriate approach, or combination of approaches, to deal with the particular research questions being investigated.

PROBLEMATISING POLICY-MAKERS' PERSPECTIVES

The first section of this chapter identified a concern of policy-makers about English standards in mathematics and the important role that international comparative studies have played in justifying this. It will be argued in this section, however, that another function of such studies is to uncover policy-maker's own implicit assumptions in respect of the standards debate and to subject these to systematic and rigorous interrogation. It has already been suggested that the previous and current Government have exploited both international comparative studies and meta-analyses of these to keep up a discourse of derision in respect of mathematics achievement and methods of teaching, which seems set to run till 2002. By this time, the current Education Secretary has pledged that three-quarters of children will reach the expected mathematics norm by the end of primary schooling. The second section highlighted the important relationship between curricula and the social-cultural context to schooling. According the current section will begin with an outline of recent changes within the school system of England and Wales.

Among the wide-ranging changes in educational organisation and practice which resulted from the *Education Reform Act*, 1988 (ERA) the imposition of a centrally controlled and directed National Curriculum is of particular importance to this chapter. The Act required all maintained schools to provide for all pupils within the years of compulsory schooling, a basic curriculum with designated core subjects of English, mathematics and science, foundation subjects of art, geography, history, music, physical education, technology, modern language (at secondary stage) and religious education. (Welsh was a core subject for Welsh-speaking schools and a foundation subject in non-Welsh-speaking schools in Wales.) Since this time there have been many revisions which culminated in a wider review of the National Curriculum (Dearing, 1994) and led to a new and slimmed-down curriculum which came into force in September, 1995. Yet another new version, the National Curriculum 2000, was unveiled in September, 1999.

The last decade has seen the introduction of national assessment of pupils on an unprecedented scale, the ERA (1988) making provision for a phrased introduction of assessment for all seven-, eleven- and fourteen-year-olds in England and Wales from 1991. Moreover, schools have been required to publish their results in the context of comparative national averages in both their annual reports to governors and their school prospectuses. The intention was to create a greater accountability in education generally, and to help parents make an informed choice of schools. This led to wide-ranging debate and a growing consensus that a fairer index of school effectiveness would be a measure of the progress made by pupils rather than their 'raw' results which reflected a range of other social factors influencing prior learning, or 'intake variables'. Measures of pupils' progress in schools in relation to similar pupils in other schools allowed 'value-added' analysis of schools' performance to be made, see Department of Education (DfE), 1995. From September, 1998 statutory baseline assessment of children's language and literacy, mathematics and personal and social development at school entry was introduced which will provide value-added information on children's progress through the first stage of formal schooling, Key Stage 1, for five- to seven-year-olds, see Qualifications and Assessment Authority (QCA), 1998.

The Labour Government's white paper *Excellence in Schools* (DfEE, 1997) announced their intention that the 'desirable outcomes' of learning for children when they reached statutory school age, the term after their fifth birthday, should be reassessed along with the new National Curriculum 2000. These outcomes were intended to provide a foundation for learning across the subjects of the National Curriculum and religious education, organised around six areas of learning:

- personal and social development
- language and literacy
- knowledge and understanding of the world
- physical development and
- creative development.

Expansion of good quality early education had become a high priority and, as noted above, pivotal to the Government's drive to raise standards in schools, particularly in literacy and numeracy. This also led to the introduction of a National Literacy Strategy (in September, 1998) and a National Numeracy Strategy (from September, 1999), which had key objectives for each school year from 'reception' year, that is, for five-year-olds to the end of primary schooling (at age eleven years). Furthermore, since September, 1998 free, part-time early years education has been made available for all four-year-olds whose parents wish it, with a similar planned rise in the number of three-year-olds receiving free part-time provision in a variety of settings over the next three years.

The first phase of the review of the the desirable outcomes (QCA, 1999) involving a period of consultation from 22 February to 30 April, 1999, focused on three broad areas of discussion:

- the aims and priorities for children aged three to five years;
- whether there should be a distinct curriculum stage for children aged three to the end of the reception year, with National Curriculum programmes of study starting for all children at the beginning of Year 1 (for six-year-olds); and
- whether curriculum guidelines for this distinct would be helpful.

Already new goals which identify expectations of achievement at the end of the foundation stage and retain the areas of learning identified above took effect from September, 2000. Detailed teaching guidance has also been drawn up by the QCA. The goals for literacy and numeracy, however, have already been determined by the key objectives for the reception year from the National Numeracy Strategy. It was stressed by Nick Tate, then Chief Executive of the QCA (1999: 1) that:

> high quality early years teaching is one the cornerstones of the Government's determination to raise standards (Tate, 1999: 1).

As I have noted elsewhere (see Kavkler et al., 2000), this argument rests on a little-examined assumption of successive Governments – that providing specifically-focused literacy and numeracy from an ever earlier age will lead to the raising of standards, to be judged in national and international results. Given policy-maker's current concern about standards of achievement and our existing early entry to full-time, compulsory schooling it might be reasonable to ask what benefits accrue from this practice when the age of school entry varies from five to seven years in different countries, with six being the most common. Accordingly the next section will consider critically the assumption that teaching of literacy and numeracy from an early age leads to the raising of standards in international terms or whether, like other European countries, we should place more emphasis on a thorough preparation for formal schooling at six years.

THE ROLE OF EARLY SCHOOLING IN THE DEVELOPMENT OF LITERACY AND NUMERACY

According to Stigler and Perry (1988: 199) one of the benefits of cross-cultural comparison is that researchers are brought to a more explicit understanding of their own implicit theories about the way children learn mathematics. Without comparison we may not question our own assumptions about traditional policies and teaching practice and may not even be aware of decisions which have been made historically, through custom and law, in the process of constructing an educational system. Policy-makers have been quick to make uncritical use of crude ranking from the TIMSS study, which placed this country below the international mean. The opportunity presented – to gain a deeper understanding of our own educational system as well as possible approaches to improve it – may not have been fully exploited. Bearing in mind the variation in school starting age in Europe, from four years to nearly eight years, one *might* expect the English early introduction to formal schooling to provide an advantage. By nine years of age, however, when our pupils gain a below-average score for mathematics in international terms, they have already been in compulsory education for nearly five years, in contrast to children in other countries who may have had as little as two or three years of formal schooling. This raises some awkward questions about the value of early formal education.

It is particularly interesting to note that despite the concern about standards in this country we did not, in fact, take part in the International Association for the Evaluation of Educational Achievement (IEA) 1992 study of reading literacy. Furthermore, this study (Elley, 1992) revealed that the age at which children began reading was associated with a gender gap in literacy. A plausible hypothesis, it concluded, was that boys were too immature to begin reading formally at age five and that their difficulties were represented in low achievement, relative to girls, at both age nine and fourteen. A further NFER study assessing reading standards (Brooks et al., 1996), comparing them with those of the IEA study, suggested that English children would have come sixteenth out of twenty-eight countries, with a 'long tail' of pupils scoring well below the national average.

The challenge to the input-output models of comparative education, as noted above, is to introduce qualitative research methods that focus on actual 'lived' educational practices and processes. The objective of micro-level case studies of a few countries is to report findings about particular instances which illuminate and, indeed, complement those obtained from large-scale international studies. The problem with micro-analyses of classroom process, of course, is that they do not generalise well to other contexts, though may provide a means of gaining insight into one's own culture.

The Hungarian educationalist Nagy (1989), for instance, who has investigated the relationship – or articulation – of kindergarten to compulsory schooling in Hungary and Sri Lanka for more than twenty years, has long argued that the outcome of a child's scholastic career is determined by entry characteristics. This echoes a point made earlier, that a country's initial accommodation to the range of attainment on school entry is likely to account to a substantial degree for its later educational achievement. Huge variation, whether through social disadvantage or developmental difference, he believed, could not be eliminated by direct instruction at the time or by later schooling. His 'alternative entry model', introduced into the Hungarian system in 1986, allowed children to be registered at school according to their stage of development rather than calendar age of six years. For him, as is believed in many other parts of Europe, under-achievement is best avoided by sound preparation for formal schooling by nursery or kindergarten which, in the case of mathematics, focuses on conceptual understanding of space, size, quantity and time, which underlies mathematical understanding.

This suggests that a more modest research agenda which aims to test out in other national and cultural settings a proposition already validated in one setting (Hall, 1990: 1) can be pursued. Whilst much has been learned from TIMSS on the broad associations between overall mathematical achievement and educational systems around the world, less attention has been directed to the impact of particular teaching regimes on children's developing arithmetic competence, problem-solving and mental calculation over time. One goal of a project to be described here was to evaluate critically the assumption that the teaching of numeracy from an early age leads to the raising of standards. This was achieved through a case study of the development of learning and teaching numeracy in two, contrasting European contexts – England and Slovenia – in order to generate for explanations for observed differences in international performance at nine years (see Kavkler, Aubrey et al., 2000).

This study was planned at the time of the Second International Assessment of Educational Progress (IAEP) in mathematics and science (Foxen, 1992) which had shown both English and Slovene pupils to be 'middling' in mathematical performance. By the time it was completed TIMSS (1997) had shown English pupils to be performing significantly below and Slovene pupils significantly above the international mean. Accordingly four hundred and eighty children overall in the main phase of the study were selected for six groups in each country, ranging from six to nearly twelve years, each level consisting of forty children: twenty high- and twenty low-attainers with equal numbers of boys and girls. Several standardized and non-standardized instruments designed for the study were applied, using both oral and written tasks.

Two-way analysis of variance showed six-year old English pupils to score significantly higher than Slovene preschoolers for a test of basic arithmetic yet by seven years there were no significant differences and thereafter the Slovene pupils forged ahead. For a standardised arithmetic test (British Abilities Scale) English six and seven-year-olds scored significantly higher, yet by eight years there were no significant differences between the countries. Mental calculation tasks also showed that by the end of the Slovene children's first year at school there was little difference in accuracy between the two groups. Furthermore, unlike their English counterparts, Slovene children were beginning to make use of more sophisticated recall-of-fact strategies. By eight years, as data from the larger project showed, there appeared to be no benefits to accrue from the early English school entry. Comparison with higher-achieving countries in Europe suggests that the English system may take too little account of pupils' developmental differences at school entry and introduce a formal curriculum too soon. The challenge, in this case, is to ensure that the educational practices pursued through our new foundation curriculum take sufficient account of children's need for careful development of conceptual understanding, in order to provide the foundation for later mathematical achievement.

More recently, the opportunity arose to take part in a more detailed analysis of children's early numeracy development between ages five and six years in a number of European countries – Flemish-speaking Belgium, Germany, Greece, Slovenia and the Netherlands. This was a limited longitudinal study of young children's early numeracy development within three testing cycles, at the mid-point and towards the end of their reception year (at five-years-of-age) and again at the mid-point of Year 1 (at six-years-of age). Assessment was carried out using the Utrecht Early Numeracy Test (Van Luit et al., 1994). This comprised eight sub-topics, five items in each, including comparison, classification, correspondence, seriation, counting, calculation and real-life number problems, with forty items in all. Three hundred pupils were selected in each national context. In the English setting, children were selected from twenty-one schools, large and small, rural and urban, with high and low concentrations of pupils eligible for free school meals and special education needs, as well as representing a broad range of educational achievement levels based on standard assessment tasks (SATs).

The multilevel modelling method of analysis used for the study provided an extension of multiple regression to incorporate the hierarchical structure of the data collected, with English groups of ten pupils (five boys and girls), nested within classes, within schools, within different areas of the south-eastern region of England. Preliminary analysis (Aubrey et al., 1999) revealed that different areas of the region and different classes of pupils showed no significant variation. Moreover no difference was found between boys and girls, though there was some indication that boys' results were more variable and less predictable. The basic multilevel regression model allowed scores to be plotted against age and this accounted for differences between scores in the different testing cycles for the different sub-topics of the test.

Sub-topic scores showed little difference between testing cycles 1 and 2, in reception year (for five-year-olds), and a large difference between cycles 2 and 3, as children moved into Year 1 (for six-year-olds). The profiles of different topics, however, varied, some declining over time and showing a different pattern from the other European countries involved. Bearing in mind the findings of the Belgium team (Guesquiere et al., 1999), that there was a significant difference in results obtained for sub-tests related to classical Piagetian skills and for those calling for counting skills, it is tempting to attribute the English pupils' different pattern of topic sub-test scores to their earlier exposure to numeracy training, in contrast with children from other European countries who have retained a strong continental kindergarten tradition of preparation for formal schooling through the development of basic concepts.

At a later date, with a more complete data-set of all countries, the analysis has been developed further. The results of this have yet to be published. Taking account of the wide variation in age of children tested across the Europe, the English pupils being youngest, the most recent analysis (Godfrey et al. in Aubrey et al., 2000) suggests a pattern to children's performance. Those countries with younger children seem to have a greater dependence of score on age. That is, their young children have lower scores but the scores increase more rapidly with age. In fact, once rates of improvement with age had been calculated and the 'best fit' underlying regression line established, no advantage was found in including differences in school or country in the model. It may be premature to draw too many conclusions from the analysis carried out, though they point towards age-dependent maturation processes rather than effects of schooling.

Bearing in mind the vastly differing social, cultural and educational experiences of children in different parts of Europe, with English pupils in compulsory education throughout the testing period, Slovene children not at all and youngsters from the other participating countries entering formal schooling at the mid-testing point, comparison of children's performance across Europe provides the most thought-provoking aspect of the analysis. The differing topic profiles may well be influenced by the differing educational experiences of different national groups. The pattern of dependence of scores on age thrown up by the multilevel modelling is, at least, consistent with the view of Nagy (1989), that developmental variation at age six years cannot be eliminated by direct teaching or the effects of later schooling. If nothing else these findings should serve to remind us that the continuously changing pedagogical practices, curriculum goals and organisational patterns associated with the English early years curriculum may not have the desired effect of raising school children's mathematical performance at nine and thirteen years. Moreover, the assumption that standards will be raised by the early introduction of numeracy teaching is at least questionable. Most important, however, the findings remind us that when changes are made to the educational system they carry implicit assumptions about the way children learn and that alternative choices could have been made.

CONCLUSIONS

This chapter began by emphasising the political perspective on comparative education and, in fact, Margaret Brown (1998: 17) of King's College has concluded that 'TIMSS ... was a 'thoroughly political activity'. It has attempted to demonstrate that researchers have a responsibility to challenge the misuse of such findings. Furthermore it has indicated that large-scale multi-national studies with global results demand small-scale and more qualitative studies, which can illuminate particular aspects of learning and teaching. These, in turn, provide a powerful means of deepening our understanding of our own educational systems, as well as a tool for critical analysis of policy-makers' decision-making. Once underlying assumptions have been uncovered, however, the rich potential in international comparison for enriching ped-agogical debate can be released and the boundaries of what is educationally possible truly explored.

REFERENCES

Aubrey, C., Godfrey, R., & Godfrey, J. (1999). *The Development of Early Numeracy in England.* Paper for poster presentation, Conference of European Association for Research on Learning and Instruction. Gothenburg, Sweden, 24–28 August.

Alexander, R., Rose, J., & Woodhead, C. (1992). *Curriculum Organisation and Classroom Practice in Primary Schools: A Discussion Paper.* London: DfEE.

Brown, M. (1998). Findings lost amid poliical jockeying. *The Times Educational Supplement, 20* (March), 17.

Bereday, G. Z. (1964). *Comparative Method in Education.* New York: Holt, Rinehart and Winston.

Broadfoot, P. (1977). The comparative contribution. A research perspective. *Comparative Education, 3*(2), 133–137.

Brooks, G., Pugh, A. K., & Schagen, I. (1996). *Reading Performance at Nine.* Slough: NFER-Open University.

Crossley, M., & Vulliamy, G. (1984). Case-study research methods and comparative education. *Comparative Education, 20*(2), 193–207.

Crossley, M., & Broadfoot, P. (1992). Comparative and international research in education: Scope, problems and potential. *British Educational Research Journal, 18*(2), 99–11.

Eckstein, M. A. (1988). Concepts and theories in comparataive education. In: T. N. Postlethwaite (Ed.), *The Encyclopaedia of Comparative Education and National Systems of Education.* Oxford: Pergamon.

Elley, W. B. (1992). *How in the World Do Students Read?* International Association for The Evaluation of Educational Achievement.

Dearing, R. (1994). *The National Curriculum and Its Assessment. A Final Report.* London: Schools Curriculum and Assessment Authority (SCAA).

Deparment for Education (1992). *Education (Schools) Act.* London: DfE.

DfE (1995). *Value Added in Education: A Briefing Paper from the Department for Education.* London: DfE.

Department of Education and Employment (1997). *Excellence in Schools.* London: DfEE.

DfEE (1998). *The National Literacy Strategy.* London: DfEE.

DfEE (1999). *The National Numeracy Strategy.* London: DfEE.

DfEE (1999). *The National Curriculum 2000.* London: DfEE.

DES (1988). *Education Reform Act.* London: DES.

Foxen, D. (1992). *Learning Mathematics and Science (The Second International Assessment of Educational Progress in England).* Slough: National Foundation for Educational Research.

Ghesquiere, P., Verschaffel, L., Torbeyns, J., & Vossen, E. (1999). *The Development of Early Numeracy in Flanders.* Paper for poster symposium European Association for Research on Learning and Instruction, 24–28 August, 1999.

Godfrey, R., & Aubrey, C. (1999). Assessing early mathematical development. *British Society for Research into Learning Mathematics.* Proceedings of the Day Conference held at St. Martin's College, 5 June.

Aubrey, C., David, T., Godfrey, R., & Thompson, T. (2000). *Early Childhood Education Research. Ethical and Methodological Issues.* London: Falmer Press.

Harris, S., Keys, W., & Fernandes, C. (1997). *Third International Mathematics and Science Study.* Slough: National Foundation for Educational Research.

Halls, W. D. (Ed.) (1990). *Comparative Education. Contemporary Issues and Trends.* London, Jessica Kingsley Publishers.

Kavker, M., Aubrey, C., Tancig S., & Magajna, L. (2000). Getting it right from the start? The influence of early school entry on later achievement in mathematics. *European Early Childhood Education Research Journal, 8*(1), 75–94.

Nagy, J. (1989). *Articulation of Pre-school with Primary School lin Hungary: An Alternative Entry Model.* Hamburg: UNESCO Institute for Education.

Noah, H. J., & Eckstein, M. A. (1969). *Towards a Science of Comparative Education.* New York: Macmillan.

Noah, H. J. (1988). Methods of comparative education. In: T. N. Postlethwaite (Ed.), *The Encyclopaedia of Comparative Education and National Systems of Education.* Oxford: Pergamon.

OFSTED (1994). *Science and Mathematics in Schools: A Review.* London: HMSO.

OFSTED (1995). *The Annual Report of Her Majesty's Chief Inspector of Schools: Standards and Quality in Education 1993/4.* London: HMSO.

OFSTED (1996). *The Annual Report of Her Majesty's Chief Inspector of Schools: Standards and Quality in Education 1994/5.* London: HMSO.

O'Leary, J. (2000). International tests show English pupils lagging. *The Times*, (Friday, 14 January), 4.

Postlethwaite, T. N. (Ed.) (1988). *The Encyclopaedia of Comparataive Education and National Systems of Education.* Oxford: Pergamon.

Prais, S., St. John Brooks, S., & Woodhead, C. et al. (2000). *Comparing Standards: The Report of the Politeia Education Commission.* London: Politeia.

QCA (1998). *Baseline Assessment Scales.* London: QCA.

QCA (1999). *Review of the DesirableLearning Outcomes for Children's Learning on Entering compulsory Schooling.* London: QCA.

Reynolds, D., & Farrell, S. (1996). *Worlds Apart. A Review of International Surveys of Educational Achievement involving England.* London: HMSO.

Stigler, J. W., & Perry, M. (1988). Cross cultural studies of mathemataics teaching and learning: Recent findings and new directions. In: D. A. Grouws, T. J. Cooney & D. Jones (Eds), *Perspectives on Reseaarch on Effective Mathemataics Teaching* (pp. 194–223). Reston, VA, Nationala Council of Teachers of Mathematics.

Tate, N. (1999). *QCA Consults on Early Years Education.* Press Release, 24 February.

Van Luit, J. E. H., Van de Rijt, B. A. M., & Pennings, A. H. (1994). *The Numeracy Test.* Deotinchem: Graviant Publishing Co.

15. RESEARCH IN THE MAJORITY WORLD

Helen Penn

This chapter explores some key concepts about research processes in majority world (third world/developing) countries. There is already a substantial general literature about such research. One of the most well known of recent texts 'Whose Reality Counts?' by Robert Chambers (1997) examines how 'scientific' findings from agricultural research have been exported from the minority (Western/developed world) to the majority world to the detriment of the latter. Chambers and others developed a technique called 'participatory rural appraisal' for soliciting the views and opinions of local people who were the objects of well-meaning agricultural aid programmes.

Early childhood researchers and practitioners tend to be unfamiliar with this wider critique of research and practice in the majority world. For the most part there is a missionary emphasis about bringing the universal precepts of 'child development' to poor people ignorant of its benefits and insights. The World Education Forum, meeting in Senegal in April 2000, supported by UNICEF, UNESCO, the World Bank and many governments, has adopted early childhood as a first step in its goal of education for all. But what kind of early childhood programmes? How should they be developed and evaluated?

This chapter discusses some of the problems in generalising research processes and findings from minority world studies of child development to the majority world. These problems will then be discussed in relation to a particular case study, an attempt to provide an early childhood intervention to farmworkers' children in Zimbabwe.

Promoting Evidence-based Practice in Early Childhood Education:
Research and its Implications, Volume 1, pages 289–308.
Copyright © 2001 by Elsevier Science Ltd.
All rights of reproduction in any form reserved.
ISBN: 0-7623-0753-6

HOW THE OTHER THREE-QUARTERS LIVE

Like the phrases 'developed-underdeveloped nations' or 'north-south' or 'first world-third world' the definition of majority-minority world is a loose one. Generally 'majority world' refers to those parts of the world, about 75%, which geographically fall outside of Europe and North America. Using the phrase 'majority world' also inverts the common understanding of the term 'ethnic minorities' which implies that those who are non-white constitute an exception to the norm. In global terms, white North-Americans and Europeans constitute an 'ethnic' minority.

The 'majority world' like any categorisation of peoples, has imprecise boundaries, and lumps people and communities together who could not be more different – for example shanty town dwellers in South Africa, and nomads in ex-communist Mongolia. Yet it is a phrase which is being accepted into common usage because it emphasises the tensions which exist between a rich minority of peoples whose consumption of resources is formidable; and a poor majority of peoples who possess very little materially, who 'tread lightly on the earth'.

There are great income variations between rich and poor people in almost every country in the world, and in some countries these differences are extreme. A recent UNICEF report 'Child Poverty in Rich Countries' (Innocenti Centre, 2000) highlights the damaging effects of such inequality on child health and other standard measures of progress. USA, U.K. and Brazil are singled out for particular criticism. The North East of Brazil, for example, which is dependent on the exploitation of marginal labourers for sugar cane production, has been described as 'a concentration camp for more than 30 million people' (Galeano, 1975: 75).

But the grossest inequalities are between the majority and minority worlds. The richest 20% of the world enjoys nearly 90% of the world's wealth, and the gap between the incomes of the richest and poorest countries continues to increase. The wealth of the four richest people in the world has doubled in the last four years, at the same time as the poverty of the poorest nations has increased (UNDP Development Report, 1999).

The development of the majority world has been intertwined with that of Europe for many centuries, although the pattern and shape of these interests has varied over time. Different regions of the world have always been interdependent. The Roman empire was an extraordinary mix of peoples, a mixing made more deliberate by the Roman system of government. The Italian renaissance was fuelled by West African gold carried along Saharan trade routes that were well established by 1400. Chinese-Indian-East African links were developed in the 12th and 13th centuries (Davidson, 1994). Meso-American kingdoms had extensive trade routes throughout South America and into North America long before the Spanish conquests (Wolf, 1997). The crusades were a European attempt to establish Christian empires in the Middle East. The direction and flow of traffic in goods and people has reflected the balance of power and prosperity (and weaponry) between various nations.

Colonialism was a vicious twist to this age-old history of trading and conquest. It was based on notions of racial supremacy, reinforced with guns and justified both by religion and science. Colonial ideas have dominated our perceptions and conceptions of the majority world.

> Embedded in the representation of peoples on the world, then were a notion of race and a notion of hierarchy, with some races being in some way higher, nearer to God ... a typology of races ... with an evolutionary component which suggests those 'higher up' have actually evolved further and those 'lower down' have not evolved so far' (Street, 1999: 52).

This notion of evolution, of 'developed' and 'less developed' countries still permeates the discourse on aid, another reason for using the descriptors minority and majority world which carry a different emphasis from that of the rhetoric of social and economic development.

The ideology of outright superiority of colonial times has been mostly abandoned, but it has been replaced by accelerating politico-economic exploitation. Technological advances – industrial production, electronic communications and motor and air transport, have made such exploitation easier. Capital has always sought the cheapest possible labour, and this labour is now more easily commandeered and exploited in situ. It is cheaper to employ children for a pittance in Bangladesh to make designer shirts which are marketed and sold in North America and Europe at a 600% profit to the entrepreneur than it is to make the same shirts in New York or London. (Chossudovsky, 1997).

Global economies are now to an extent regulated by the World Bank, the World Trade Organisation and similar international cartels. The World Bank acts as a kind of international pawnbroking system; it is there to make a profit out of poverty, whatever its current rhetoric about combating it. It loans money to the poorest countries, mostly at commercial rates of interest, which they can only repay by diverting resources to the production of cash crops, or by raiding natural resources such as forests, or by promoting industries such as tourism (George & Sabelli, 1994; Chussudovsky, 1999; Sklair, 1994).

At the same time, this economic system is predicated on consumer choice. Consumers in the minority world assume as their right patterns of consumption that badly deplete the world's natural resources. Climatic change, erosion and pollution have reached near-catastrophic levels. War and conflict, fuelled by competition over resources and by a profitable arms trade supplied by the minority world, have led to the flight of refugees and waves of immigration from one country to another. An estimated 60 million people in the world are refugees from conflict. In almost all majority world countries there have been dramatic population shifts from the countryside to the city, as cash crops, for consumption in the minority world, have superceded local domestic agriculture. Cities do not have the resources to cope with these influxes, shanty towns spring up and sprawl, and violence escalates. In Sachs' (1999) phrase, the doomsday clock stands at five to twelve.

The consequences for children of this escalating inequality are serious indeed. There are many international reports that document the position of children in the majority world. An unacceptable number die at birth or soon after. Child death is a commonplace; the *daily* deaths of children exceed the total child population of the U.K. Many of those that survive have limited and falling access to education and health care, particularly girl children in poor Asian countries. Children are the most vulnerable victims of warfare – a high percentage of refugees are children (Machel, 1996).

There is a widespread view in the majority world that children should contribute to the household, either through their labour or through earnings. (It is only in the minority world we regard children as incapable of contribution). But children's availability and willingness are exploited by those in search of cheap labour. Many of the goods used and consumed on a daily basis in the minority world, such as food, flowers, and clothing, depend for their production on cheap child labour in poor countries. Amost all cities have growing populations of street children. Increasing poverty and indebtedness in the majority world have led to the resurgence of endemic diseases once under control, such as tuberculosis, and to the failure to deal with new ones such as aids. An estimated one in four children in sub-Saharan Africa is infected by AIDS, and still more are affected by it, a truly shocking figure.

As the Indian ecologist, Vandana Shiva (2000) has pointed out, this catalogue of suffering, disaster and chaos is not natural; it is mostly man-made and preventable. The grossly unequal distribution and consumption and of resources between the minority and majority world has been highlighted by some commentators as the major ethical and economic issue facing the world in the twenty-first century (Rahnema, 1998; Rist, 1997). It is *impossible* to consider the position of young children in the majority world without taking this inequality into account, although many accounts of early childhood seem to do so (Stephens, 1995). As the All-Africa Council of churches has commented:

Every child born in Africa is born with a financial burden which a lifetime's work cannot repay. The debt is a new form of slavery as vicious as the slave trade.[1]

Research and development programmes for children in majority world countries can only make a tiny local impact, if any, against this backdrop of inequality. To an extent this is also the situation in unequal rich nations. As Kagan also points out, inequality and class are ignored as predictors of outcome in the USA in favour of limited intervention programmes with the poor (Kagan, 1998: see below).

WHOSE IDEAS?

As suggested above, material inequality is justified by ideology, often cloaked in the guise of scientific validity. Some perspectives and understandings are more powerful than others, irrespective of any claims to logic or truth. The influence or hegemony of powerful groups – their truth claims and understandings – affects policy, provision and research far beyond their own intellectual or national borders. Foucault (1980) has commented vividly on how knowledge and power are inextricably linked.

A recent review of early childhood programmes, carried out by Myers for the recent World Education Forum Conference at Dakar commented on the monopoly of Minority World ideas and the tensions this has provoked.

Frameworks and knowledge . . . continue to originate, for the most part in the Minority World. Accordingly a tension often arises between 'received truth' linked to Minority World knowledge base and values guiding an agency, and local knowledge linked to another set of values rooted in some part of the majority world. These may overlap, but are different (Myers, 1999: 10).

There has been a dramatic expansion in early childhood provision in most of the world's cities but what understandings of children and what models of services have fuelled this expansion? Practitioners in the minority world mostly hold to the view that there are universal and essential truths about young children and how to care for and educate them, which apply everywhere in the world, with minor cultural variations. Often these 'truths' are based on contradictory theoretical viewpoints, extrapolated on pick and mix basis. Piagetian, Behaviourist, Vygotskian and other ideas are freely drawn upon with little understanding of any inherent contradictions (Serpell, 1999).

DEVELOPMENTALLY APPROPRIATE PRACTICE?

The over-riding assumption, which appears everywhere in the minority world literature on early childhood practice, is that the ages and stages children go through, and the familial contexts in which learning takes place, are similar everywhere. Precepts of practice forged for children in the minority world are invariably applied unchanged to the majority world. Leading American educators have claimed that 'children are pretty much the same everywhere and the people teaching them have pretty much the same ideas' (Weikart, 1999; Katz, 1999). Can the knowledge and understanding about young children that has been built up in the minority world be generalised to include all children? Many early childhood experts in the minority world consider this to be the case:

> Given the right opportunities and the right learning environment children will develop in similar ways whatever their background. Culture may affect, and sometimes even determine, the topics, methodologies and techniques we use, but there is an underlying universality. As long as we keep in mind that everything we do is concerned with the development of the whole child, we are all doing the same sorts of things for the same sorts of reasons (Why Children Matter, Bernard van Leer Foundation, 1994: 9).

Child development as a discipline is an area of study and knowledge that is mainly based on positivist assumptions. It assumes an empirical methodology, whereby 'facts' can be systematically established, compared, and accumulated to build a wider picture of children's capacities. It uses the biological model of growth and development as a metaphor for psychological development, and assumes that there are psychological processes which mirror the body's changes. Brain research serves to bolster this biological metaphor of growth in childhood, even though the evidence about 'developing brains' is very slight indeed (see chapter 1 in this volume and Bruer, 1999).

The dominant discourse in developmental psychology is that psychological processes can be investigated through the study of the individual behaviour and learning of children; and by aggregating the findings of many studies about highly specific aspects of behaviour, universal norms can be established. Children are assumed to pass through the same ages and stages whether in remote parts of Nepal or in Chicago.

> Developmental psychologists have searched for natural sequences of ages and stages in the child's understandings of the physical, social and moral world's. Problems have arisen because this approach has rested, more often than not, upon an exclusively biological orientation. The biological metaphor ignores the social and historical aspects of the child's development and takes them as secondary. The traditional biological approach has been characteristically finalistic, centring attention on what children are to *become* and concerned with the child's march towards adulthood (Cahan et al., 1993, p. 219.)[2]

The 'science' of child development, which is a complex theoretical and empirical body of knowledge is not necessarily concerned with practical application of research findings. Nevertheless it is continually drawn upon to inform practice. Providing the study is an empirical one, evidence from research, however specific or discrete the investigation, are extrapolated to build up a picture of what children need.[3] The National Association for the Education of Young Children (NAEYC), which is the main voice for the profession in America has published a best-selling manual 'Developmentally Appropriate Practice'. (Bredekamp, 1987/97) This lists the ages and stages children pass through, and the kinds of practices which adults should adopt in order to enable them to pass through those stages successfully. For each segment of behaviour and for each aspect of practice, 'scientific research evidence' is quoted, even although such research has often been generated within very different theoretical frames. The notion of 'developmentally appropriate practice' is pervasive and appears in manuals and books for people working with children throughout the world.

Close textual reading of Developmentally Appropriate Practice and other similar documents suggest that they also draw heavily on highly specific societal assumptions. These include the paramountcy of individualism and selfhood, the concept of a permanent nuclear household with a prime carer and a dependent child as a model for development, the need to encourage choice from a wide range of material goods, the separation of mind and body, and so on. The practice advocated is not neutrally and scientifically established but rooted in specific assumptions about the nature of investigation, and about the structures of childhood and society (Penn, 1999).

A further widely held assumption in the child development literature and in its applications, is that adults bringing up young children, as parents, teachers and childcare workers, have a unique, profound and formative influence in a child's early years (Rich Harris, 1995) The pattern and sequence of child development may be more or less the same everywhere, but it can be speeded up by particular kinds of interventions like parent education programmes; and slowed down or even stymied, by the lack of such intervention. Conversely 'poor parenting', left untreated, can lead to low self-esteem, lack of aspirations, and anti-social behaviour in children. If professionals can only find the right parenting programme, the right kind of intervention, to use when children are especially young and malleable, many of the ill effects of poverty could be offset. Kagan suggests that this is an American fantasy.

> ... so many people believe in infant determinism (because) it ignores the power of social class membership. Though a child's social class is the best predictor of future vocation, academic accomplishments and psychiatric health, Americans wish to believe that their society is open, egalitarian, without rigid class boundaries. To acknowledge the power of class is to question this ethical canon (Kagan, 1998: 147).

BORN IN THE USA?

Findings from the child development research literature then are widely used to inform and evaluate practice in the field of early childhood, both in then USA and elsewhere. Yet this child development research rests on a very narrow base. Ninety-nine percent of the academic work in child development is undertaken by American psychologists. The sample of children they have investigated and on whom they base their theories are themselves a largely narrow sample within an American context which is over-weighted towards white, middle-class children (Woodhead, 1998).

But from any wider perspective, conduct of behaviour in the USA is highly context specific. The USA is a society whose values may be taken to represent one extreme of a neo-liberal economic continuum. It has a particular political economy which makes certain assumptions about the role of the individual and the role of the state and the inter-relationships between them. For example it accepts extreme disparities between rich and poor as normal and interprets such disparities as a reflection of personal achievement or lack of it. It has one of the worst childcare systems (OECD, 2001) as well as the highest percentage of men in prison, and the highest number of executions, in the minority world. The USA has refused to sign the UN declaration on the rights of the child (the only country in the world besides Somalia to refuse to do so) or to agree to the establishment of an international court of human rights, despite considerable international pressure. Presumably the USA acts in this way because its legislators consider the opinions of the rest of the world to be of little consequence. The economic and military power of the USA is such that it is an unassailable position to enforce its own ideological position.[4]

Can precepts for a universal science of child development, or at least precepts on how to best bring up children, be drawn from sampling on such a population? Can the avenues of enquiry, the research questions and the technologies of investigation that arise from such a very particular and dominating society, be relevant elsewhere? Within the field, awkward questions about the shortcomings of representativeness and enquiry carry little weight. The findings from the USA constitute the most substantial body of knowledge currently in existence about young children and their circumstances. The World Bank on its website refers *exclusively* to research from the USA as the baseline for its 'knowledge base' about early childhood throughout the world. The World Bank funds 29 major early childhood programmes in the majority world, totalling over $1000 million. It draws on this research as a rationale for the loans, arguing that early intervention – especially parental education – can in the long run, increase economic productivity.

DOES CHILD DEVELOPMENT ADDRESS CULTURE?

There is an increasing recognition that 'culture' or 'socio-cultural context' is important in shaping children's lives. Bronfenbrenner (1979) has provided a model in which the individual child is surrounded by concentric rings of influence, of which the outer rings are variously described as 'cultural context'. This is a way of accommodating the notion of 'cultural difference' without moving from the universalistic, individualistic notion of a child. International Non Governmental Organisations (INGOs)[5] manuals frequently refer to Bronfenbrenner as evidence that they are taking 'culture' into account.

Others such as Michael Cole (1996) take the concept of culture further, and view all learning as essentially social and cultural – children only learn with and from others. Cole and his group have been developing notions of apprenticeship and expertise, peripheral participation and situated learning; analysing how children and adults become inducted into the ideas of the social and work groups of which they are a part (Chaiklin & Lave, 1996). Culture, in this analysis, is profoundly transformative and not an additional variable to take into account in the development of the individual. Cole argues for the reverse of Bronfenbrenner's position: it is meaningless to talk of individual being and thought outside of culture (Resnick et al., 1996).

Eldering and Leseman (1999) address questions about cross cultural and international perspectives. They argue that research studies in this field fall along an axis one end of which is cultural relativism and the other behavioural universalism. Cultural relativism is the position that culture and behaviour are inseparable, and there is only meaning to behaviour within given cultural populations. Behavioural universalism is the view that the same behaviour traits and patterns appear in children wherever they are, perhaps with minor variations, and these can be charted accurately through cross-cultural surveys. But only Serpell in that volume raises any ethical questions, and those are of a limited nature.

There is also a body of work from Havard carried out in the 1960s and 1970s by the Whitings (1975), and more recently by Levine and his group, working mainly in East Africa (Levine et al., 1992). The emphasis of this work, which is very scholarly, is to systematically contrast the childrearing patterns of different groups of people, using well-established methodologies such as timed observations, and psychological and physiological measurement. (Local assistants are used, although their contribution is rarely cited in subsequent publications. However this work also does not explore, except in the most limited sense, any ethical questions). For the purposes of research enquiry, the studies essentially regard culture as bounded and static. This tribe has adopted these ways of behaving, that tribe does it differently, etc.

Woodhead (1996) was commissioned by the Bernard van Leer Foundation to address the question of cultural relativity in early childhood programmes. He investigated projects in France, Kenya, India and Venezuela. He arrived at the concept of 'culturally appropriate practice'. That is he identified a whole range of components of early childhood programmes such as staffing and worker satisfaction, parental satisfaction, ratios, resourcing, child participation etc. He argued that practice could only be judged in terms of the best that was locally available; it would be wrong to expect that a project in Venezuela or Kenya could aim at the same 'standards' as one in France. This position has not been well received, by those who argue from a universalist position about children's needs and entitlements. Put at its crudest, the contra- argument is 'why should we accept anything less as a goal for children in a poor country than we would for children in a rich country?'

But both the cultural relativity and the cultural uniformity models need unpacking, ethically and epistemologically. How does one conduct relation-ships of any kind if one is a representative of a privileged minority? How does one use knowledge garnered from one small section of the globe, and apply it in another? These questions are not new, especially in sociology or anthropology. (Foucault, 1982; Clifford & Marcus, 1986; Hood et al., 1999).

IS THERE ANY SUCH THING AS CULTURE?

If culture is important, then what is it, how can it be defined? Is culture static and bounded, or is it best thought of, in the metaphor of the Kenyan critic Ngugi wa Thiongo, as a river, always changing, flowing and merging, but nevertheless a recognisable entity? What are its key reference points, where are its borders? Developmental psychology has so recently acknowledged culture that the notion that the concept of culture itself is highly problematic is only beginning to be recognised. Bruner (1996: 14), for example, acknowledges that culture *'rarely conforms to anything resembling a cookbook of recipes or formulas for it is a universal of all cultures that they contain factional or institutional interests.'* Mercer (1992) argues that 'culture' is a usable concept only if culture involves changing and contested meanings, and takes account of power and status.

Within anthropology the notion of culture is more suspect. Rosaldo (1989) for instance, argues that is a mistake to think that cultural borders are ever fixed; there is a continual ebb and flow and reshaping of ideas. Most people, he argues, inhabit these cultural borderlands. Cultural and social life is both inherited and always being changed. In the theatre this view of 'culture' as forever being amalgamated and reshaped is embodied vividly by the dramatist-impressario Peter Brookes. His Mahabharata triology was a triumph of reinventive incorporation, a truly multi-racial cast reinterpreting a classic of Indian literature played to audiences in Glasgow, Paris and Kampala. Brookes argues that mingling rich traditions like this enhances artistic endeavour. There is even a term to describe this cultural plurality, the 'transborder world' (Pieterse & Parekh, 1995).

But 'transbordering' is rarely on such equal terms. Some ideas carry more weight than others irrespective of any claim to truth or logic. In the minority world of North America and Europe, it is *other* people who are seen as having these quaint blocks of irrational, or sometimes destructive, beliefs and practices; funny colourful clothes; strange, strong foods, and idiomatic or incomprehensible speech patterns. We call this conglomeration 'culture', in a way which Street (1999) has argued is akin to racism.

> Even though the concept of culture appears not to be rooted in biology (race) it is in fact very often premised on assumptions about fixity and permanence: the idea that somebody, for instance, might come from Nigeria and settle in England, somehow bringing along a bag with Nigerian culture in it, with which he or she is then stuck . . . a person belongs to a given culture, that is how they are, they must think that way and behave that way (Street, 1999: 54).

For those on the other side of the cultural fence, especially children, the pressures are not merely to exercise benign tolerance for someone else's 'culture' but to conform, to adapt and to metamorphose.

Nancy Scheper-Hughes (1993) offers a similar perspective to Rosaldo in stressing the complexities of negotiating 'cultural borderlands'. She has written a brilliant and widely acclaimed 20-year account of the everyday life of women and children in a shanty town of Alto do Cruseiro in the north-east of Brazil, '*Death without Weeping.*' She tries to understand the neglect women appear to show their young children, and the apparent casualness and indifference with which they react to frequent infant death, behaviour which would appear to be abusive by conventional North American or European standards. She concludes that the way the women respond is not a matter of poor 'cultural' parenting practices, which need correction, but a mirror image of the way in which the shanty women themselves are treated by their wider society as being worthless and of no account. Being able to accommodate to and accept the unrelenting grimness and misery of their everyday life enables them to survive. She claims, (as does Rosaldo, writing of Chicano populations) that those who are on the receiving end of oppression nevertheless find ways to defend themselves with subversiveness and wit. They are often resilient in the face of tremendous odds.

A major issue then in trying to understand 'culture' is to see how a powerful view of what is right and necessary and normal impacts on those who do not or cannot share it. This is much harder for those that inflict it than for those on whom it is inflicted. '*Short of genius, a rich man cannot imagine poverty*' (Peguy, 1943).

This process of cultural confrontation is historical; it is not peculiar to our times. Various groups of people who have held a particular material advantage have continuously expanded and overflowed beyond their borders, enslaving or subjugating others, as Wolf documents so carefully in his book *People Without History*. 'Culture' in his view is 'forever assembled, dismantled, and reassembled' (1997: 391). 'Culture' is not merely about trying to understand and make allowances for 'the other', someone different from ourselves. 'Culture' is also almost always, to use Rosaldo's words, 'a field of contention' in which the key words are 'change, experience, conflict and struggle' (1989: 105). Or as the anthropologist Sharon Stephens writes:

> what sort of social visions and notions of culture underlie assertions within international rights discourses that every child has a right to cultural identity? To what extent is this identity conceived of as singular and exclusive, and what sorts of priorities are asserted in cases where various forms of cultural identity – regional, national, ethnic minority or indigenous – come up against one another? (Stephens, 1995: 3).

In other words there are not only empirical issues, but unavoidable ethical and moral issues in trying to confront and intervene in the practices of others. Scheper Hughes lucidly remarks:

> The problem is of course, how to articulate a standard or divergent standards, for the beginnings of a moral and an ethical reflection on cultural practices that takes into account but does not privilege our own cultural presuppositions (1993: 21).

DOING RESEARCH IN THE MAJORITY WORLD: THE EXAMPLE OF FARMWORKERS IN ZIMBABWE

All the research I have undertaken in the majority world has been evaluative, that is I have been asked to assess the effectiveness of various kinds of small scale interventions in early childhood carried out by INGOs (International Non-Governmental Organisations) in majority world countries, or offer meta reviews of existing evidence (Penn, 1998). At first I felt privileged to have the opportunity to carry out such work, but I have become increasingly aware of the ethical shortcomings of my position as a minority world 'expert' hired at dollar rates by an INGO in a country with which I am not familiar. I have described my methods of working elsewhere (Hood et al., 1999). Essentially these are to accumulate information from as many sources as possible, and contextualise the initiative I am being asked to evaluate, and feed back my analysis to those who have commissioned it. Most recently I have included autobiographical material and commentary from those local people with whom I have been working (Penn, 2001).

The initiative I describe here was an attempt by an INGO to provide basic support to the young children of farmworkers in Zimbabwe. The position of white farms in Zimbabwe is contentious. The best farming land was appropriated by white settlers in the 1920s and 1930s, and the struggle for independence in Zimbabwe was closely tied up with land reclamation issues. The Lancaster House agreement, which granted Zimbabwe independence from the U.K. ratified the status quo. The farms have continued in white ownership until the agreement expired, which it has just done. The bitterness of the Zimbabwean Government towards the Lancaster House agreement has recently erupted but it has long been a fact of political life. One expression of this bitterness has been the refusal by the Government to provide any education in situ on the farms, since they saw it as investing public resources on private property. Children had either to travel out of the farms to attend state primary schools, with transport provided by the farmer, or the farmer himself had to provide the schooling. An estimated 20% of children were thus excluded from schooling. Farm workers are also disenfranchised and not entitled to vote in elections (Loewensen, 1992).

The farm was the owner's fiefdom, and he could treat the workers as well or as badly as he wished, including the use of physical punishment. There was a minumum wage, but many workers, especially women, were classed as temporary or transient and were not entitled to it. Some of the farms are under contract to multi-nationals, with a manager responsible for delivery quotas. I visited one farm under contract to one well-known multi-national company. There were well-watered lawns surrounding a model factory and workers in smart company uniforms. But behind the scenes there was little or no sanitation and two water taps for over 1000 people. The manager claimed to be providing transport for children to school outside the farm, but according to one of our informants was doing no such thing. In another farm, schooling was provided, but the farmer was a fundamentalist Christian and was using textbooks which used the biblical story of the seven days of creation as a basis for agricultural training. At the other extreme, one liberal farmer provided good housing, sanitation and running water, ran an excellent primary school, and was supporting the daughter of one of his farm workers through university. Given the political uncertainty and the very variable conditions, many native Zimbabweans refused to work on the farms. Much of the farm labour has been migrant employees from neighbouring Mozambique and Malawi, and on almost all farms there has been considerable turnover of labour.

The situation for young children had become an especial problem as agribusiness gained a hold. Women workers had traditionally taken children with them to the fields. But the heavy use of sprays and fertilisers made the fields unsafe, and flower production in particular was extremely hazardous for young children (Vukasin, 1992).

In this situation, the INGO had arrived at a very practical solution. The aid worker was herself a white Zimbabwean, married to a black Zimbabwean, and had a small farm. She suggested that if the farmer would allocate a small plot of land, it would be possible to cordon off a safe play area for children, with basic sanitation, and basic play equipment. One or two women could be designated as health/childcare workers to look after the children in the play area, and provide them with a simple meal, with farmworkers contributing produce from a communal garden plot.[6] This minimalist approach worked fairly well under the restricted circumstances. The farmers were not asked to do too much, and the programme was unambitious; it aimed only to provide a safe space, some shade, and some robust play equipment (tyres and planks) for the children. There was no systematic attempt to provide education or training, since resources were very scarce, staff were untrained, and to offer education then raised the question about access to schooling.

The ratios of adults to children were, by conventional minority world standards very poor, one adult to 50 children, or higher. The linguistic complexities of working in a multi-lingual setting, and the lack of money and time for any training for staff, the lack of manufactured playthings for children, meant that the children were left to their own devices, and appeared resourceful and had many games of their own to play. In fact the notion that young children are not resourceful is a particular conceptualisation of minority world childhood (Boyden & Mann, 2000). Some locally recruited men and women acted as support workers, visited the farms and helped build the equipment and set up the arrangements. Depending on the area, up to 20% of farms joined in the scheme.

However there were also other schemes to support farmworkers children. A rival INGO had made these claims about its intervention in a project called Kushanda.[7]

> This is the story of dozens of small rural commuities in Zimbabwe which are working together to give their children a chance for a better future. A chance to develop their full potential and to acquire the skills needed to break the vicious cycle of poverty that has held

their families in its grip for generations. Through establishing village-based early childhood education and care centres these communities are seeking to ensure that their preschool children are safe; get proper health care; receive a supplementary nutritious diet; interact with at least one reliable adult; have interesting activities which contribute to their physical and mental development; and have other children to play with, thereby encouraging healthy development (Booker, 1995: 15).

This statement draws on a number of unjustified assumptions about the history of poverty in the area, the existence of a coherent (and linguistic) community, the neglect by parents of their children, and about the activities of children themselves. For example children in majority world countries are commonly part of a multi-generational household, and live and learn in their daily lives as a contributing member of their household and mixed-age peer group. The bored, unstimulated individual lonely child dependent on the kindly intervention of an adult carer maybe a feature of home life in the minority world but it is an incomprehensible image in much of the majority world. (Note how this reflects the situation in Venezuela portrayed in chapter 3 of this volume).

But above all, it is the notion that through such early childhood intervention poverty can be combated that is misleading and disempowering. The white owned farmland in Zimbabwe is productive land. Within living memory, before their land was taken over for agribusiness and tobacco, black Zimbabwean farmers produced a food surplus for local consumption (Loewenson, 1992; Dede Wilks, 1996; Mugwesi & Balleis, 1994). The refugees from the war in Mozambique, the migrant labourers from Malawi, and black Zimbabweans working on the white farms in order to supplement their own meagre barren smallholdings, were not a stable, integrated farm or village community nor were they likely to become so through the agency of the childcare centre. The problem about subsequent access to schooling remained (Nyagura & Mupawaenda, 1994). The sole oblique reference to social injustice in the programme evaluation was this comment:

Owing to the unique dynamics of farm life, the farm owners, and often their wives, can be important actors in ensuring that a preschool operates on the premises. While Kushanda staff members can on occasions find themselves thrust into difficult positions between the workers and the owners, they always keep in mind the objective of securing the resources necessary to provide better quality ECEC services for the communities' pre-school children (Booker, 1995: 82).

The situation is one many INGOs find themselves in, not only in Zimbabwe. They seek to better the conditions of a local population, but do not wish to intervene, or be seen to take sides in a difficult, tense and politicised environment. It is one thing to acknowledge this position and to uphold other, more indirect forms of advocacy as well as continued, but realistic involvement in a local programme. It is another to blind oneself to it, and to adopt a rhetoric which naively supports the status quo.

The INGO who commissioned me were, however, impressed by the Kushanda report. They decided to develop a curriculum for the children in their centres. The original worker had withdrawn and white European-trained staff had been employed. A start had already been made by offering a training programme to farm care-workers. This consisted of a very short and garbled account of 'ages and stages' and an attempt to use piles of old newspapers to make paper maché imitations of expensive western plastic toys which were deemed necessary to the children's development. Illiterate women were thus expected to tear up and glue the only newsprint with which they came into contact in order to make these 'toys'. If finished, the paper maché toys were rarely used, but carefully displayed on a ledge far out of the children's reach!

The newly appointed staff who now led the project wanted to meet mothers of children attending the play spaces and discuss their 'cultural practices' so they could incorporate them into the practice of the existing centres. They intended to develop the curriculum in accordance with the best precepts of developmentally appropriate practice with a liberal nod to socio-cultural context.

I was asked to evaluate the existing centres, and suggest in what ways they could expand their activities. Mostly our visits to the farms were a kind of royal progress, a procession of cars with INGO staff and local support workers eager to demonstrate their success, a kind of 'developmental tourism' typical of INGOs and well described by Chambers (1997). He points out that for an 'important ' person, that is one who might have resources to distribute, the act of visiting remote places is in itself problematic and a distortion of the everyday. We did however manage to have a few meetings on the farms with cowed, silent and exhausted groups of mothers.

In the end I wrote a short report which used local data and reports to emphasise the inequalities of the situation, and the political difficulties which were likely to ensue (as indeed they have). I made some very practical suggestions about soliciting the views of children and their mothers on the farms using participatory methods. I also suggested how they might compile a checklist of activities and monitor how they were carried out. But my overall conclusion, and unfortunately one I could not adequately convey, was that the project workers themselves made assumptions about early childhood, about how and what children learnt and from whom, about what role material goods played in that learning, and about what the effects or outcomes of that learning might be. The very basis of the evaluation was highly problematic.

CONCLUSION

This story of trying to 'research' early childhood development programmes on Zimbabwean farms illustrates many of the more general points I wish to make. First of all the wider context of injustice colours many situations and one cannot pretend that it does not exist. Moral ambiguity pervades such research, and the ethics, as well as the practicalities, of research encounters need to be addressed.

Secondly, the notion of culture is highly questionable, and as Street (1999) has pointed out, veers on racial stereotyping. What is the 'culture' of refugees from Mozambique, who find themselves alongside Malawian emigrants on a farm whose daily arrangements are controlled by a white Zimbabwean farmer? What definitions of 'culture' might cover such circumstances, and how might it be investigated?

Thirdly, 'developmentally appropriate practice' as defined in USA terms is simply not practical, let alone appropriate. For instance recommending a ratio of one adult to a small group of children is laughable in such a situation. The very basis of children's agency and dependency has to be rethought in order to reflect and comprehend majority world realities.

The Zimbabwean farms may be a very particular case, but the dilemmas of conducting any kind of research into early childhood under such circumstances, whether it is evaluative or has some wider scientific purpose, are the same.

NOTES

1. Fifty Years is Enough. Factsheet produced by the Inter-Church coalition on Africa, on the 50th anniversary of the founding of the World Bank. Toronto.

2. The attraction of brain research for so many early childhood advocates, despite the lack of direct evidence, is that it appears to strengthens the link between biology and cognitive development, and provides a stronger rationale both for universal laws and more intervention.

3. For instance experiments, carried out in the 1950s on the visual cortex of kittens, which showed that blindfolding newborn kittens irretreviably impaired visual development, were cited as relevant evidence in a major report in Canada arguing for early intervention programmes with children under three! (Fraser Mustard, 1999).

4. A recent article in the Guardian newspaper carried replies from Americans in response to an article making these same points about American society. E.g. *I couldn't care less about any country other than my own. The U.S. uses a lot of more of the world's resources than any other country- so WHAT? WE're feeding the world and our economy is supporting every wannabe economy on the third world. We don't need you. You need us. Its about time you Eurotrash paid us the respect we deserve* Guardian. August 25th 2000: 17.

5. There are a number of international non-governmental organisations who have specialised in-or pay particular attention to early childhood. These include the Bernard van Leer Foundation, the various branches of Save the Children, and the Soros Foundation, which operates in transitional(ex-communist) countries.

6. – in one instance the children were fed on asparagus soup, made with substandard asparagus spears.The asparagus spears were intended for an English food chain but some fell short of the required standard of the English market by not being perfectly symmetrical, and the company agreed to donate them to the children.

7. Rivalry and competition between INGOs is commonplace in the majority world, and often results in INGOs over-selling their work in order to justify their intervention over and above that of another INGO. In Pristina in Kosovo for example there are more than 150 INGOs claiming to work with local people.

REFERENCES

Booker, S. (1995). *We Are Your children*. The Hague: Bernard van Leer Foundation, Early Childhood Development: Practice and Reflections. No. 7.

Boyden, J., & Mann, G. (2000). *Children in Adversity*. Oxford: Background Paper for the Children in Adversity Conference, Oxford Refugee Studies Centre, September 2000.

Bredekamp, S. (Ed.) (1987). *Developmentally Appropriate Practice in Early Childhood Programmes Serving Children Birth through Age 8*. Washington: National Association for the Education of Young Children.

Bronfenbrenner, U. (1979). *The Ecology of Human Development*. Cambridge, Mass: Harvard University Press.

Bruer, J. (1999). *The Myth of the First Three Years: A New Understanding of Early Brain Development and Lifelong Learning*. New York: The Free Press.

Bruner, J. (1996). *The Culture of Education*. Cambridge, Mass: Harvard University Press.

Cahan, E., Meckling, J., Sutton Smith, S., & White, S. (1993) The Elusive Historical Child. In: G. Elder, J. Modell & R. Parke. (Eds), *Children in Time and Place: Developmental and Historical Insights*. Cambridge: CUP.

Chaiklin, S., & Lave, J. (1996). *Understanding Practice: Perspectives on Activity and Context*. Cambridge: CUP.

Chambers, R. (1997). *Whose Reality Counts?* London: Intermediate Technology Books.

Chossudovsky, M. (1997). *The Globalisation of Poverty: Impacts of IMF and World Bank Reforms*. London: Zed Books.

Clifford, J., & Marcus, G. (1986). *Writing Culture:The Poetics and the Politics of Ethnography*. Berkeley: University of California Press.

Cole, M. (1996). *Cultural Psychology*. Havard: Bellknap Press.

Davidson, B. (1994). *The Search for Africa: A History in the Making*. London: James Currey.

Dede Esi Amanor Wilks (Ed.) (1996). *In Search of Hope for Zimbabwe's Farm Workers*. London: Panos/Dateline Southern Africa.

Eldering, L., & Leseman, P. (1999). *Effective Early Education: Cross Cultural Perspectives*. London: Falmer.

Foucault, M. (1980). *Power/Knowledge: Selected Interviews and Other Writings*. Brighton: Harvester Press.

Galeano, E. (1975). *Open Veins of Latin America: Five Centuries of the Pillage of a Continent*. New York: Monthly Review.

George, S., & Sabelli, F. (1994). *Faith and Credit: The World Bank's Secular Empire*. London: Penguin.

Hood, S., Mayall, B., & Oliver, S. (Eds) (1999). *Critical Issues in Social Research: Power and Prejudice*. Buckinghamshire: Open University Press.

Kagan, J. (1998). *Three Seductive Ideas*. Cambridge: Harvard University Press.

Katz, L. (1998). Presentation at the International Seminar of the annual NAEYCE conference, Toronto 1998.

LeVine, R., Dixon, S., Levine, S. et al. (1994). *Childcare and Culture:Lessons from Africa*. Cambridge: Cambridge University Press.

Loewenson, R. (1992). *Modern Plantation Agriculture: Corporate Wealth and Labour Squalor*. London: Zed Books.

Machel, G. (1996). *The UN Study on the Impact of Armed Conflict on Children*. New York: United Nations Dept. Of Information.

Mercer, N. (1992). Culture, Context and the Construction of Knowledge in the Classroom. In: P. Light & G.Butterworth (Eds), *Context and Cognition: Ways of Learning and Knowing* (pp. 28–46). London: Harvester Wheatsheaf.

Mugwesi, T., & Balleis, P. (1994). *The Forgotten People: The Living and Health Conditions of Farm Workers and their Families*. Harare: Silveira House Social Series No. 6.

Myers, R. (1999). *Summary and Update: The EFA Global Thematic Review of Early Childhood Care and Development*. World Education Forum. www.unesco/org/wef

Ngugi Wa Thiong'o (1993). *Moving the Centre.The Struggle for Cultural Freedoms*. Portsmouth: Heinemann.

Nyagura, L. M., & Mupawaenda, A. C. (1994). *A Study of Factors affecting the Education of Women and Girls in the Commercial Farming Areas of Zimbabwe*. Harare: Unpublished paper.

OECD (forthcoming). *Review of Early Childhood Education and Care*. Paris: OECD.

Penn, H. (1997). *Review of Early Childhood Programmes in Developing and transitional Countries*. Paper prepared for U.K. Department for International Development.

Penn, H. (1999). *How Should We Care for Babies and Toddlers*. Toronto: CRRU, Centre for Urban and Community Studies, University of Toronto.

Penn, H. (2001). Negotiating Childhood in Mongolia. In: L. Alanen & B. Mayall (Eds), *Negotiating Adult-Child Relationships*. London: Falmer.

Peguy, C. (1943). *Socialism and the Modern World*. London: Basic Verities.

Pieterse, J. N., & Parekh, B. (Eds) (1995). *The Decolonisation of the Imagination: Culture, Knowledge and Power*. London: Zed Books.

Rahnema, M. with Bawtree, V. (Eds) (1997). *The Post Development Reader*. London: Zed Books.

Resnick, L., Levine, J., & Teasley, S. (Eds) (1996). *Perspectives on Socially Shared Cognition*. Washington: American Psychological Association (3rd ed.).

Rich Harris, J. (1995). Where is the Children's Environment? A Group Socialisation Theory of Development. *Psychological Review, 102*(3), 458–489.

Rist, G (1997). *The History of Development: From Western Origins to Global Faith*. London: Zed Books.

Rosaldo, R. (1989). *Culture and Truth: The Remaking of Social Analysis*. Boston: Beacon Press.

Sachs, W. (1999). *Planet Dialectics*. London: Zed Books.

Scheper-Hughes, N. (1993). *Death Without Weeping*. Los Angeles: University of California Press.

Serpell, R. (1999). *Theoretical Conceptions of Human Development*. In: L. Eldering & P.Leseman (Eds), *op cit* (pp. 41–66).

Shiva, V. (2000). *Poverty and Globalisation*. BBC Reith Lecture. April 2000.

Sklair, L. (Ed.) (1994). *Capitalism and Development*. London: Routledge.

Stephens, S. (1995). *Children and the Politics of Culture*. New Jersey: Princeton University Press.

Street, B. (1999). Meanings of Culture in Development: A Case Study from Literacy. In: F. E. Leach & A. Little (Eds), *Education, Cultures and Economics* (pp. 49–68). London: Falmer.

UNDP (1999). *Human Development Report*. Oxford: OUP.

UNICEF (2000). *Child Poverty in Rich Countries*. Florence: Innocenti Centre.

Vukasin, H (Ed.) (1992). *We carry a heavy load: Rural Women in Zimbabwe speak out: Summary Report of the Survey of Rural Women*. Harare: Zimbabwe Women's Bureau.

Weikart, D. (1998). Presentation at the International Seminar of the annual NAEYCE conference, Toronto 1998.

Whiting, B., & Whiting, J. (1975). *Children of Six Cultures*. Cambridge: Harvard University Press.

Wolf, E. (1997). *Europe and the People without History*. Los Angeles: University of California Press.

Woodhead, M. (1998), Quality in Early Childhood Programmes-a contextually appropriate approach. *International Journal of Early Years Education*, 6(1), 5–17.

Woodhead, M. (1996). *In Search of the Rainbow: Pathways to Quality in Large Scale Programmes for Young Disadvantaged Children*. The Hague; Bernard van Leer Foundation.

ABOUT THE AUTHORS

Carol Aubrey is a Professor of Education in the Centre for Educational Research at Canterbury Christ Church University College, U.K.

Lars-Erik Berg works as an Associate Professor in the Department of Sociology at the University of Göteborg, Sweden.

Stig Broström is Associate Professor in Early Childhood Education at the Danish University of Education in Copenhagen.

Pamela Calder is a Senior Lecturer at the University of the South Bank, London, and coordinator of the UK's national Early Childhood Studies degrees network.

Tricia David was, until her recent retirement, a Professor of Education in the Centre for Educational Research at Canterbury Christ Church University College, U.K.

Patricia Jessup is a doctoral candidate in Educational Studies in the School of Education at the University of Michigan and she has been designated a 'new scholar' by the Council on Anthropology and Education of the American Anthropological Association.

Ann Lewis is Professor of Special Education and Educational Psychology at the University of Birmingham, England, and a Chartered Psychologist.

Sally Lubeck is Associate Professor of Educational Studies and coordinator of the early childhood programme at the School of Education, The University of Michigan.

Glenda MacNaughton is an Associate Professor in the Department of Learning and Educational Development at the Faculty of Education, University of Melbourne, Australia.

Dr Anne Meade currently chairs the Working Group developing a ten-year strategic plan for Early Childhood Policy for the Government of New Zealand.

Arelys Moreno de Yanez is a Venezuelan psychologist. She has taught at the Instituto Universitario Avepane and the Universidad Catolica Andres Bello and is currently working with the Bernard van Leer Foundation as an independent consultant.

Peter Moss (U.K.) is Professor of Early Childhood Services at the Thomas Coram Research Unit, London University Institute of Education.

Dr Olusola Obisanya works for the Nigerian Educational Research and Development Council in Lagos, Nigeria.

Helen Penn is Professor of Early Childhood Studies at the University of East London, U.K.

Bridie Raban holds the Mooroolbeek Foundation Chair of Early Childhood Education at the University of Melbourne, Australia. Recently Professor Raban was seconded as the first Research Fellow with the Australian Commonwealth Government.

Celia Valiente is a Lecturer in Sociology at the Departamento de Ciencia Política y Sociología at the Universidad Carlos III de Madrid in Spain.

Leonardo Yanez has taught Social and Child Psychology at university level. In Venezuela he has been a consultant to the Ministry of the Family, the Ministry of Education and the Foundation for the Child. Leonardo is at present coordinating a Bernard van Leer Foundation project involving ten countries, exploring what makes ECEC programmes effective.

INDEX